Haruka
-Beyond the Stream of Time-

3

Story & Art by **Tohko Mizuno**

Haruka
—Beyond the Stream of Time—

3

CONTENTS

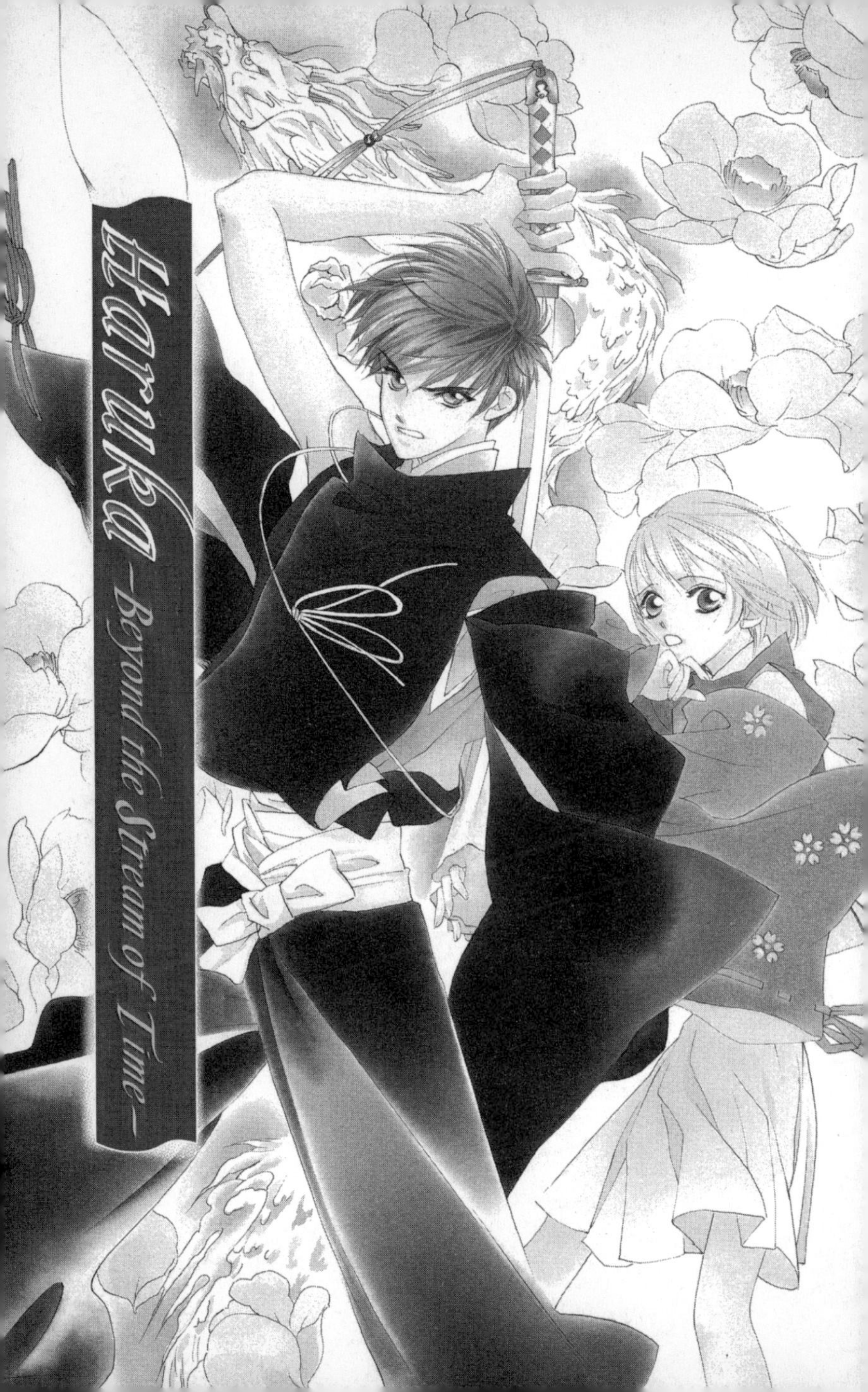
Haruka -Beyond the Stream of Time-

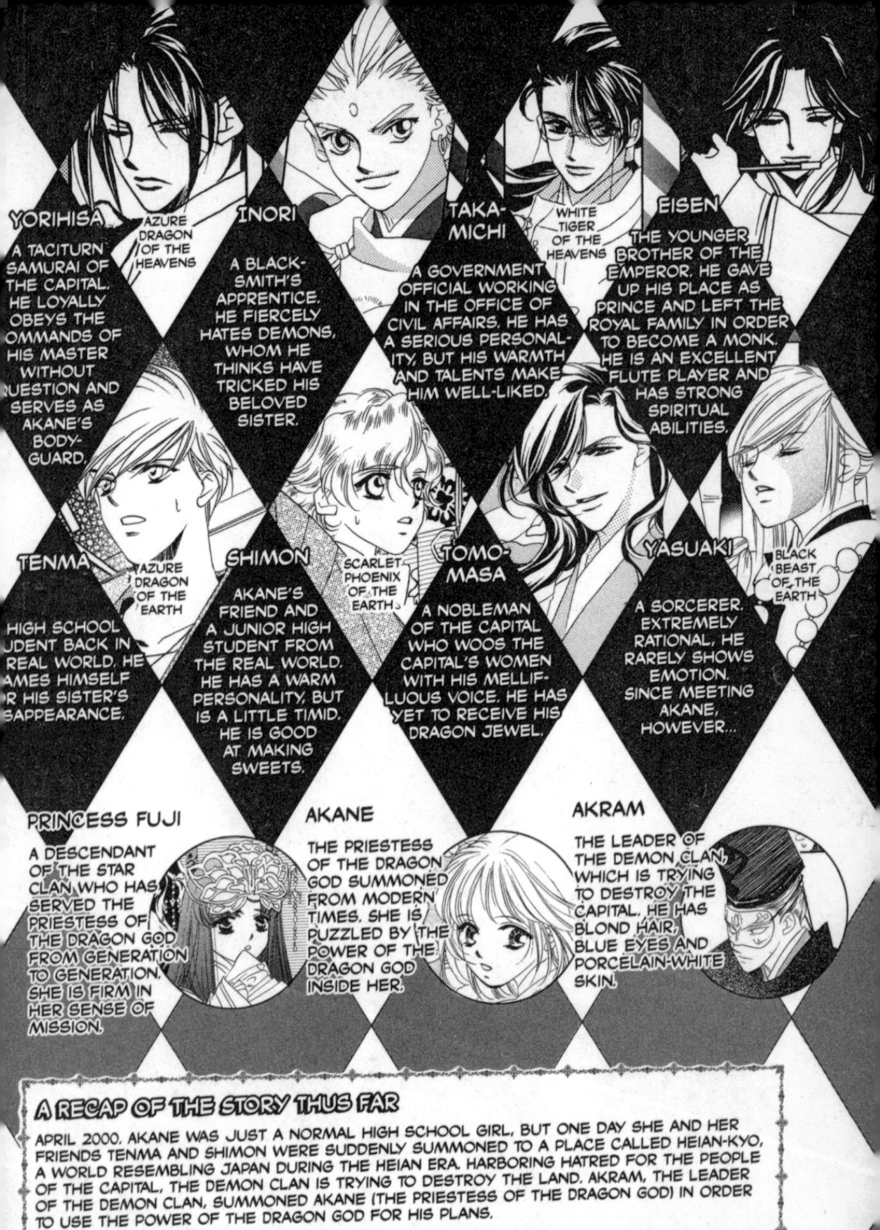
YORIHISA
AZURE DRAGON OF THE HEAVENS
A TACITURN SAMURAI OF THE CAPITAL. HE LOYALLY OBEYS THE OMMANDS OF HIS MASTER WITHOUT UESTION AND SERVES AS AKANE'S BODY-GUARD.
INORI
A BLACK-SMITH'S APPRENTICE. HE FIERCELY HATES DEMONS, WHOM HE THINKS HAVE TRICKED HIS BELOVED SISTER.
TAKA-MICHI
WHITE TIGER OF THE HEAVENS
A GOVERNMENT OFFICIAL WORKING IN THE OFFICE OF CIVIL AFFAIRS. HE HAS A SERIOUS PERSONAL-ITY, BUT HIS WARMTH AND TALENTS MAKE HIM WELL-LIKED.
EISEN
THE YOUNGER BROTHER OF THE EMPEROR. HE GAVE UP HIS PLACE AS PRINCE AND LEFT THE ROYAL FAMILY IN ORDER TO BECOME A MONK. HE IS AN EXCELLENT FLUTE PLAYER AND HAS STRONG SPIRITUAL ABILITIES.
TENMA
AZURE DRAGON OF THE EARTH
HIGH SCHOOL UDENT BACK IN REAL WORLD. HE AMES HIMSELF R HIS SISTER'S SAPPEARANCE.
SHIMON
SCARLET PHOENIX OF THE EARTH
AKANE'S FRIEND AND A JUNIOR HIGH STUDENT FROM THE REAL WORLD. HE HAS A WARM PERSONALITY, BUT IS A LITTLE TIMID. HE IS GOOD AT MAKING SWEETS.
TOMO-MASA
A NOBLEMAN OF THE CAPITAL WHO WOOS THE CAPITAL'S WOMEN WITH HIS MELLIF-LUOUS VOICE. HE HAS YET TO RECEIVE HIS DRAGON JEWEL.
YASUAKI
BLACK BEAST OF THE EARTH
A SORCERER. EXTREMELY RATIONAL, HE RARELY SHOWS EMOTION. SINCE MEETING AKANE, HOWEVER...
PRINCESS FUJI
A DESCENDANT OF THE STAR CLAN WHO HAS SERVED THE PRIESTESS OF THE DRAGON GOD FROM GENERATION TO GENERATION. SHE IS FIRM IN HER SENSE OF MISSION.
AKANE
THE PRIESTESS OF THE DRAGON GOD SUMMONED FROM MODERN TIMES. SHE IS PUZZLED BY THE POWER OF THE DRAGON GOD INSIDE HER.
AKRAM
THE LEADER OF THE DEMON CLAN, WHICH IS TRYING TO DESTROY THE CAPITAL. HE HAS BLOND HAIR, BLUE EYES AND PORCELAIN-WHITE SKIN.

A RECAP OF THE STORY THUS FAR

APRIL 2000. AKANE WAS JUST A NORMAL HIGH SCHOOL GIRL, BUT ONE DAY SHE AND HER FRIENDS TENMA AND SHIMON WERE SUDDENLY SUMMONED TO A PLACE CALLED HEIAN-KYO, A WORLD RESEMBLING JAPAN DURING THE HEIAN ERA. HARBORING HATRED FOR THE PEOPLE OF THE CAPITAL, THE DEMON CLAN IS TRYING TO DESTROY THE LAND. AKRAM, THE LEADER OF THE DEMON CLAN, SUMMONED AKANE (THE PRIESTESS OF THE DRAGON GOD) IN ORDER TO USE THE POWER OF THE DRAGON GOD FOR HIS PLANS.

THE ONLY THING THAT CAN SAVE THE PEOPLE OF THE CAPITAL FROM THIS CRISIS IS THE POWER OF THE DRAGON GOD. PRINCESS FUJI ASKED AKANE TO USE THE DRAGON GOD'S POWER TO PROTECT THE CAPITAL. SHE ALSO TOLD AKANE THAT EIGHT MEN CALLED THE EIGHT GUARDIANS WOULD GATHER AROUND HER IN ORDER TO PROTECT HER AS THE PRIESTESS.

MEANWHILE, AKANE WAS FEELING ATTRACTED TO AKRAM... BUT WHEN TENMA SAW THE OTHER MEMBERS OF THE EIGHT GUARDIANS PROTECTING AKANE, HE LOST HIS COOL AND BLURTED OUT HIS LOVE FOR HER!

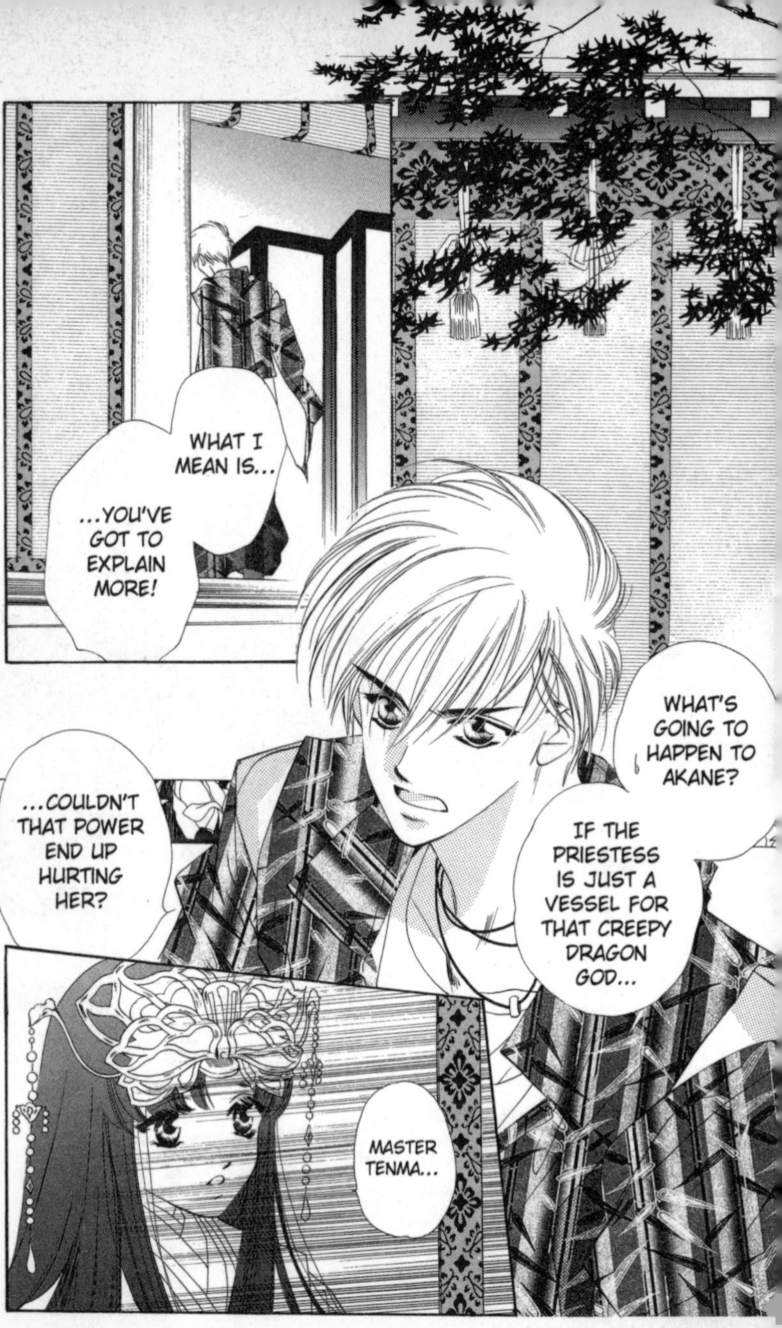
WHAT I MEAN IS...
...YOU'VE GOT TO EXPLAIN MORE!
WHAT'S GOING TO HAPPEN TO AKANE?
IF THE PRIESTESS IS JUST A VESSEL FOR THAT CREEPY DRAGON GOD...
...COULDN'T THAT POWER END UP HURTING HER?
MASTER TENMA...

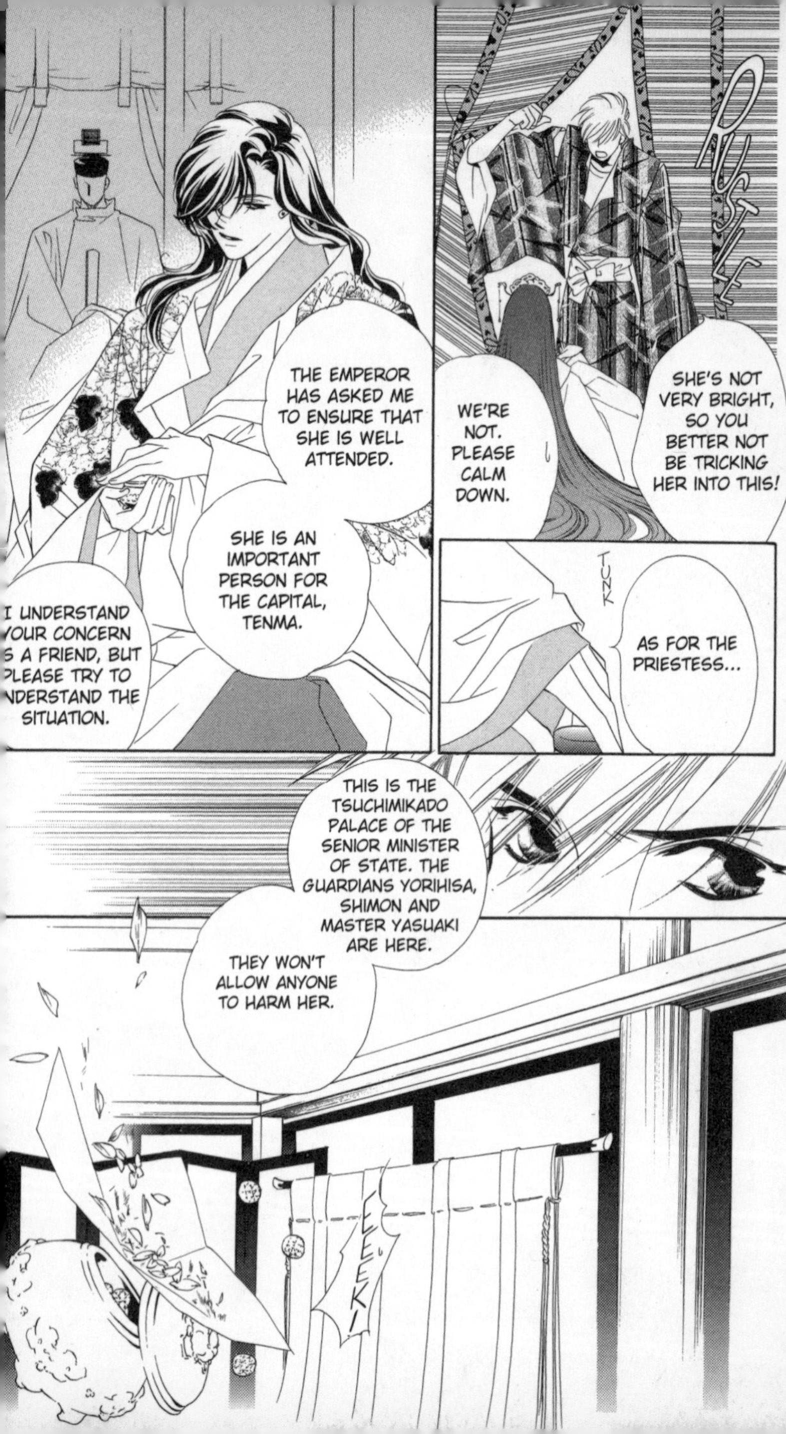
RUSTLE
SHE'S NOT VERY BRIGHT, SO YOU BETTER NOT BE TRICKING HER INTO THIS!
WE'RE NOT. PLEASE CALM DOWN.
TUNK
AS FOR THE PRIESTESS...
THE EMPEROR HAS ASKED ME TO ENSURE THAT SHE IS WELL ATTENDED.
SHE IS AN IMPORTANT PERSON FOR THE CAPITAL, TENMA.
I UNDERSTAND YOUR CONCERN S A FRIEND, BUT PLEASE TRY TO NDERSTAND THE SITUATION.
THIS IS THE TSUCHIMIKADO PALACE OF THE SENIOR MINISTER OF STATE. THE GUARDIANS YORIHISA, SHIMON AND MASTER YASUAKI ARE HERE.
THEY WON'T ALLOW ANYONE TO HARM HER.
EEEEK!

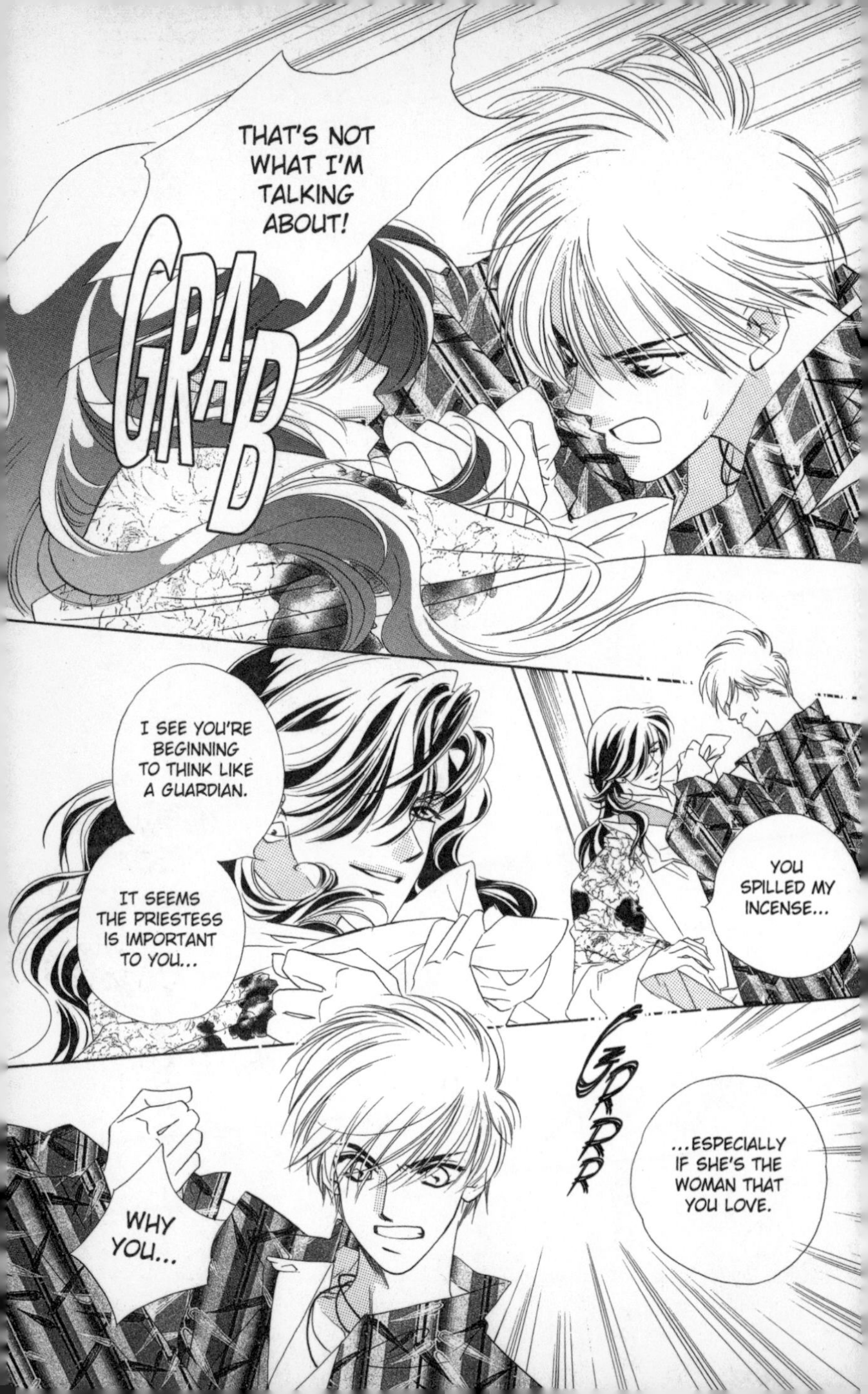
THAT'S NOT WHAT I'M TALKING ABOUT!
GRAB
YOU SPILLED MY INCENSE...
I SEE YOU'RE BEGINNING TO THINK LIKE A GUARDIAN.
IT SEEMS THE PRIESTESS IS IMPORTANT TO YOU...
...ESPECIALLY IF SHE'S THE WOMAN THAT YOU LOVE.
GRRRR
WHY YOU...

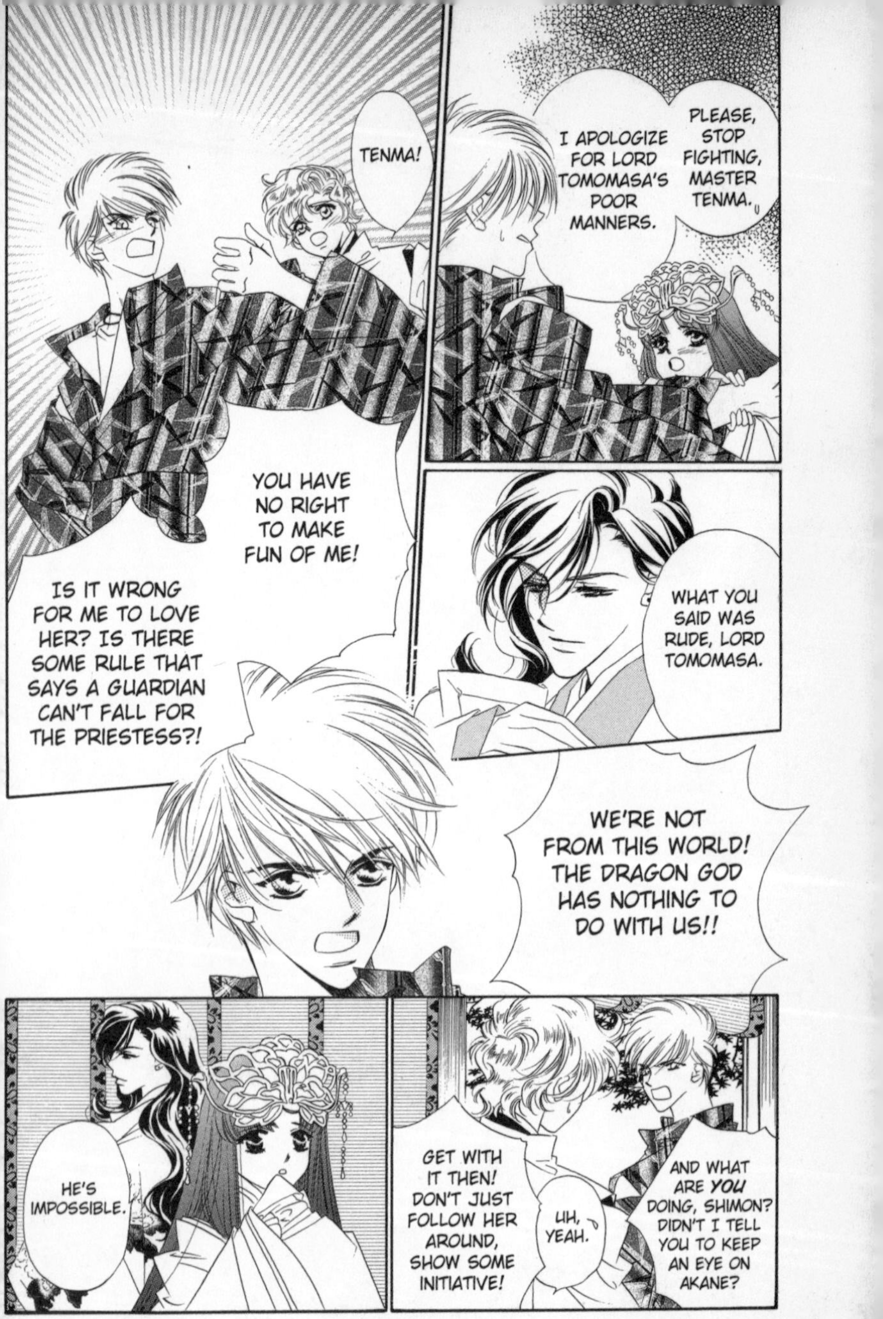
PLEASE, STOP FIGHTING, MASTER TENMA.
I APOLOGIZE FOR LORD TOMOMASA'S POOR MANNERS.
WHAT YOU SAID WAS RUDE, LORD TOMOMASA.
TENMA!
YOU HAVE NO RIGHT TO MAKE FUN OF ME!
IS IT WRONG FOR ME TO LOVE HER? IS THERE SOME RULE THAT SAYS A GUARDIAN CAN'T FALL FOR THE PRIESTESS?!
WE'RE NOT FROM THIS WORLD! THE DRAGON GOD HAS NOTHING TO DO WITH US!!
AND WHAT ARE *YOU* DOING, SHIMON? DIDN'T I TELL YOU TO KEEP AN EYE ON AKANE?
UH, YEAH.
GET WITH IT THEN! DON'T JUST FOLLOW HER AROUND, SHOW SOME INITIATIVE!
HE'S IMPOSSIBLE.

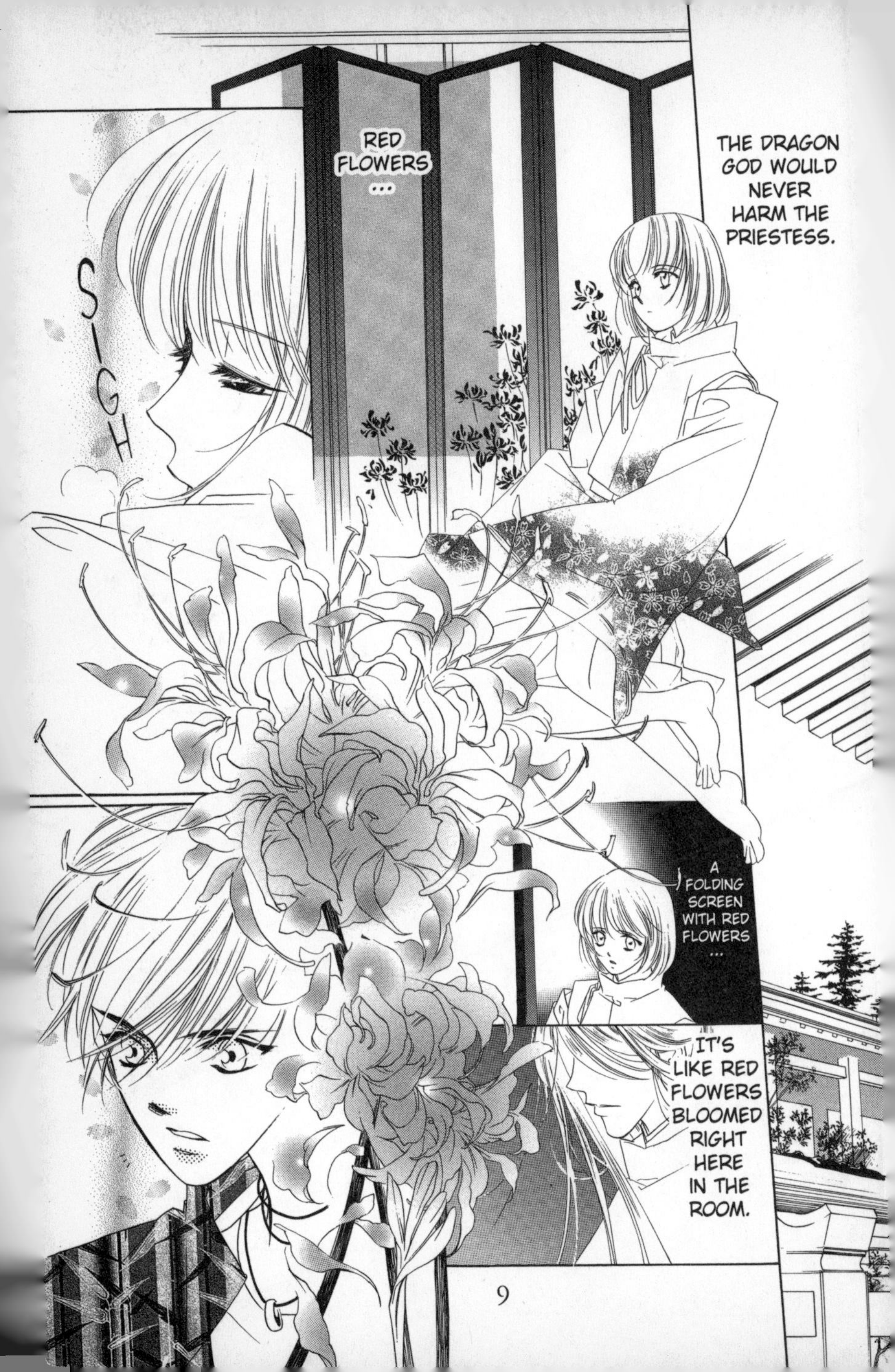
THE DRAGON GOD WOULD NEVER HARM THE PRIESTESS.
RED FLOWERS ...
SIGH
A FOLDING SCREEN WITH RED FLOWERS ...
IT'S LIKE RED FLOWERS BLOOMED RIGHT HERE IN THE ROOM.

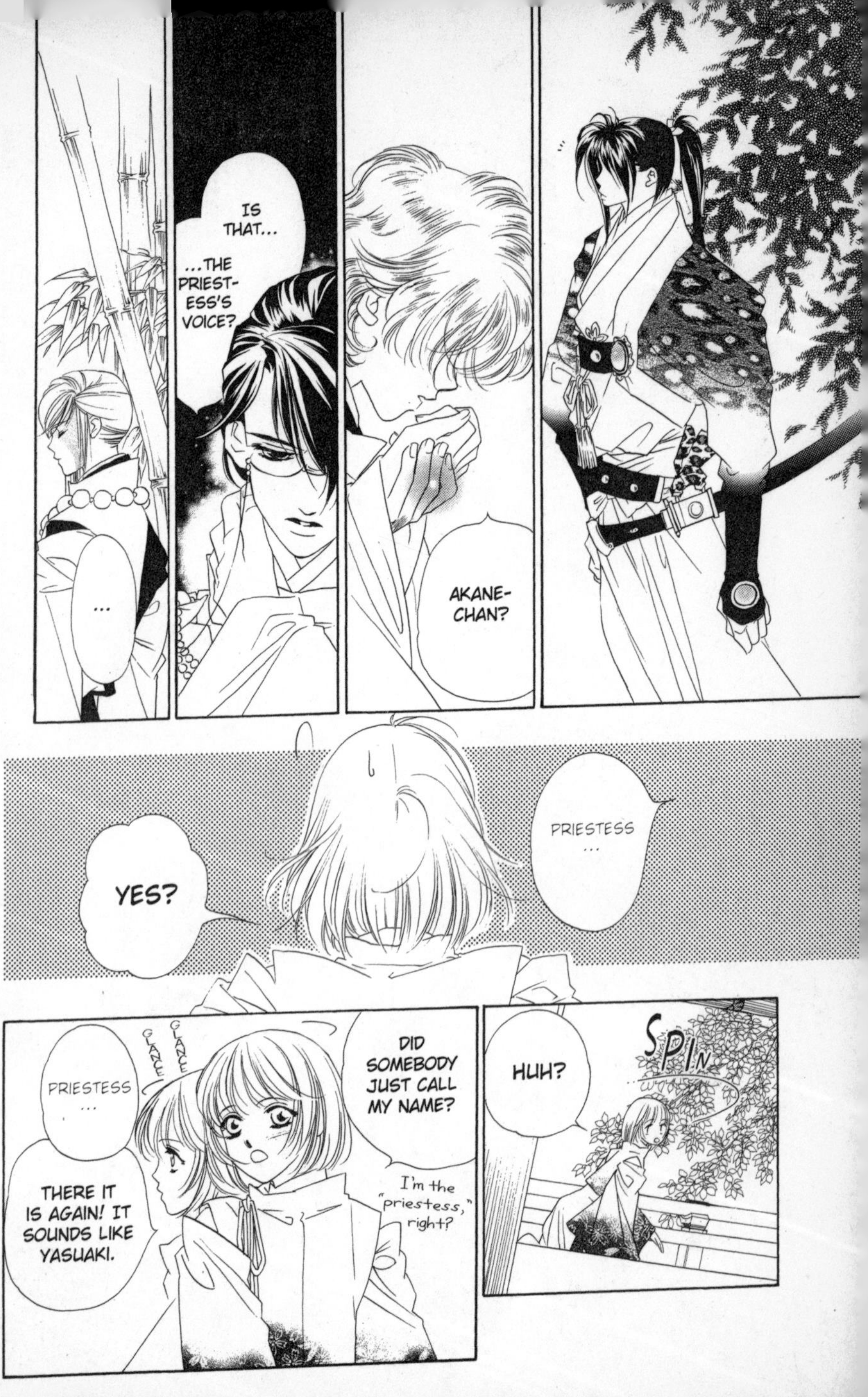
AKANE-CHAN?
IS THAT...
...THE PRIESTESS'S VOICE?
...
PRIESTESS ...
YES?
SPIN
HUH?
DID SOMEBODY JUST CALL MY NAME?
I'm the "priestess," right?
GLANCE GLANCE
PRIESTESS ...
THERE IT IS AGAIN! IT SOUNDS LIKE YASUAKI.

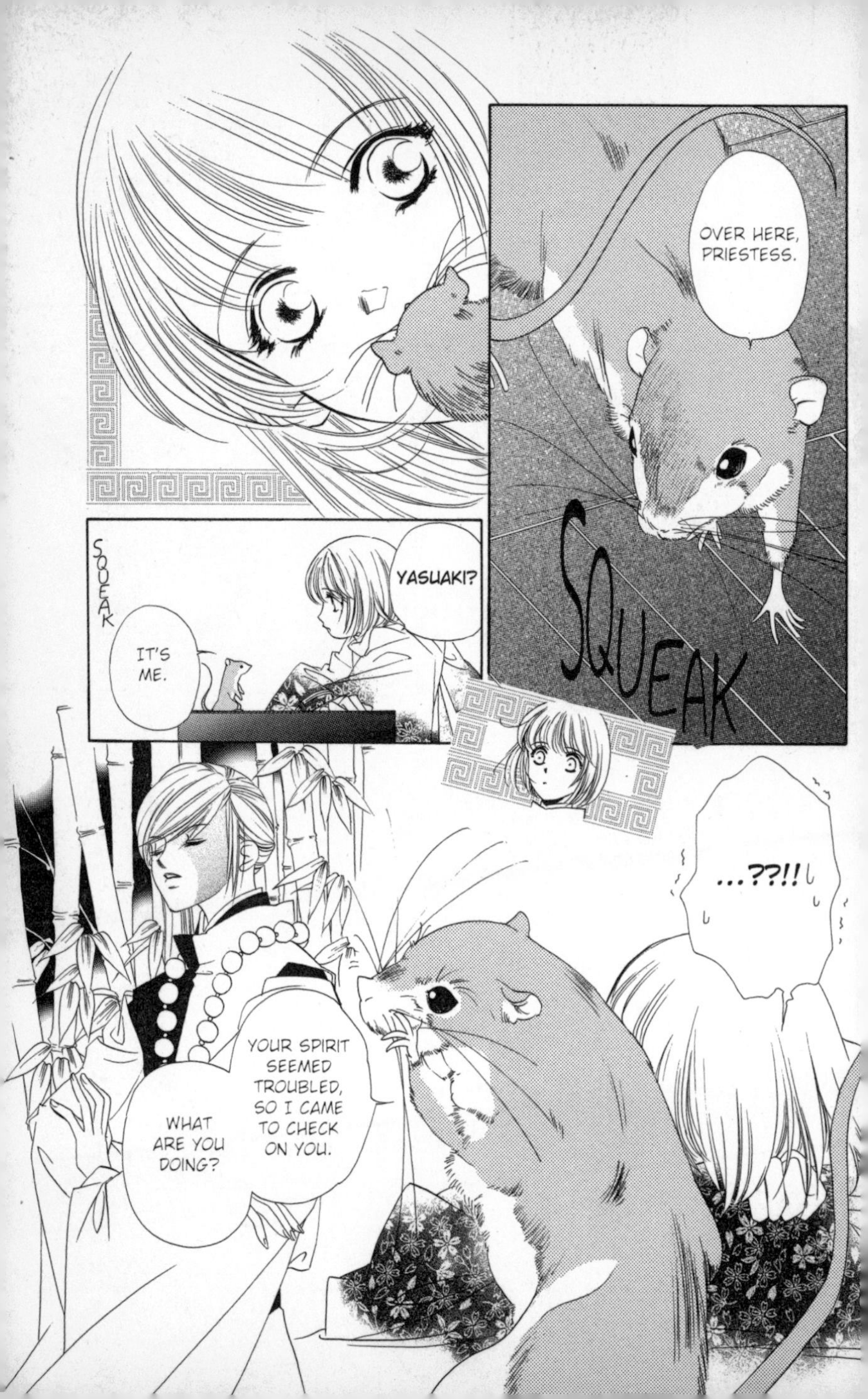

OVER HERE, PRIESTESS.
SQUEAK
YASUAKI?
IT'S ME.
SQUEAK
...??!!
YOUR SPIRIT SEEMED TROUBLED, SO I CAME TO CHECK ON YOU.
WHAT ARE YOU DOING?

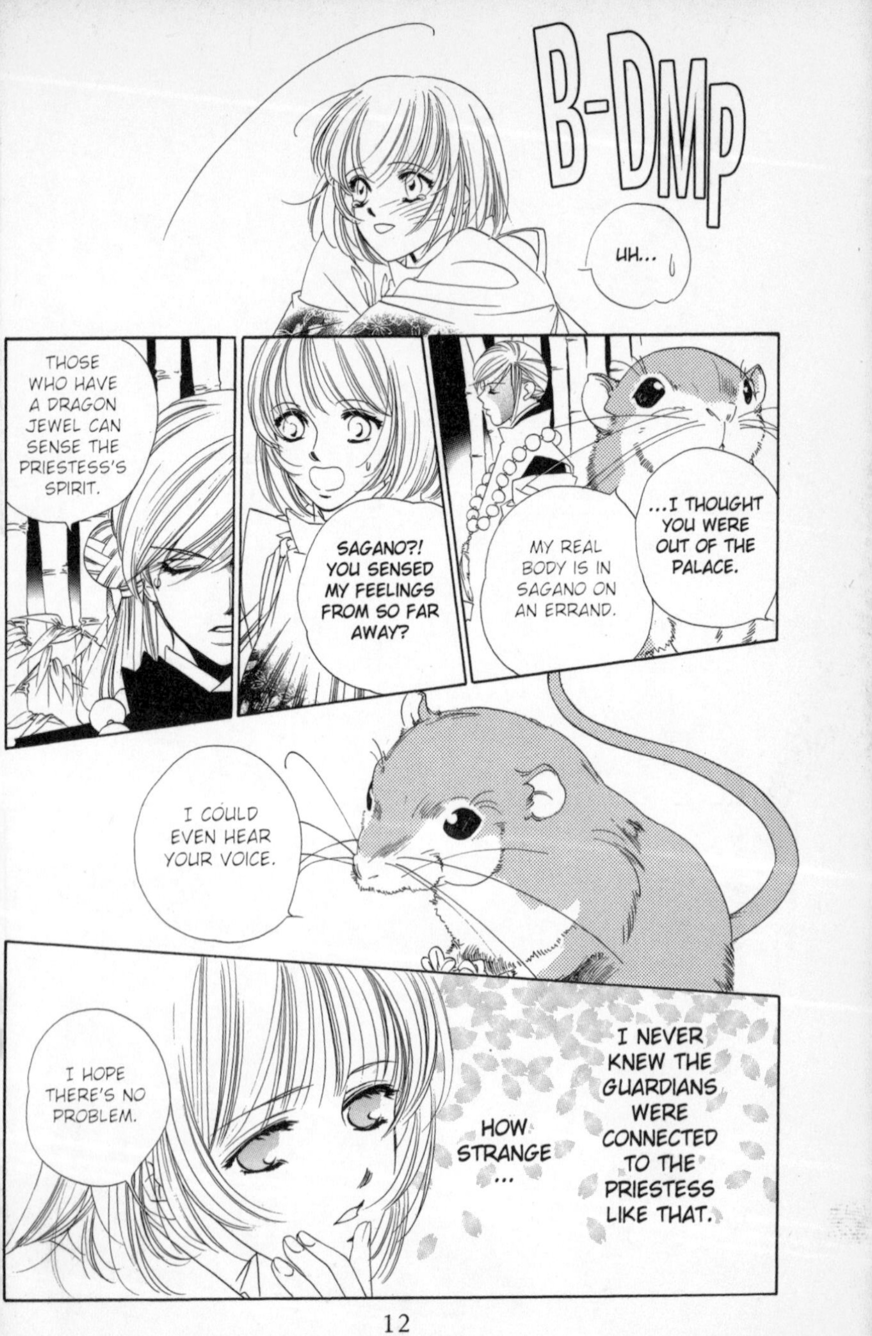
B-DMP
UH...
...I THOUGHT YOU WERE OUT OF THE PALACE.
MY REAL BODY IS IN SAGANO ON AN ERRAND.
SAGANO?! YOU SENSED MY FEELINGS FROM SO FAR AWAY?
THOSE WHO HAVE A DRAGON JEWEL CAN SENSE THE PRIESTESS'S SPIRIT.
I COULD EVEN HEAR YOUR VOICE.
I NEVER KNEW THE GUARDIANS WERE CONNECTED TO THE PRIESTESS LIKE THAT.
HOW STRANGE...
I HOPE THERE'S NO PROBLEM.

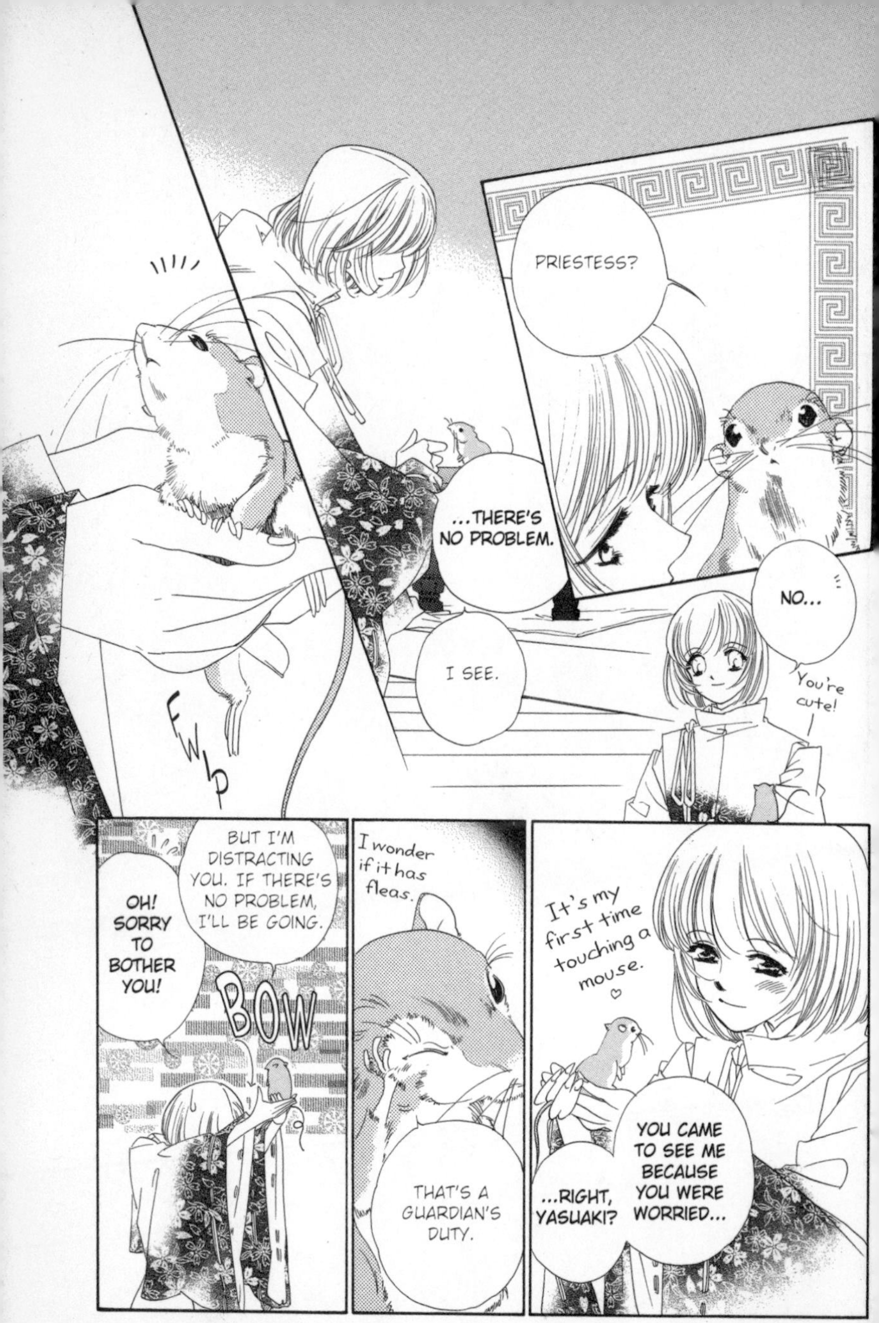
PRIESTESS?
NO...
You're cute!
...THERE'S NO PROBLEM.
I SEE.
FWIP
It's my first time touching a mouse.
YOU CAME TO SEE ME BECAUSE YOU WERE WORRIED...
...RIGHT, YASUAKI?
I wonder if it has fleas.
THAT'S A GUARDIAN'S DUTY.
BUT I'M DISTRACTING YOU. IF THERE'S NO PROBLEM, I'LL BE GOING.
OH! SORRY TO BOTHER YOU!
BOW

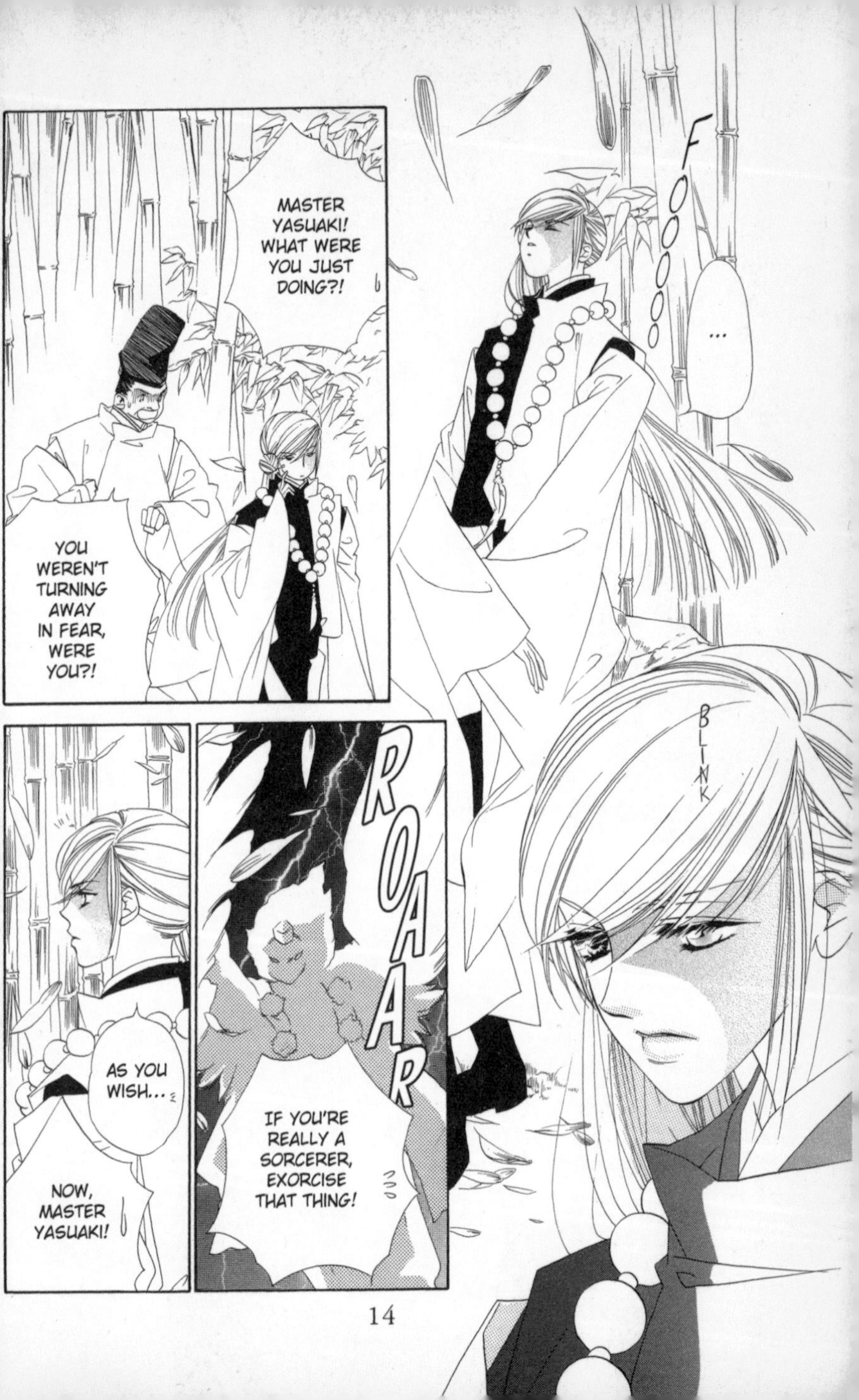
FOOOOOO
...
MASTER YASUAKI! WHAT WERE YOU JUST DOING?!
YOU WEREN'T TURNING AWAY IN FEAR, WERE YOU?!
BLINK
ROAAR
IF YOU'RE REALLY A SORCERER, EXORCISE THAT THING!
AS YOU WISH...
NOW, MASTER YASUAKI!

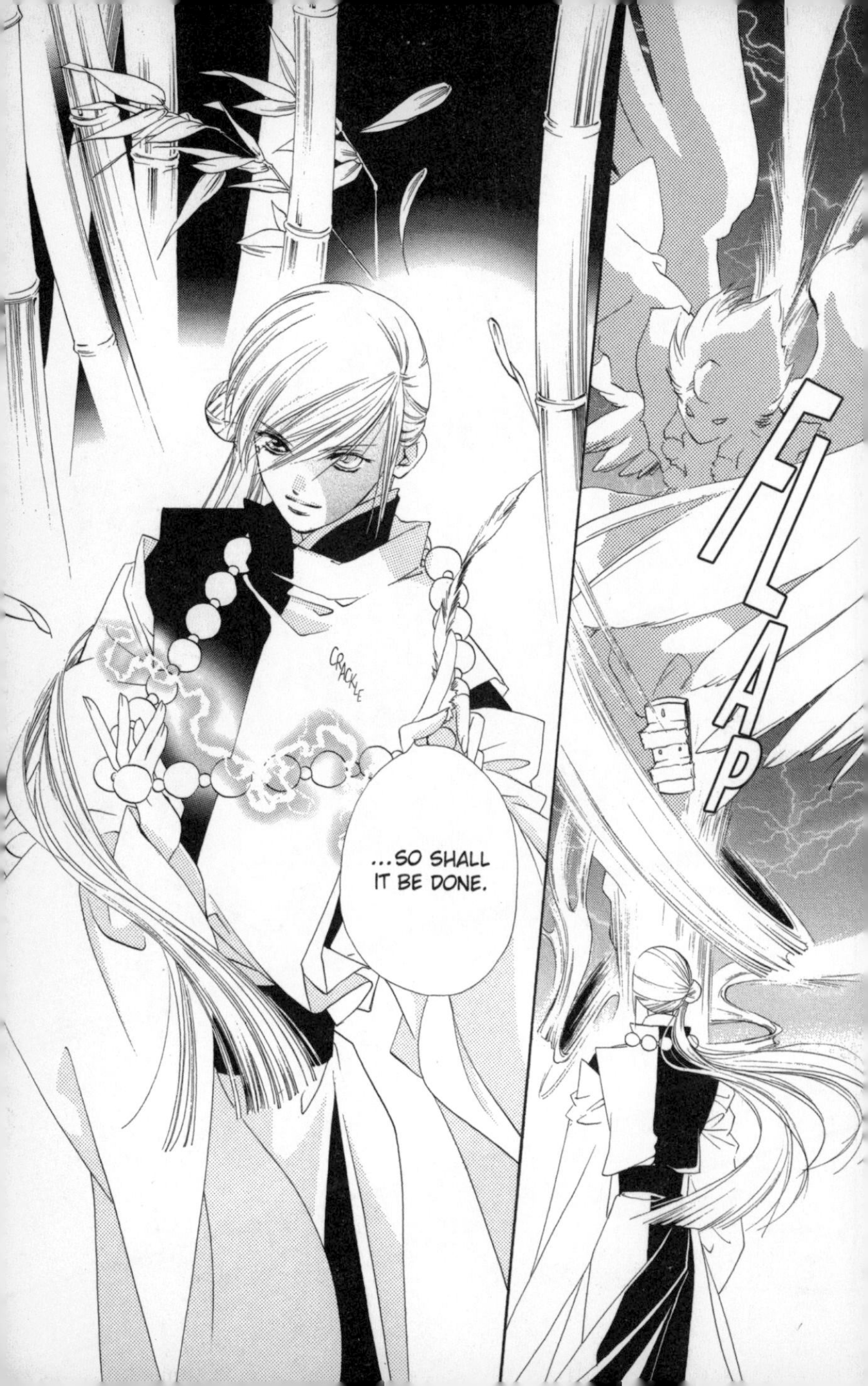
FLAP
CRACKLE
...SO SHALL IT BE DONE.

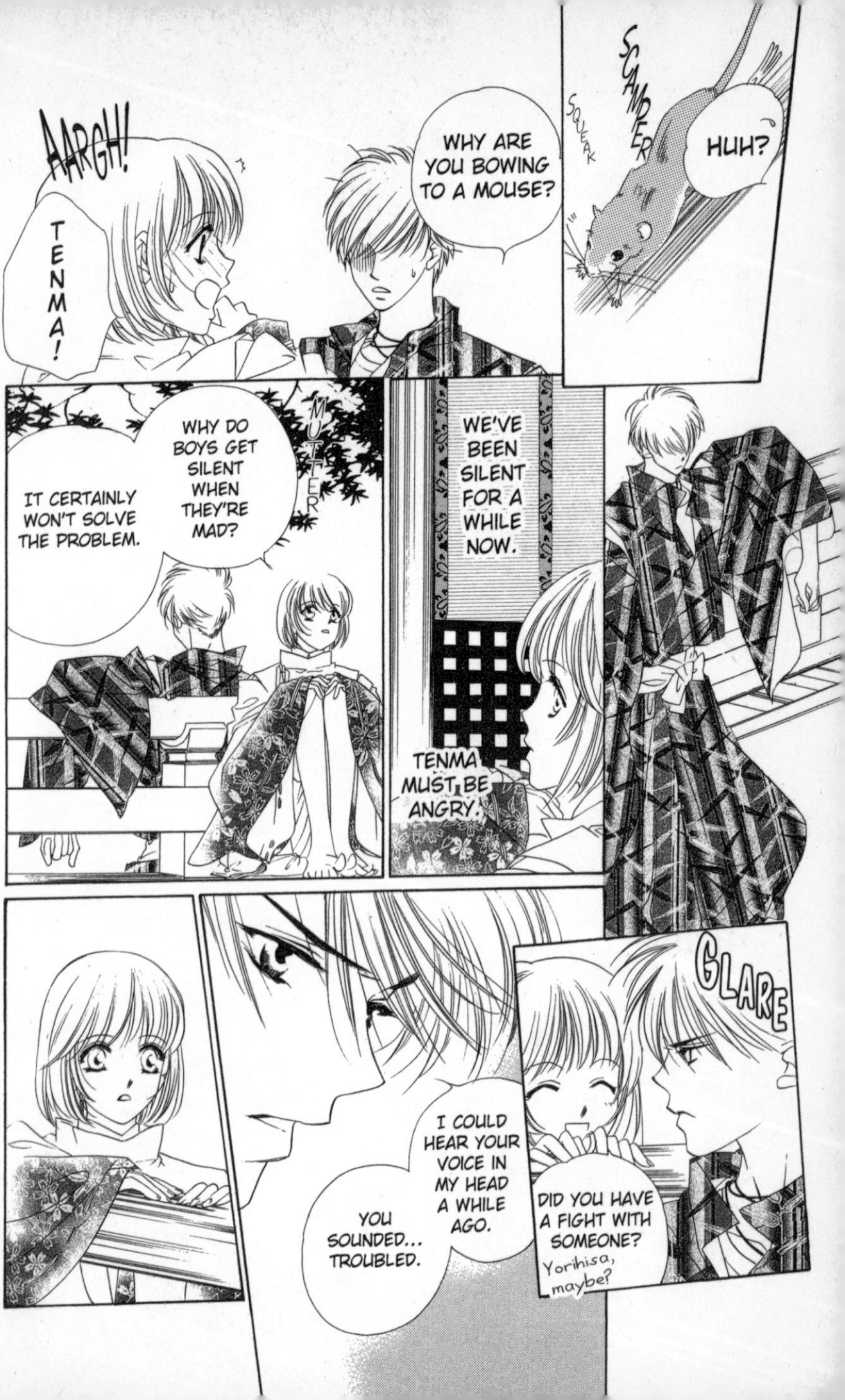
SCAMPER
SQUEAK
HUH?
WHY ARE YOU BOWING TO A MOUSE?
AARGH!
TENMA!
WE'VE BEEN SILENT FOR A WHILE NOW.
TENMA MUST BE ANGRY.
MUTTER
WHY DO BOYS GET SILENT WHEN THEY'RE MAD?
IT CERTAINLY WON'T SOLVE THE PROBLEM.
GLARE
DID YOU HAVE A FIGHT WITH SOMEONE?
Yorihisa, maybe?
I COULD HEAR YOUR VOICE IN MY HEAD A WHILE AGO.
YOU SOUNDED... TROUBLED.

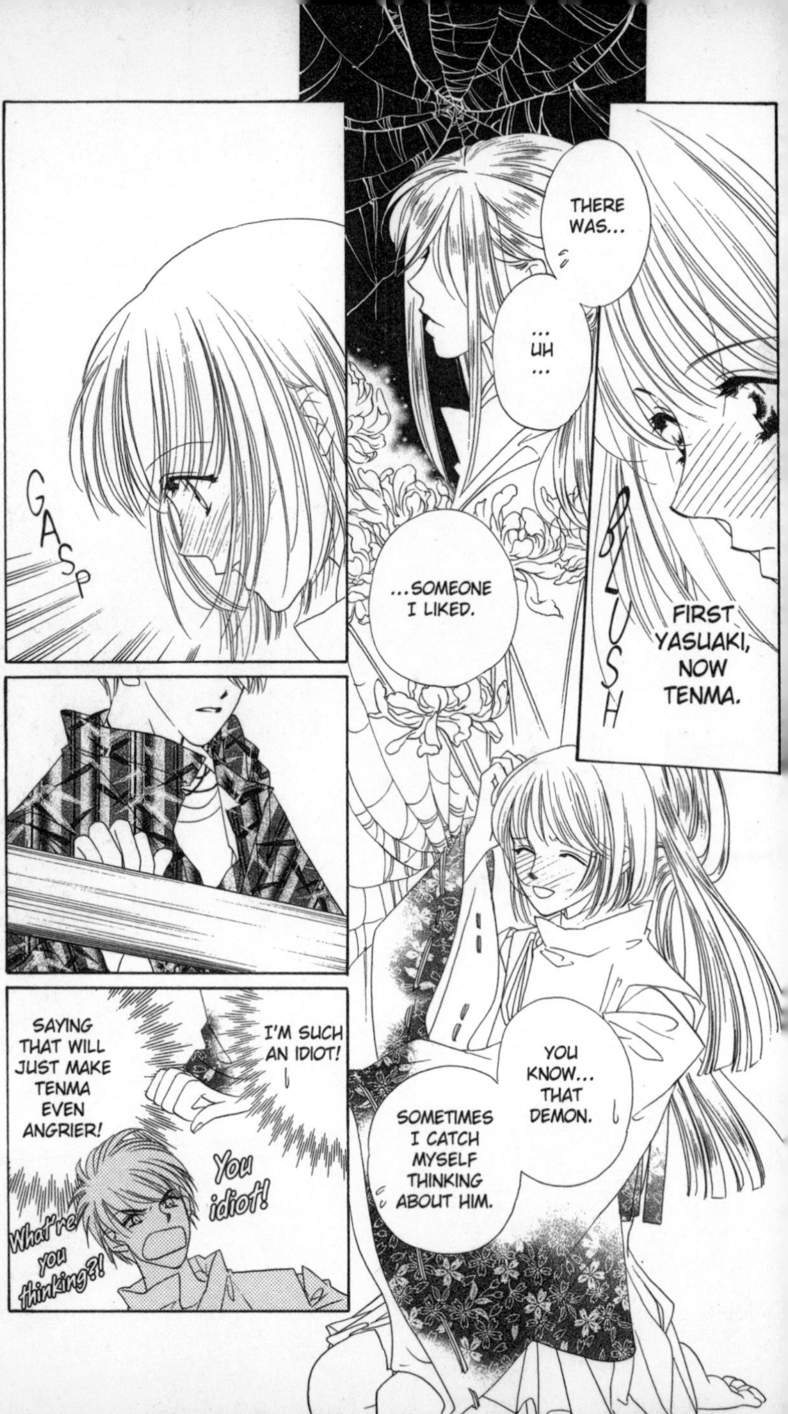
THERE WAS...
... UH ...
...SOMEONE I LIKED.
BLUSH
FIRST YASUAKI, NOW TENMA.
YOU KNOW... THAT DEMON.
SOMETIMES I CATCH MYSELF THINKING ABOUT HIM.
GASP
I'M SUCH AN IDIOT!
SAYING THAT WILL JUST MAKE TENMA EVEN ANGRIER!
You idiot!
What're you thinking?!

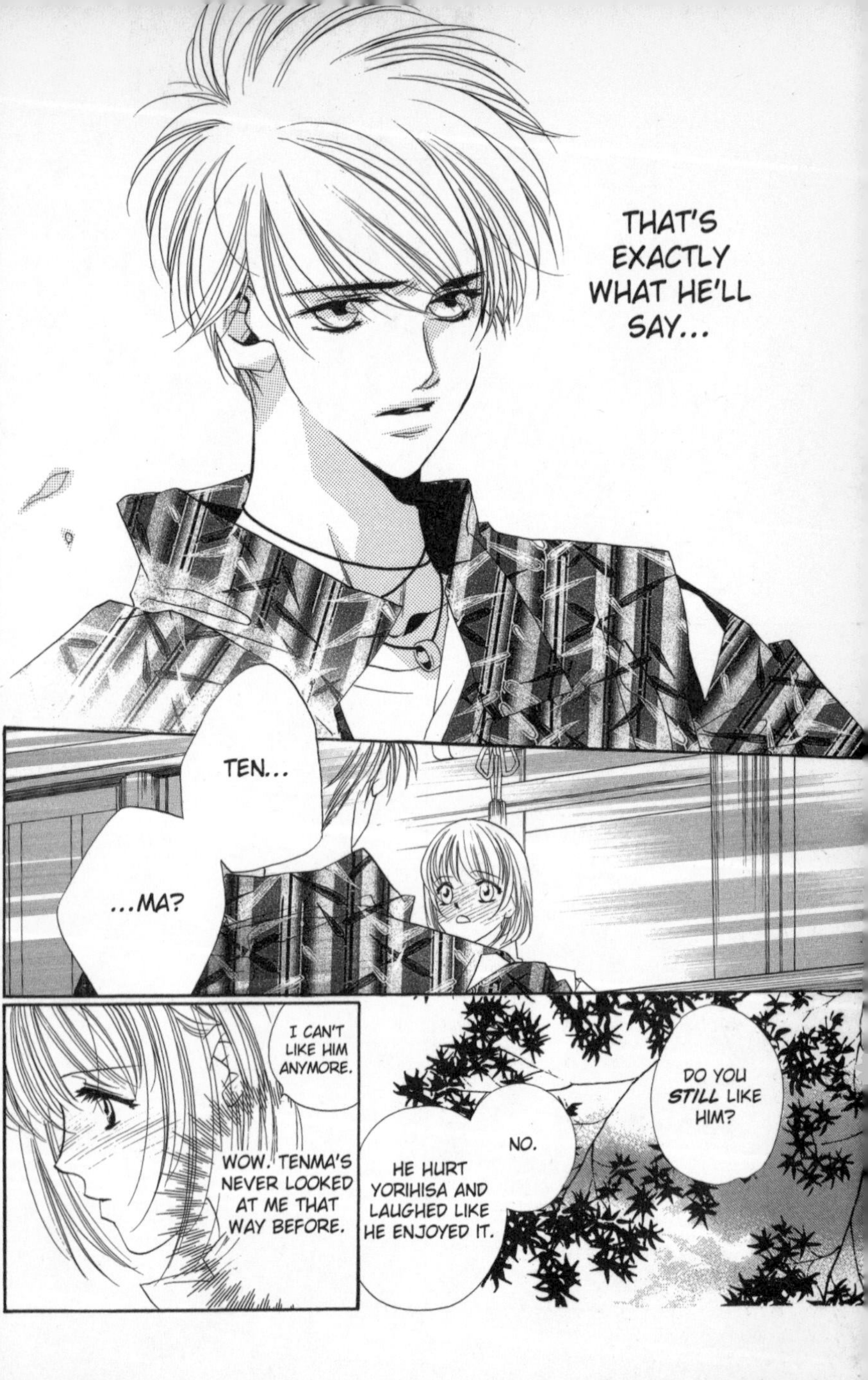
THAT'S EXACTLY WHAT HE'LL SAY...
TEN...
...MA?
DO YOU STILL LIKE HIM?
NO.
HE HURT YORIHISA AND LAUGHED LIKE HE ENJOYED IT.
I CAN'T LIKE HIM ANYMORE.
WOW. TENMA'S NEVER LOOKED AT ME THAT WAY BEFORE.

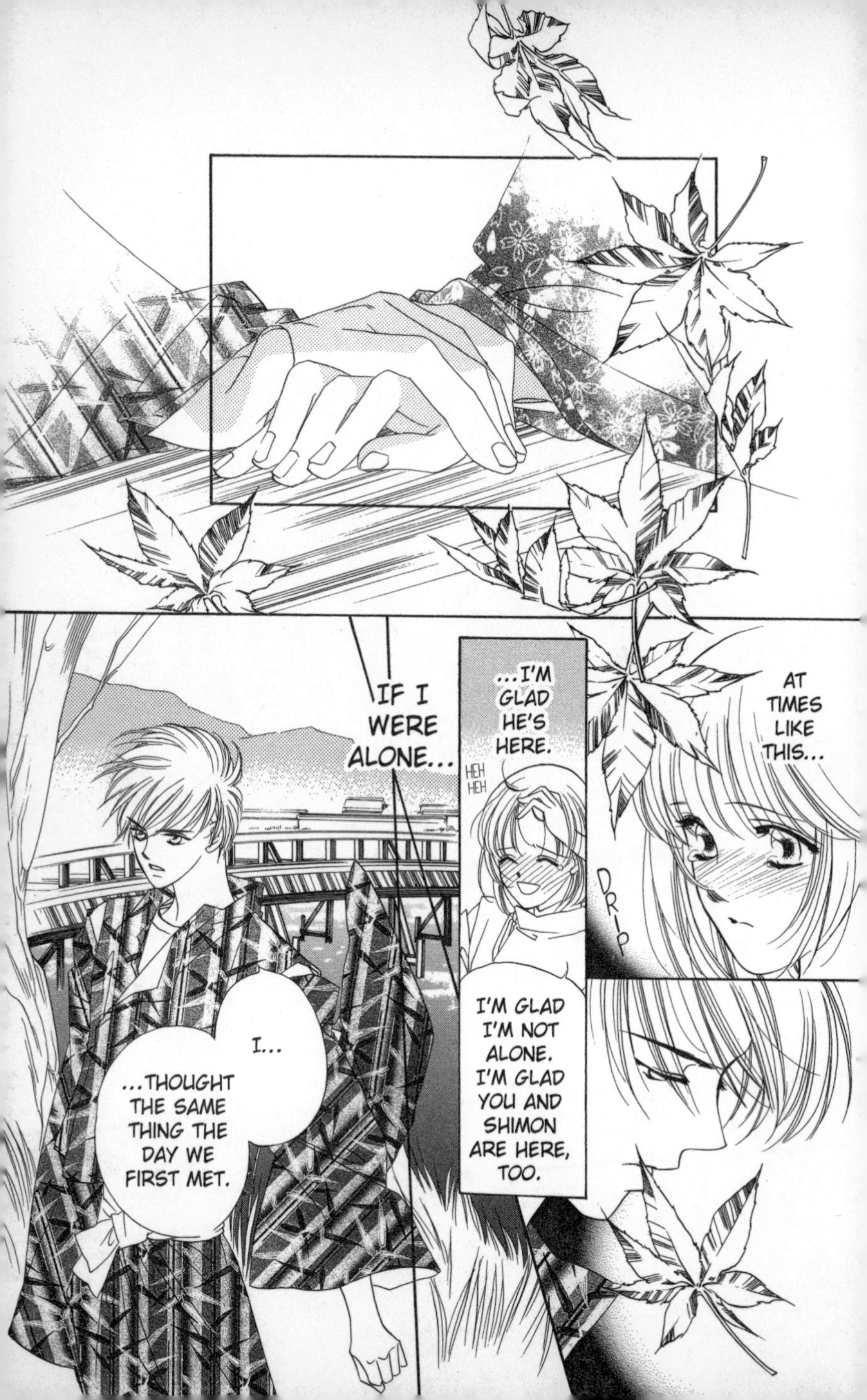
AT TIMES LIKE THIS...
DRIP
...I'M GLAD HE'S HERE.
HEH HEH
IF I WERE ALONE...
I'M GLAD I'M NOT ALONE. I'M GLAD YOU AND SHIMON ARE HERE, TOO.
I...
...THOUGHT THE SAME THING THE DAY WE FIRST MET.

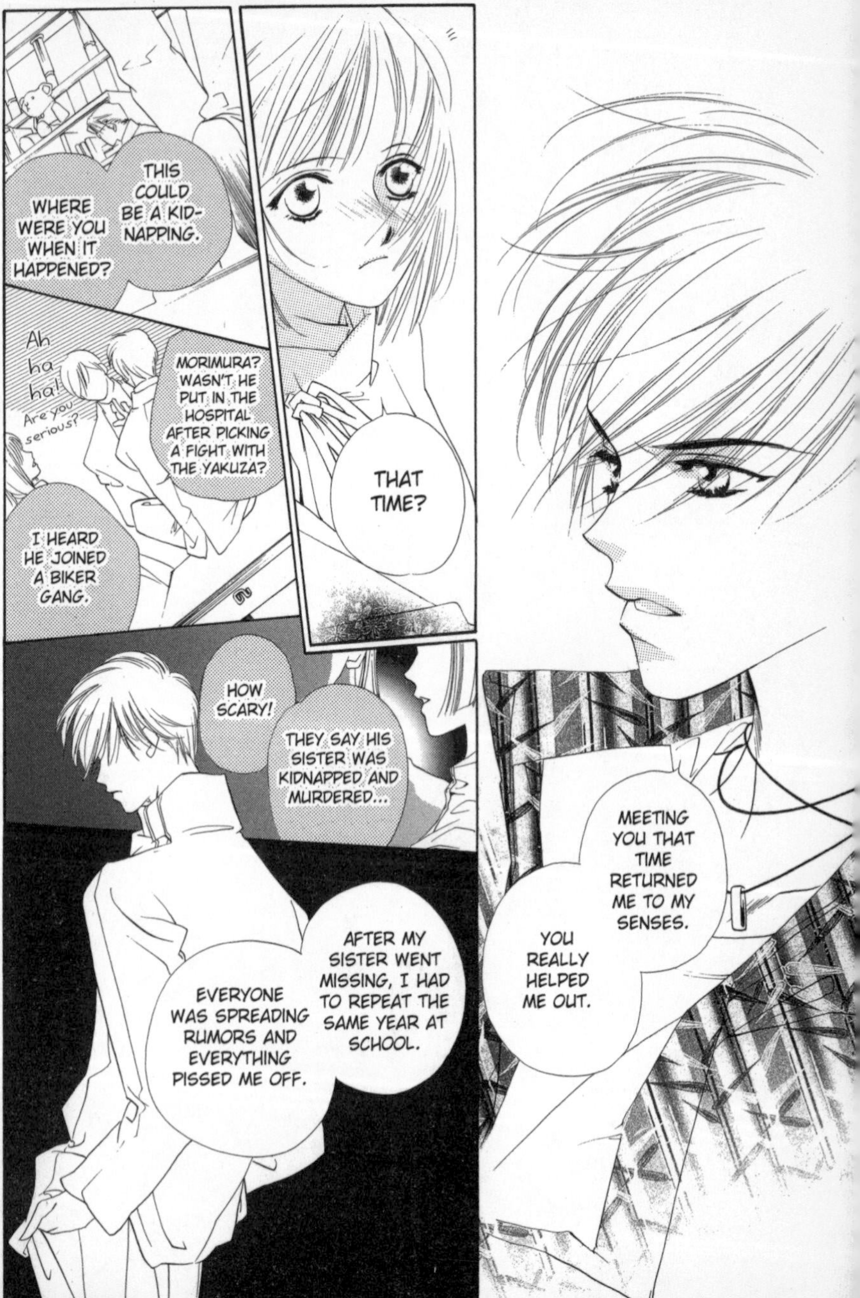
THAT TIME?
THIS COULD BE A KID-NAPPING.
WHERE WERE YOU WHEN IT HAPPENED?
MORIMURA? WASN'T HE PUT IN THE HOSPITAL AFTER PICKING A FIGHT WITH THE YAKUZA?
Ah ha ha! Are you serious?
I HEARD HE JOINED A BIKER GANG.
HOW SCARY!
THEY SAY HIS SISTER WAS KIDNAPPED AND MURDERED...
AFTER MY SISTER WENT MISSING, I HAD TO REPEAT THE SAME YEAR AT SCHOOL.
EVERYONE WAS SPREADING RUMORS AND EVERYTHING PISSED ME OFF.
MEETING YOU THAT TIME RETURNED ME TO MY SENSES.
YOU REALLY HELPED ME OUT.

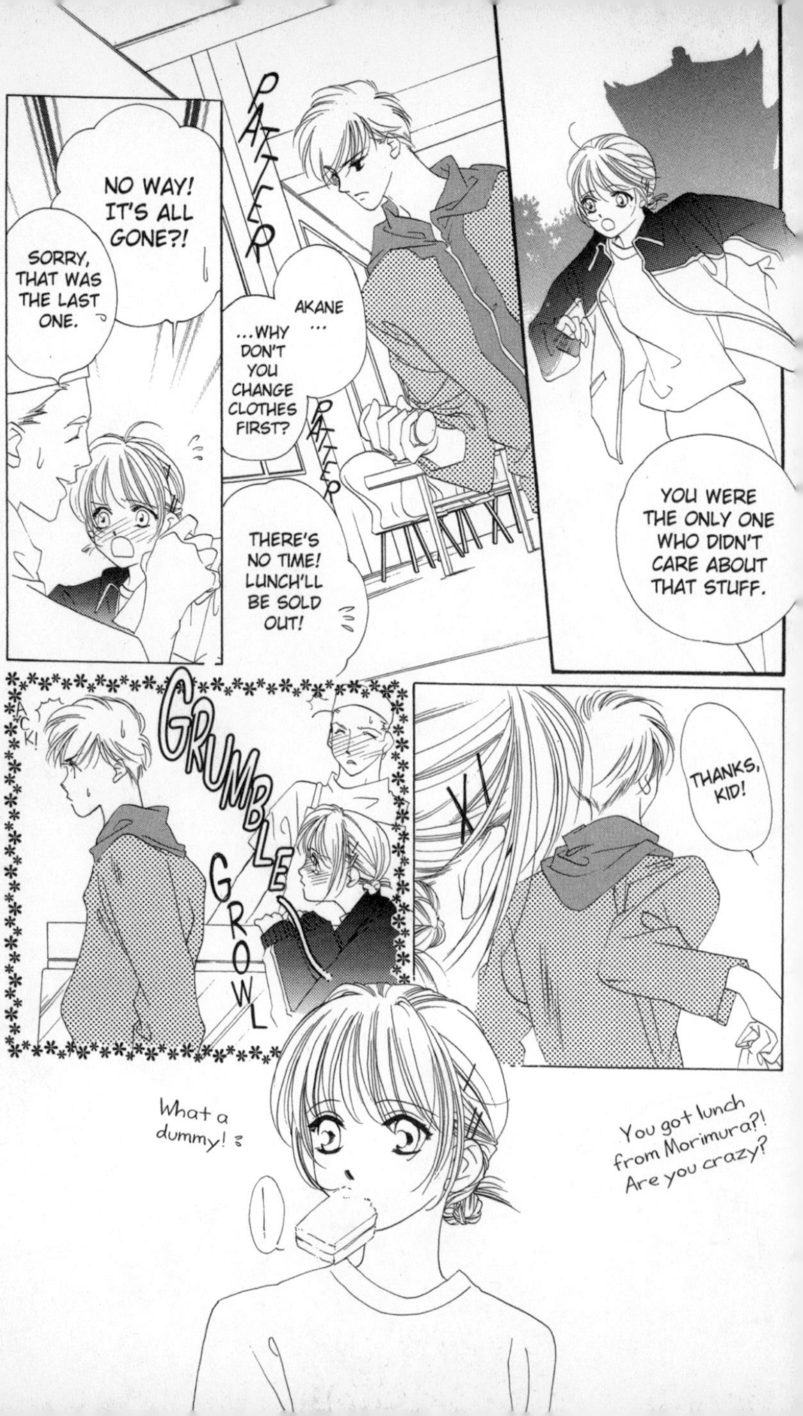
YOU WERE THE ONLY ONE WHO DIDN'T CARE ABOUT THAT STUFF.
PATTER
AKANE ...
...WHY DON'T YOU CHANGE CLOTHES FIRST?
PATTER
THERE'S NO TIME! LUNCH'LL BE SOLD OUT!
NO WAY! IT'S ALL GONE?!
SORRY, THAT WAS THE LAST ONE.
THANKS, KID!
ACK!
GRUMBLE
GROWL
You got lunch from Morimura?! Are you crazy?
What a dummy!

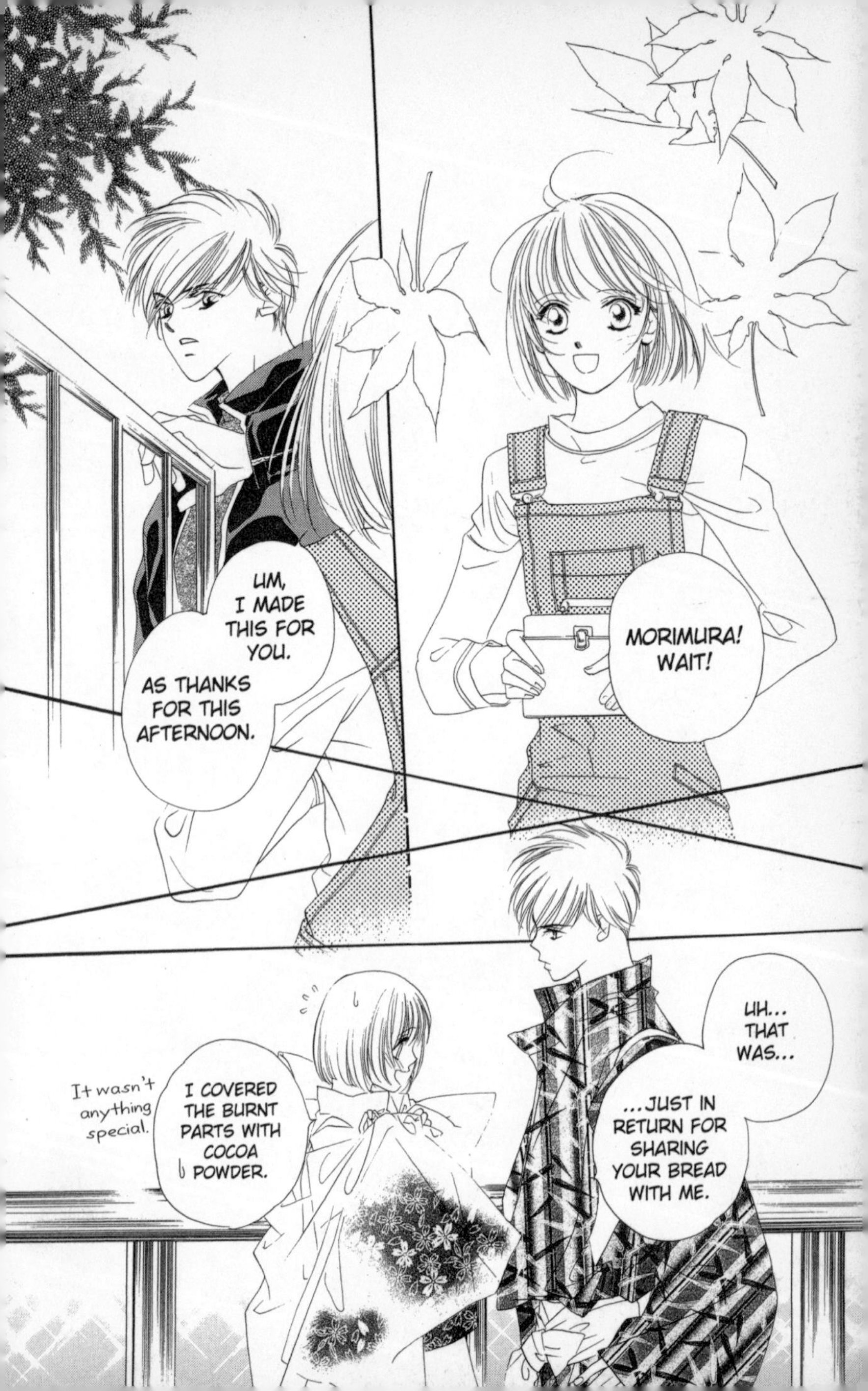
MORIMURA! WAIT!
UM, I MADE THIS FOR YOU.
AS THANKS FOR THIS AFTERNOON.
UH... THAT WAS...
...JUST IN RETURN FOR SHARING YOUR BREAD WITH ME.
I COVERED THE BURNT PARTS WITH COCOA POWDER.
It wasn't anything special.

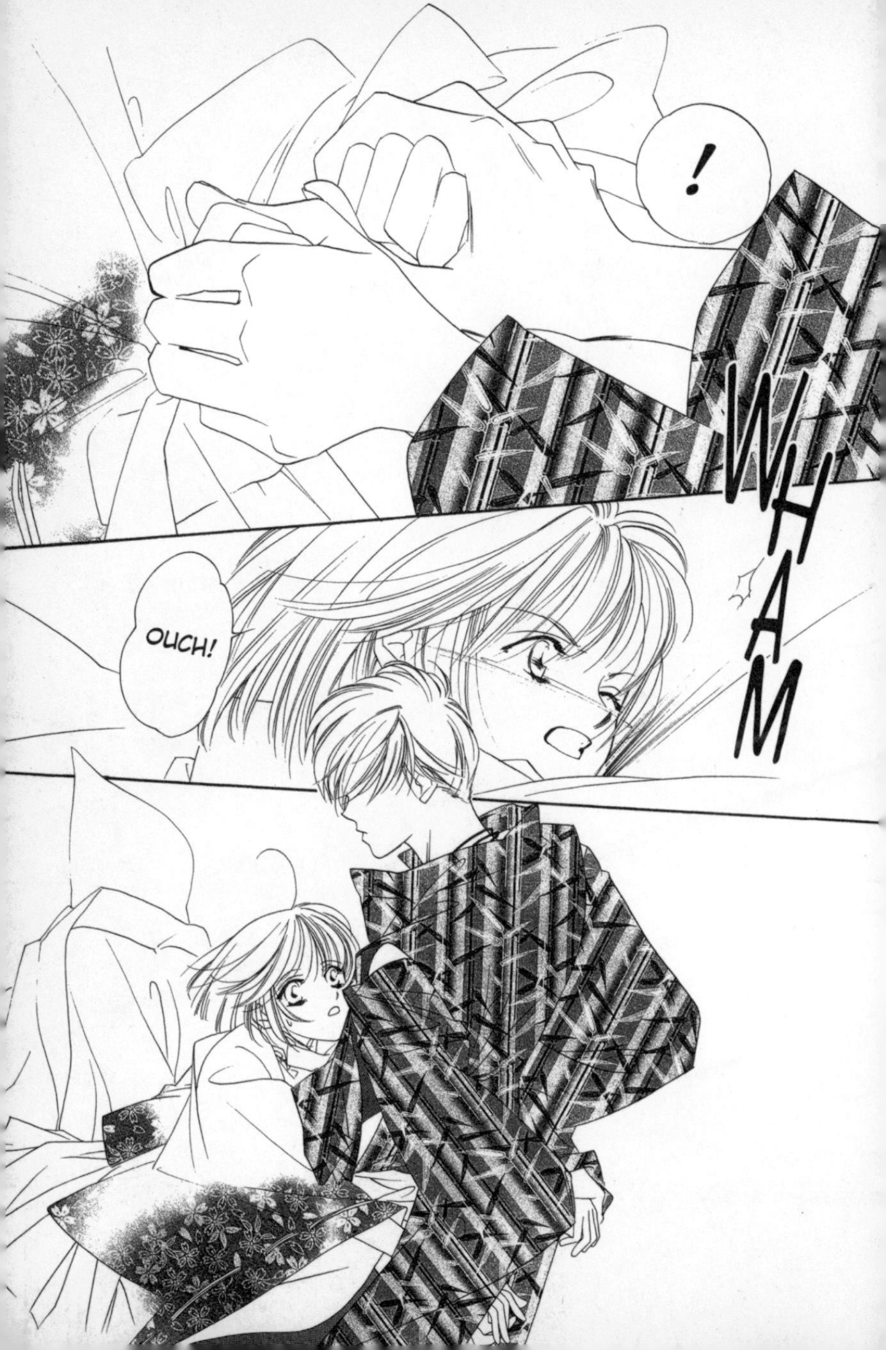
!
WHAM
OUCH!

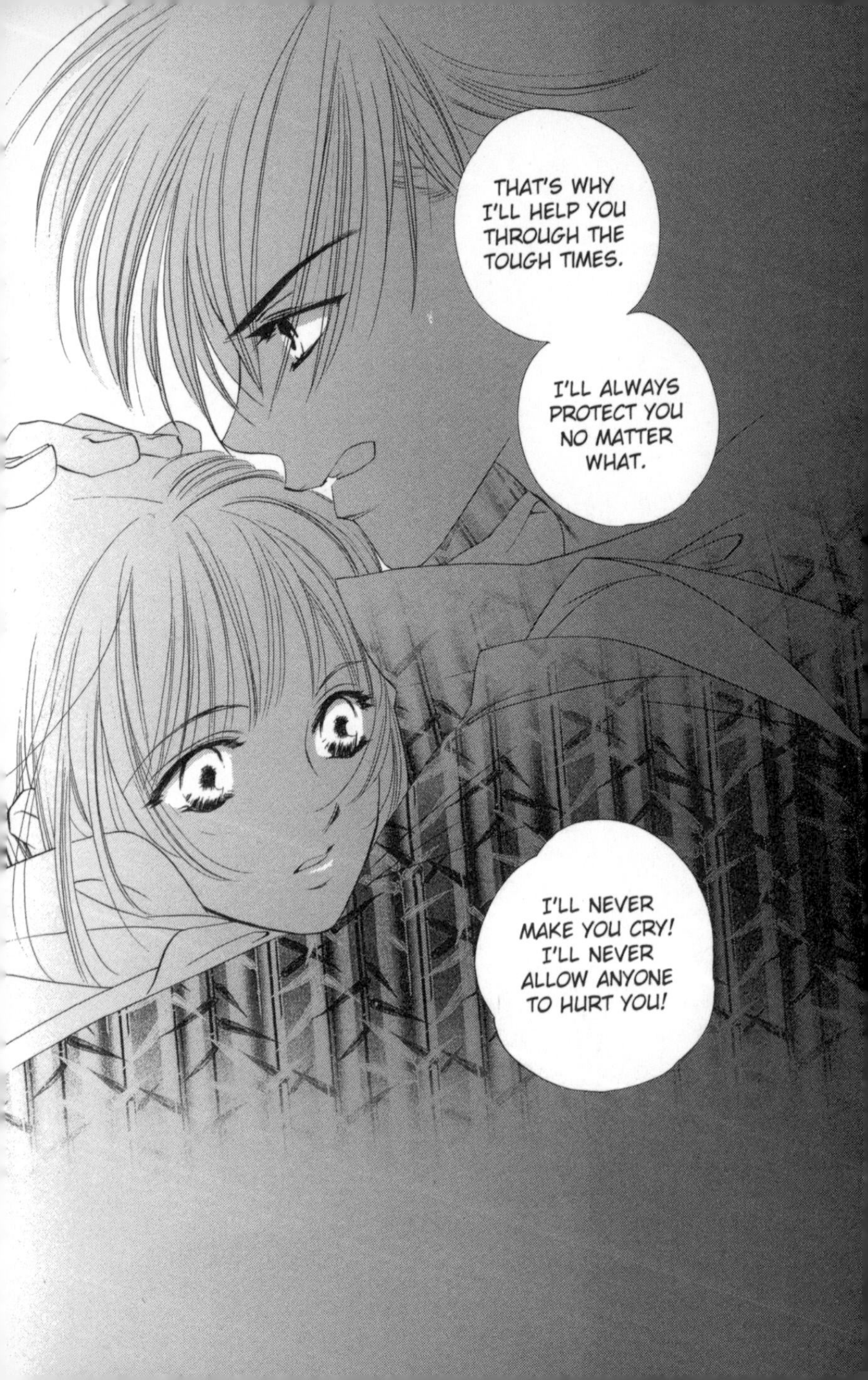
THAT'S WHY I'LL HELP YOU THROUGH THE TOUGH TIMES.
I'LL ALWAYS PROTECT YOU NO MATTER WHAT.
I'LL NEVER MAKE YOU CRY! I'LL NEVER ALLOW ANYONE TO HURT YOU!

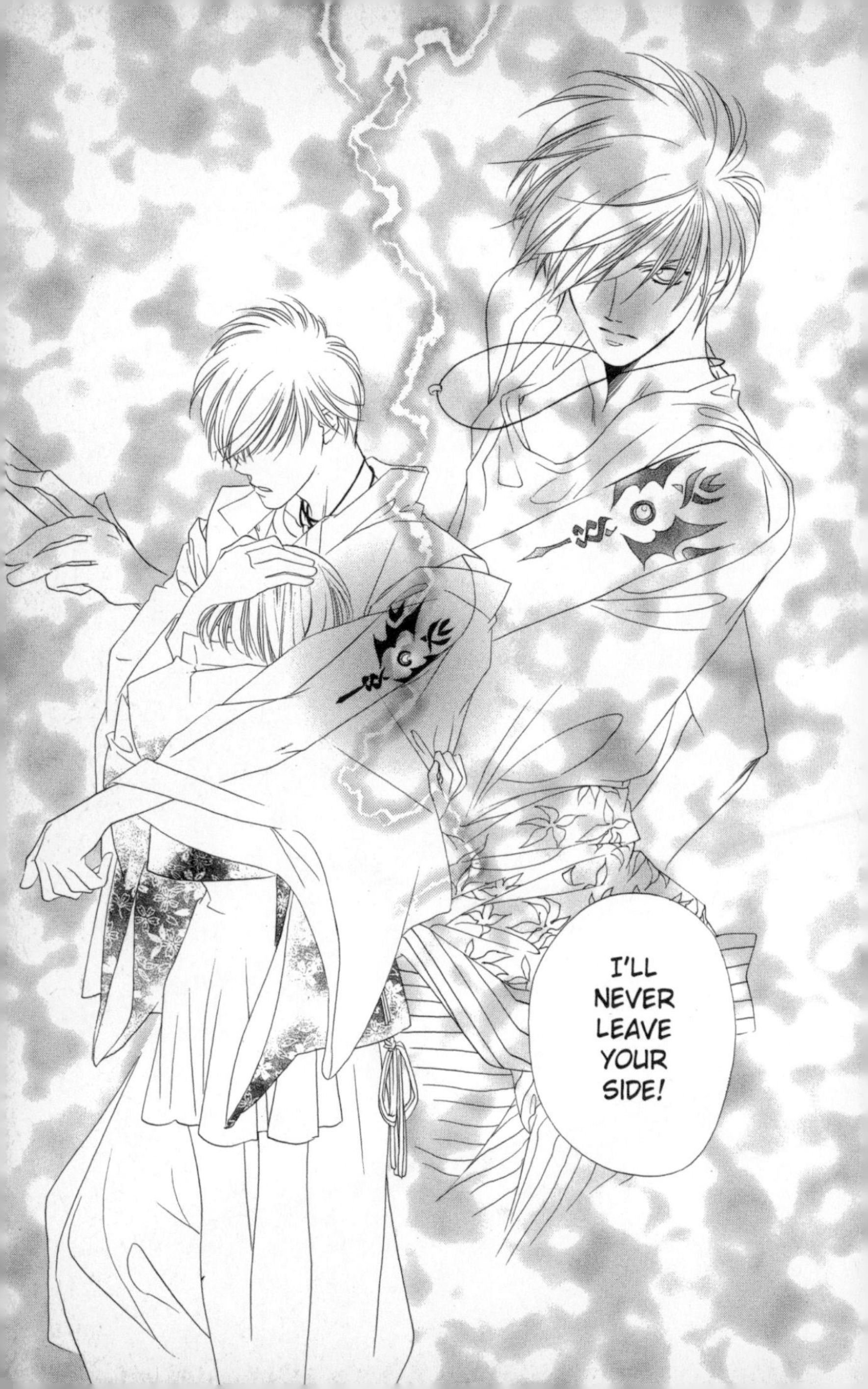
I'LL NEVER LEAVE YOUR SIDE!

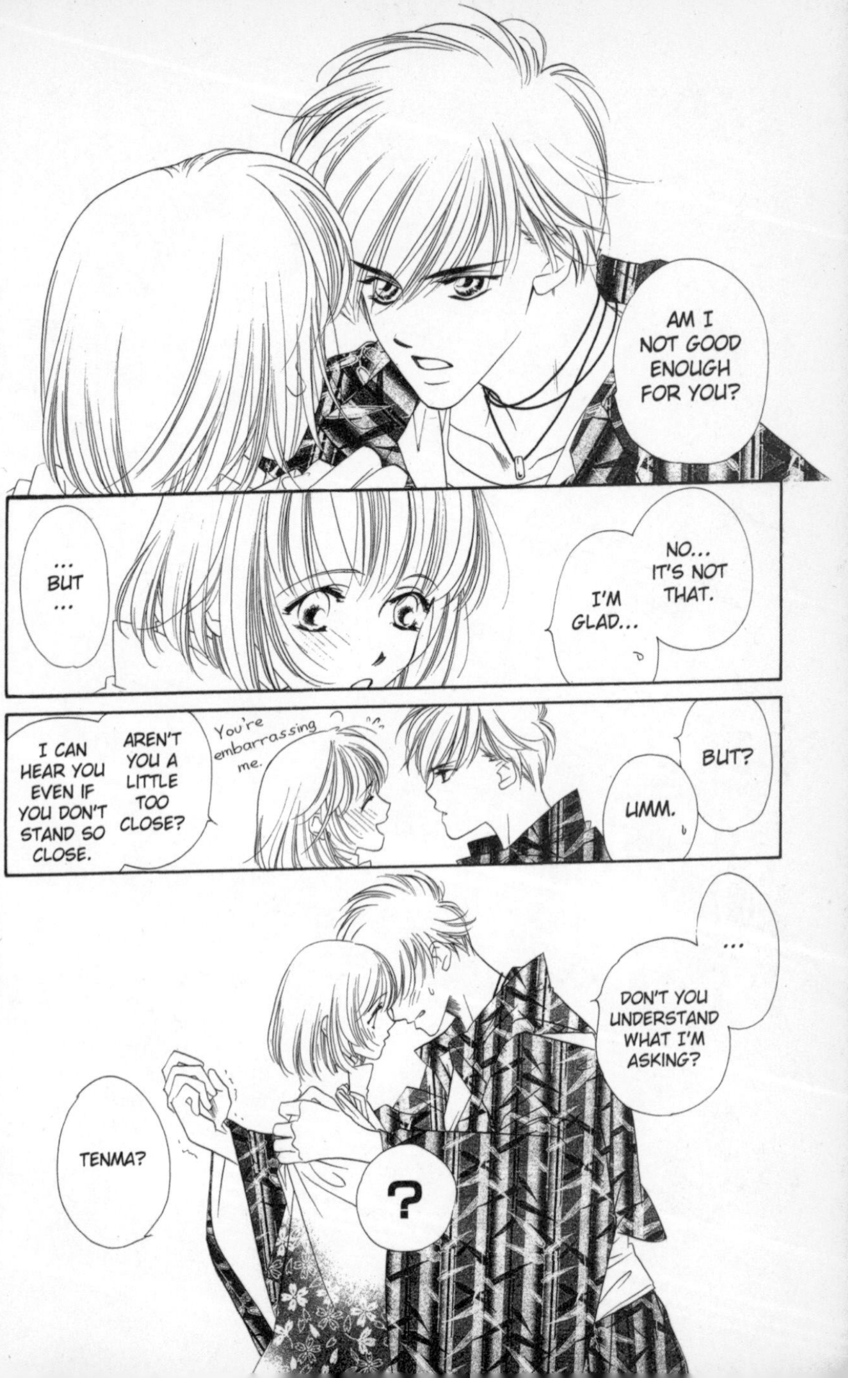
AM I NOT GOOD ENOUGH FOR YOU?
NO... IT'S NOT THAT.
I'M GLAD...
... BUT ...
BUT?
UMM.
You're embarrassing me.
AREN'T YOU A LITTLE TOO CLOSE?
I CAN HEAR YOU EVEN IF YOU DON'T STAND SO CLOSE.
...
DON'T YOU UNDERSTAND WHAT I'M ASKING?
TENMA?
?

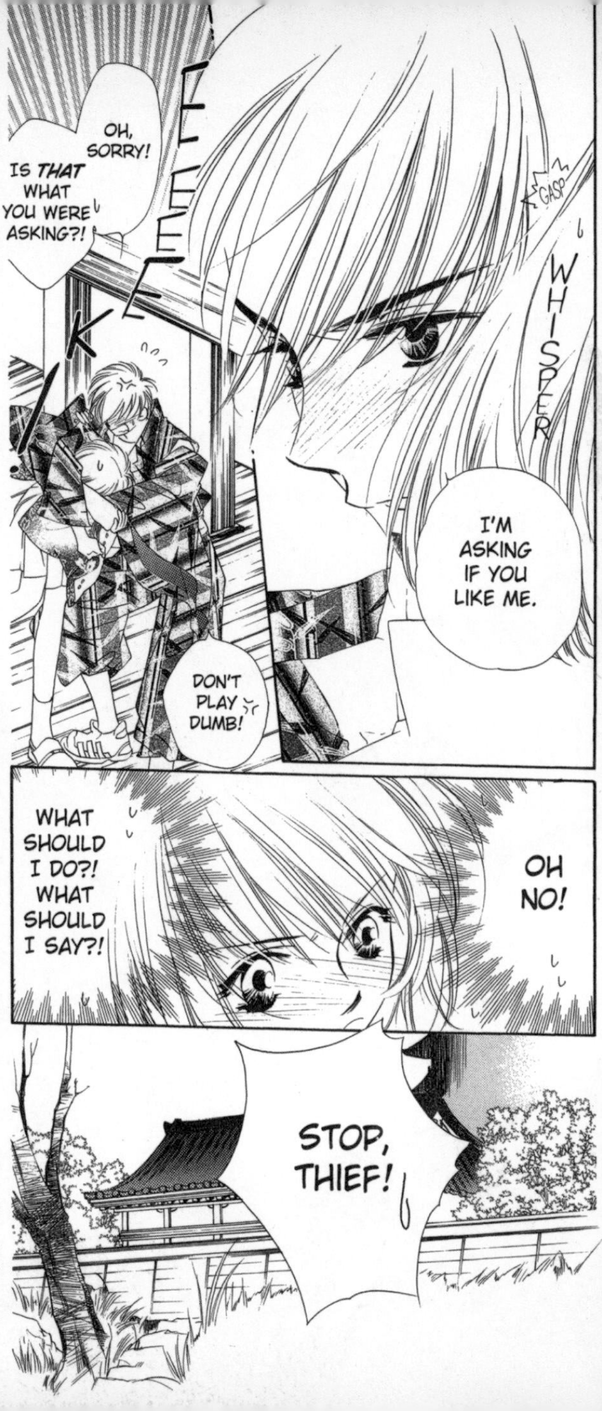
GASP
WHISPER
I'M ASKING IF YOU LIKE ME.
EEEEEEK!
OH, SORRY!
IS *THAT* WHAT YOU WERE ASKING?!
DON'T PLAY DUMB!
OH NO!
WHAT SHOULD I DO?! WHAT SHOULD I SAY?!
STOP, THIEF!
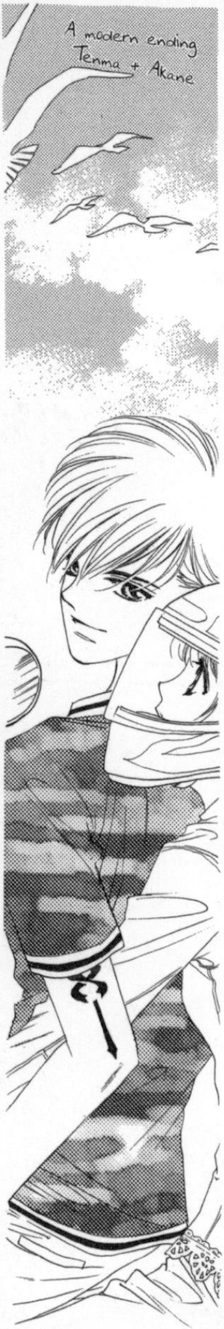
A modern ending
Tenma + Akane

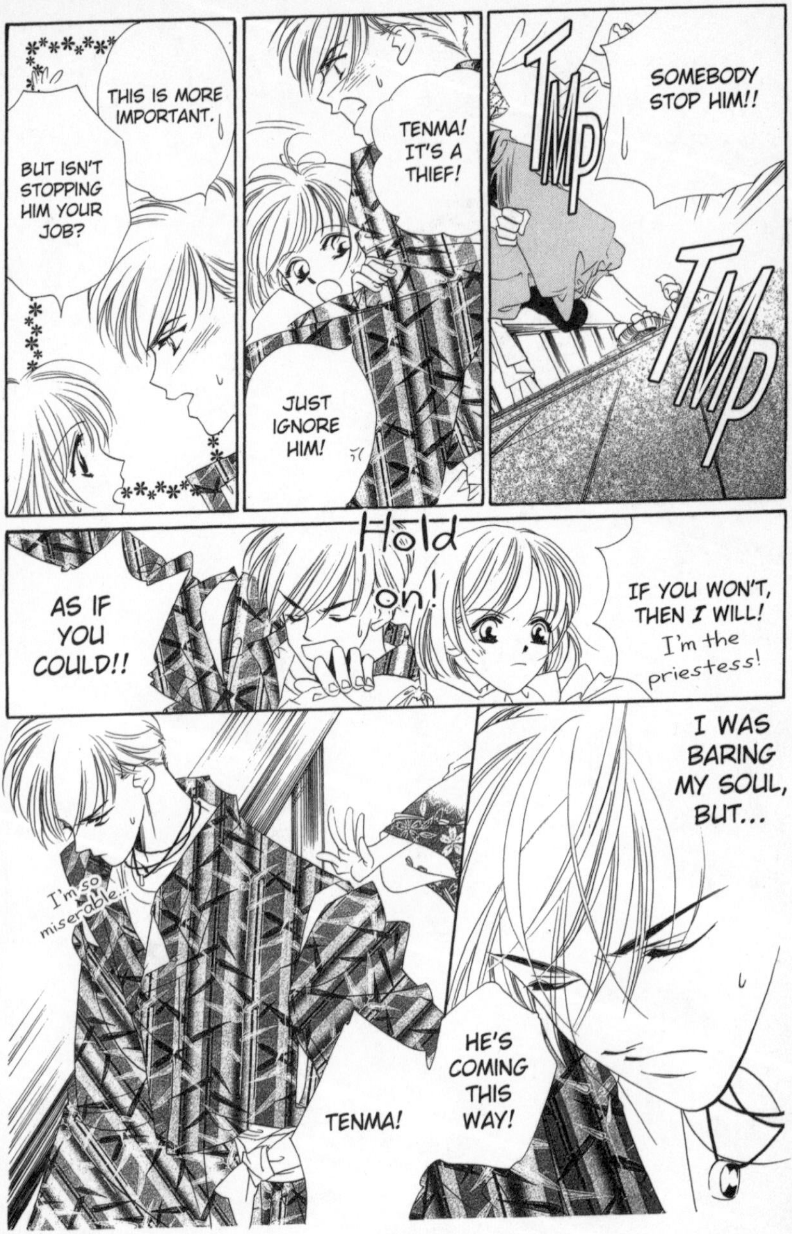
TMP
SOMEBODY STOP HIM!!
TMP
TENMA! IT'S A THIEF!
JUST IGNORE HIM!
THIS IS MORE IMPORTANT.
BUT ISN'T STOPPING HIM YOUR JOB?
IF YOU WON'T, THEN *I* WILL! I'm the priestess!
Hold on!
AS IF YOU COULD!!
I WAS BARING MY SOUL, BUT...
HE'S COMING THIS WAY!
TENMA!
I'm so miserable...

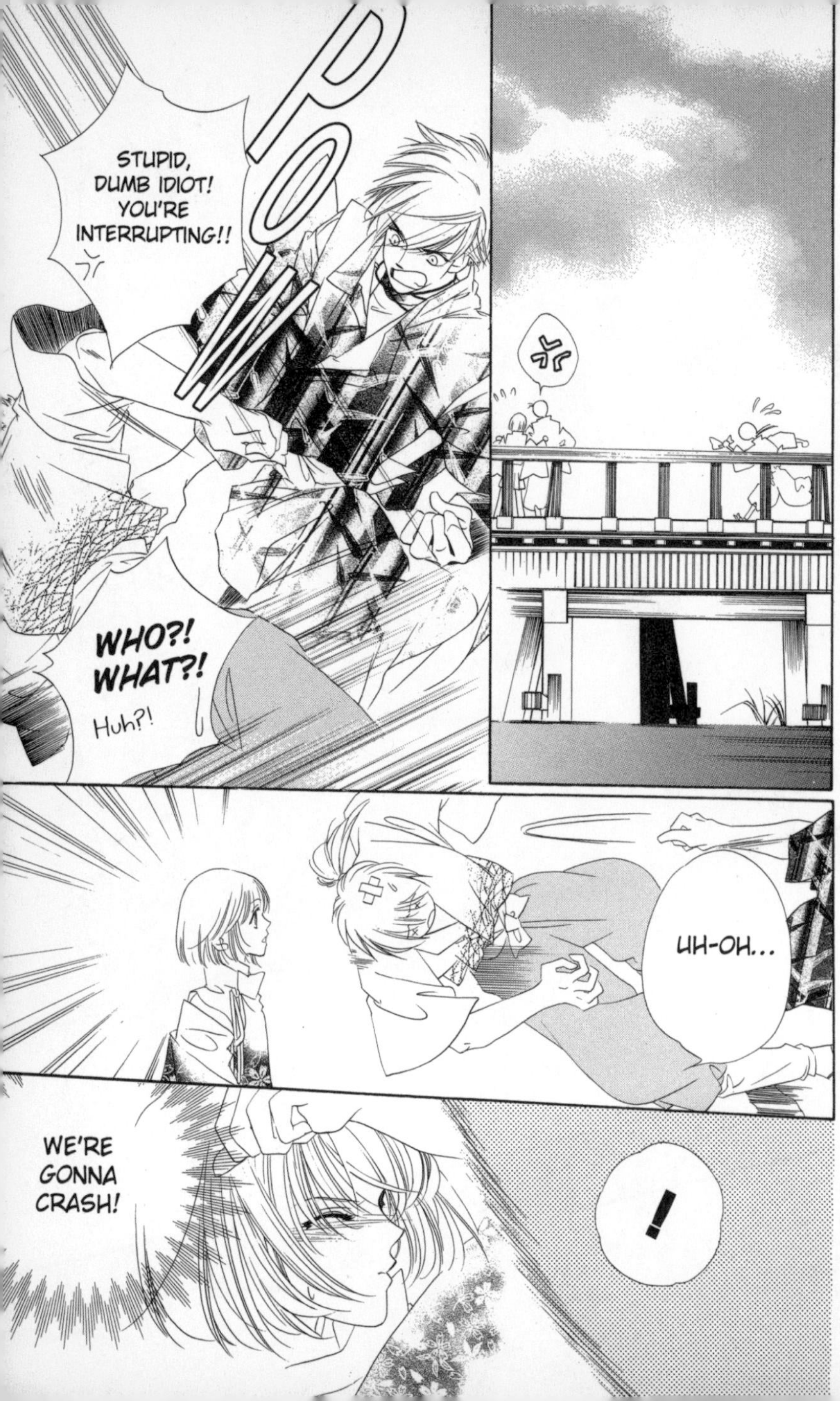
POW
STUPID, DUMB IDIOT! YOU'RE INTERRUPTING!!
WHO?! WHAT?!
Huh?!
UH-OH...
!
WE'RE GONNA CRASH!

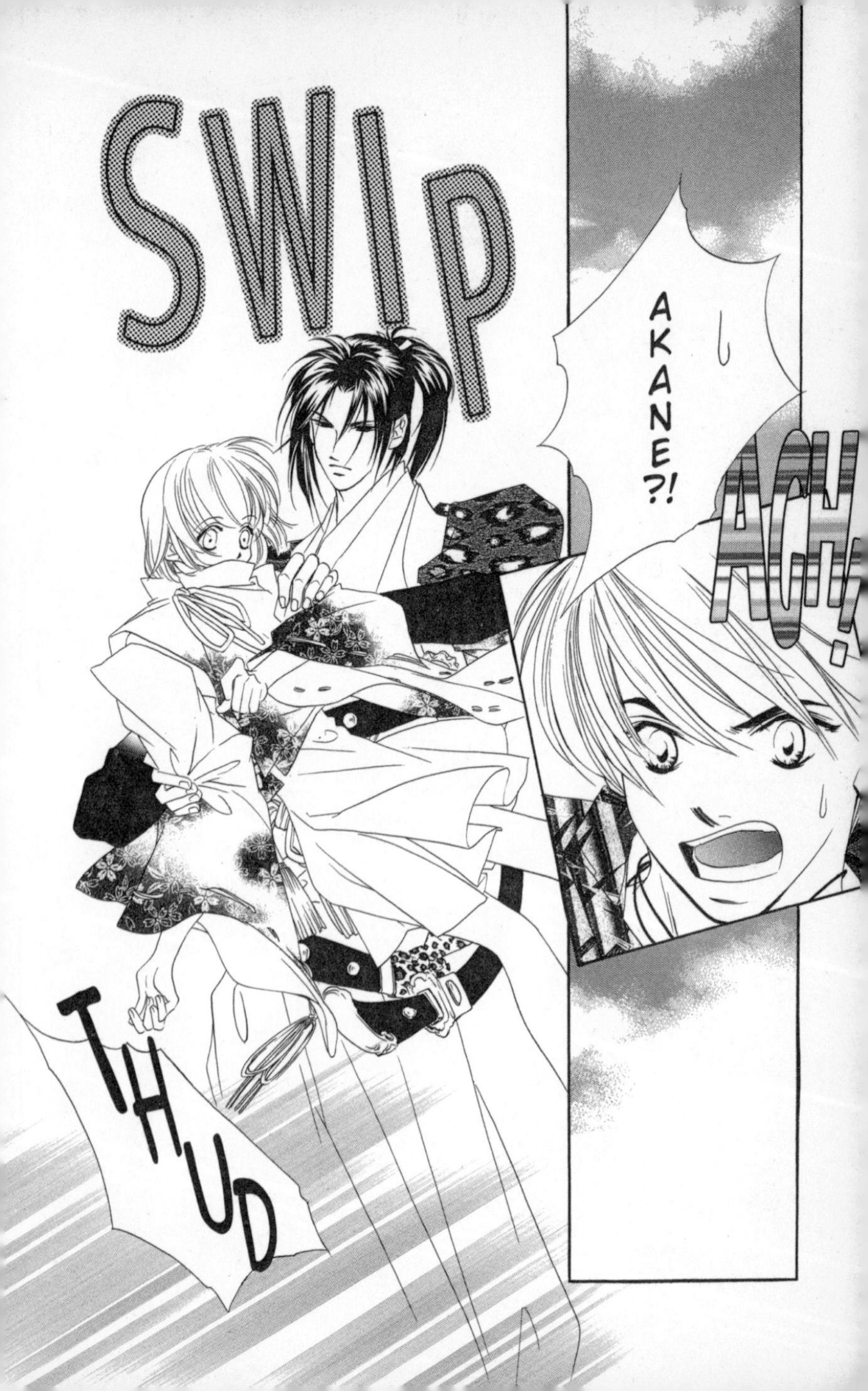
AKANE?!
ACH!
SWIP
THUD

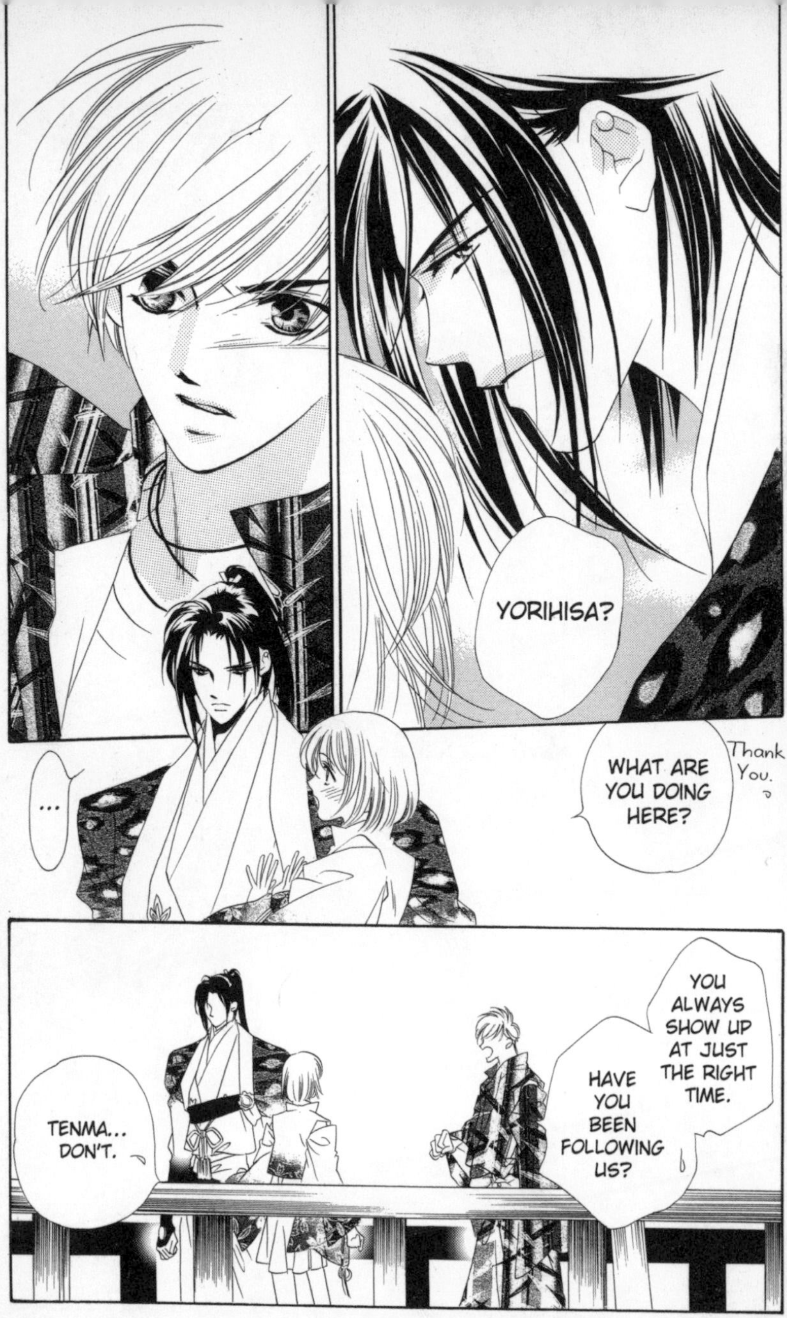
YORIHISA?
Thank You.
WHAT ARE YOU DOING HERE?
...
YOU ALWAYS SHOW UP AT JUST THE RIGHT TIME.
HAVE YOU BEEN FOLLOWING US?
TENMA... DON'T.

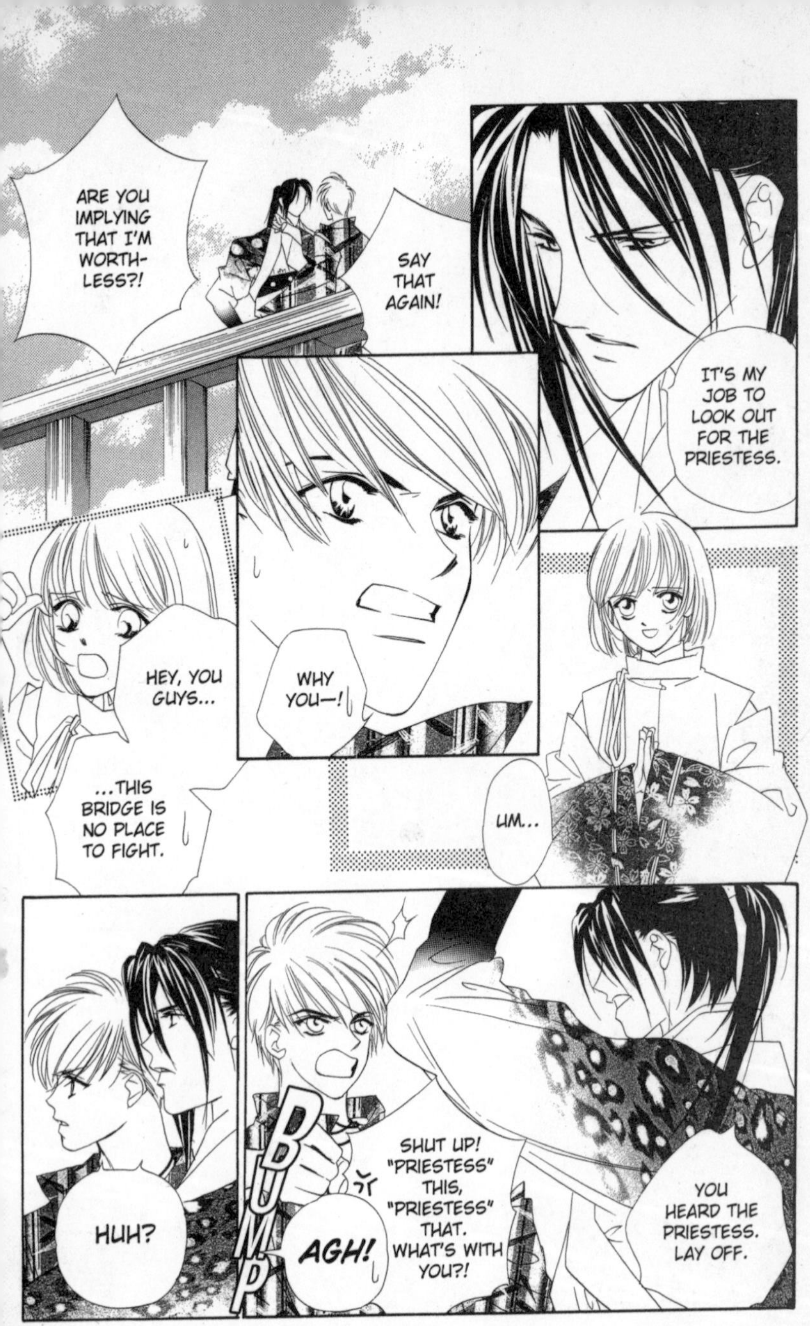
IT'S MY JOB TO LOOK OUT FOR THE PRIESTESS.
SAY THAT AGAIN!
ARE YOU IMPLYING THAT I'M WORTH-LESS?!
UM...
WHY YOU—!
HEY, YOU GUYS...
...THIS BRIDGE IS NO PLACE TO FIGHT.
YOU HEARD THE PRIESTESS. LAY OFF.
SHUT UP! "PRIESTESS" THIS, "PRIESTESS" THAT. WHAT'S WITH YOU?!
BUMP
AGH!
HUH?

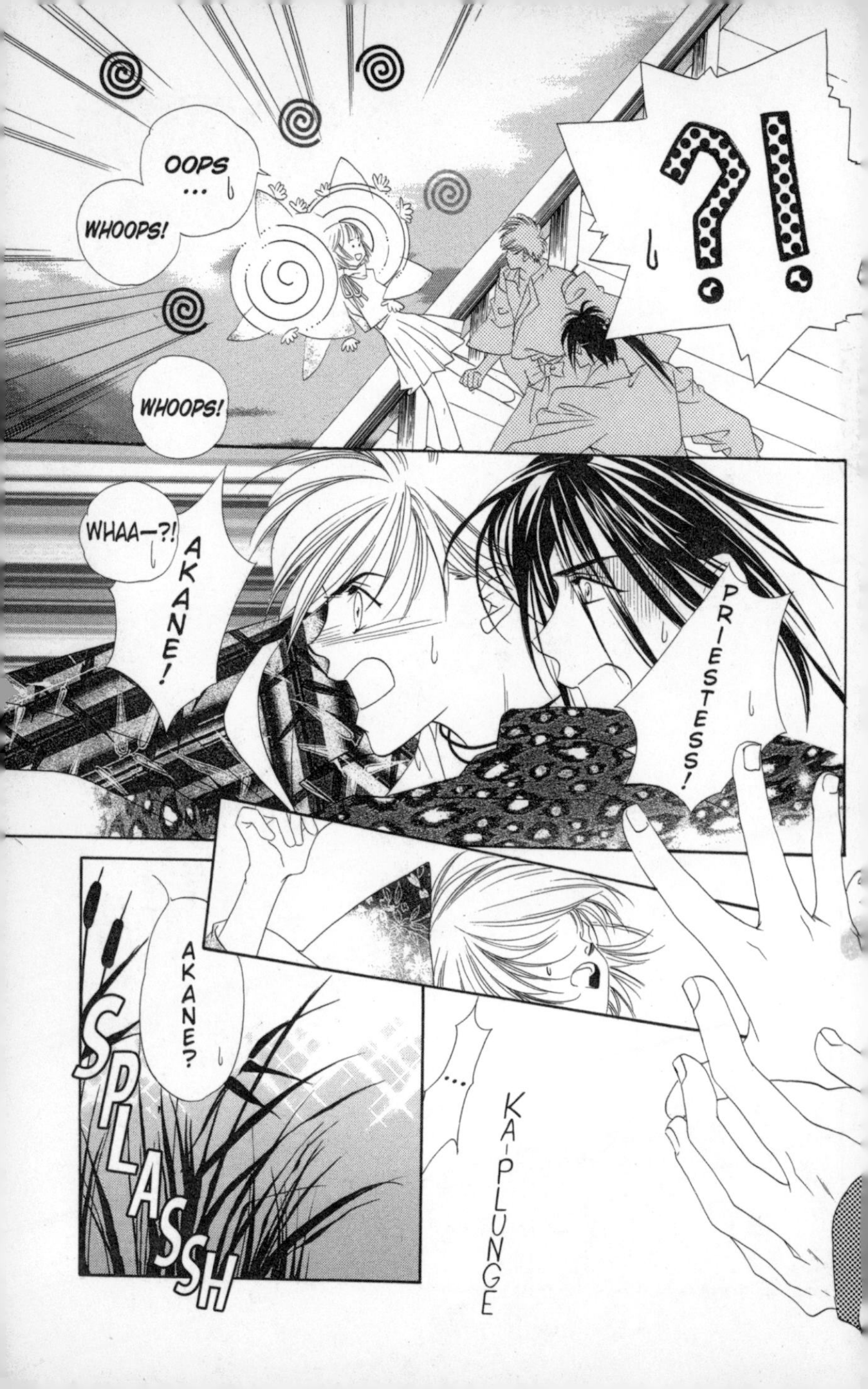
?!
OOPS ... WHOOPS!
WHOOPS!
PRIESTESS!
AKANE!
WHAA—?!
...
KA-PLUNGE
AKANE?
SPLASSH

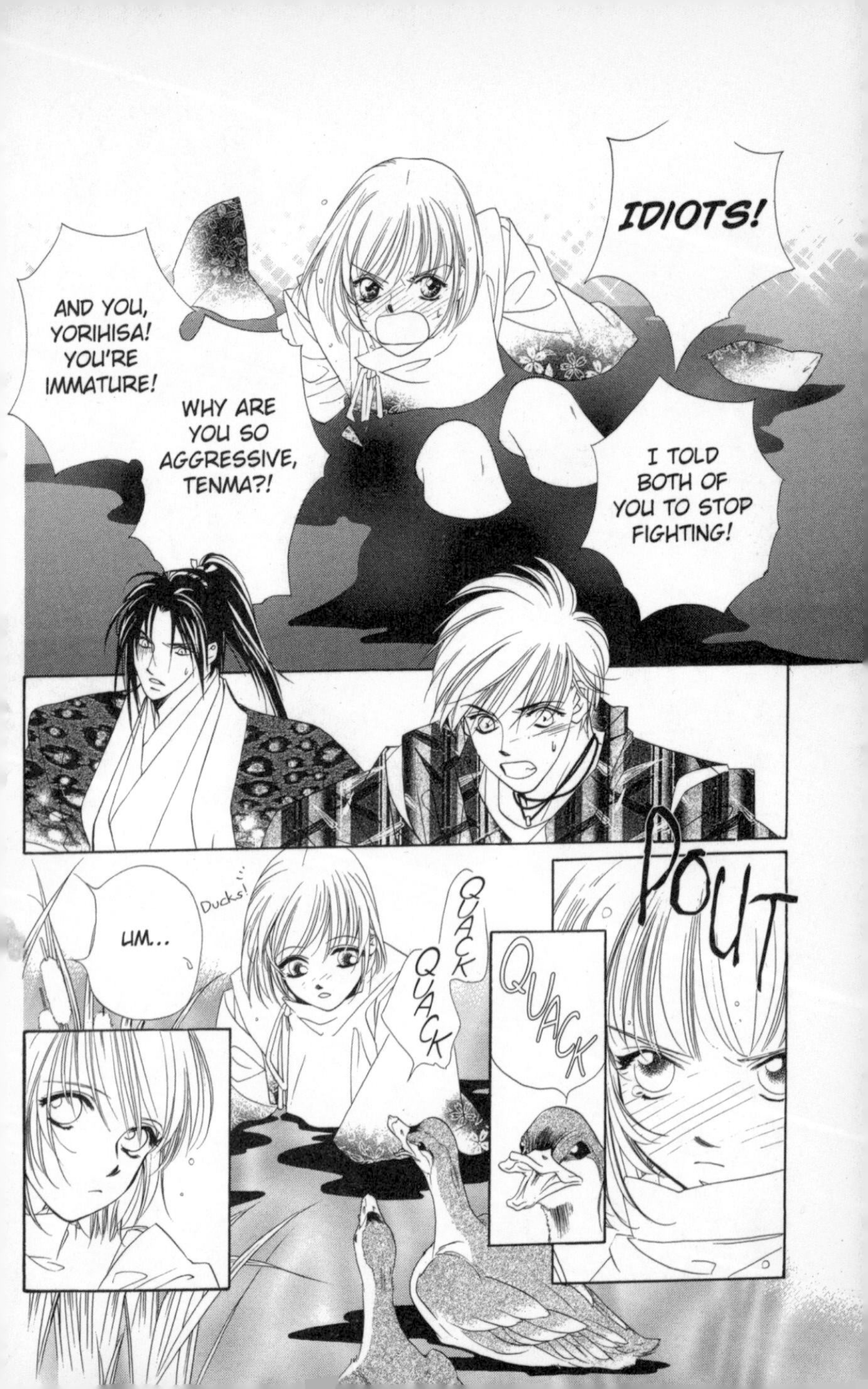
IDIOTS!
I TOLD BOTH OF YOU TO STOP FIGHTING!
WHY ARE YOU SO AGGRESSIVE, TENMA?!
AND YOU, YORIHISA! YOU'RE IMMATURE!
POUT
QUACK
QUACK QUACK
Ducks!
UM...

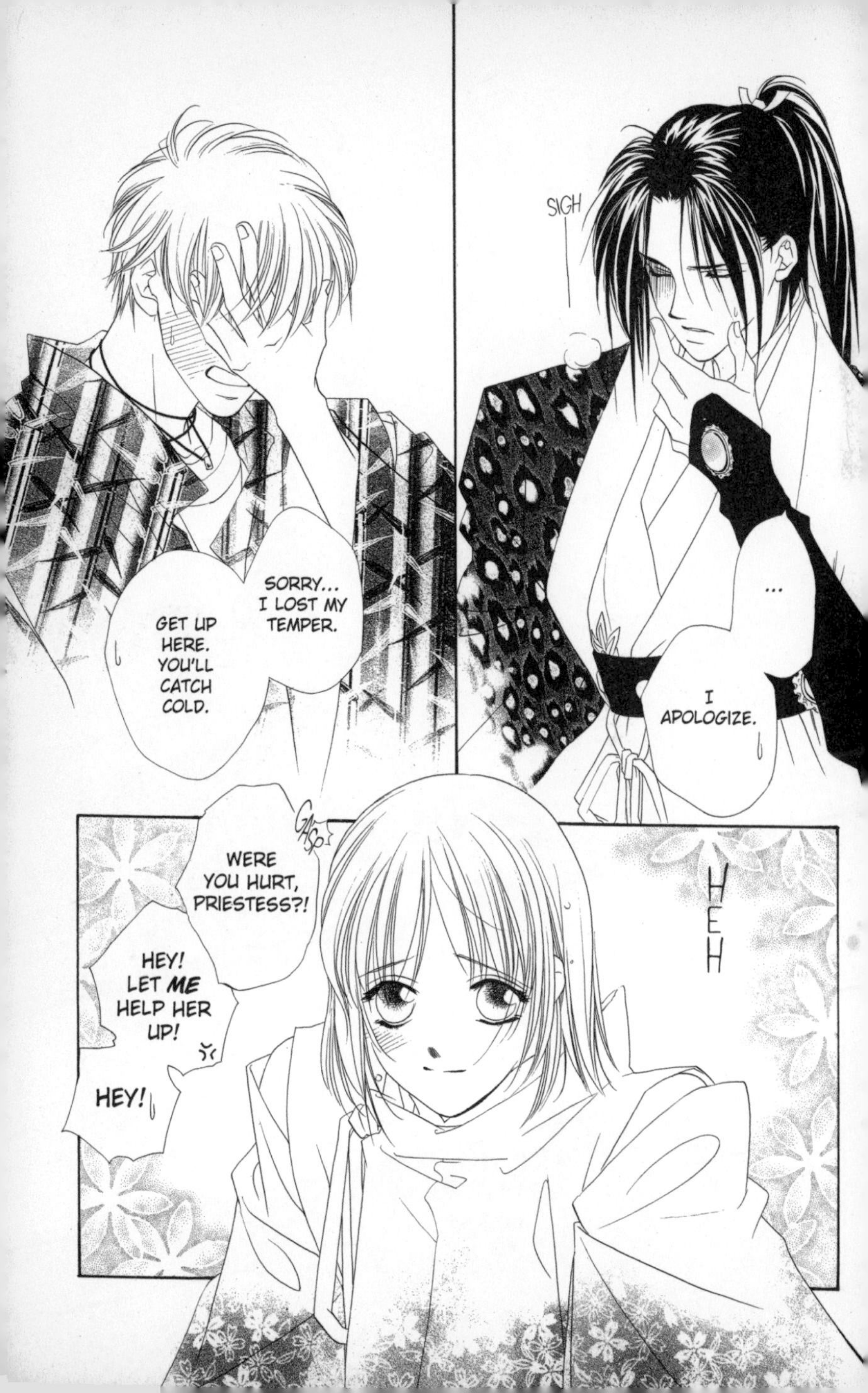
SIGH
...
I APOLOGIZE.
SORRY... I LOST MY TEMPER.
GET UP HERE. YOU'LL CATCH COLD.
HEH
GASP
WERE YOU HURT, PRIESTESS?!
HEY! LET *ME* HELP HER UP!
HEY!

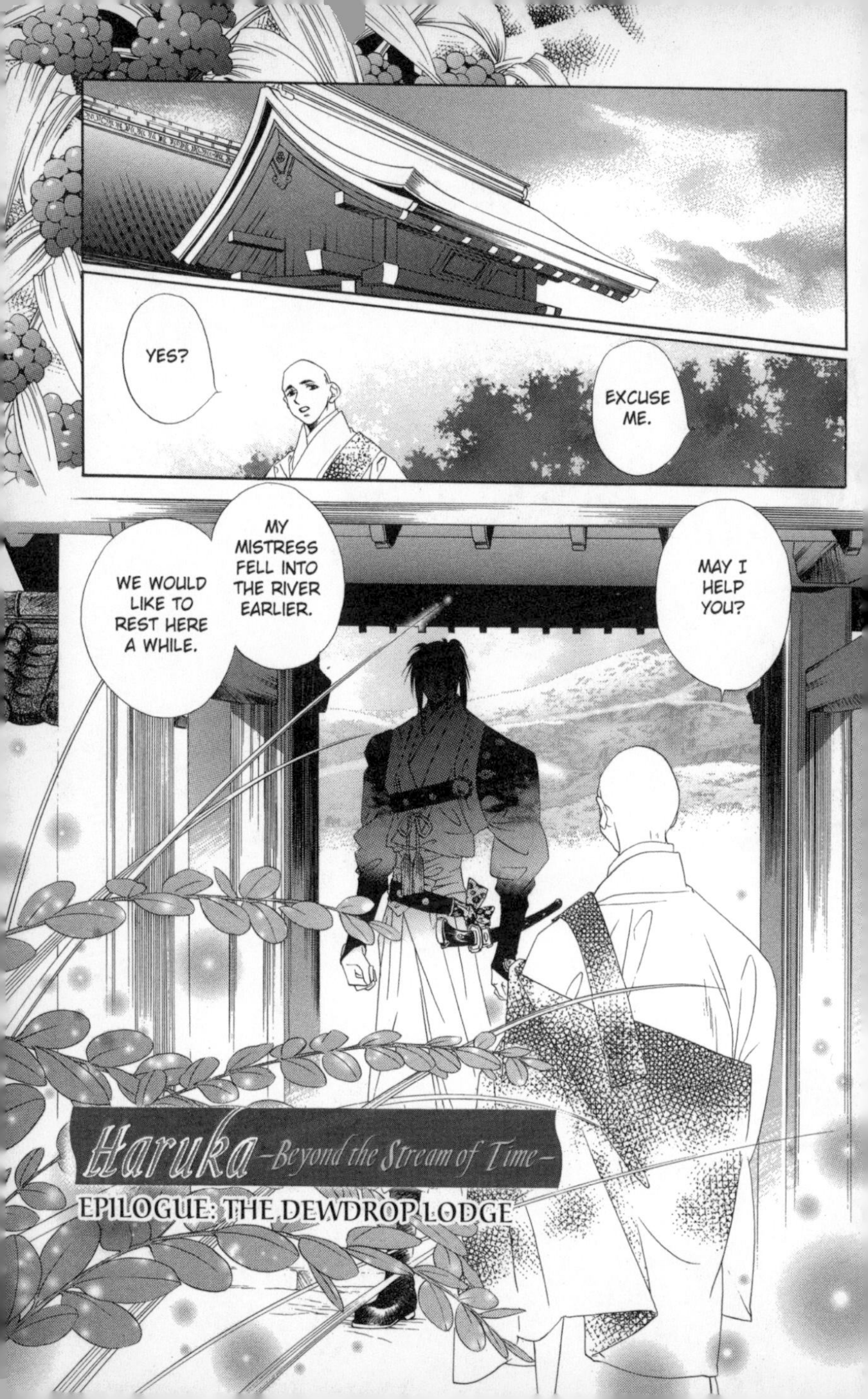
EXCUSE ME.
YES?
MAY I HELP YOU?
MY MISTRESS FELL INTO THE RIVER EARLIER.
WE WOULD LIKE TO REST HERE A WHILE.
Haruka –Beyond the Stream of Time–
EPILOGUE: THE DEWDROP LODGE

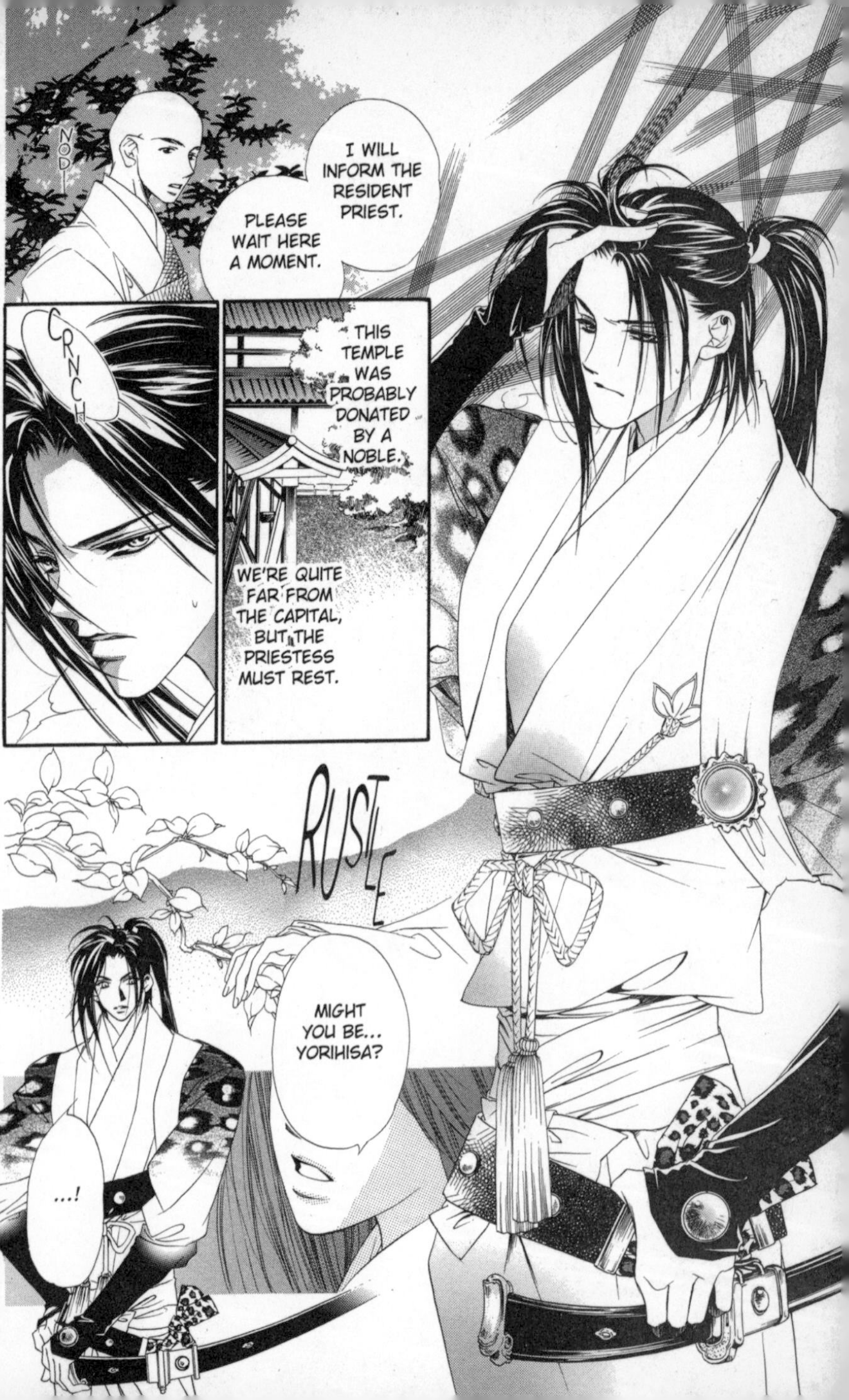
I WILL INFORM THE RESIDENT PRIEST.
PLEASE WAIT HERE A MOMENT.
NOD
THIS TEMPLE WAS PROBABLY DONATED BY A NOBLE.
WE'RE QUITE FAR FROM THE CAPITAL, BUT THE PRIESTESS MUST REST.
CRNCH
RUSTLE
MIGHT YOU BE... YORIHISA?
...!

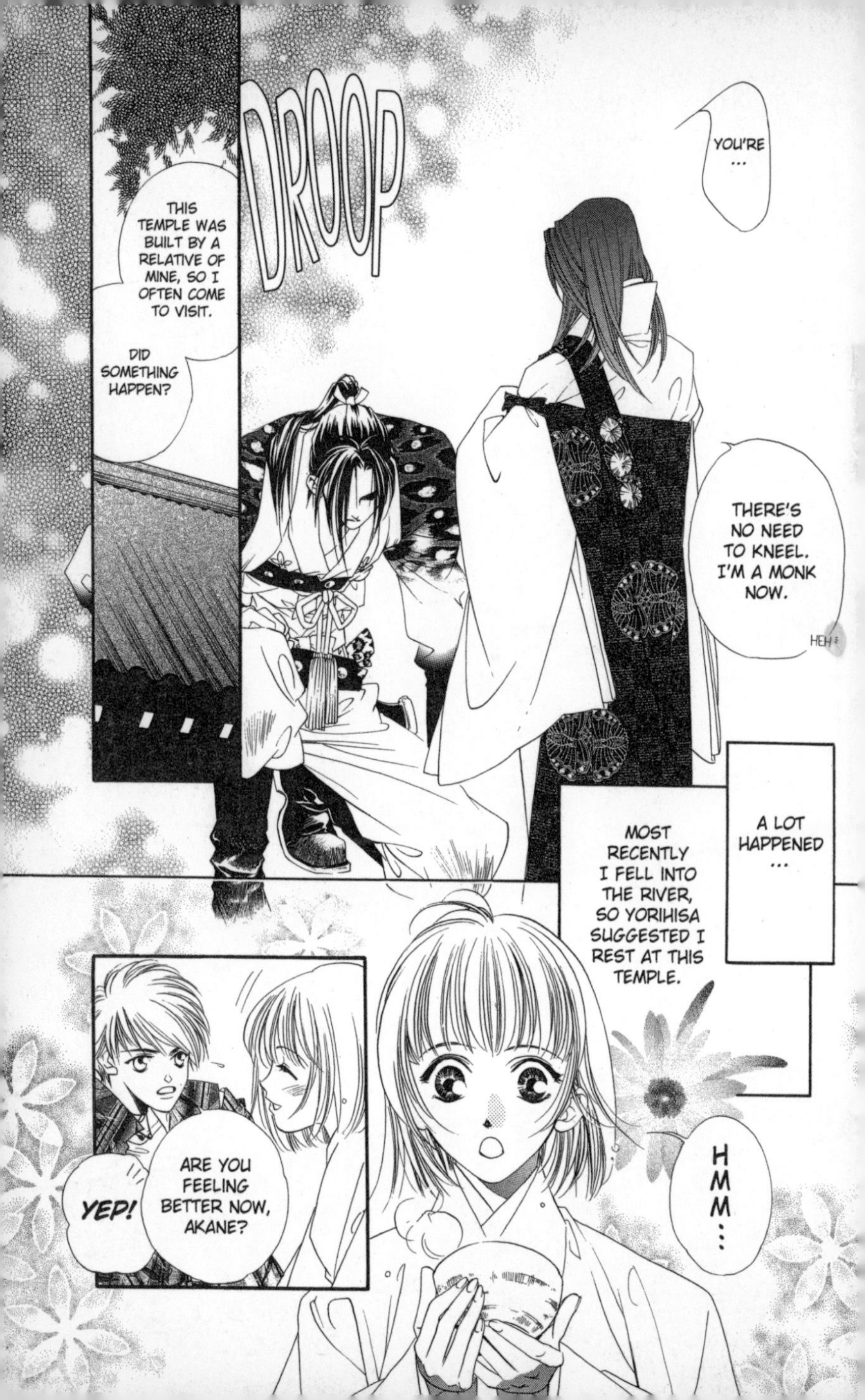
YOU'RE ...
DROOP
THERE'S NO NEED TO KNEEL. I'M A MONK NOW.
HEH
THIS TEMPLE WAS BUILT BY A RELATIVE OF MINE, SO I OFTEN COME TO VISIT.
DID SOMETHING HAPPEN?
A LOT HAPPENED ...
MOST RECENTLY I FELL INTO THE RIVER, SO YORIHISA SUGGESTED I REST AT THIS TEMPLE.
HMM...
ARE YOU FEELING BETTER NOW, AKANE?
YEP!

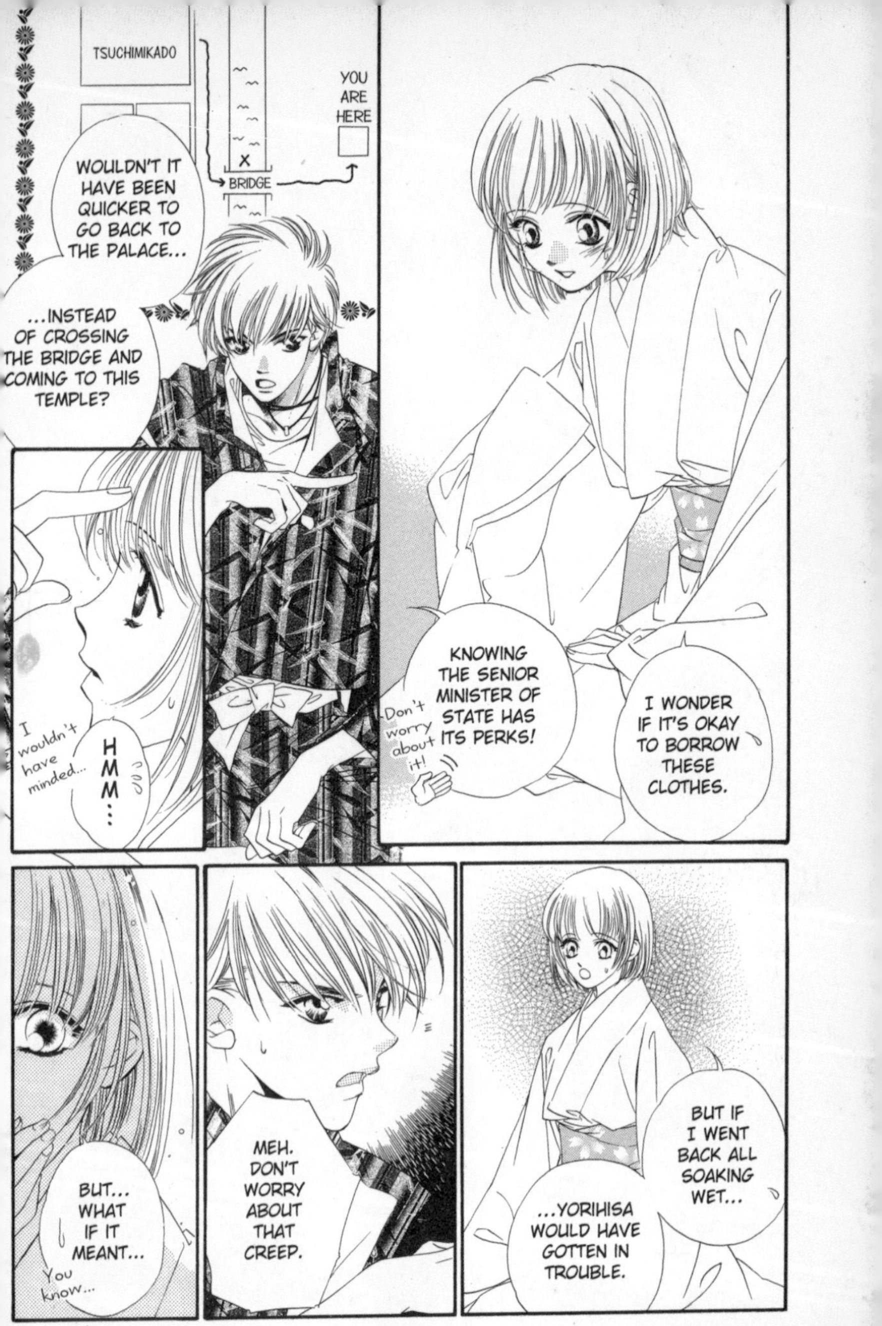
I WONDER IF IT'S OKAY TO BORROW THESE CLOTHES.
KNOWING THE SENIOR MINISTER OF STATE HAS ITS PERKS!
Don't worry about it!
TSUCHIMIKADO
BRIDGE
YOU ARE HERE
WOULDN'T IT HAVE BEEN QUICKER TO GO BACK TO THE PALACE...
...INSTEAD OF CROSSING THE BRIDGE AND COMING TO THIS TEMPLE?
HMM...
I wouldn't have minded...
BUT IF I WENT BACK ALL SOAKING WET...
...YORIHISA WOULD HAVE GOTTEN IN TROUBLE.
MEH. DON'T WORRY ABOUT THAT CREEP.
BUT... WHAT IF IT MEANT...
You know...

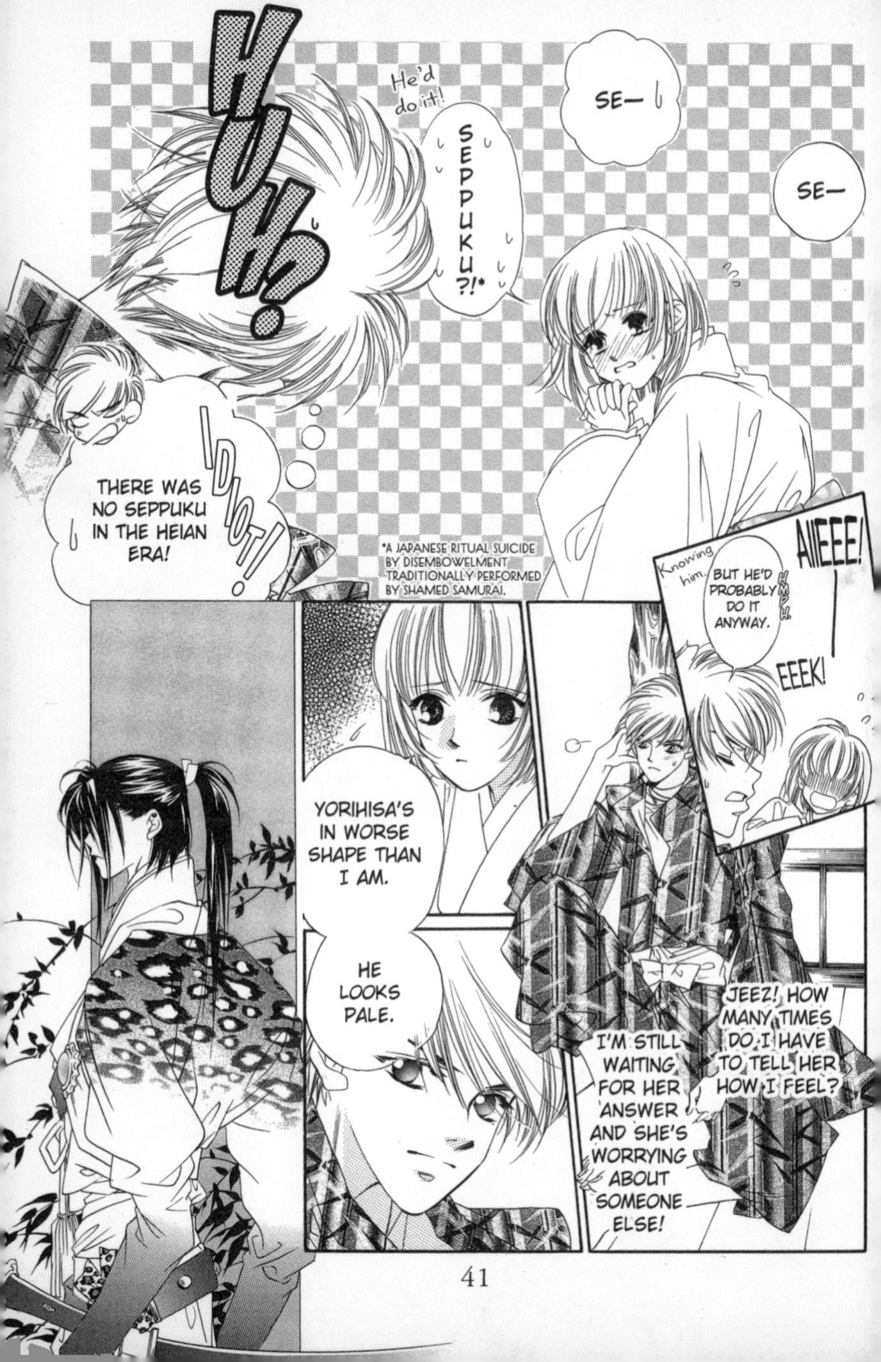

SE—
SE—
He'd do it!
SEPPUKU?!*
HUH?!
IDIOT!
THERE WAS NO SEPPUKU IN THE HEIAN ERA!
*A JAPANESE RITUAL SUICIDE BY DISEMBOWELMENT TRADITIONALLY PERFORMED BY SHAMED SAMURAI.
AIEEE!
EEEK!
HMPH.
Knowing him.
BUT HE'D PROBABLY DO IT ANYWAY.
JEEZ! HOW MANY TIMES DO I HAVE TO TELL HER HOW I FEEL?
I'M STILL WAITING FOR HER ANSWER AND SHE'S WORRYING ABOUT SOMEONE ELSE!
YORIHISA'S IN WORSE SHAPE THAN I AM.
HE LOOKS PALE.

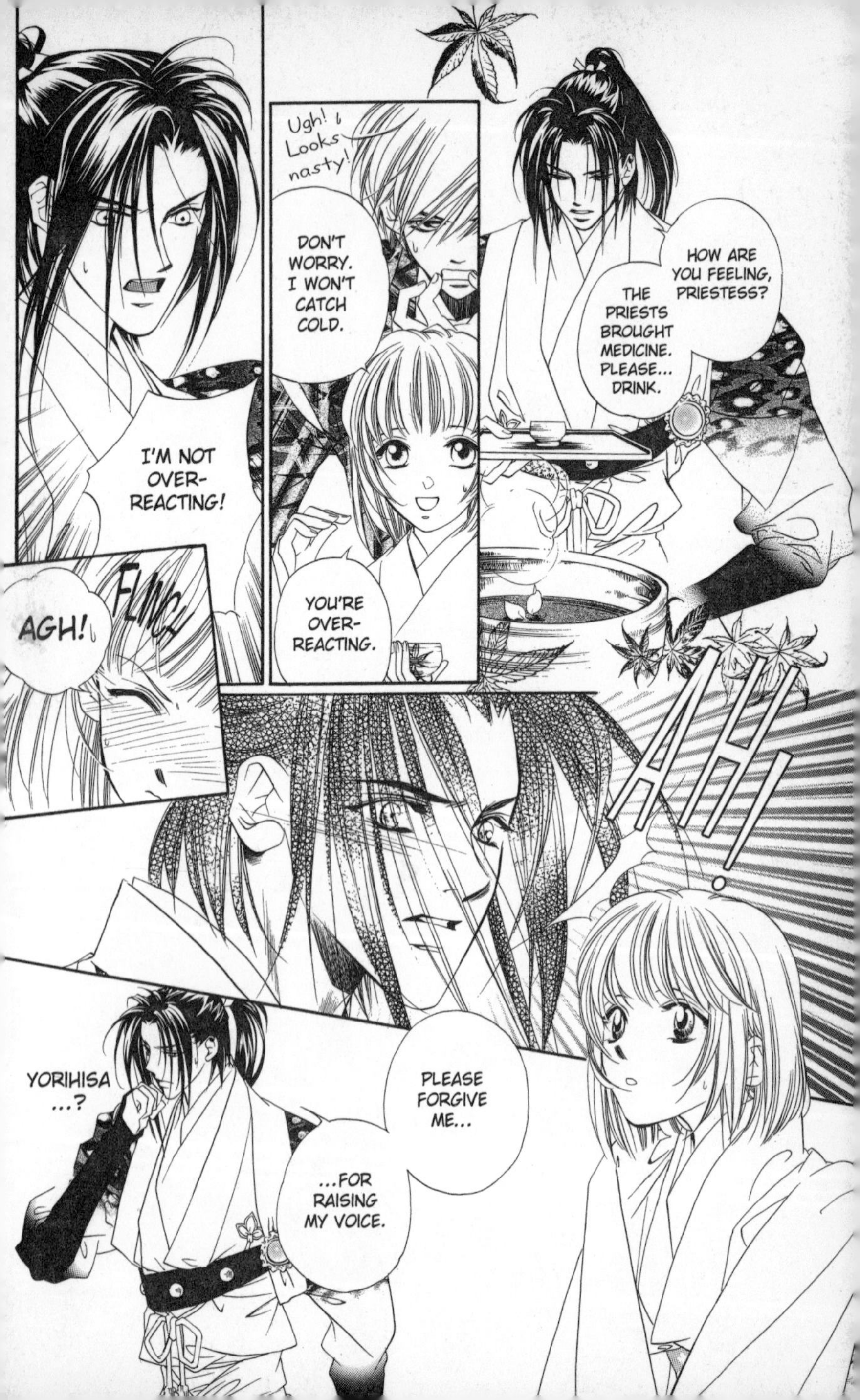
HOW ARE YOU FEELING, PRIESTESS?
THE PRIESTS BROUGHT MEDICINE. PLEASE... DRINK.
Ugh! Looks nasty!
DON'T WORRY. I WON'T CATCH COLD.
YOU'RE OVER-REACTING.
I'M NOT OVER-REACTING!
FLINCH
AGH!
AH!!
PLEASE FORGIVE ME...
...FOR RAISING MY VOICE.
YORIHISA ...?

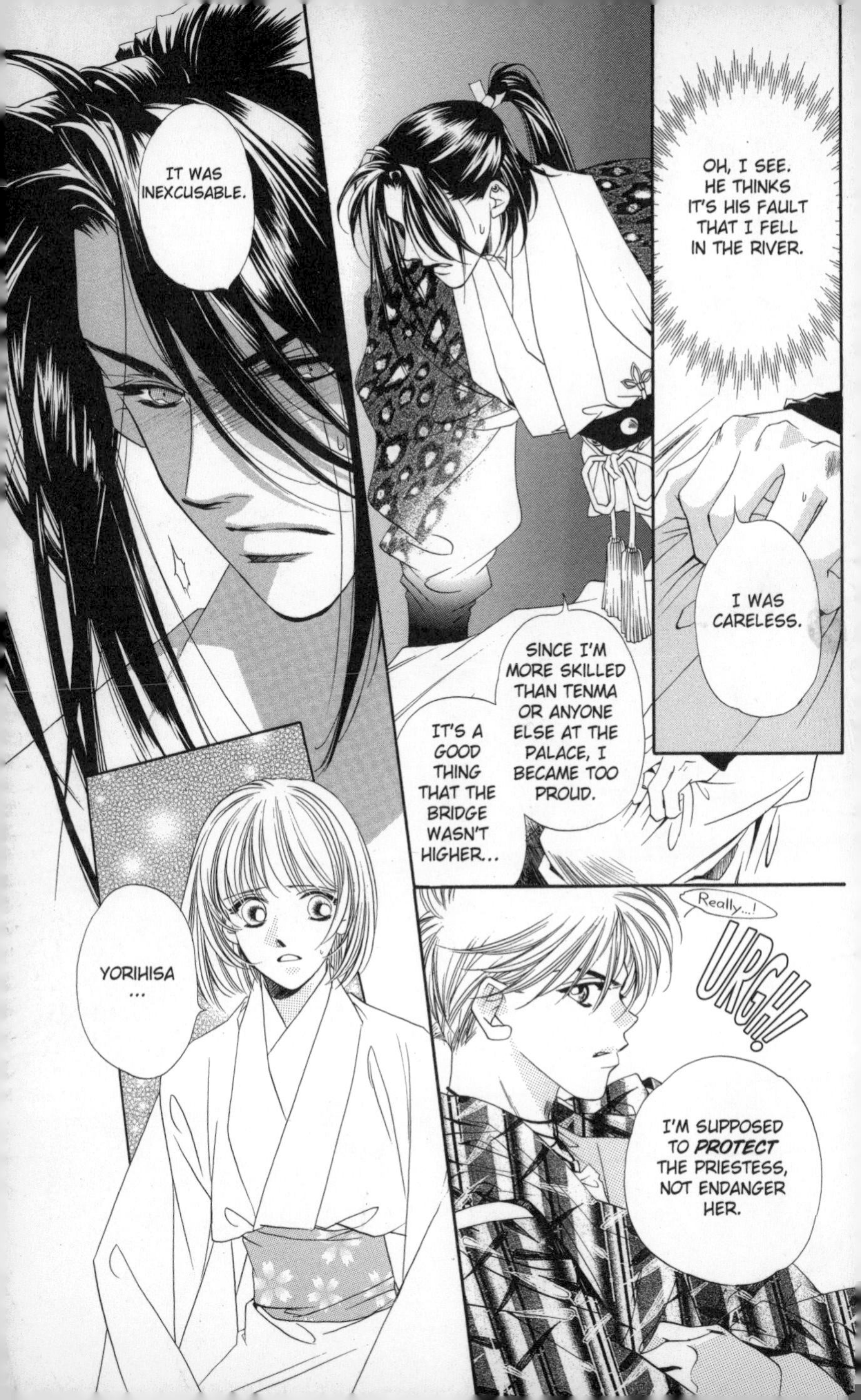
OH, I SEE. HE THINKS IT'S HIS FAULT THAT I FELL IN THE RIVER.
I WAS CARELESS.
SINCE I'M MORE SKILLED THAN TENMA OR ANYONE ELSE AT THE PALACE, I BECAME TOO PROUD.
IT'S A GOOD THING THAT THE BRIDGE WASN'T HIGHER...
IT WAS INEXCUSABLE.
Really...!
URGH!
I'M SUPPOSED TO **PROTECT** THE PRIESTESS, NOT ENDANGER HER.
YORIHISA ...

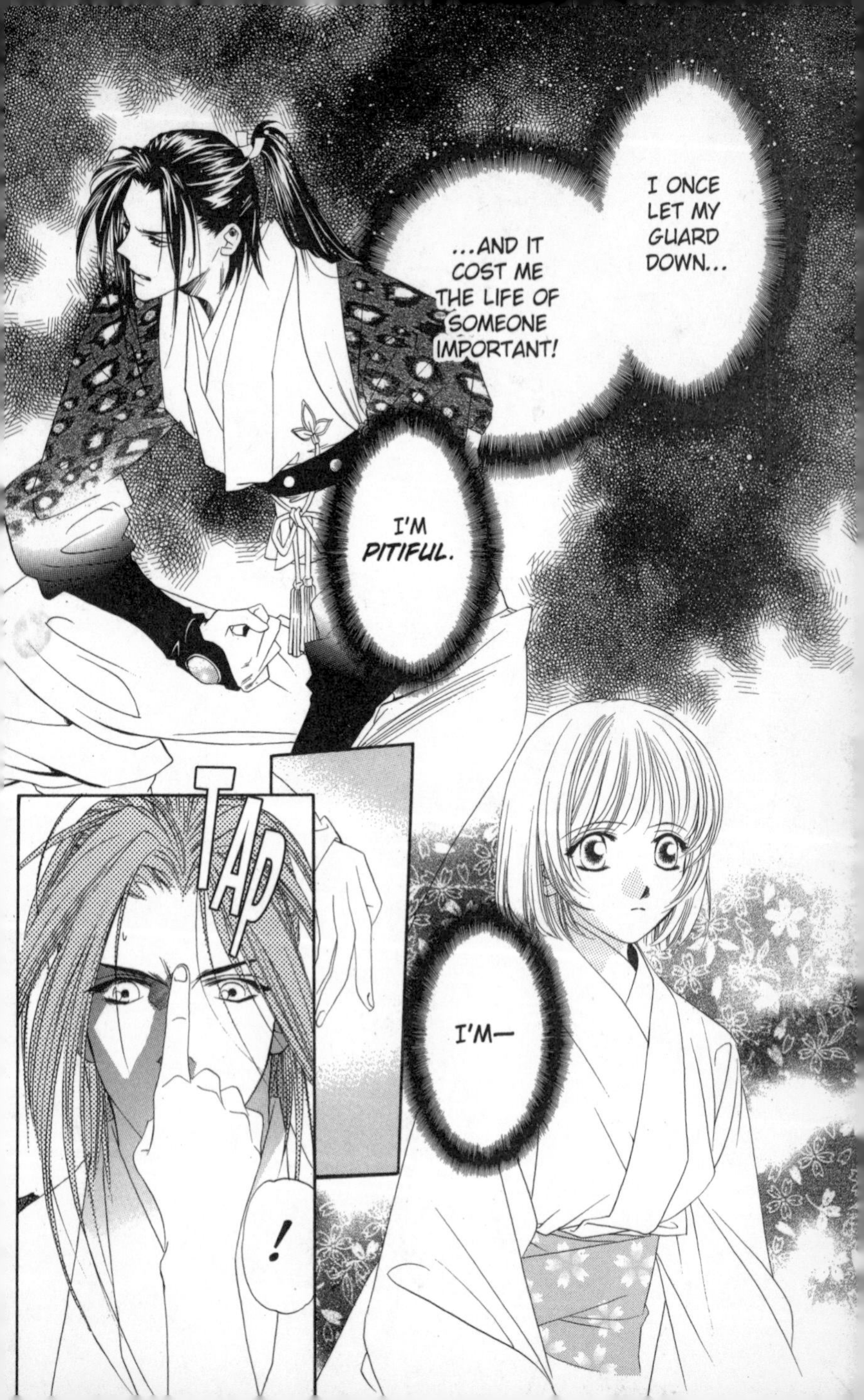
I ONCE LET MY GUARD DOWN...
...AND IT COST ME THE LIFE OF SOMEONE IMPORTANT!
I'M *PITIFUL.*
I'M—
TAP
!

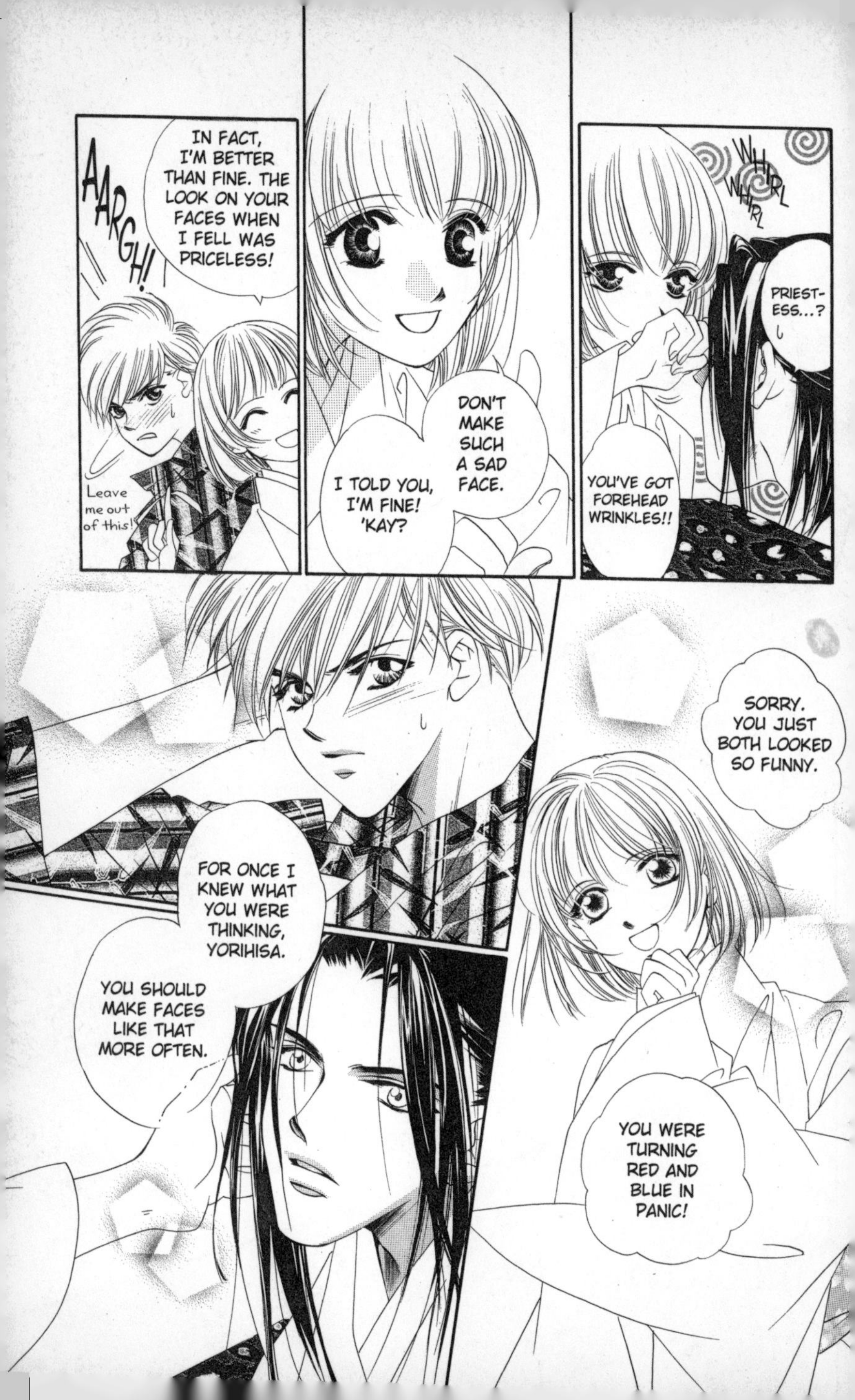
WHIRL WHIRL
PRIEST-ESS...?
YOU'VE GOT FOREHEAD WRINKLES!!
DON'T MAKE SUCH A SAD FACE.
I TOLD YOU, I'M FINE! 'KAY?
IN FACT, I'M BETTER THAN FINE. THE LOOK ON YOUR FACES WHEN I FELL WAS PRICELESS!
AARGH!
Leave me out of this!
SORRY. YOU JUST BOTH LOOKED SO FUNNY.
YOU WERE TURNING RED AND BLUE IN PANIC!
FOR ONCE I KNEW WHAT YOU WERE THINKING, YORIHISA.
YOU SHOULD MAKE FACES LIKE THAT MORE OFTEN.

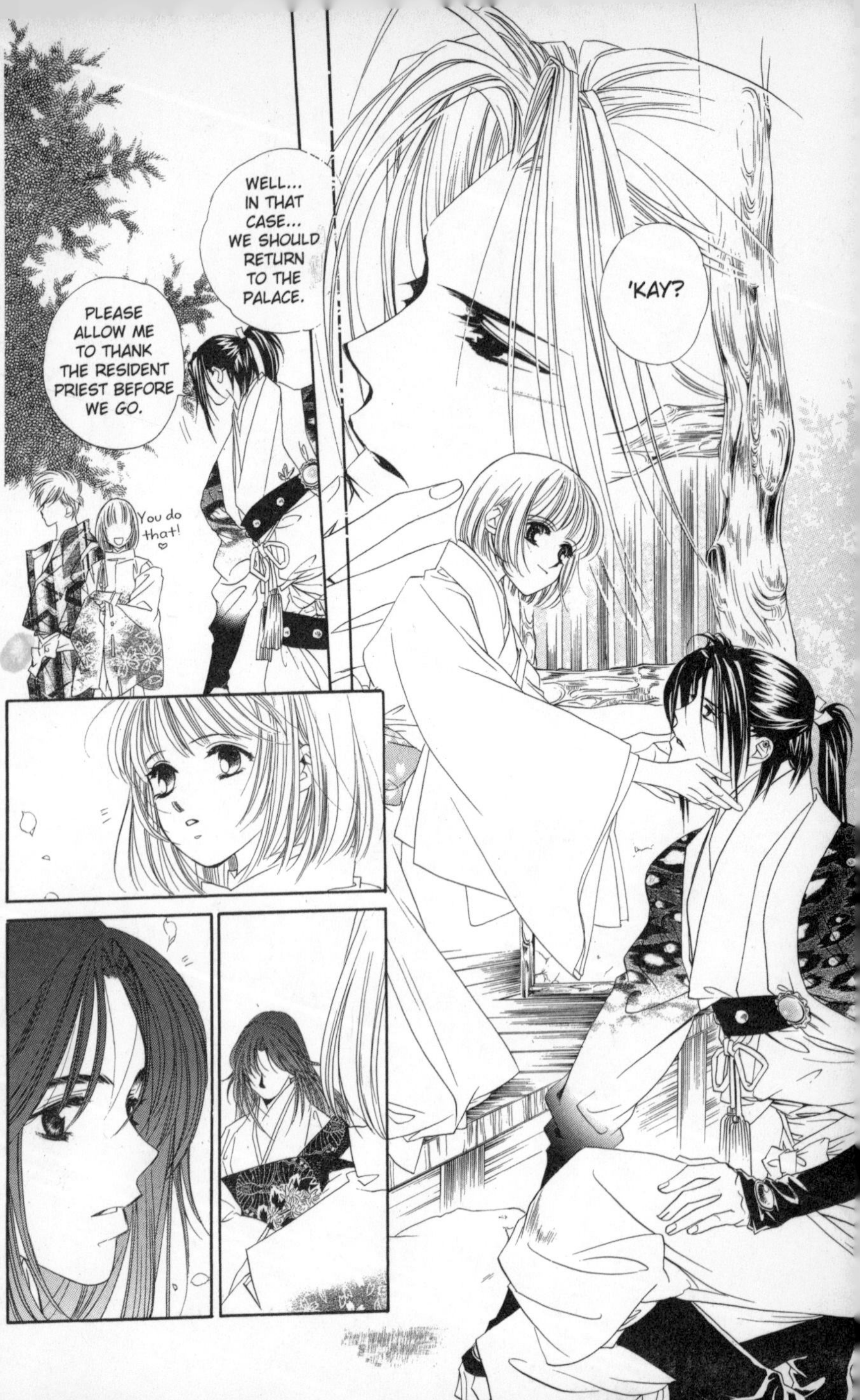
'KAY?
WELL... IN THAT CASE... WE SHOULD RETURN TO THE PALACE.
PLEASE ALLOW ME TO THANK THE RESIDENT PRIEST BEFORE WE GO.
You do that!

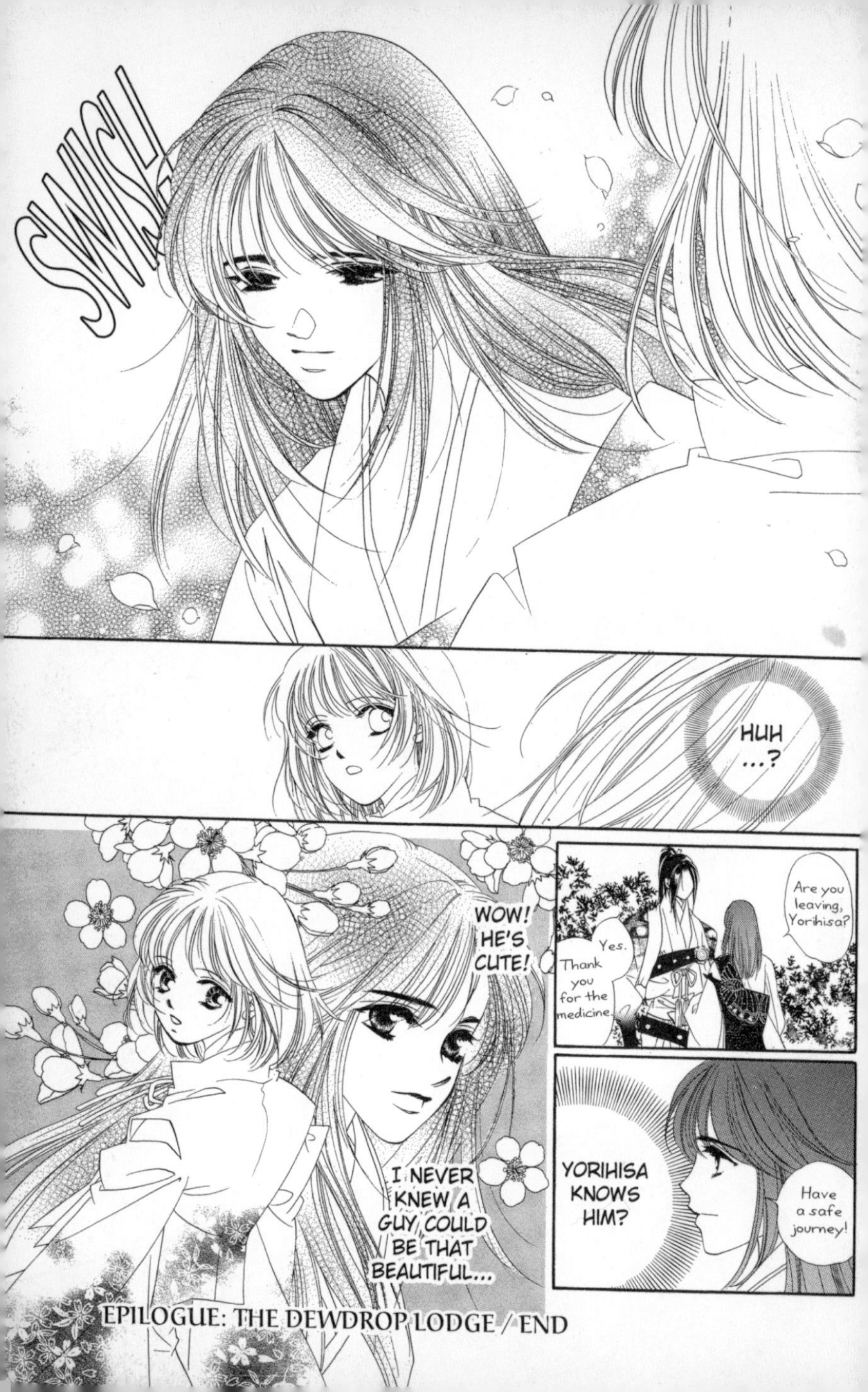
SWISH
HUH ...?
Are you leaving, Yorihisa?
Yes. Thank you for the medicine.
Have a safe journey!
YORIHISA KNOWS HIM?
WOW! HE'S CUTE!
I NEVER KNEW A GUY COULD BE THAT BEAUTIFUL...
EPILOGUE: THE DEWDROP LODGE / END

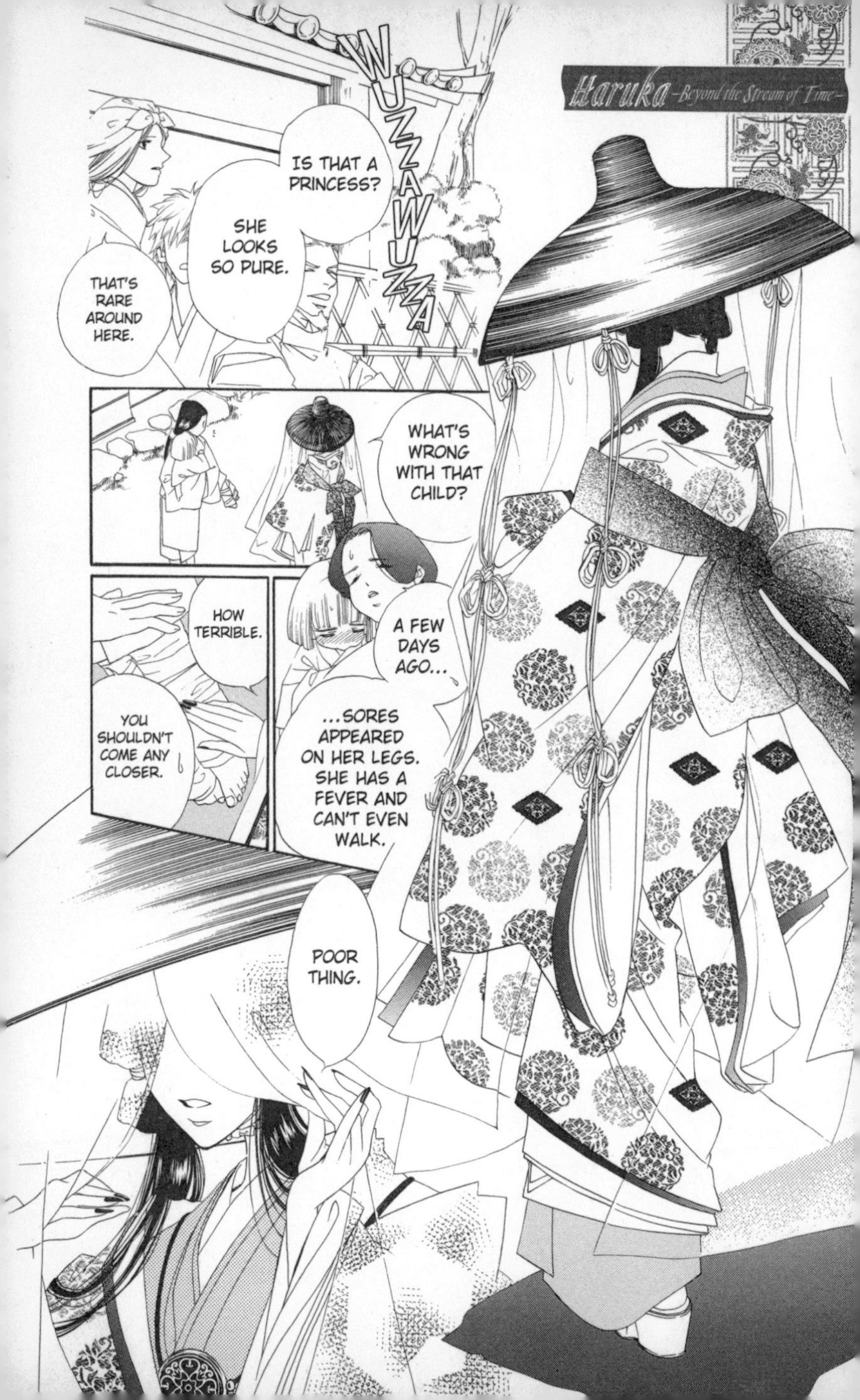
WUZZAWUZZA
IS THAT A PRINCESS?
SHE LOOKS SO PURE.
THAT'S RARE AROUND HERE.
WHAT'S WRONG WITH THAT CHILD?
A FEW DAYS AGO...
...SORES APPEARED ON HER LEGS. SHE HAS A FEVER AND CAN'T EVEN WALK.
HOW TERRIBLE.
YOU SHOULDN'T COME ANY CLOSER.
POOR THING.

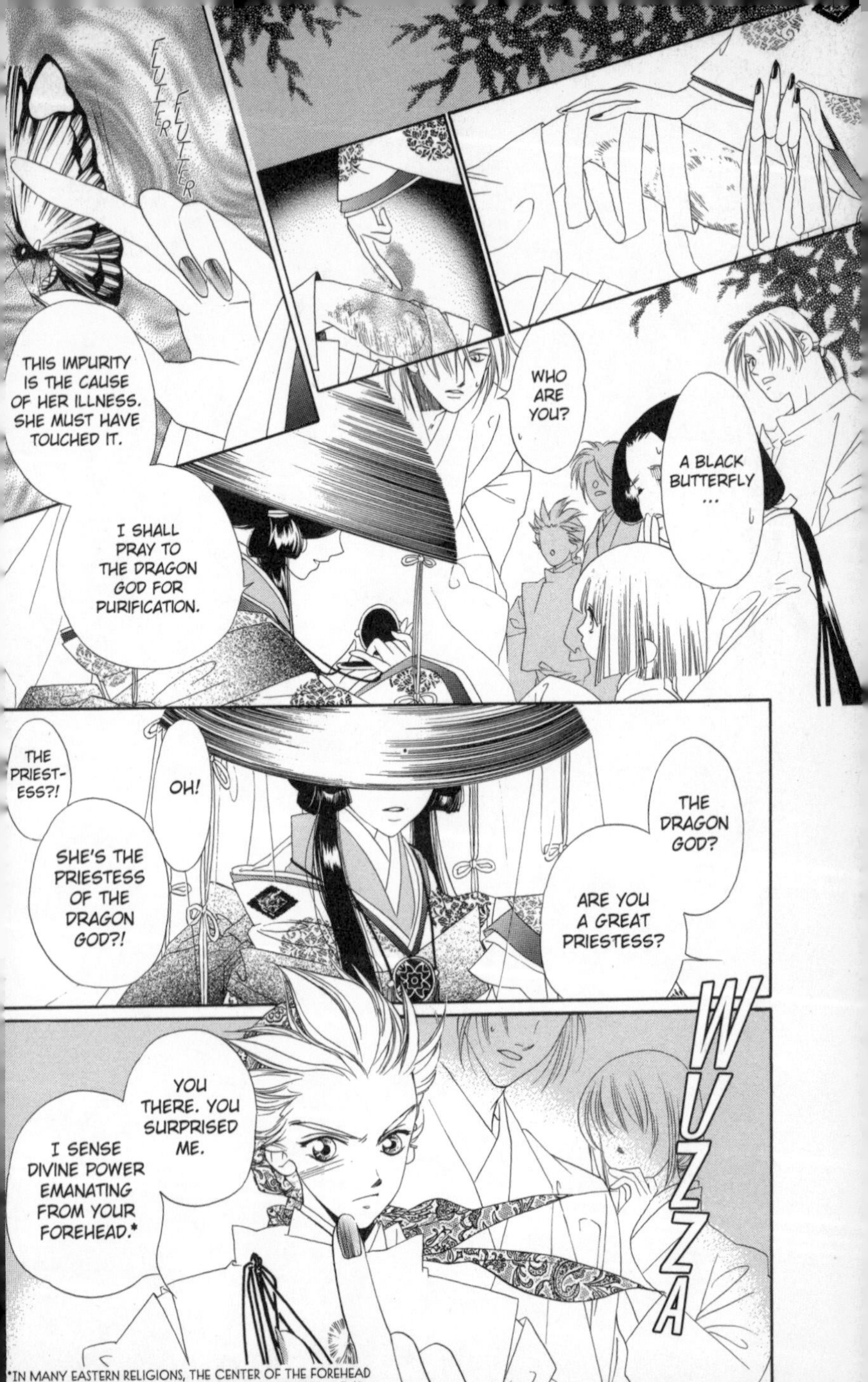
FLUTTER FLUTTER
THIS IMPURITY IS THE CAUSE OF HER ILLNESS. SHE MUST HAVE TOUCHED IT.
A BLACK BUTTERFLY...
WHO ARE YOU?
I SHALL PRAY TO THE DRAGON GOD FOR PURIFICATION.
THE DRAGON GOD?
ARE YOU A GREAT PRIESTESS?
OH!
THE PRIEST-ESS?!
SHE'S THE PRIESTESS OF THE DRAGON GOD?!
WUZZA
YOU THERE. YOU SURPRISED ME.
I SENSE DIVINE POWER EMANATING FROM YOUR FOREHEAD.*

*IN MANY EASTERN RELIGIONS, THE CENTER OF THE FOREHEAD IS CONSIDERED A PLACE OF GREAT SPIRITUAL POWER.

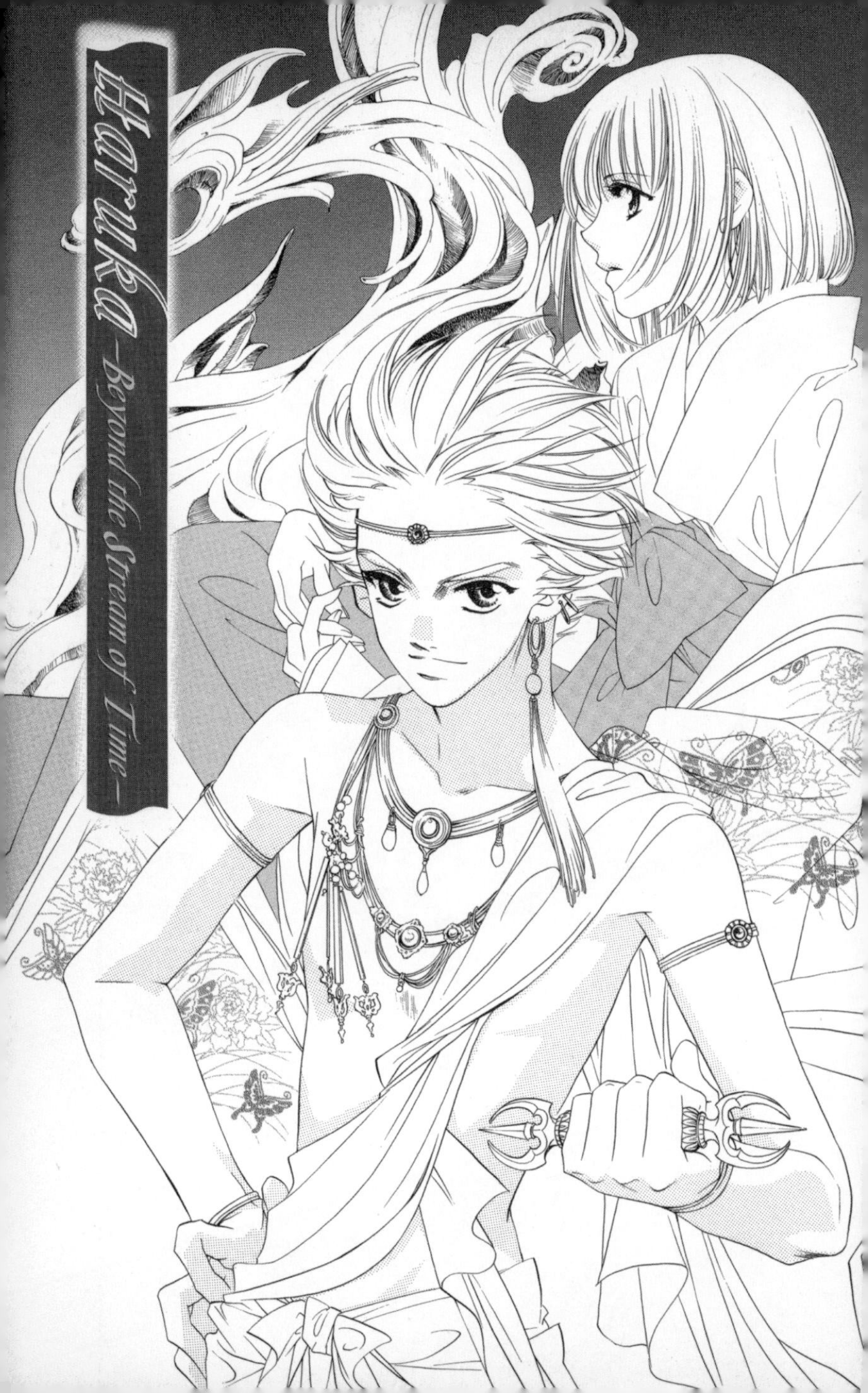
Haruka -Beyond the Stream of Time-

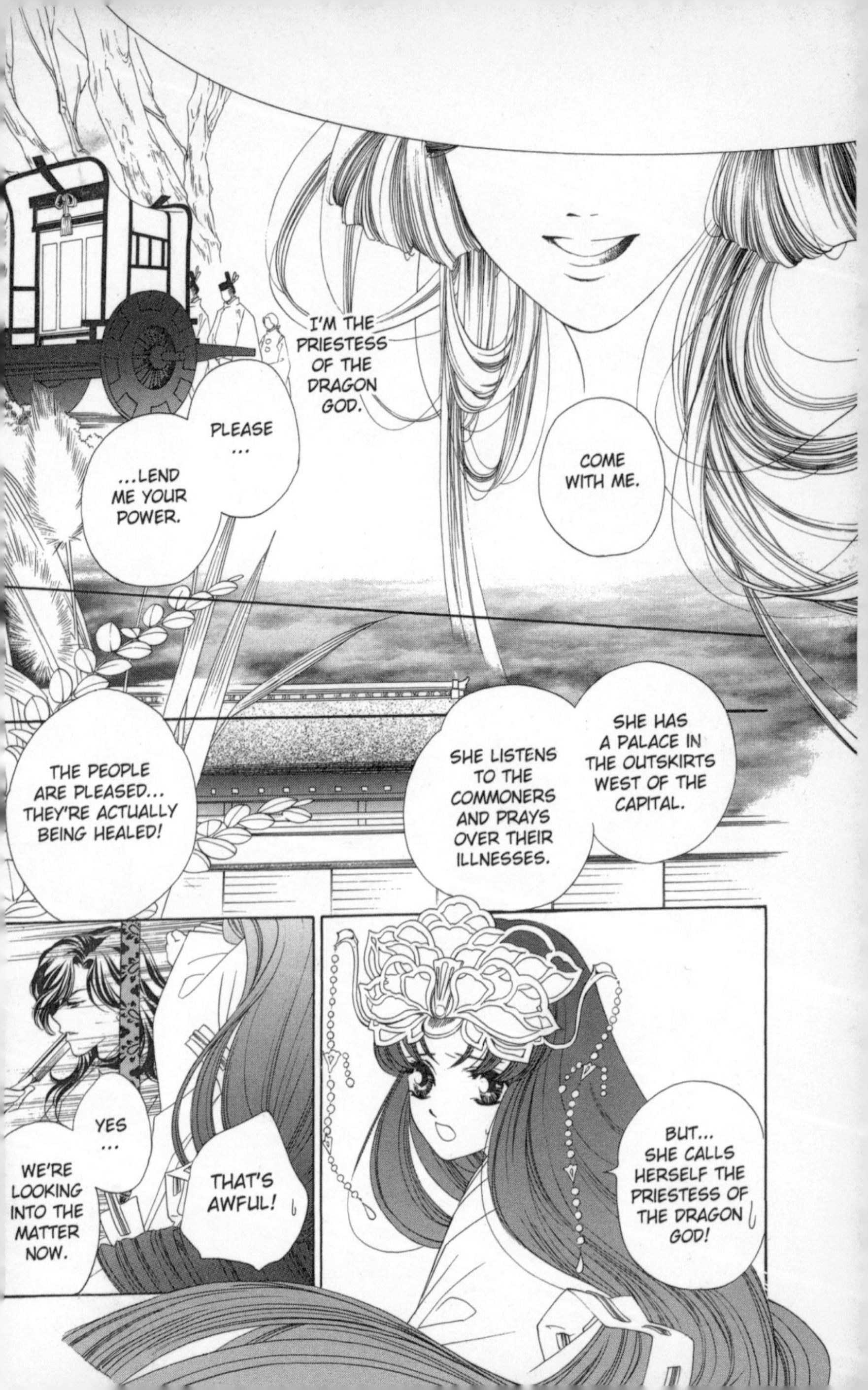
I'M THE PRIESTESS OF THE DRAGON GOD.
COME WITH ME.
PLEASE... ...LEND ME YOUR POWER.
SHE HAS A PALACE IN THE OUTSKIRTS WEST OF THE CAPITAL.
SHE LISTENS TO THE COMMONERS AND PRAYS OVER THEIR ILLNESSES.
THE PEOPLE ARE PLEASED... THEY'RE ACTUALLY BEING HEALED!
BUT... SHE CALLS HERSELF THE PRIESTESS OF THE DRAGON GOD!
THAT'S AWFUL!
YES... WE'RE LOOKING INTO THE MATTER NOW.

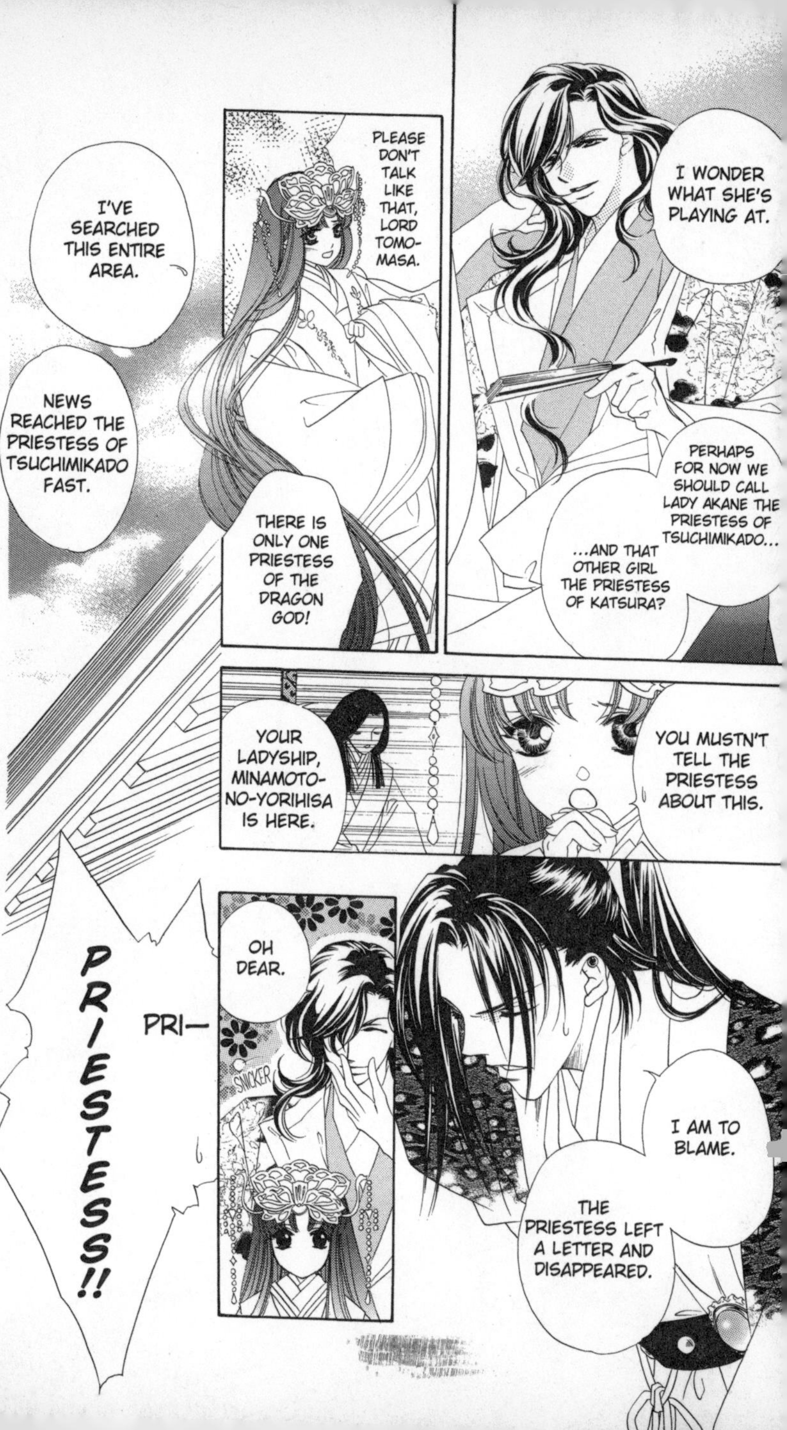
I WONDER WHAT SHE'S PLAYING AT.
PERHAPS FOR NOW WE SHOULD CALL LADY AKANE THE PRIESTESS OF TSUCHIMIKADO...
...AND THAT OTHER GIRL THE PRIESTESS OF KATSURA?
PLEASE DON'T TALK LIKE THAT, LORD TOMO-MASA.
THERE IS ONLY ONE PRIESTESS OF THE DRAGON GOD!
I'VE SEARCHED THIS ENTIRE AREA.
NEWS REACHED THE PRIESTESS OF TSUCHIMIKADO FAST.
YOU MUSTN'T TELL THE PRIESTESS ABOUT THIS.
YOUR LADYSHIP, MINAMOTO-NO-YORIHISA IS HERE.
I AM TO BLAME.
THE PRIESTESS LEFT A LETTER AND DISAPPEARED.
OH DEAR.
SNICKER
PRI—
PRIESTESS!!

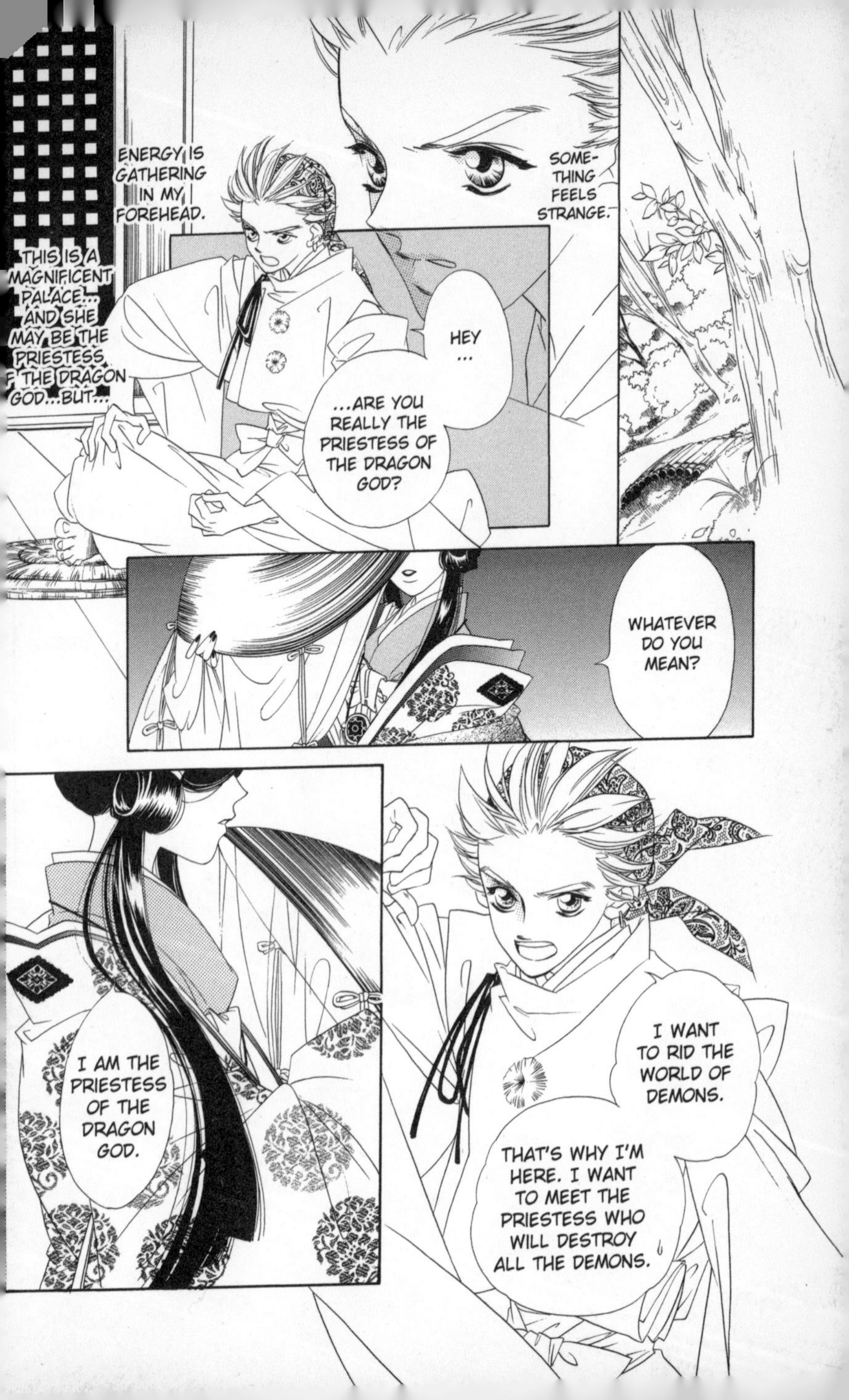
SOME-THING FEELS STRANGE.
ENERGY IS GATHERING IN MY FOREHEAD.
THIS IS A MAGNIFICENT PALACE... AND SHE MAY BE THE PRIESTESS F THE DRAGON GOD...BUT...
HEY...
...ARE YOU REALLY THE PRIESTESS OF THE DRAGON GOD?
WHATEVER DO YOU MEAN?
I WANT TO RID THE WORLD OF DEMONS.
THAT'S WHY I'M HERE. I WANT TO MEET THE PRIESTESS WHO WILL DESTROY ALL THE DEMONS.
I AM THE PRIESTESS OF THE DRAGON GOD.

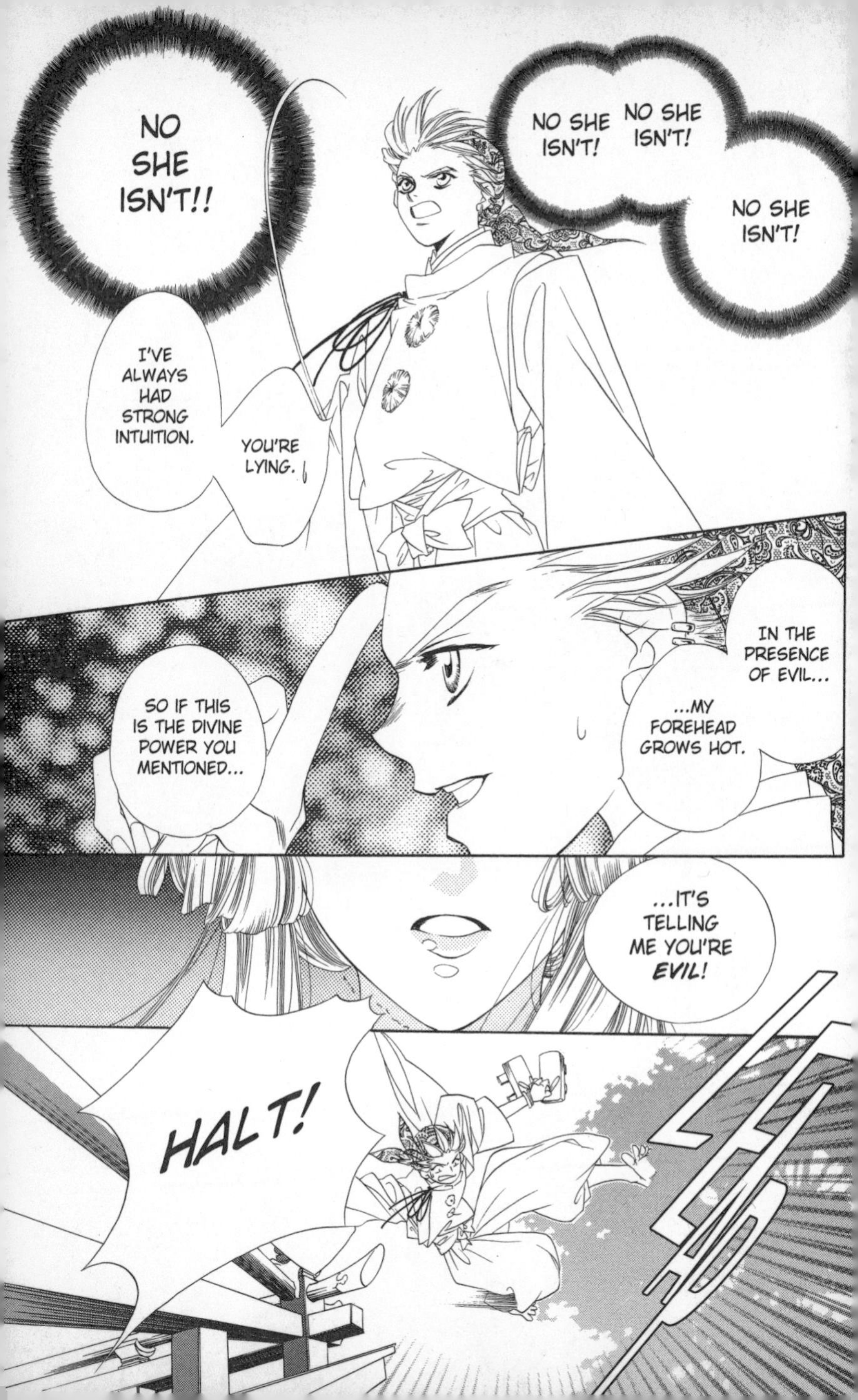
NO SHE ISN'T! NO SHE ISN'T! NO SHE ISN'T!
NO SHE ISN'T!!
YOU'RE LYING.
I'VE ALWAYS HAD STRONG INTUITION.
IN THE PRESENCE OF EVIL...
...MY FOREHEAD GROWS HOT.
SO IF THIS IS THE DIVINE POWER YOU MENTIONED...
...IT'S TELLING ME YOU'RE *EVIL*!
HALT!

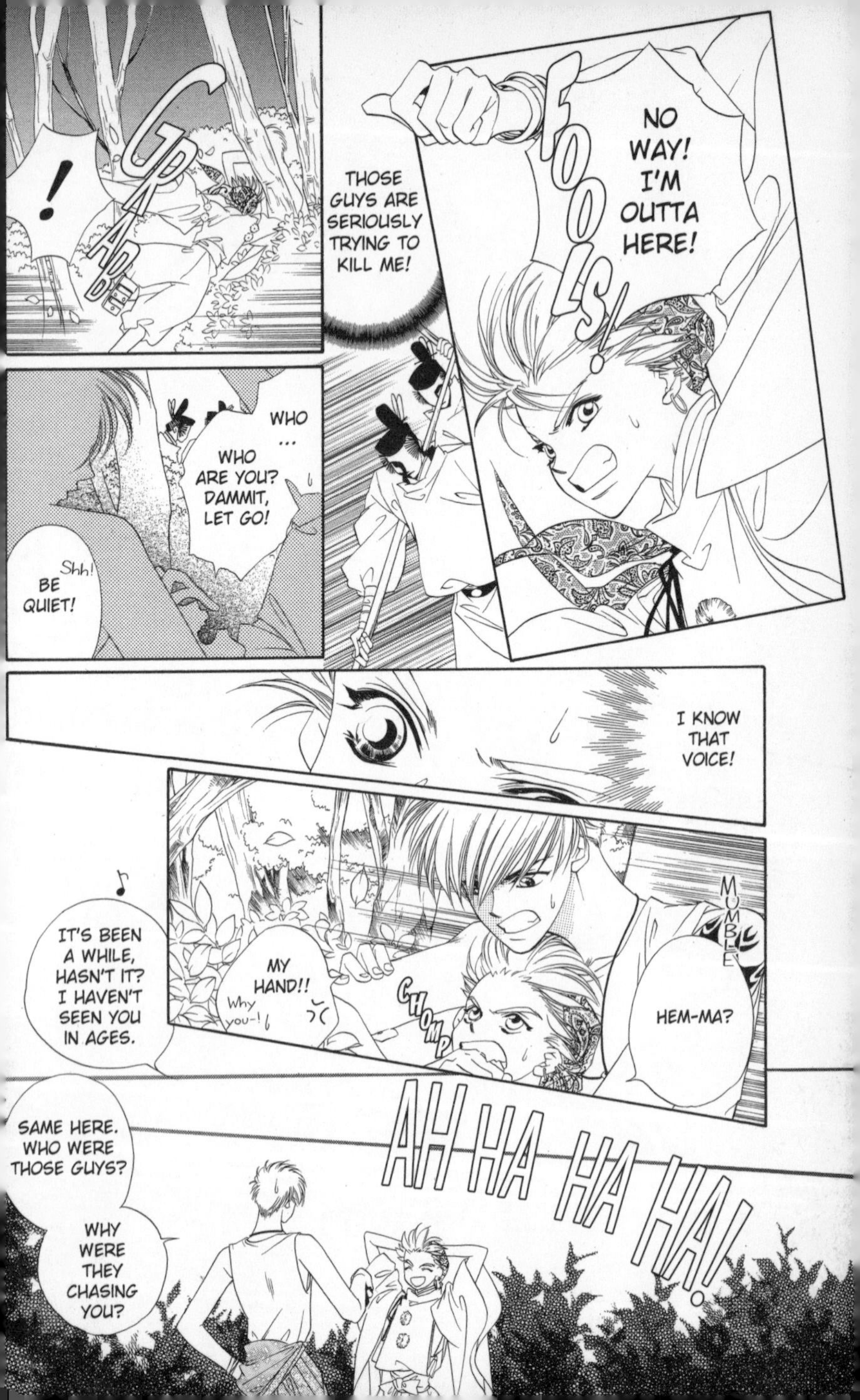
FOOLS!
NO WAY! I'M OUTTA HERE!
THOSE GUYS ARE SERIOUSLY TRYING TO KILL ME!
!
GRAB!!
WHO ...
WHO ARE YOU? DAMMIT, LET GO!
Shh!
BE QUIET!
I KNOW THAT VOICE!
MUMBLE
HEM-MA?
CHOMP
MY HAND!!
Why you-!
IT'S BEEN A WHILE, HASN'T IT? I HAVEN'T SEEN YOU IN AGES.
AH HA HA HA!
SAME HERE. WHO WERE THOSE GUYS?
WHY WERE THEY CHASING YOU?

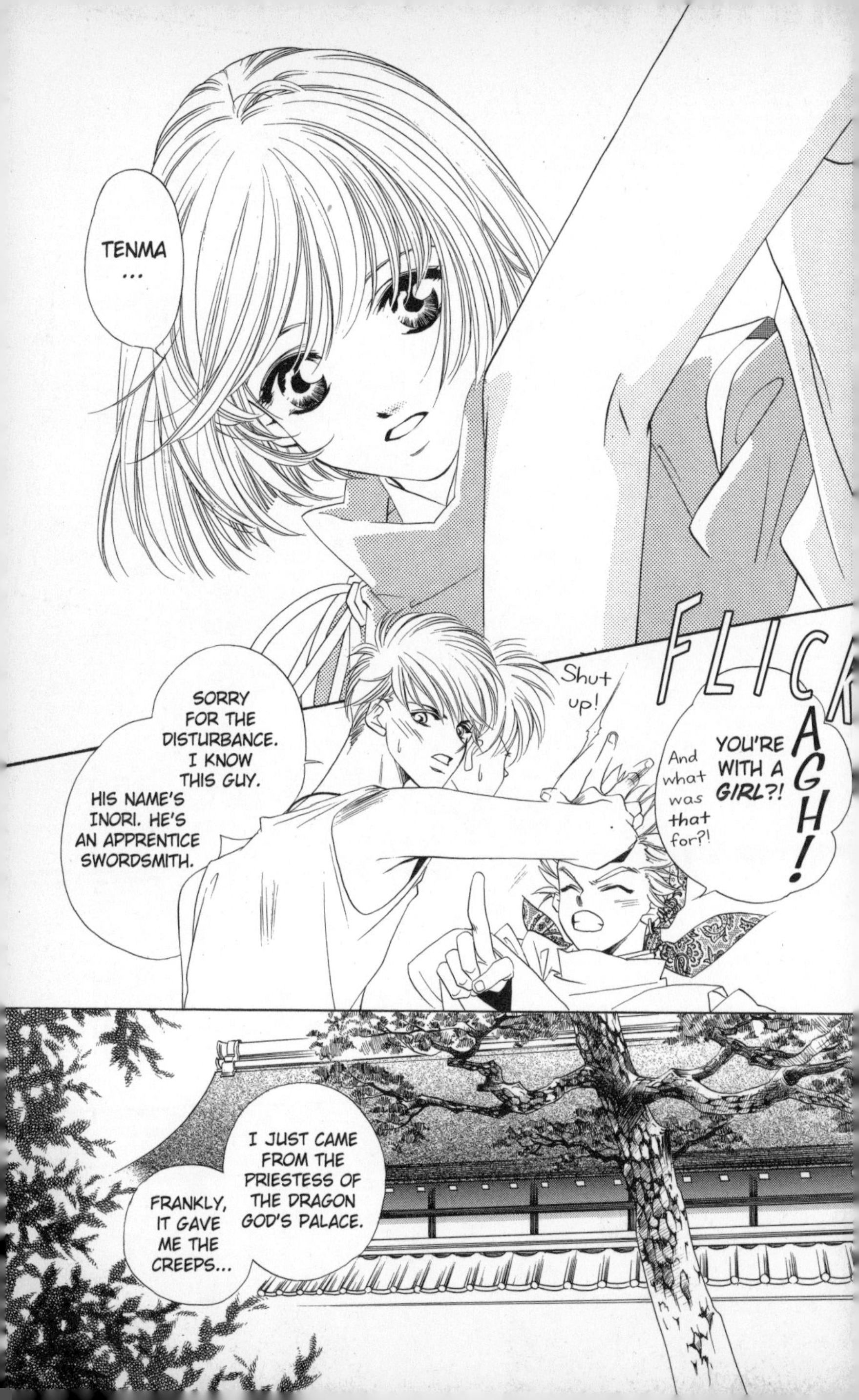
TENMA ...
FLICK
AGH!
YOU'RE WITH A GIRL?!
And what was that for?!
Shut up!
SORRY FOR THE DISTURBANCE. I KNOW THIS GUY.
HIS NAME'S INORI. HE'S AN APPRENTICE SWORDSMITH.
I JUST CAME FROM THE PRIESTESS OF THE DRAGON GOD'S PALACE.
FRANKLY, IT GAVE ME THE CREEPS...

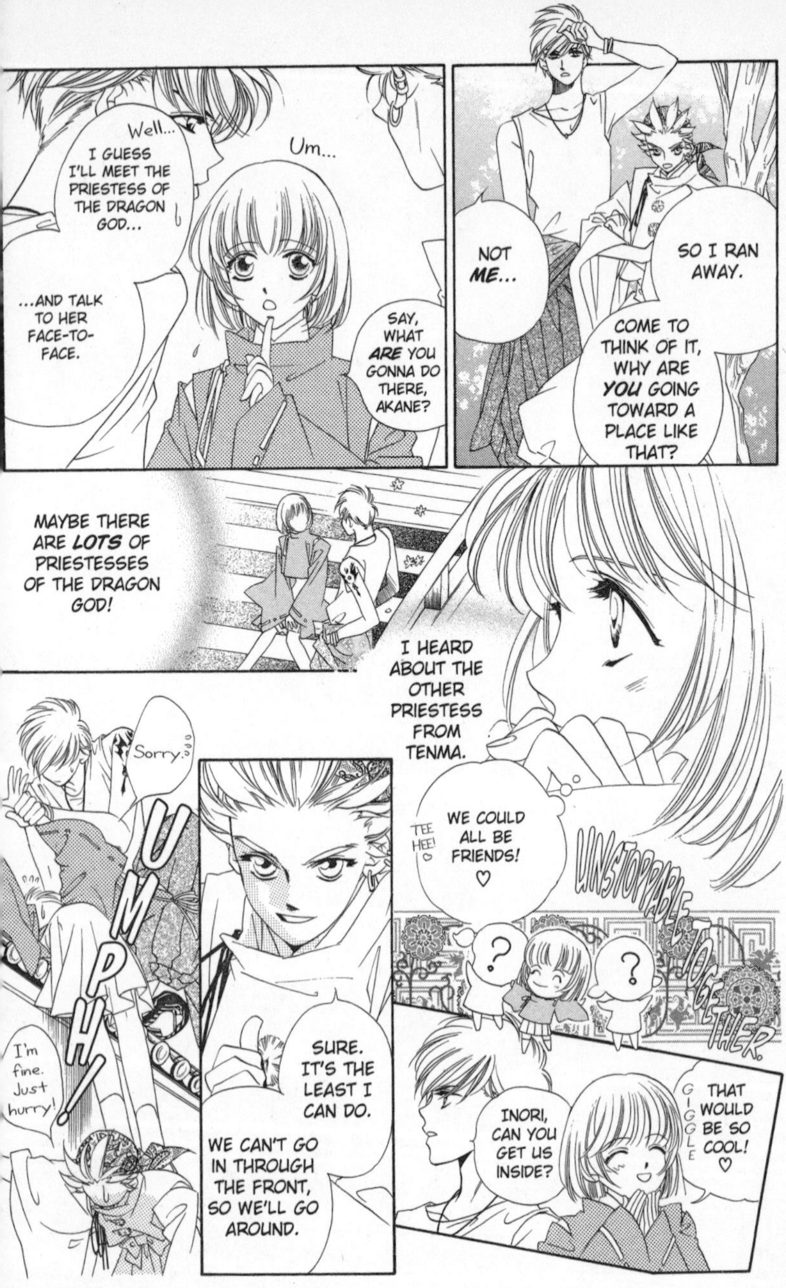

SO I RAN AWAY.
NOT ME...
COME TO THINK OF IT, WHY ARE YOU GOING TOWARD A PLACE LIKE THAT?
Um...
SAY, WHAT ARE YOU GONNA DO THERE, AKANE?
Well... I GUESS I'LL MEET THE PRIESTESS OF THE DRAGON GOD...
...AND TALK TO HER FACE-TO-FACE.
I HEARD ABOUT THE OTHER PRIESTESS FROM TENMA.
MAYBE THERE ARE LOTS OF PRIESTESSES OF THE DRAGON GOD!
WE COULD ALL BE FRIENDS! ♡
TEE HEE! ♡
UNSTOPPABLE TOGETHER.
THAT WOULD BE SO COOL! ♡
GIGGLE
INORI, CAN YOU GET US INSIDE?
SURE. IT'S THE LEAST I CAN DO.
WE CAN'T GO IN THROUGH THE FRONT, SO WE'LL GO AROUND.
Sorry.
UMPHH!
I'm fine. Just hurry!

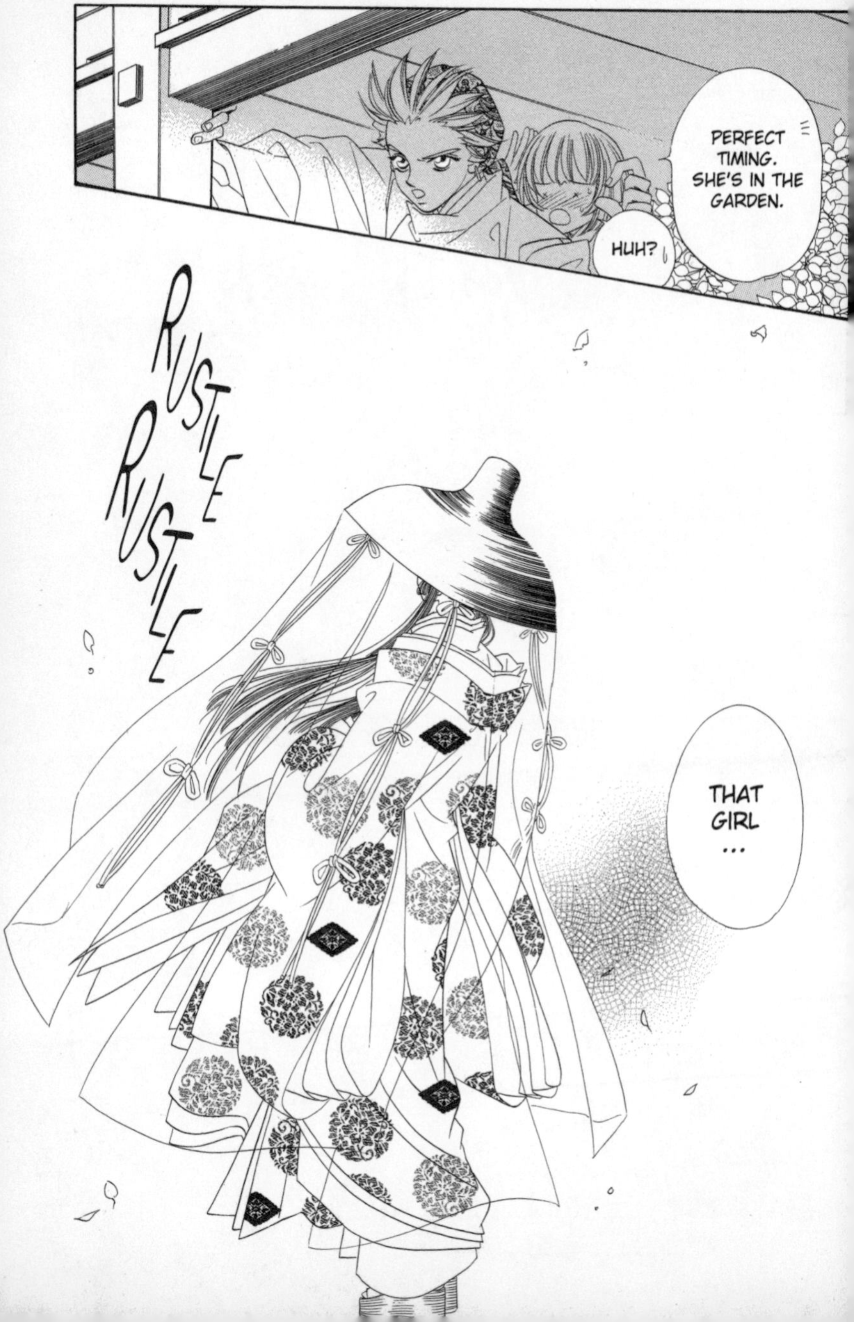
PERFECT TIMING. SHE'S IN THE GARDEN.
HUH?
RUSTLE RUSTLE
THAT GIRL ...

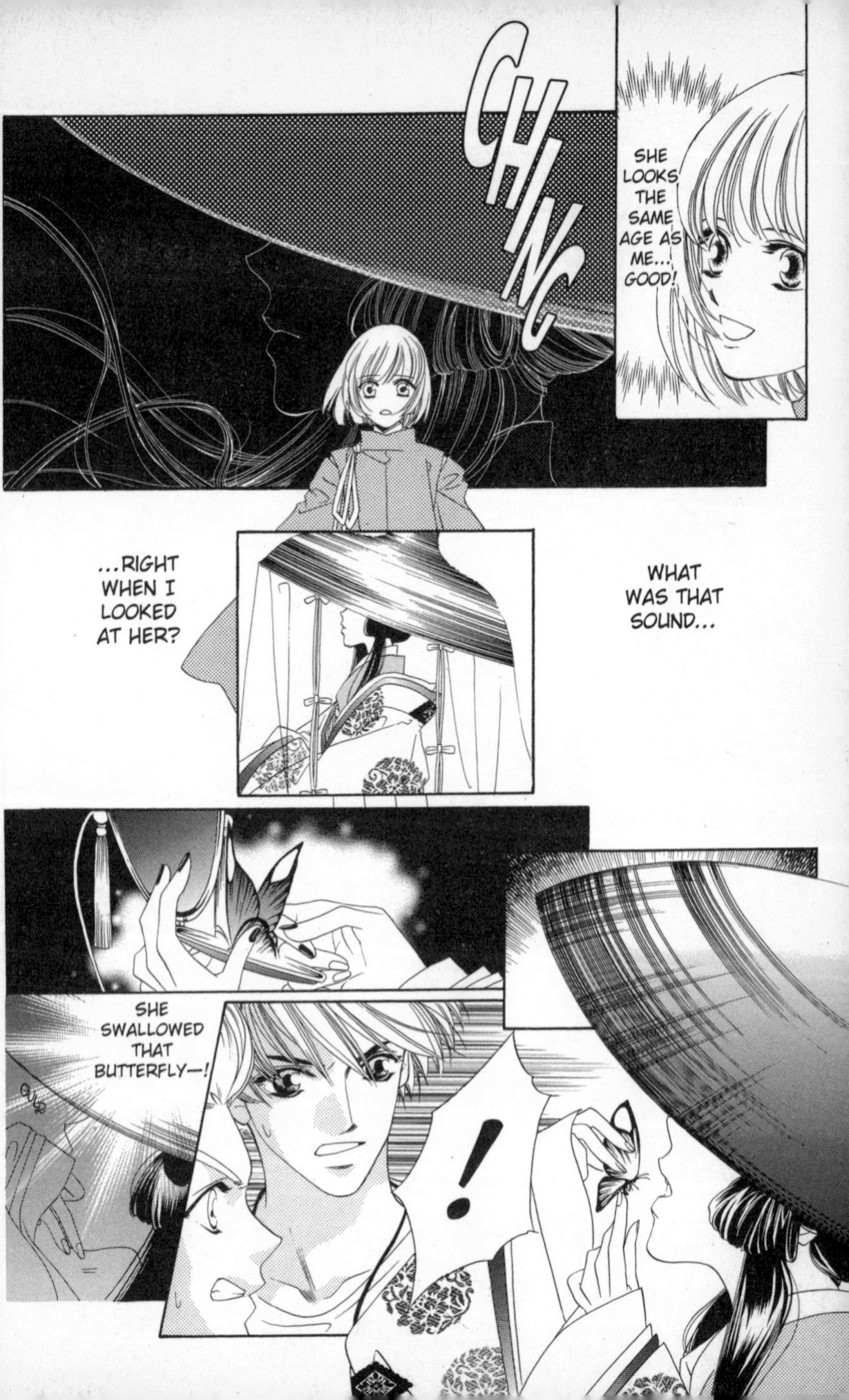
SHE LOOKS THE SAME AGE AS ME... GOOD!
CHING
WHAT WAS THAT SOUND...
...RIGHT WHEN I LOOKED AT HER?
!
SHE SWALLOWED THAT BUTTERFLY—!

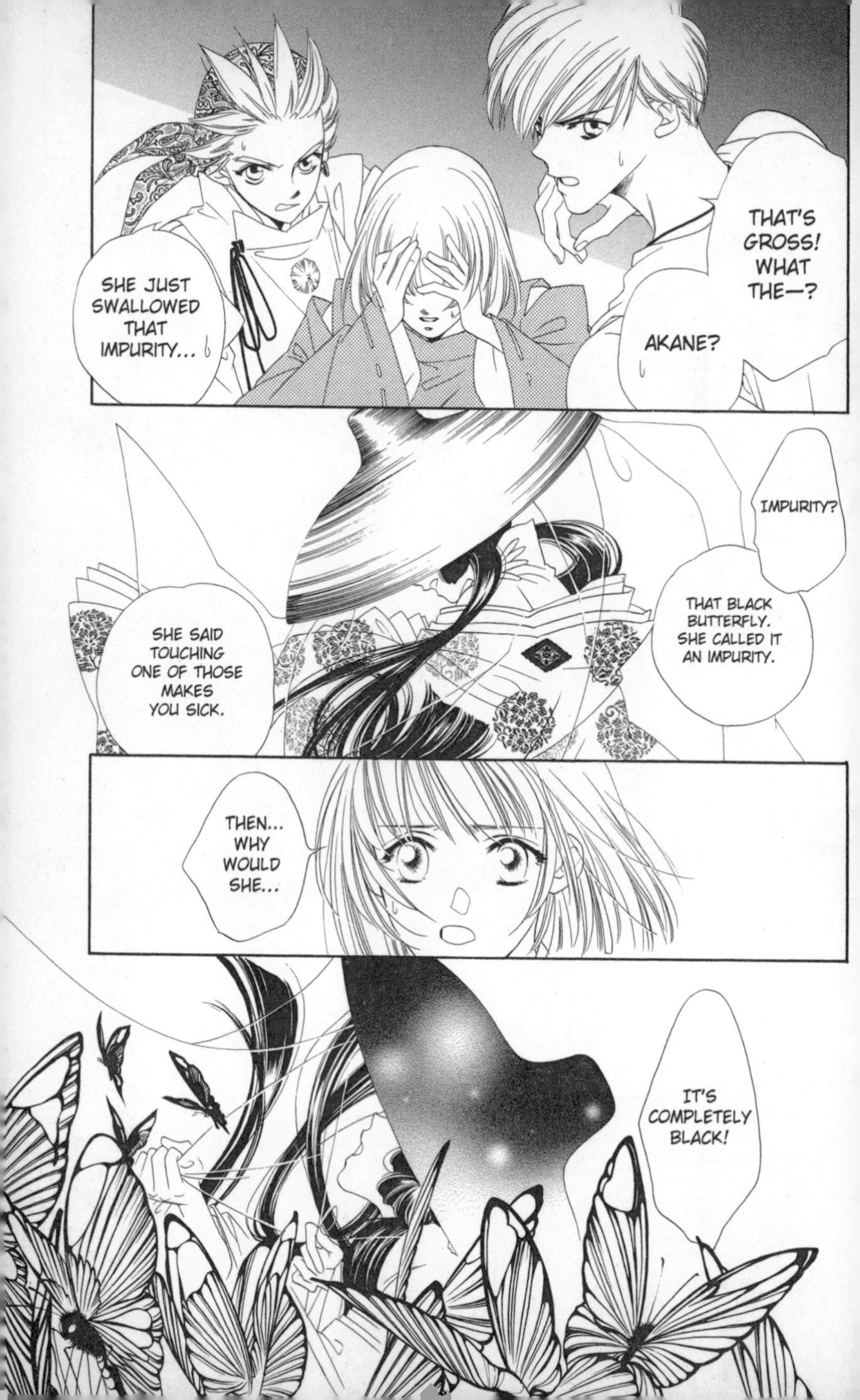
THAT'S GROSS! WHAT THE—?
AKANE?
SHE JUST SWALLOWED THAT IMPURITY...
IMPURITY?
THAT BLACK BUTTERFLY. SHE CALLED IT AN IMPURITY.
SHE SAID TOUCHING ONE OF THOSE MAKES YOU SICK.
THEN... WHY WOULD SHE...
IT'S COMPLETELY BLACK!

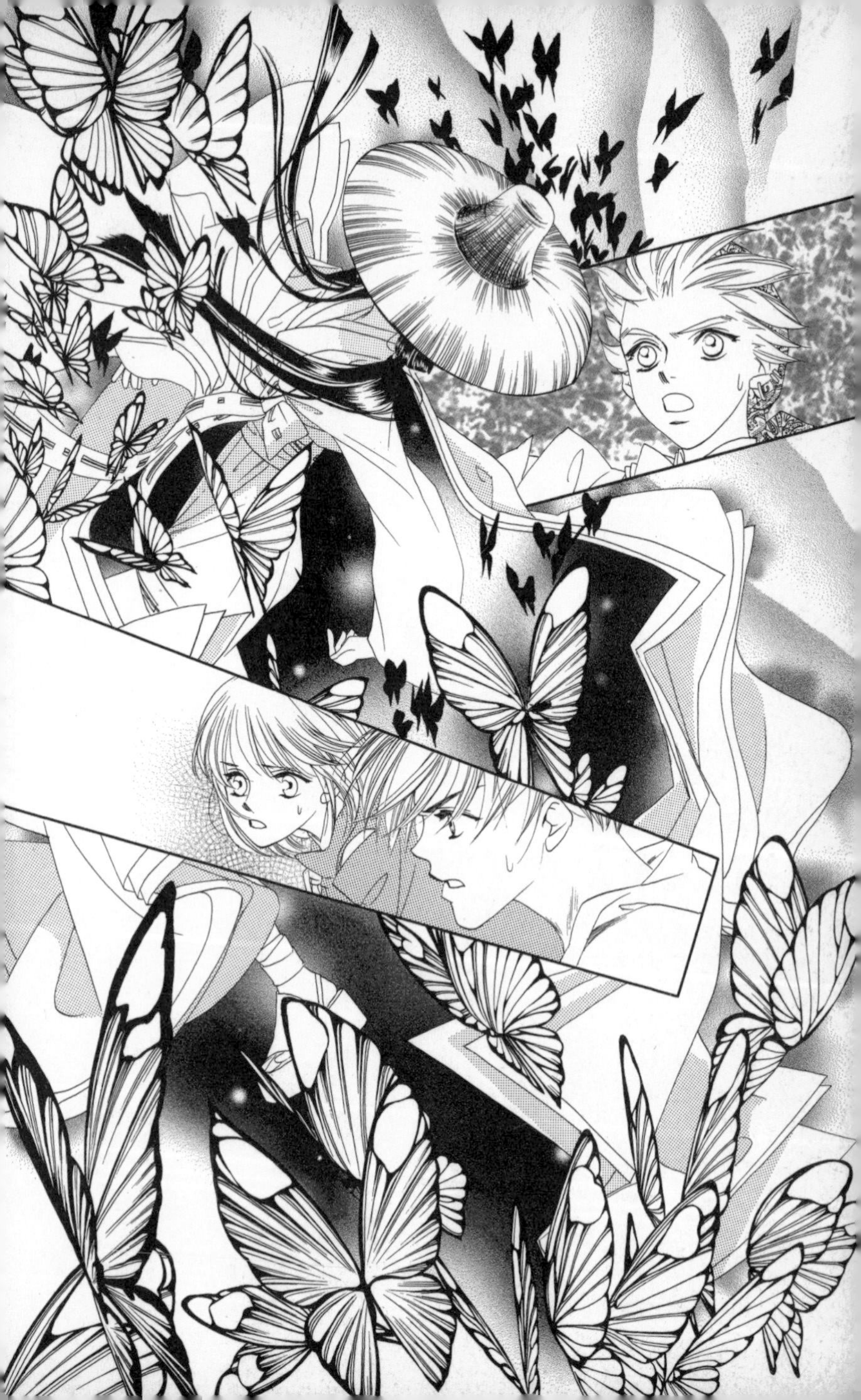

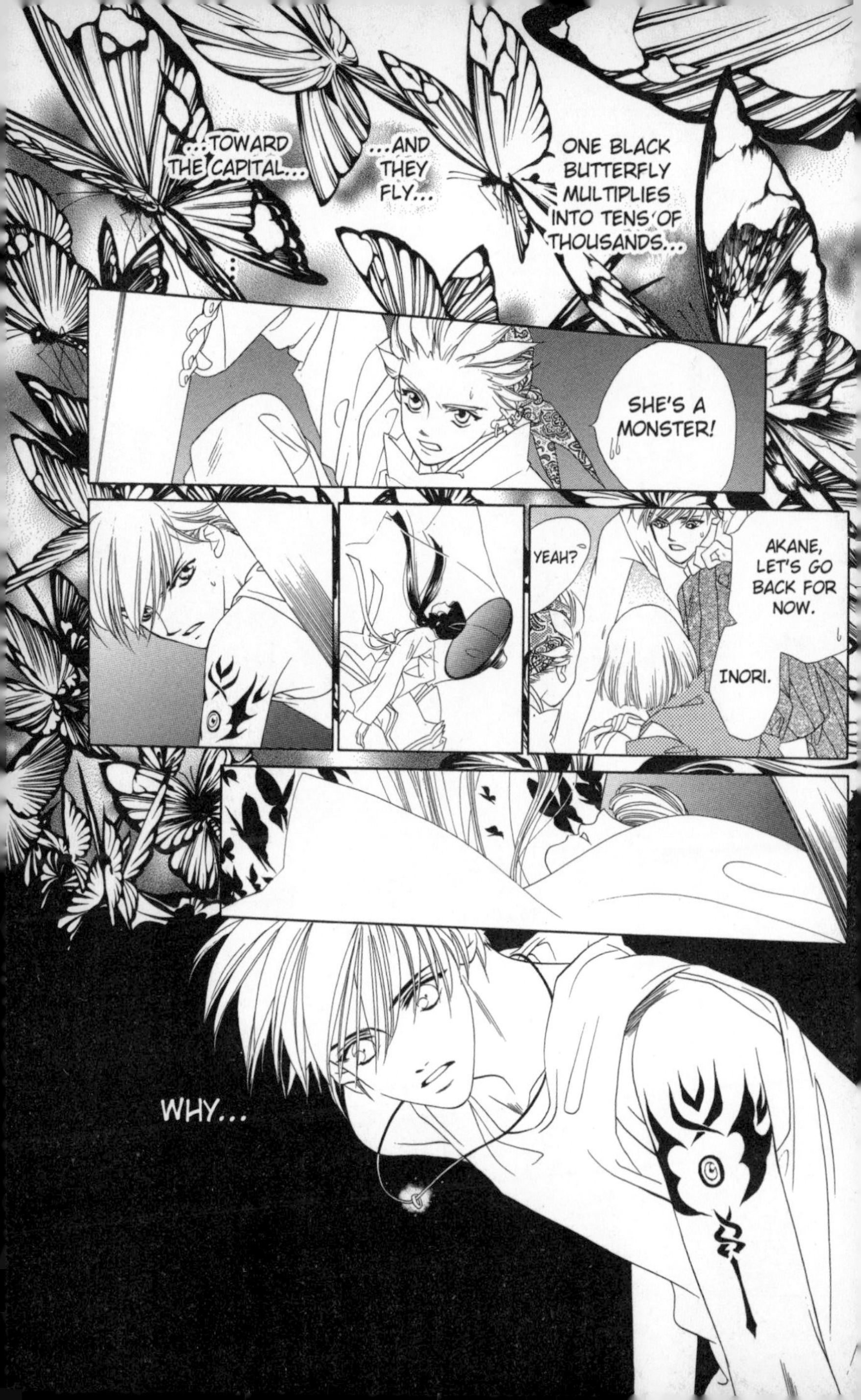

ONE BLACK BUTTERFLY MULTIPLIES INTO TENS OF THOUSANDS...
...AND THEY FLY...
...TOWARD THE CAPITAL...
SHE'S A MONSTER!
AKANE, LET'S GO BACK FOR NOW.
YEAH?
INORI.
WHY...

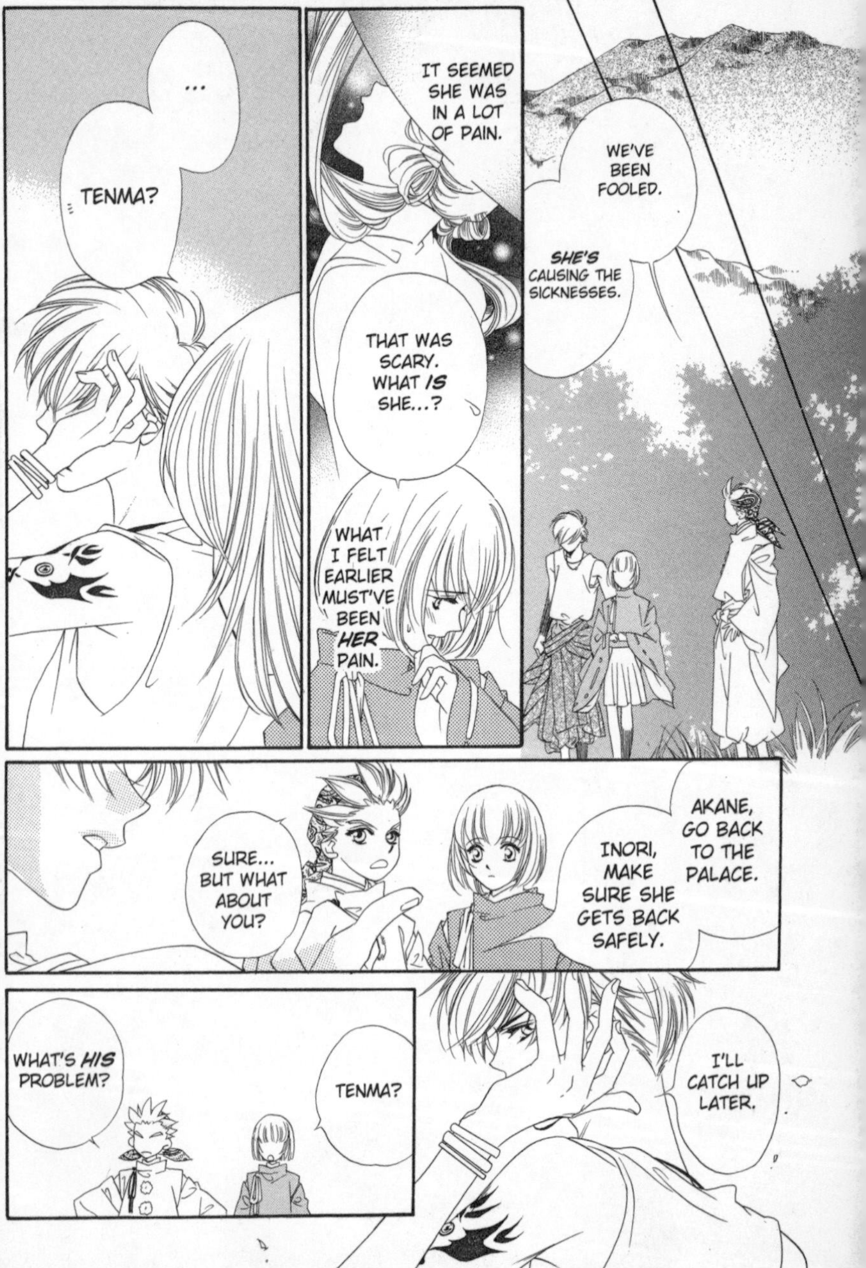
WE'VE BEEN FOOLED.
SHE'S CAUSING THE SICKNESSES.
IT SEEMED SHE WAS IN A LOT OF PAIN.
THAT WAS SCARY. WHAT IS SHE...?
WHAT I FELT EARLIER MUST'VE BEEN HER PAIN.
...
TENMA?
AKANE, GO BACK TO THE PALACE.
INORI, MAKE SURE SHE GETS BACK SAFELY.
SURE... BUT WHAT ABOUT YOU?
I'LL CATCH UP LATER.
TENMA?
WHAT'S HIS PROBLEM?

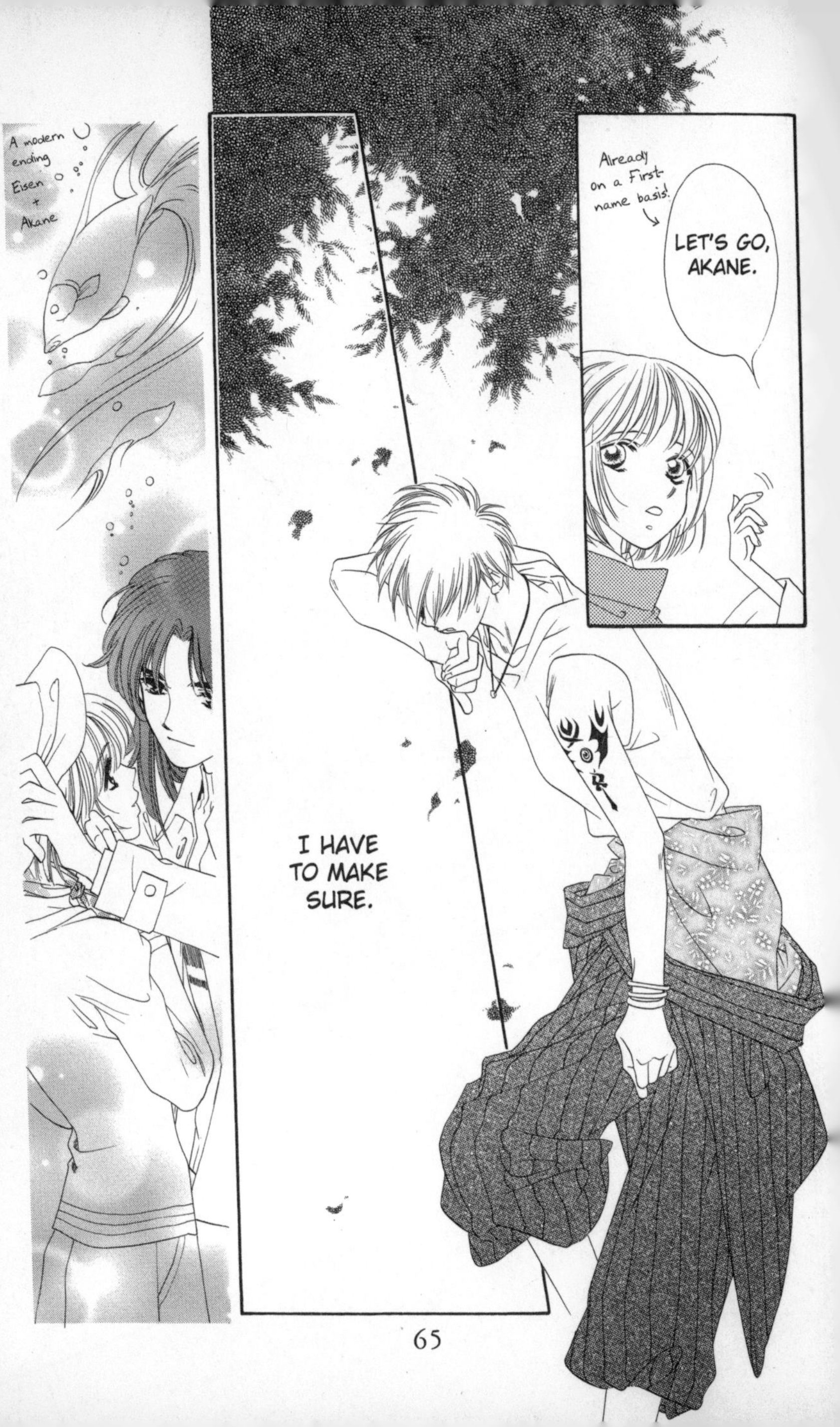
LET'S GO, AKANE.
Already on a First-name basis!
I HAVE TO MAKE SURE.
A modern ending Eisen + Akane

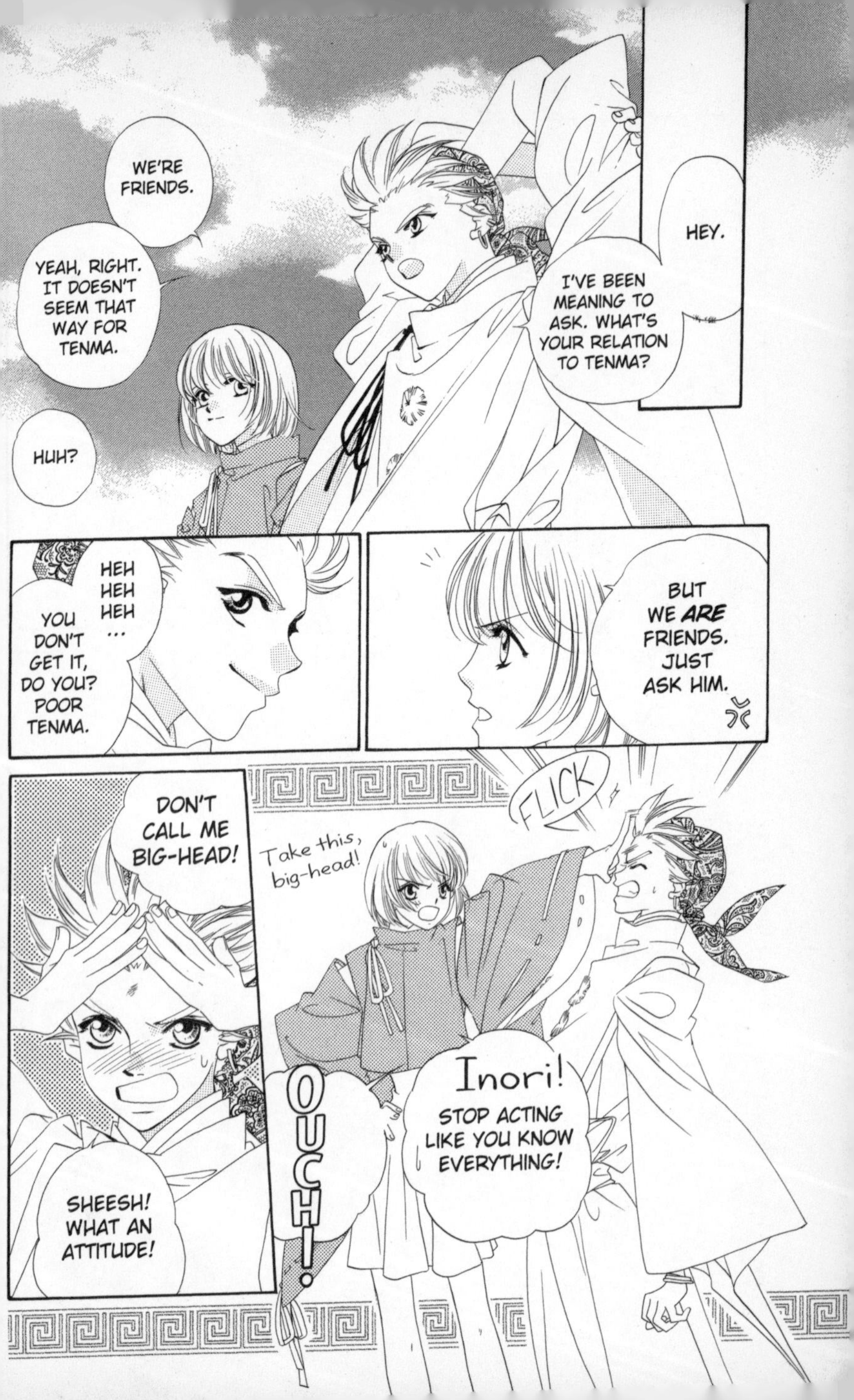
HEY.
I'VE BEEN MEANING TO ASK. WHAT'S YOUR RELATION TO TENMA?
WE'RE FRIENDS.
YEAH, RIGHT. IT DOESN'T SEEM THAT WAY FOR TENMA.
HUH?
BUT WE ***ARE*** FRIENDS. JUST ASK HIM.
HEH HEH HEH...
YOU DON'T GET IT, DO YOU? POOR TENMA.
FLICK
Take this, big-head!
Inori! STOP ACTING LIKE YOU KNOW EVERYTHING!
OUCH!
DON'T CALL ME BIG-HEAD!
SHEESH! WHAT AN ATTITUDE!

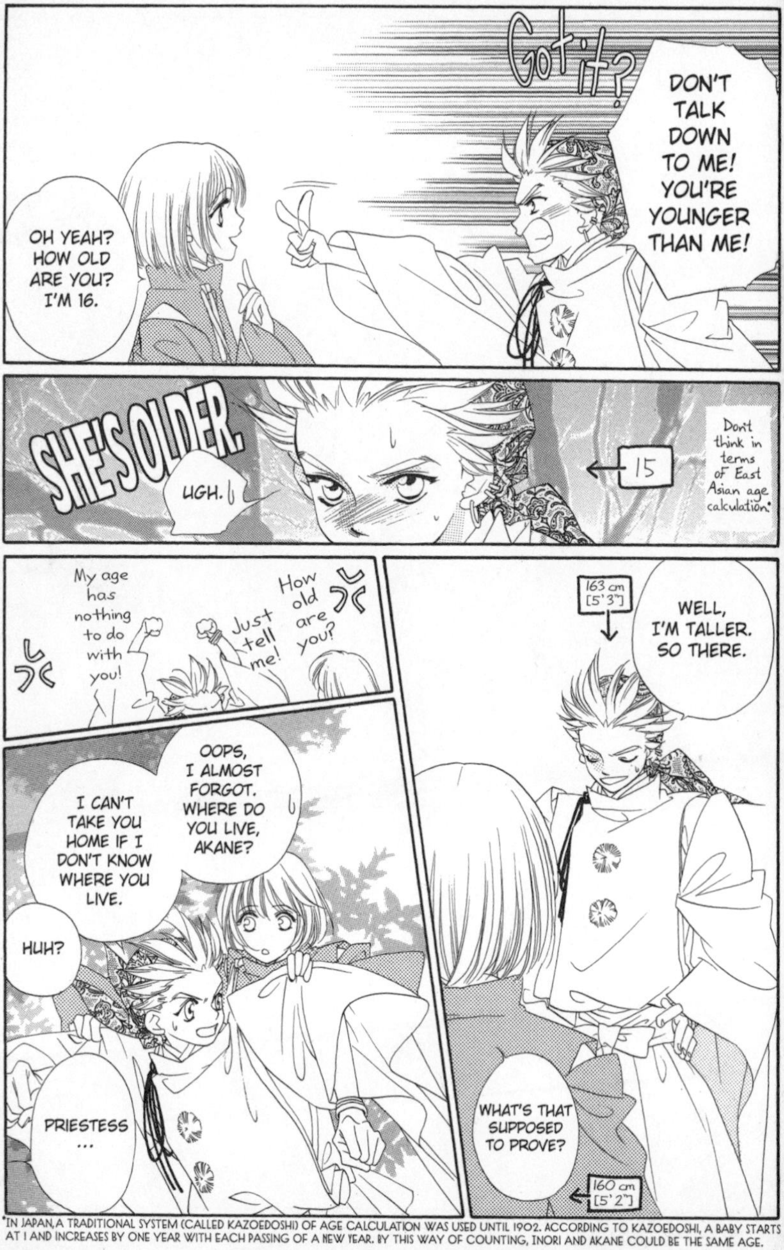
Got it?
DON'T TALK DOWN TO ME! YOU'RE YOUNGER THAN ME!
OH YEAH? HOW OLD ARE YOU? I'M 16.
Don't think in terms of East Asian age calculation*
15
UGH.
SHE'S OLDER.
163 cm [5'3"]
WELL, I'M TALLER. SO THERE.
WHAT'S THAT SUPPOSED TO PROVE?
160 cm [5'2"]
How old are you?
Just tell me!
My age has nothing to do with you!
OOPS, I ALMOST FORGOT. WHERE DO YOU LIVE, AKANE?
I CAN'T TAKE YOU HOME IF I DON'T KNOW WHERE YOU LIVE.
HUH?
PRIESTESS ...

*IN JAPAN, A TRADITIONAL SYSTEM (CALLED KAZOEDOSHI) OF AGE CALCULATION WAS USED UNTIL 1902. ACCORDING TO KAZOEDOSHI, A BABY STARTS AT 1 AND INCREASES BY ONE YEAR WITH EACH PASSING OF A NEW YEAR. BY THIS WAY OF COUNTING, INORI AND AKANE COULD BE THE SAME AGE.

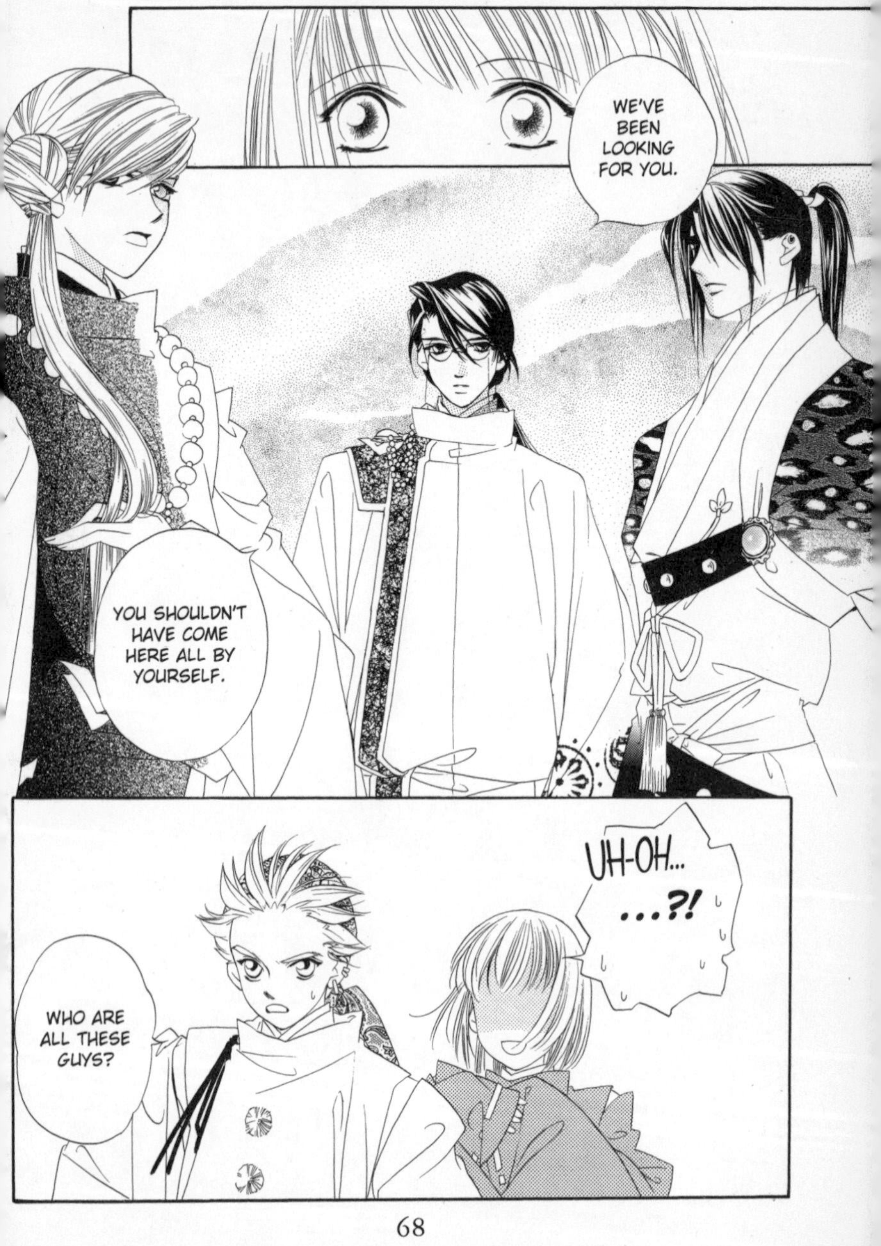
WE'VE BEEN LOOKING FOR YOU.
YOU SHOULDN'T HAVE COME HERE ALL BY YOURSELF.
UH-OH... ...?!
WHO ARE ALL THESE GUYS?

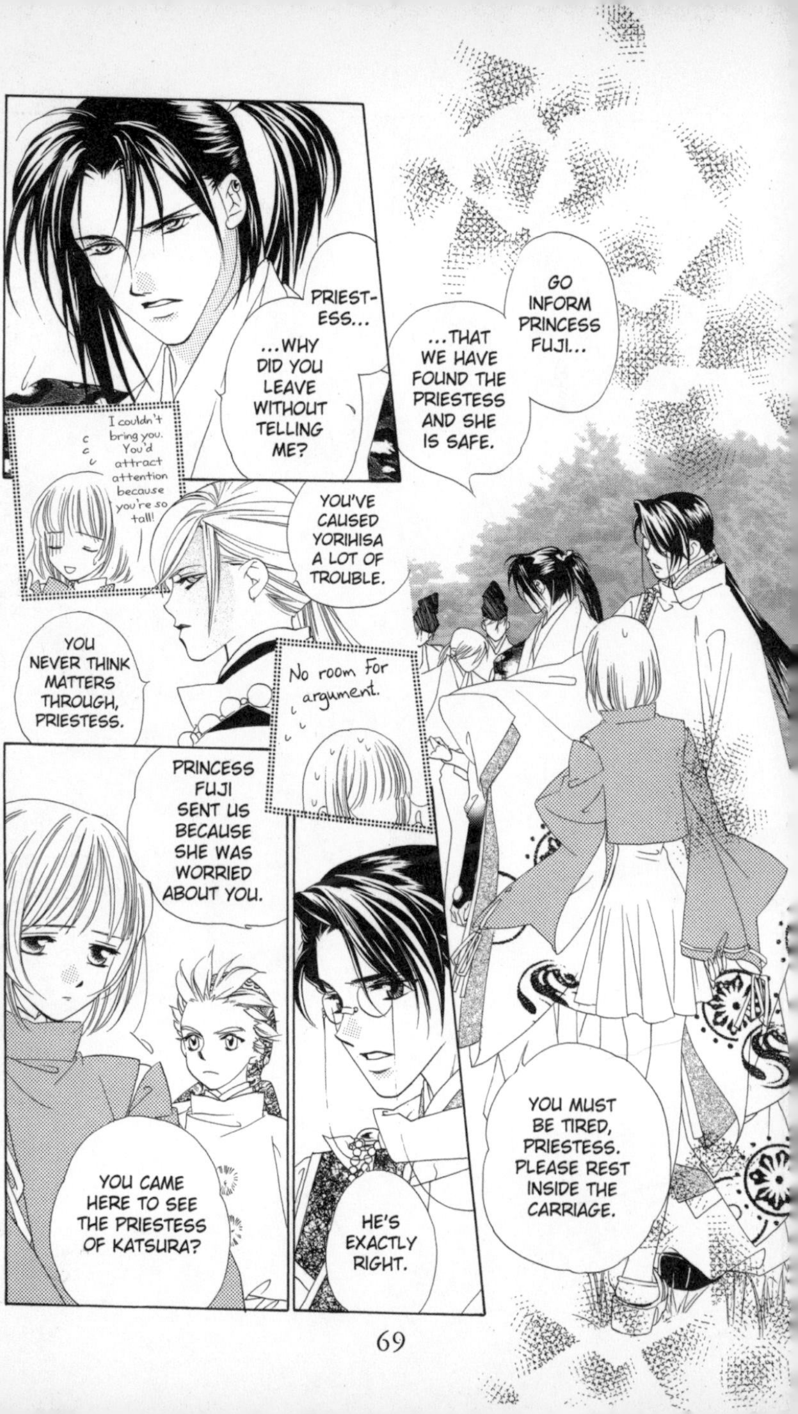
GO INFORM PRINCESS FUJI...
...THAT WE HAVE FOUND THE PRIESTESS AND SHE IS SAFE.
YOU MUST BE TIRED, PRIESTESS. PLEASE REST INSIDE THE CARRIAGE.
PRIEST-ESS...
...WHY DID YOU LEAVE WITHOUT TELLING ME?
I couldn't bring you. You'd attract attention because you're so tall!
YOU'VE CAUSED YORIHISA A LOT OF TROUBLE.
YOU NEVER THINK MATTERS THROUGH, PRIESTESS.
No room for argument.
HE'S EXACTLY RIGHT.
PRINCESS FUJI SENT US BECAUSE SHE WAS WORRIED ABOUT YOU.
YOU CAME HERE TO SEE THE PRIESTESS OF KATSURA?

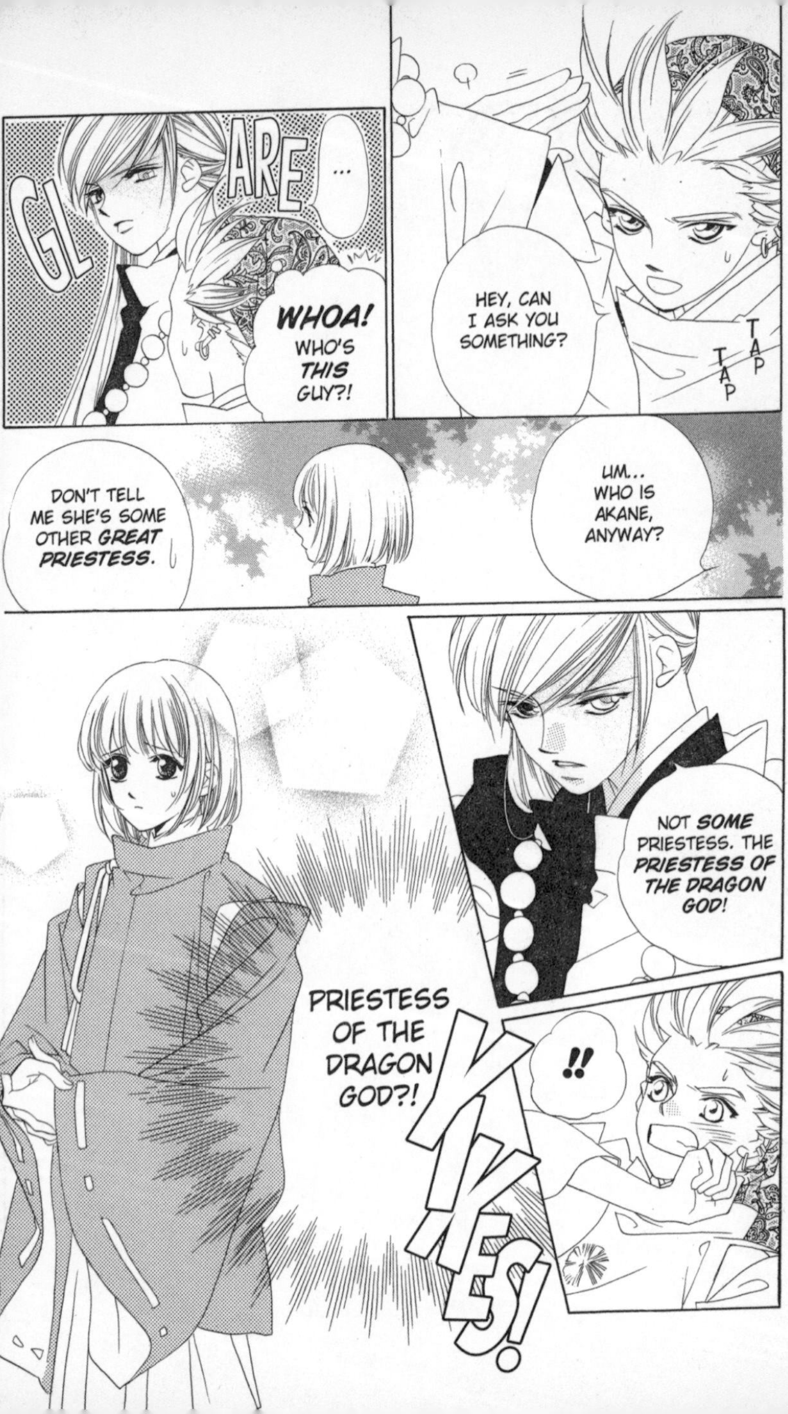

HEY, CAN I ASK YOU SOMETHING?
TAP TAP
GLARE
...
WHOA! WHO'S THIS GUY?!
UM... WHO IS AKANE, ANYWAY?
DON'T TELL ME SHE'S SOME OTHER GREAT PRIESTESS.
NOT SOME PRIESTESS. THE PRIESTESS OF THE DRAGON GOD!
!!
YIKES!
PRIESTESS OF THE DRAGON GOD?!

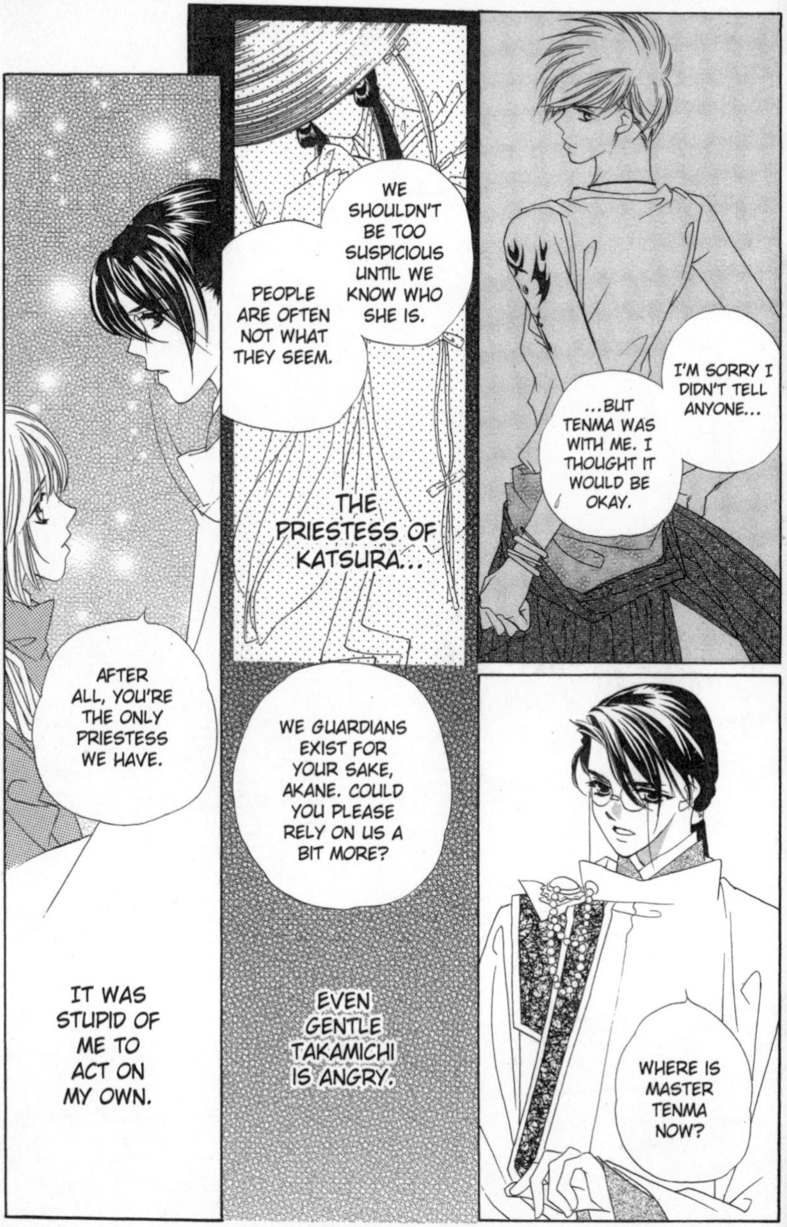
I'M SORRY I DIDN'T TELL ANYONE...
...BUT TENMA WAS WITH ME. I THOUGHT IT WOULD BE OKAY.
WE SHOULDN'T BE TOO SUSPICIOUS UNTIL WE KNOW WHO SHE IS.
PEOPLE ARE OFTEN NOT WHAT THEY SEEM.
THE PRIESTESS OF KATSURA...
WHERE IS MASTER TENMA NOW?
WE GUARDIANS EXIST FOR YOUR SAKE, AKANE. COULD YOU PLEASE RELY ON US A BIT MORE?
EVEN GENTLE TAKAMICHI IS ANGRY.
AFTER ALL, YOU'RE THE ONLY PRIESTESS WE HAVE.
IT WAS STUPID OF ME TO ACT ON MY OWN.

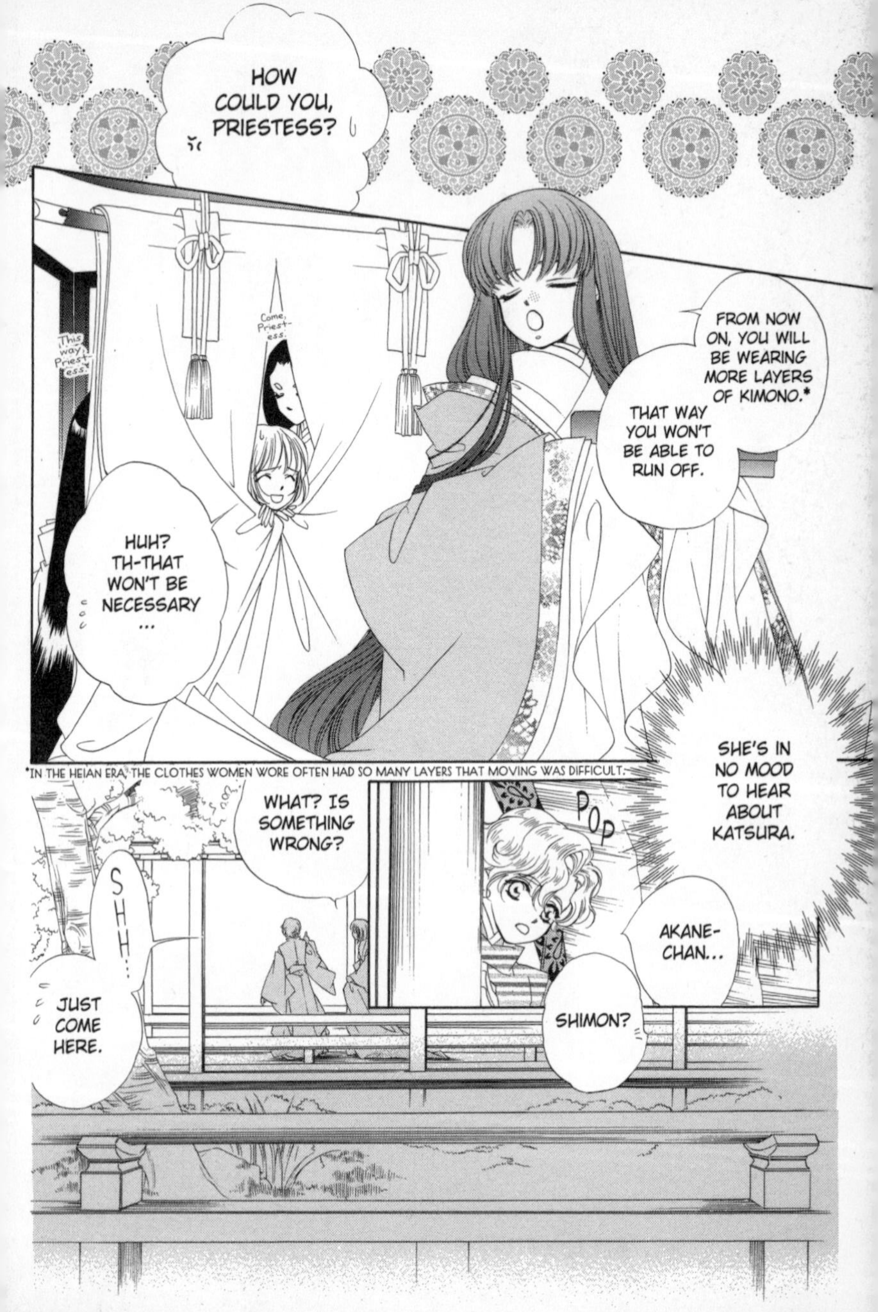
HOW COULD YOU, PRIESTESS?
FROM NOW ON, YOU WILL BE WEARING MORE LAYERS OF KIMONO.*
THAT WAY YOU WON'T BE ABLE TO RUN OFF.
Come, Priestess.
This way, Priestess.
HUH? TH-THAT WON'T BE NECESSARY...
SHE'S IN NO MOOD TO HEAR ABOUT KATSURA.
POP
AKANE-CHAN...
SHIMON?
WHAT? IS SOMETHING WRONG?
SHH!
JUST COME HERE.

*IN THE HEIAN ERA, THE CLOTHES WOMEN WORE OFTEN HAD SO MANY LAYERS THAT MOVING WAS DIFFICULT.

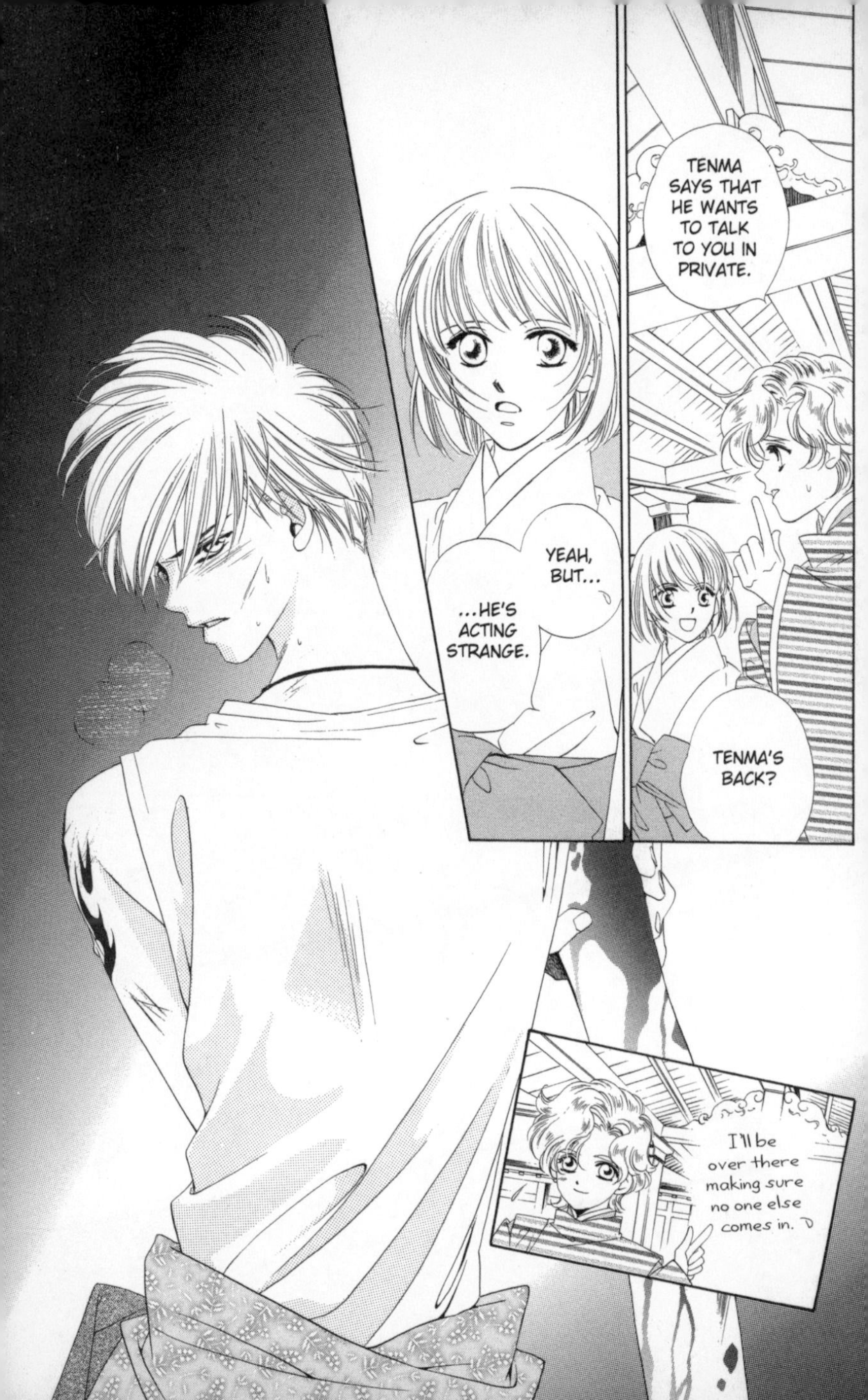
TENMA SAYS THAT HE WANTS TO TALK TO YOU IN PRIVATE.
TENMA'S BACK?
YEAH, BUT...
...HE'S ACTING STRANGE.
I'll be over there making sure no one else comes in.

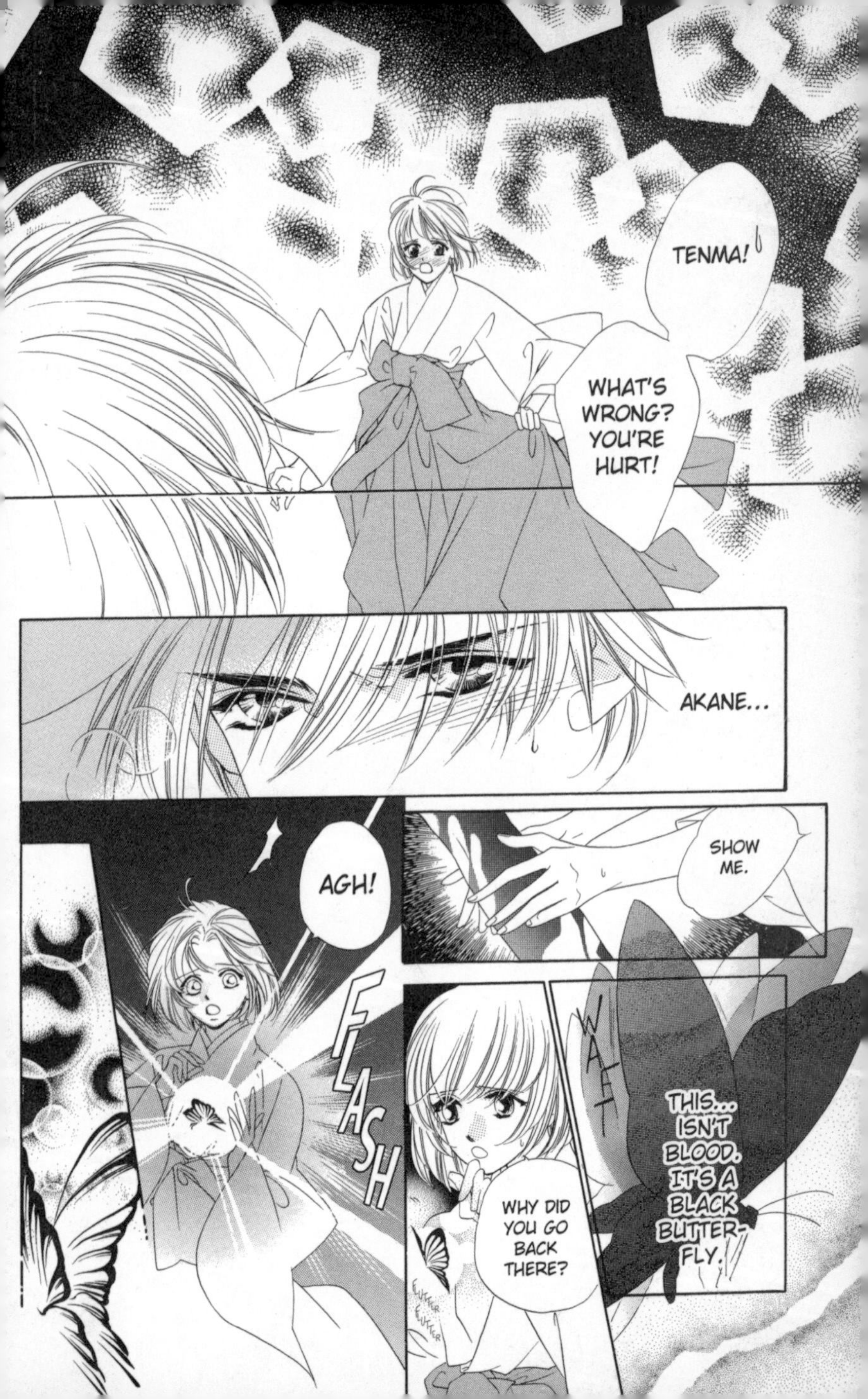
TENMA!
WHAT'S WRONG? YOU'RE HURT!
AKANE...
SHOW ME.
WAIT
THIS... ISN'T BLOOD. IT'S A BLACK BUTTER-FLY.
WHY DID YOU GO BACK THERE?
FLUTTER FLUTTER
AGH!
FLASH

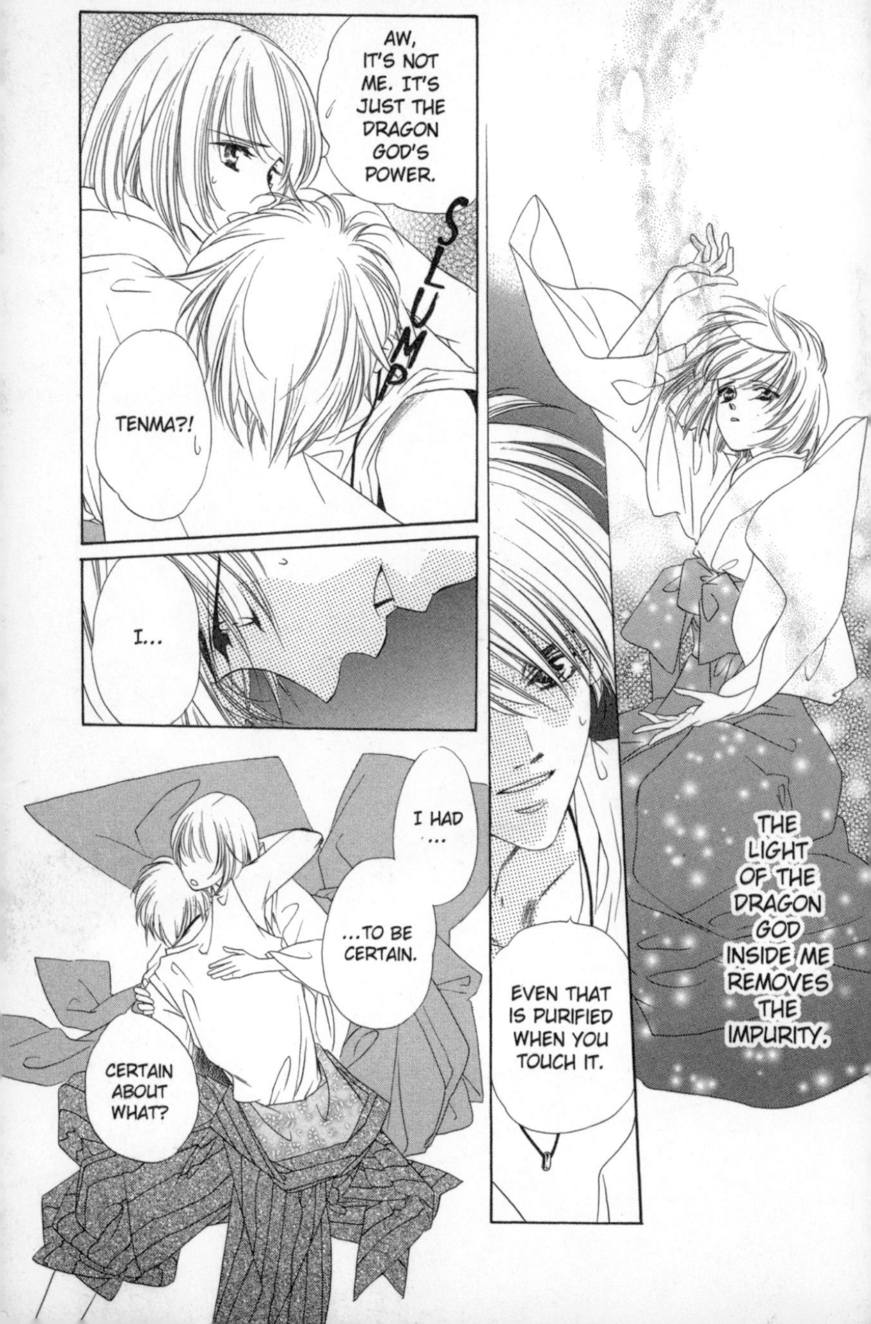
THE LIGHT OF THE DRAGON GOD INSIDE ME REMOVES THE IMPURITY.
EVEN THAT IS PURIFIED WHEN YOU TOUCH IT.
AW, IT'S NOT ME. IT'S JUST THE DRAGON GOD'S POWER.
SLUMP
TENMA?!
I...
I HAD...
...TO BE CERTAIN.
CERTAIN ABOUT WHAT?

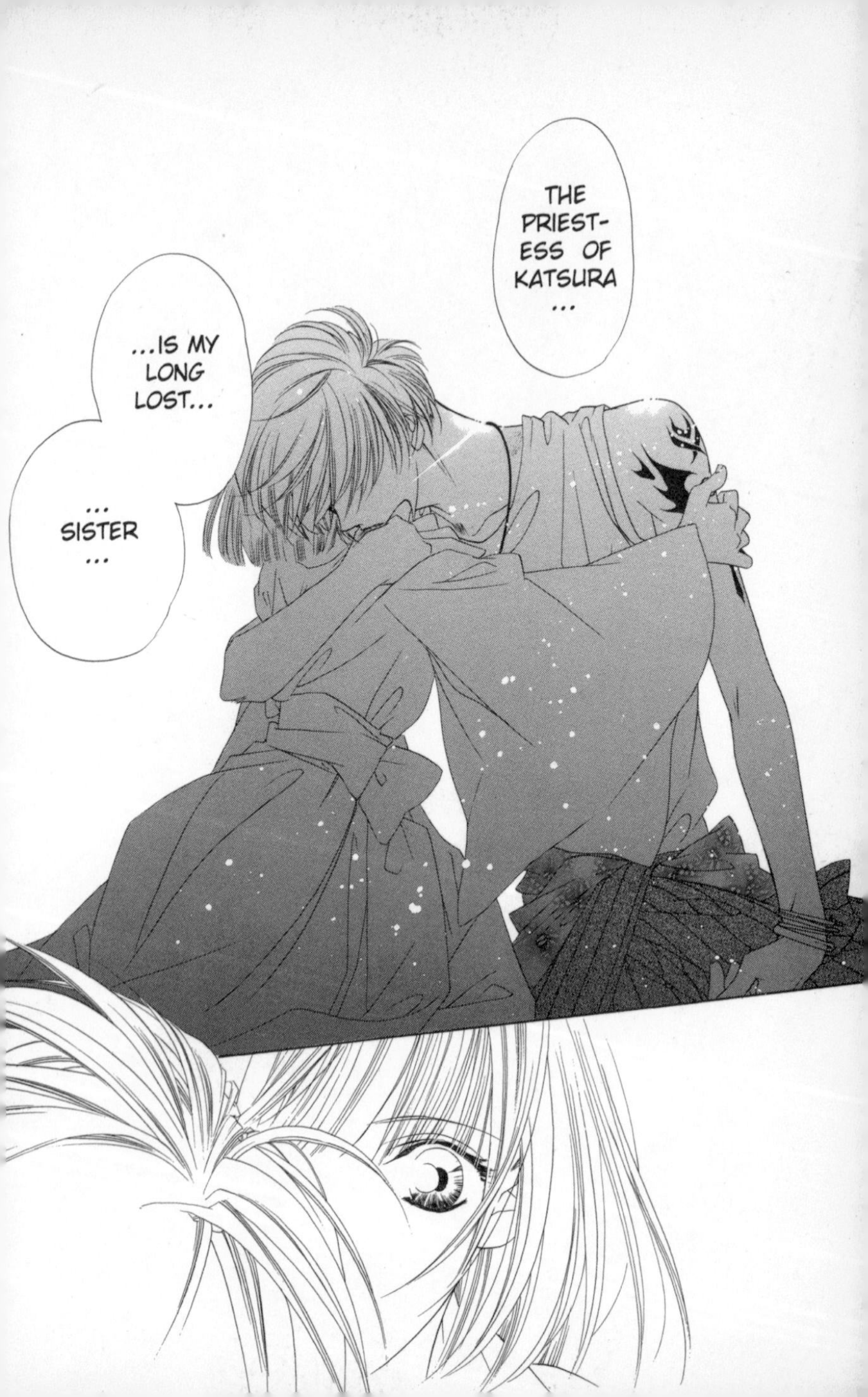
THE PRIEST-ESS OF KATSURA ...
...IS MY LONG LOST...
... SISTER ...

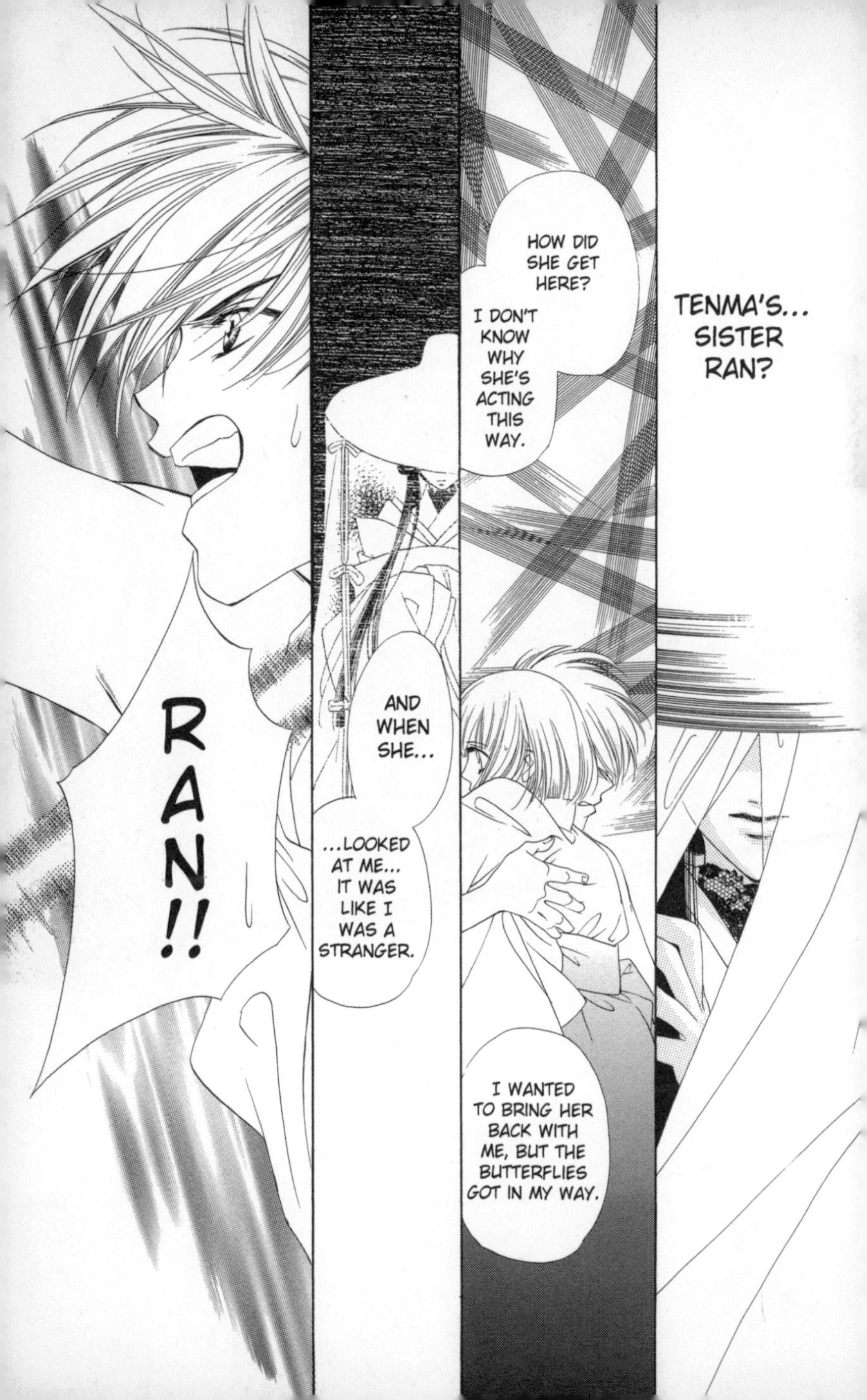
TENMA'S... SISTER RAN?
HOW DID SHE GET HERE?
I DON'T KNOW WHY SHE'S ACTING THIS WAY.
I WANTED TO BRING HER BACK WITH ME, BUT THE BUTTERFLIES GOT IN MY WAY.
AND WHEN SHE...
...LOOKED AT ME... IT WAS LIKE I WAS A STRANGER.
RAN!!

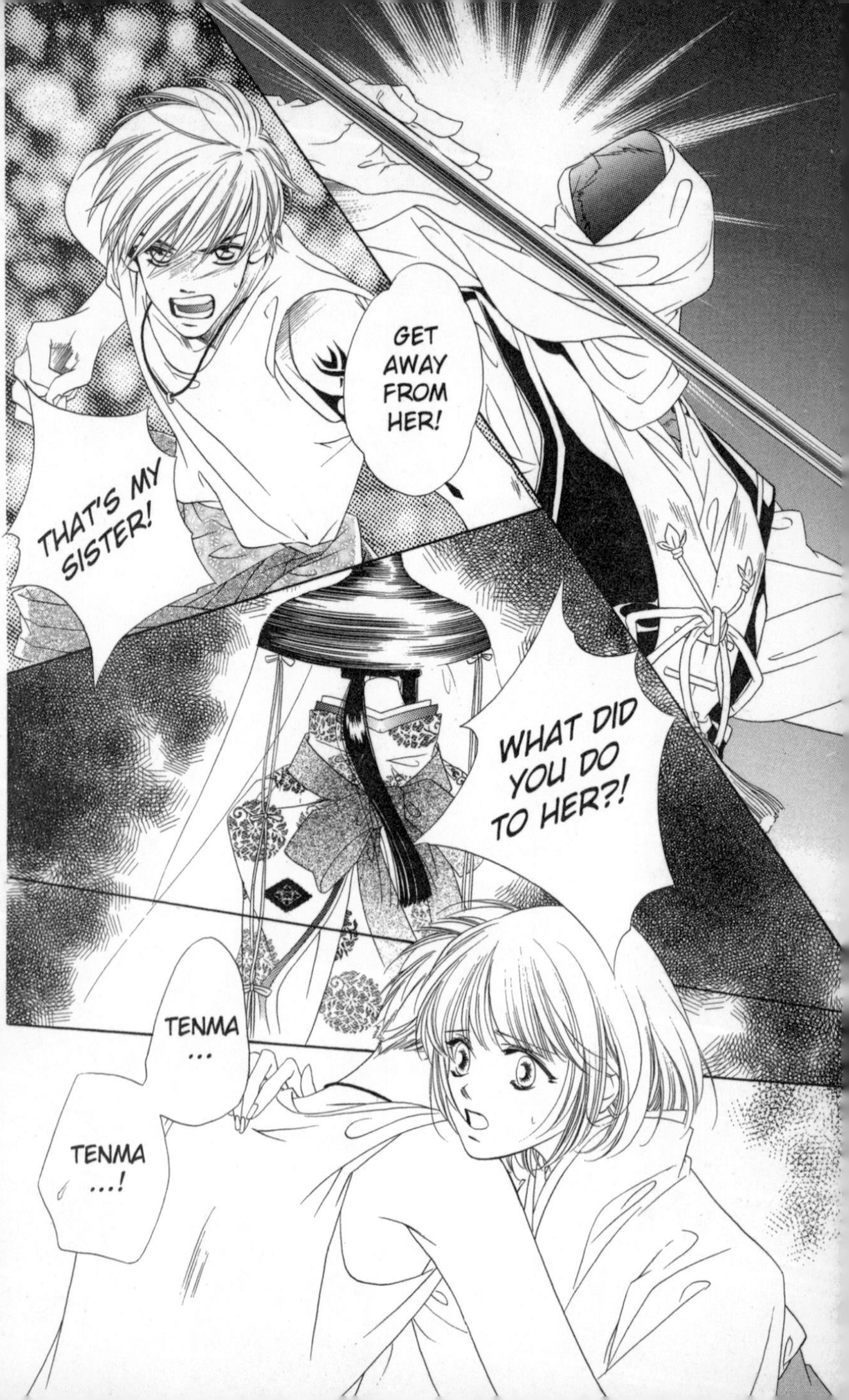
GET AWAY FROM HER!
THAT'S MY SISTER!
WHAT DID YOU DO TO HER?!
TENMA ...
TENMA ...!

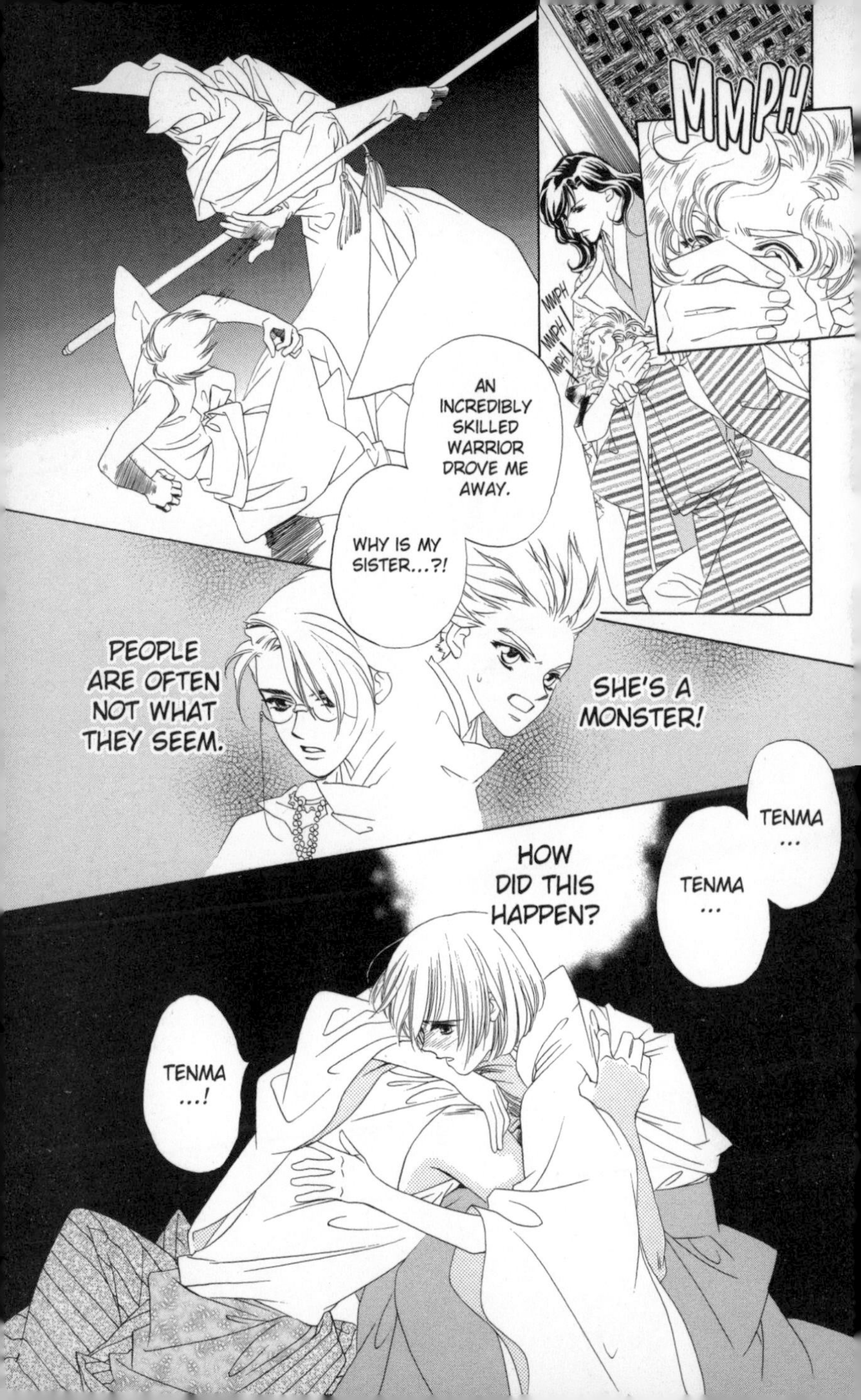
MMPH
MMPH
MMPH
MMPH
AN INCREDIBLY SKILLED WARRIOR DROVE ME AWAY.
WHY IS MY SISTER...?!
SHE'S A MONSTER!
PEOPLE ARE OFTEN NOT WHAT THEY SEEM.
TENMA...
TENMA...
HOW DID THIS HAPPEN?
TENMA...!

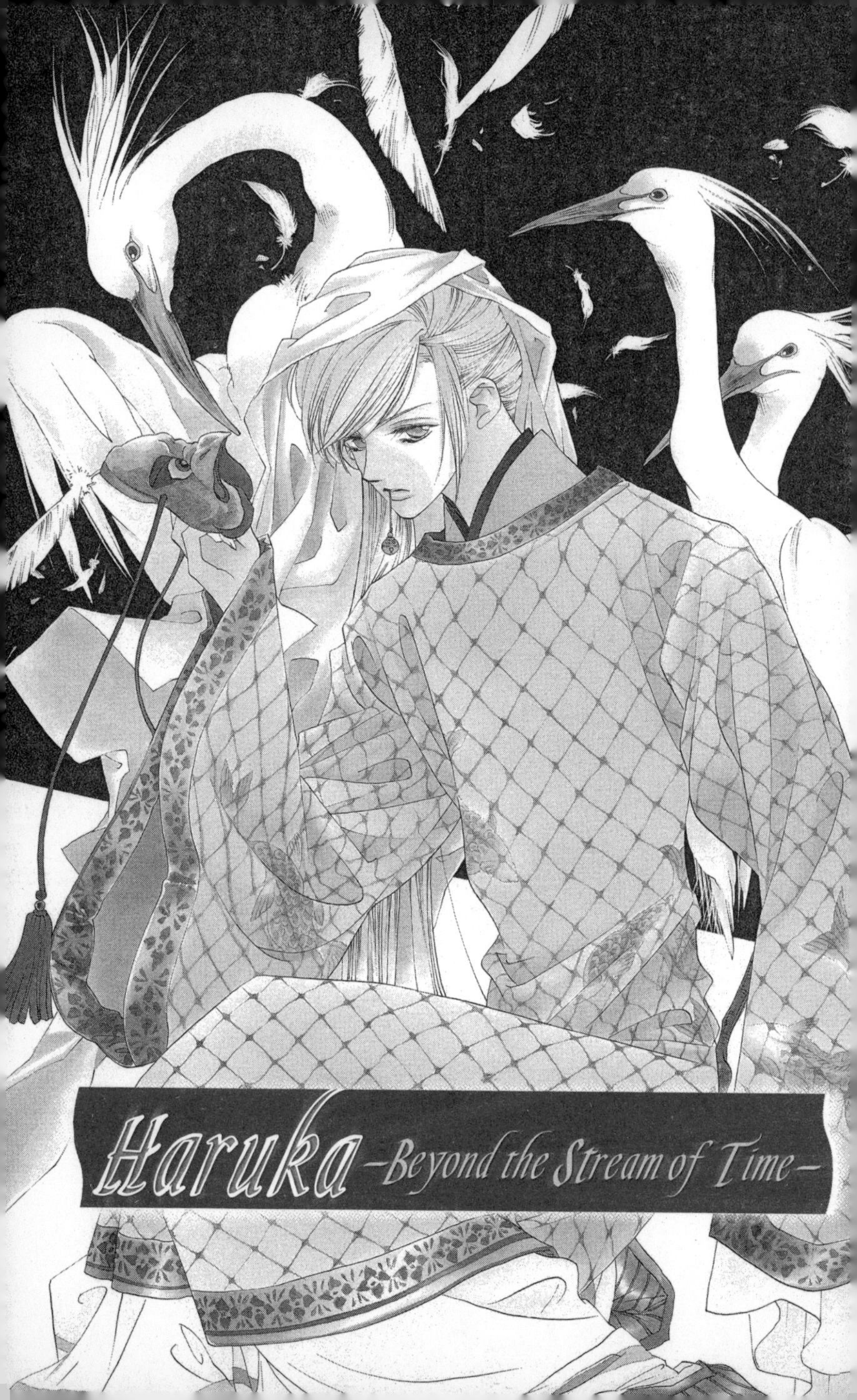
Haruka -Beyond the Stream of Time-

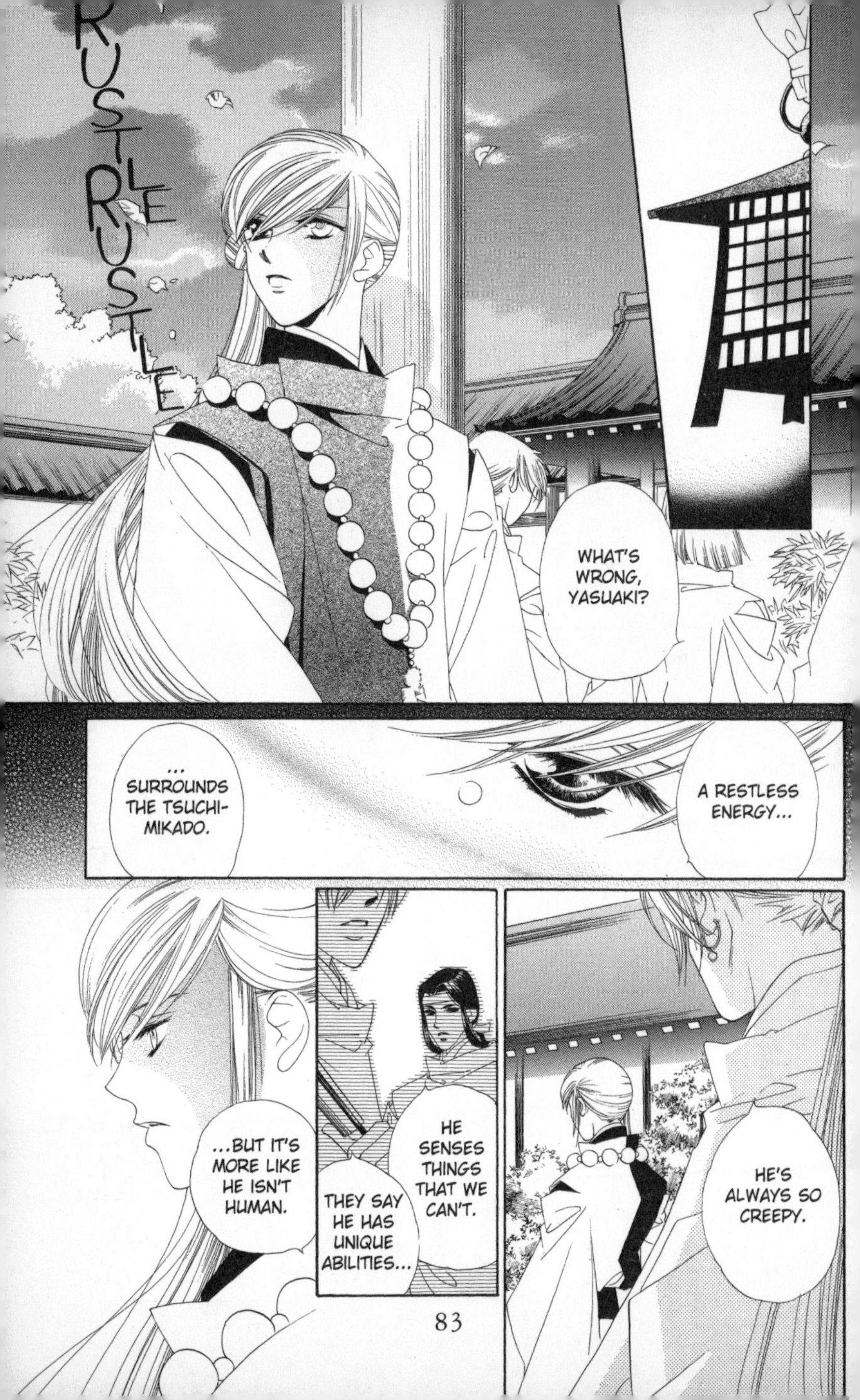
WHAT'S WRONG, YASUAKI?
RUSTLE RUSTLE
A RESTLESS ENERGY...
...SURROUNDS THE TSUCHI-MIKADO.
HE'S ALWAYS SO CREEPY.
HE SENSES THINGS THAT WE CAN'T.
THEY SAY HE HAS UNIQUE ABILITIES...
...BUT IT'S MORE LIKE HE ISN'T HUMAN.

WHY ARE YOU HERE?
IT'S THE OTHER PRIESTESS.
TENMA'S SISTER...?
YOU'RE IN MY WAY.
BA-THUMP
?!

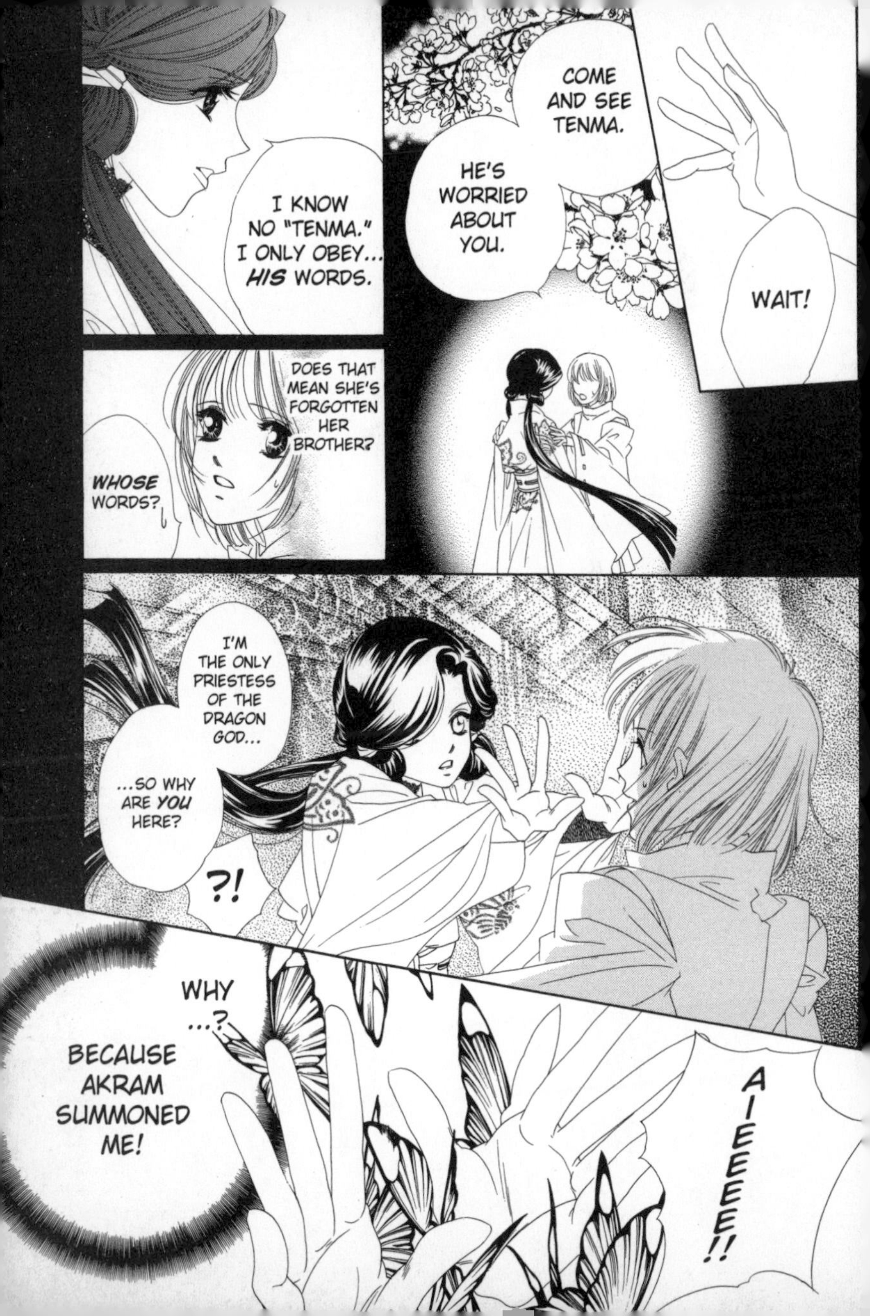
WAIT!
COME AND SEE TENMA.
HE'S WORRIED ABOUT YOU.
I KNOW NO "TENMA." I ONLY OBEY... *HIS* WORDS.
DOES THAT MEAN SHE'S FORGOTTEN HER BROTHER?
WHOSE WORDS?
I'M THE ONLY PRIESTESS OF THE DRAGON GOD...
...SO WHY ARE *YOU* HERE?
?!
AIEEEEE!!
WHY ...?
BECAUSE AKRAM SUMMONED ME!

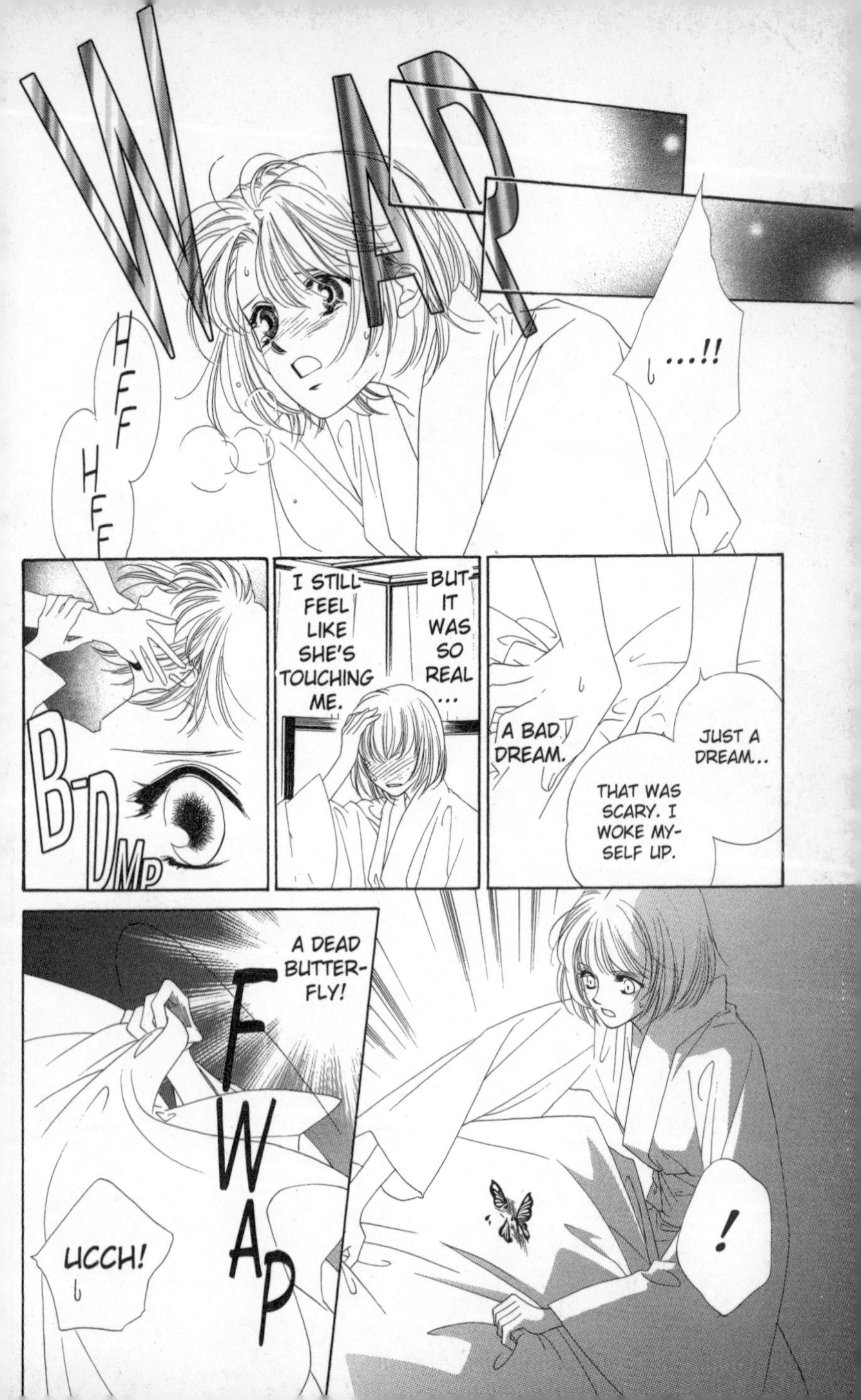
WAP
...!!
HFF HFF
JUST A DREAM...
A BAD DREAM.
THAT WAS SCARY. I WOKE MY-SELF UP.
BUT IT WAS SO REAL...
I STILL FEEL LIKE SHE'S TOUCHING ME.
B-DMP
!
A DEAD BUTTER-FLY!
FWAP
UCCH!

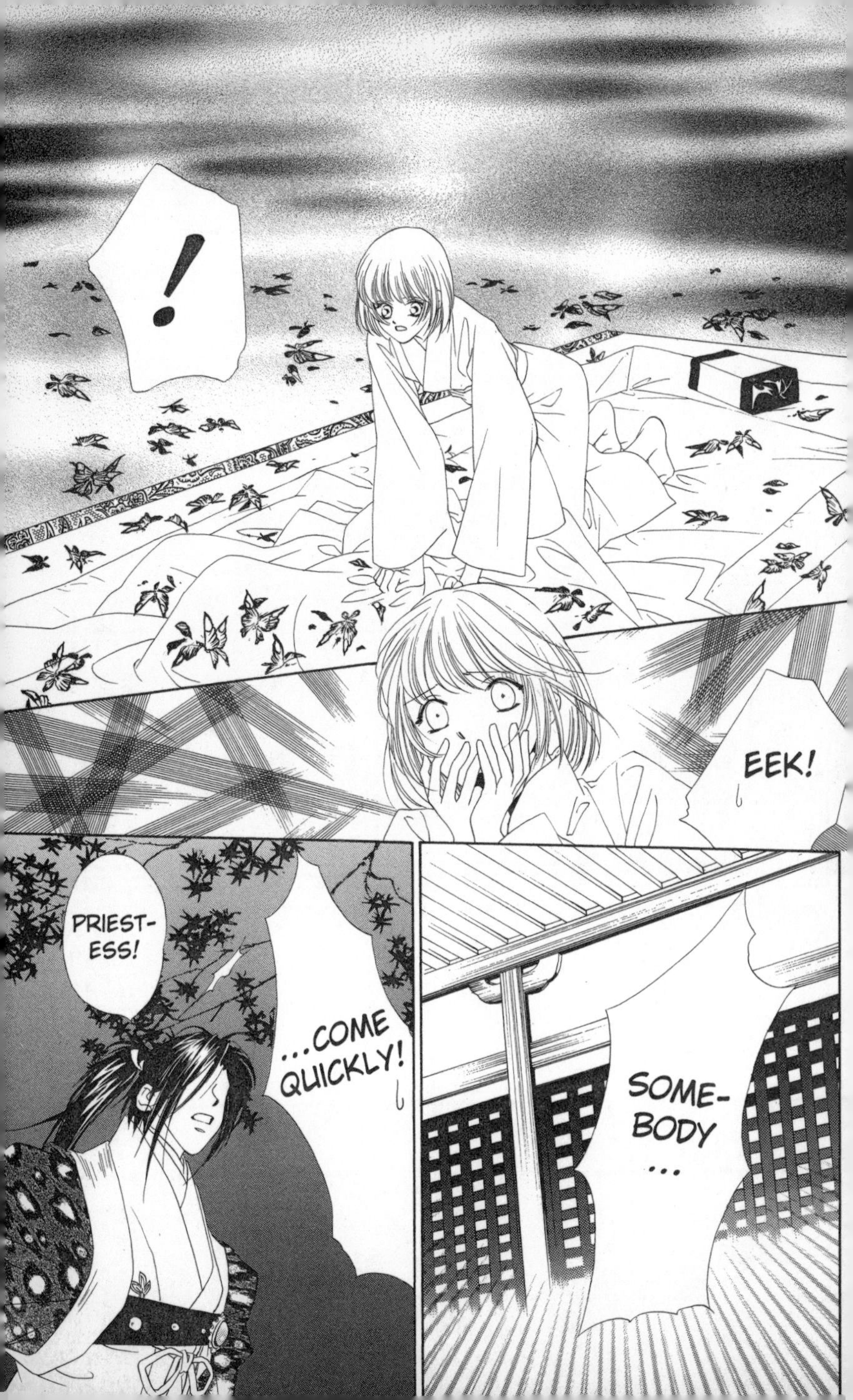
!
EEK!
SOME-BODY ...
PRIEST-ESS!
...COME QUICKLY!

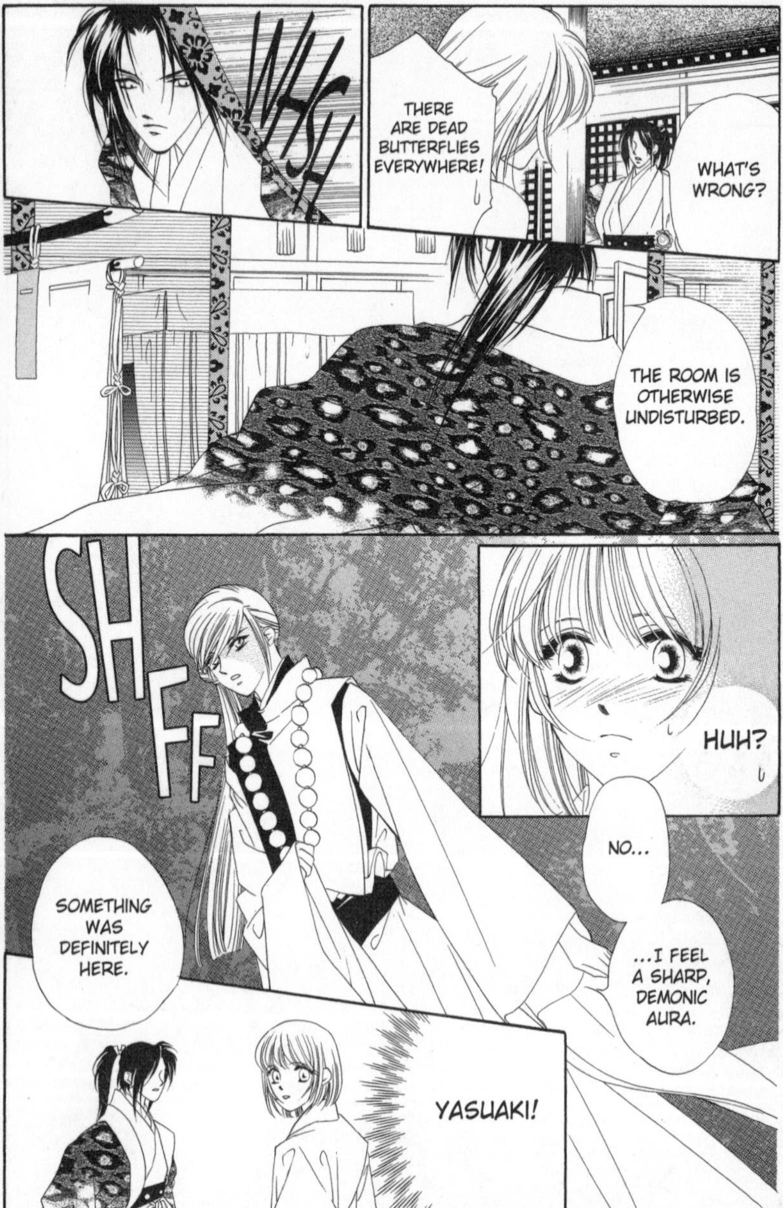
WHAT'S WRONG?
THERE ARE DEAD BUTTERFLIES EVERYWHERE!
WHSH
THE ROOM IS OTHERWISE UNDISTURBED.
HUH?
SHFF
NO...
...I FEEL A SHARP, DEMONIC AURA.
SOMETHING WAS DEFINITELY HERE.
YASUAKI!

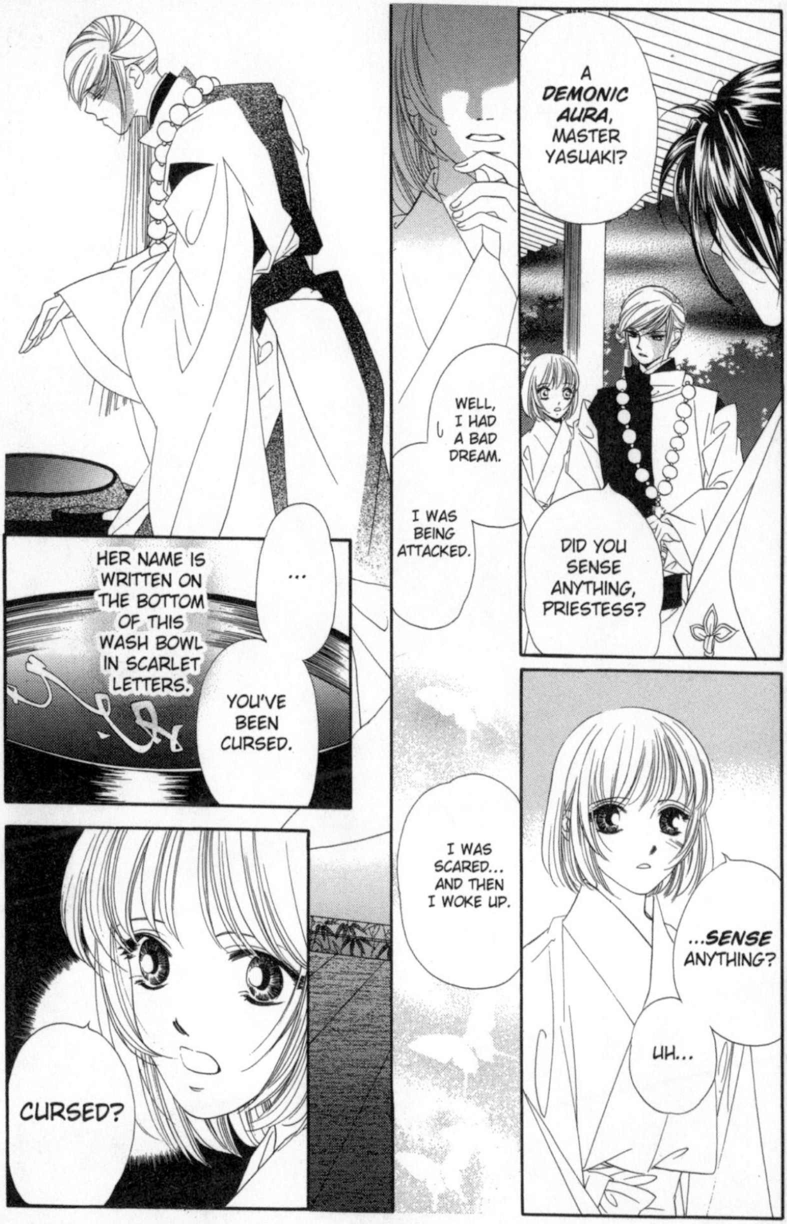
A DEMONIC AURA, MASTER YASUAKI?
DID YOU SENSE ANYTHING, PRIESTESS?
WELL, I HAD A BAD DREAM.
I WAS BEING ATTACKED.
...SENSE ANYTHING?
UH...
I WAS SCARED... AND THEN I WOKE UP.
...
HER NAME IS WRITTEN ON THE BOTTOM OF THIS WASH BOWL IN SCARLET LETTERS.
YOU'VE BEEN CURSED.
CURSED?

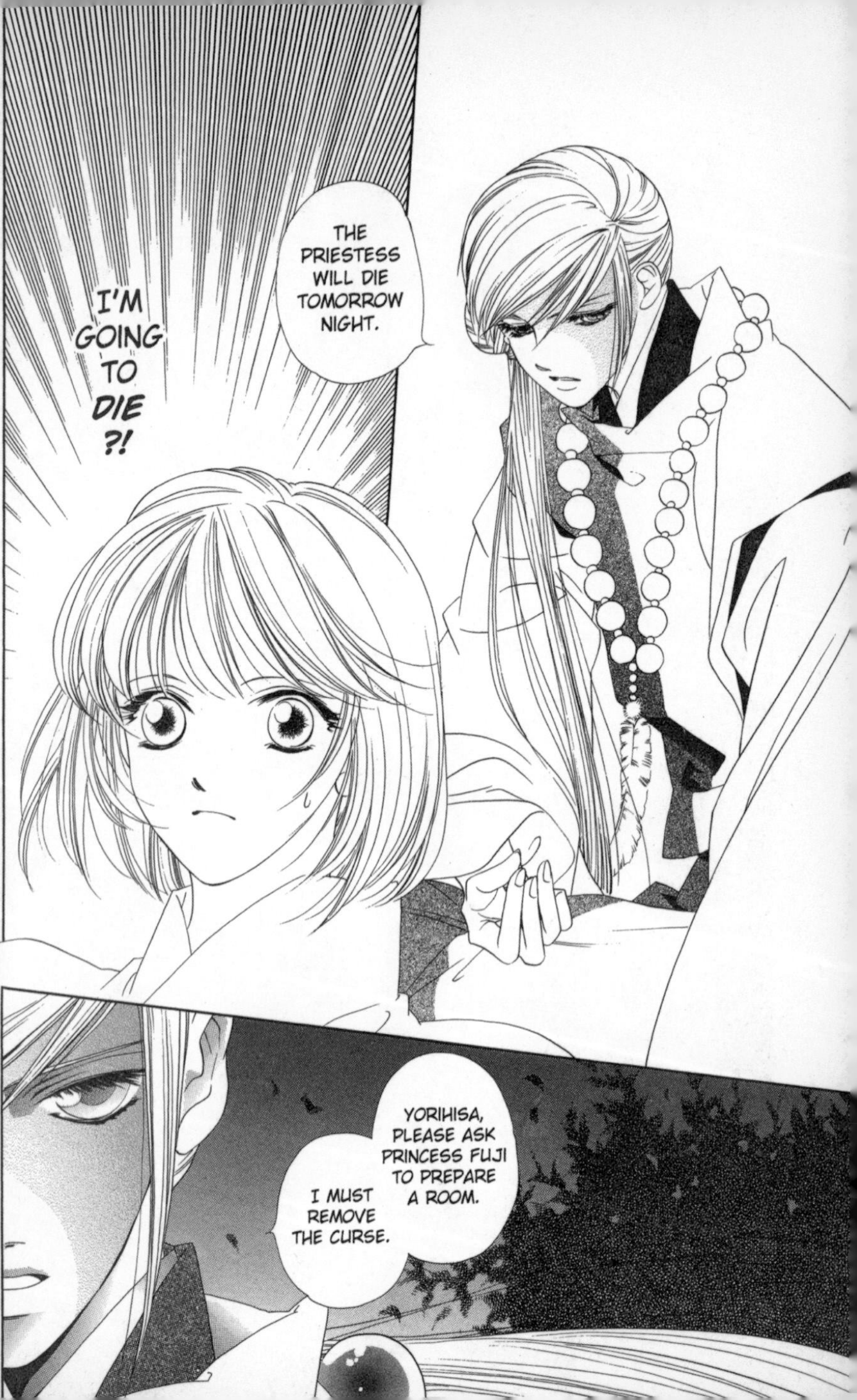
THE PRIESTESS WILL DIE TOMORROW NIGHT.
I'M GOING TO DIE ?!
YORIHISA, PLEASE ASK PRINCESS FUJI TO PREPARE A ROOM.
I MUST REMOVE THE CURSE.

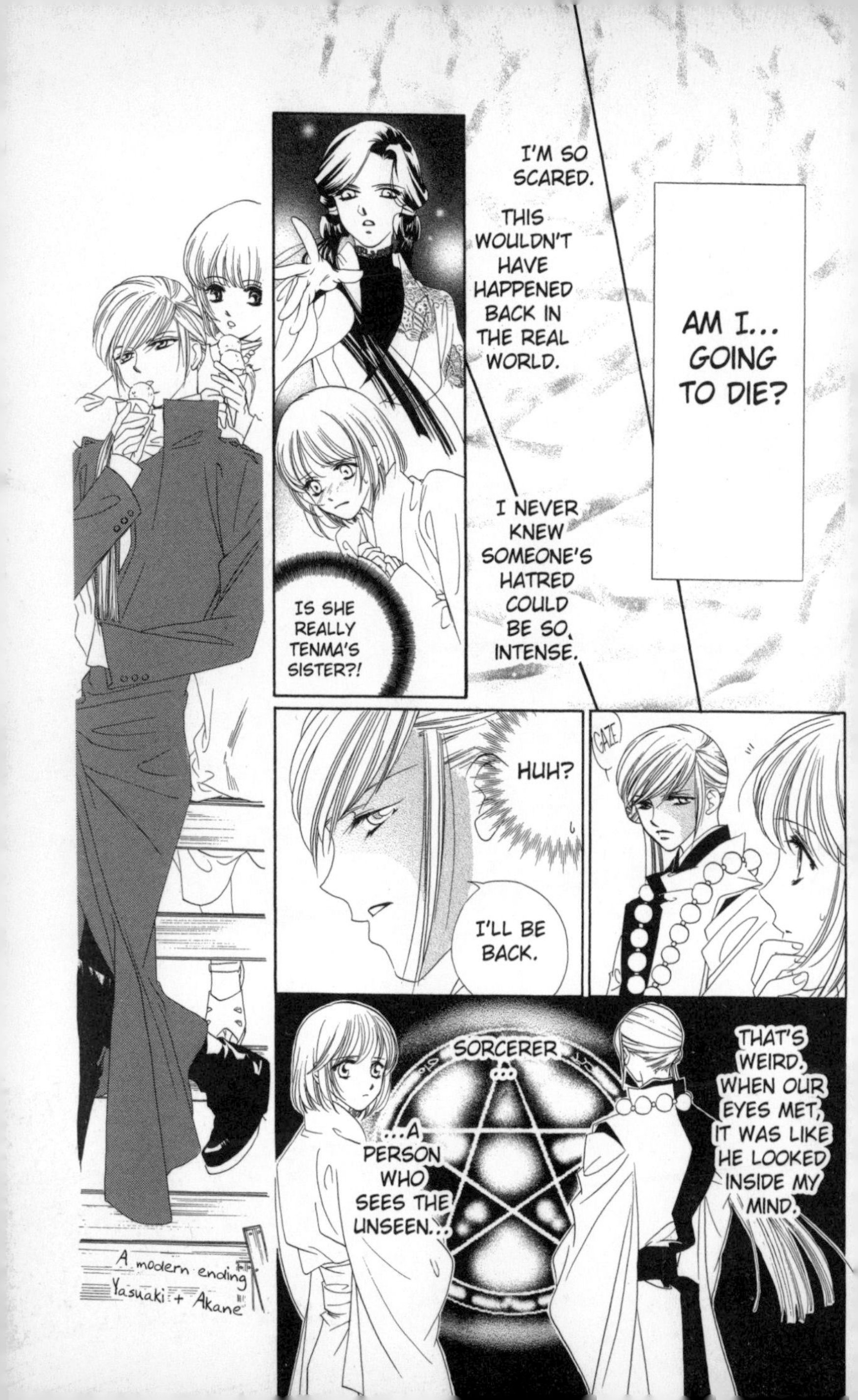
AM I... GOING TO DIE?
I'M SO SCARED.
THIS WOULDN'T HAVE HAPPENED BACK IN THE REAL WORLD.
I NEVER KNEW SOMEONE'S HATRED COULD BE SO INTENSE.
IS SHE REALLY TENMA'S SISTER?!
GAZE
HUH?
I'LL BE BACK.
THAT'S WEIRD. WHEN OUR EYES MET, IT WAS LIKE HE LOOKED INSIDE MY MIND.
SORCERER
...A PERSON WHO SEES THE UNSEEN...
A modern ending
Yasuaki + Akane

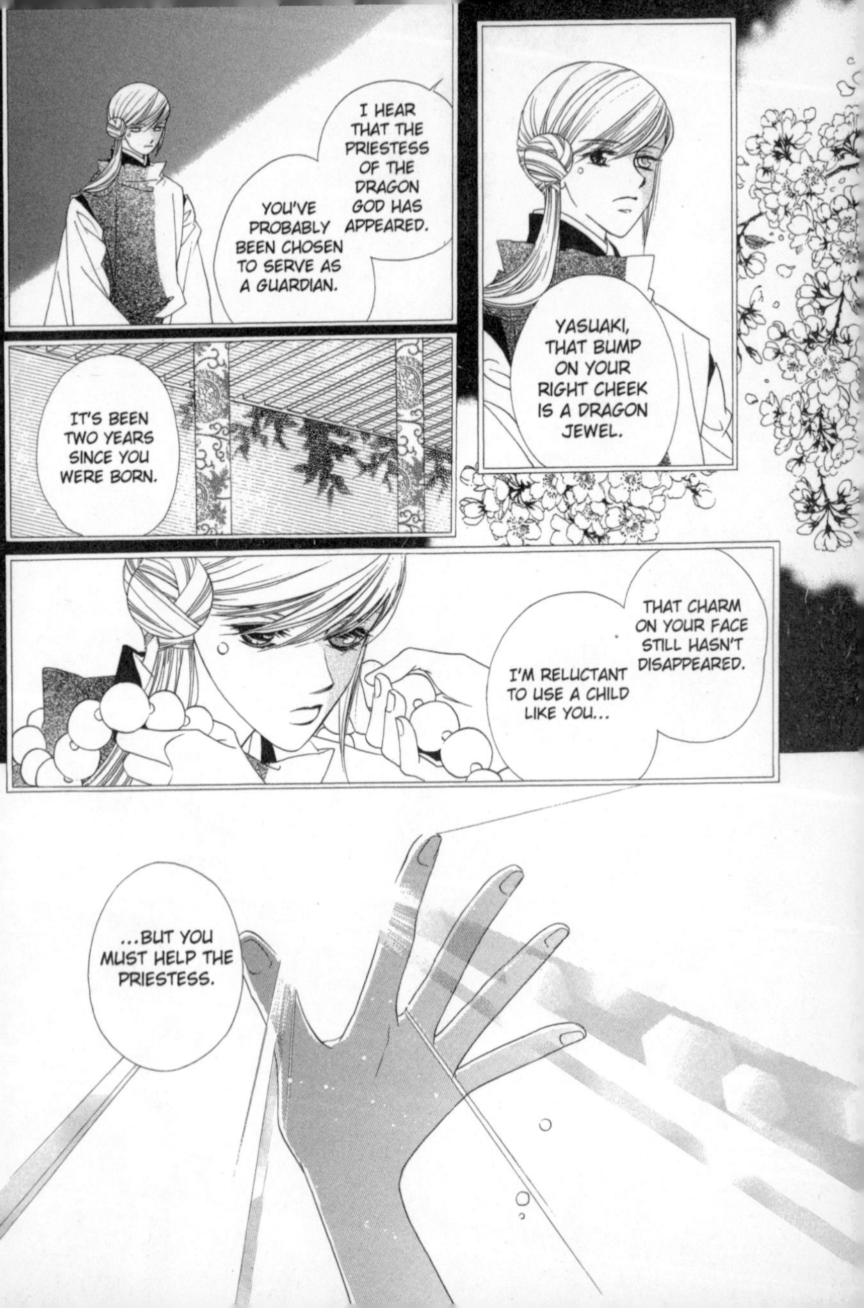
YASUAKI, THAT BUMP ON YOUR RIGHT CHEEK IS A DRAGON JEWEL.
I HEAR THAT THE PRIESTESS OF THE DRAGON GOD HAS APPEARED.
YOU'VE PROBABLY BEEN CHOSEN TO SERVE AS A GUARDIAN.
IT'S BEEN TWO YEARS SINCE YOU WERE BORN.
THAT CHARM ON YOUR FACE STILL HASN'T DISAPPEARED.
I'M RELUCTANT TO USE A CHILD LIKE YOU...
...BUT YOU MUST HELP THE PRIESTESS.

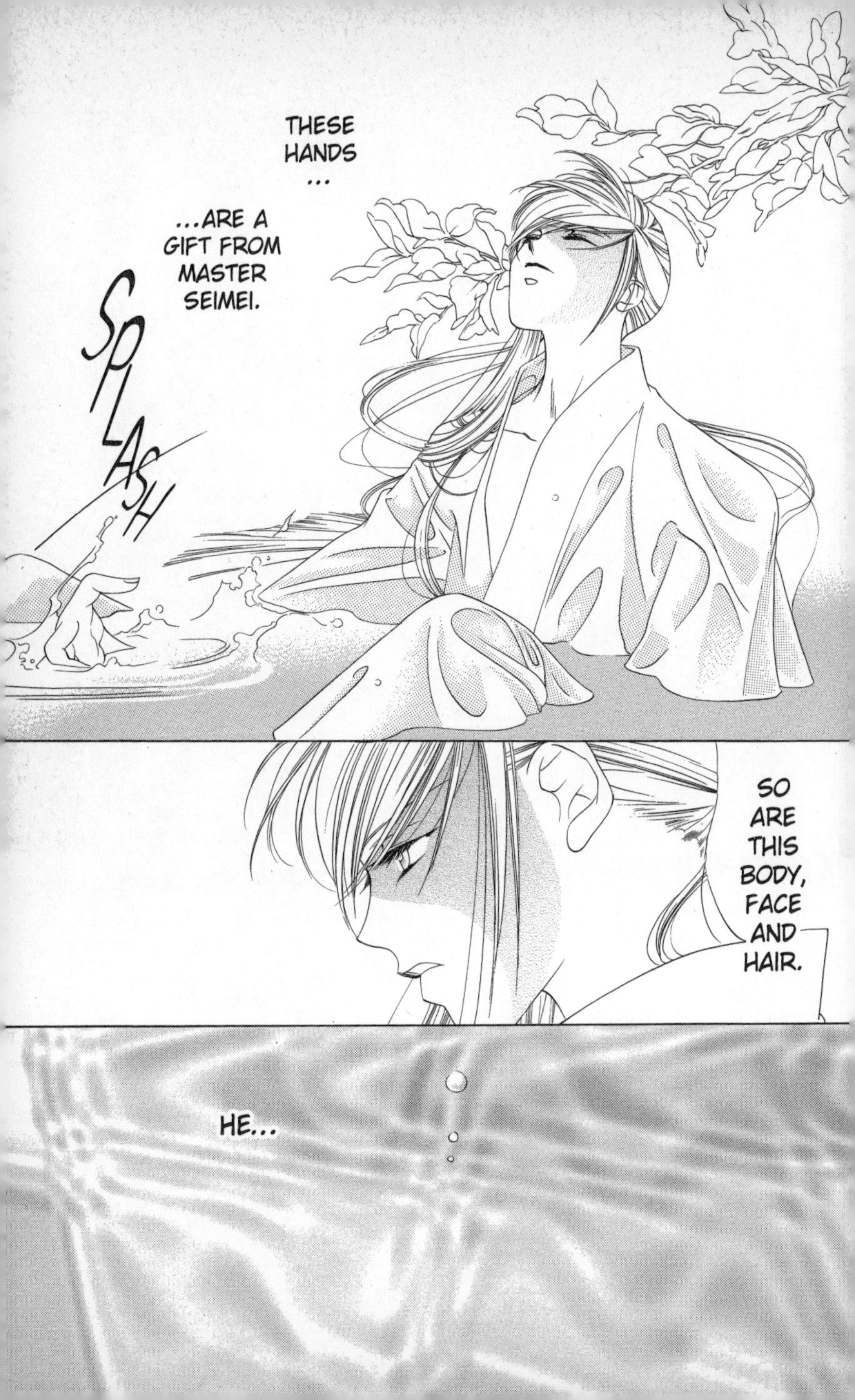
THESE HANDS ...
...ARE A GIFT FROM MASTER SEIMEI.
SPLASH
SO ARE THIS BODY, FACE AND HAIR.
HE...

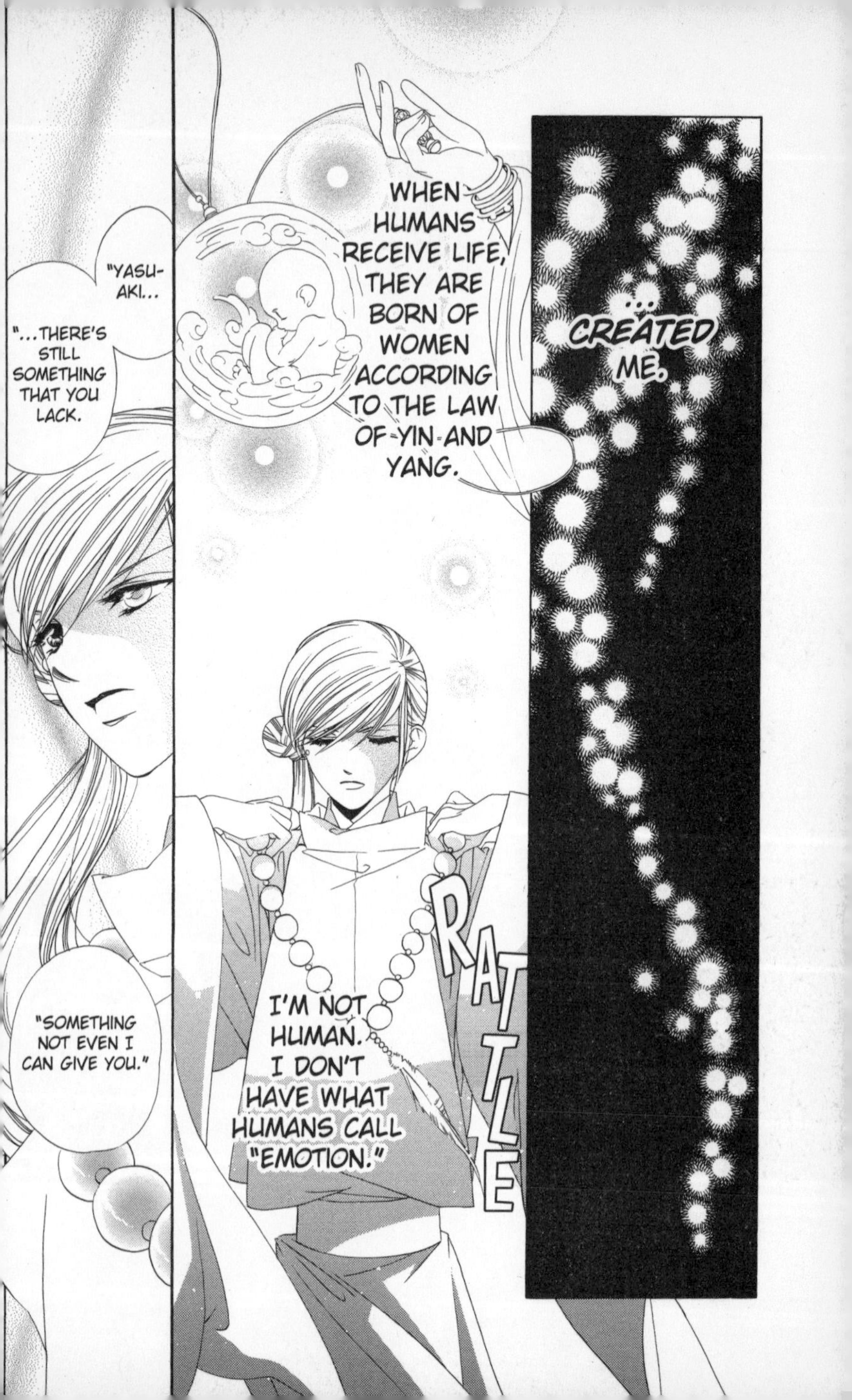
WHEN HUMANS RECEIVE LIFE, THEY ARE BORN OF WOMEN ACCORDING TO THE LAW OF YIN AND YANG.
...CREATED ME.
RATTLE
I'M NOT HUMAN. I DON'T HAVE WHAT HUMANS CALL "EMOTION."
"YASU-AKI...
"...THERE'S STILL SOMETHING THAT YOU LACK.
"SOMETHING NOT EVEN I CAN GIVE YOU."

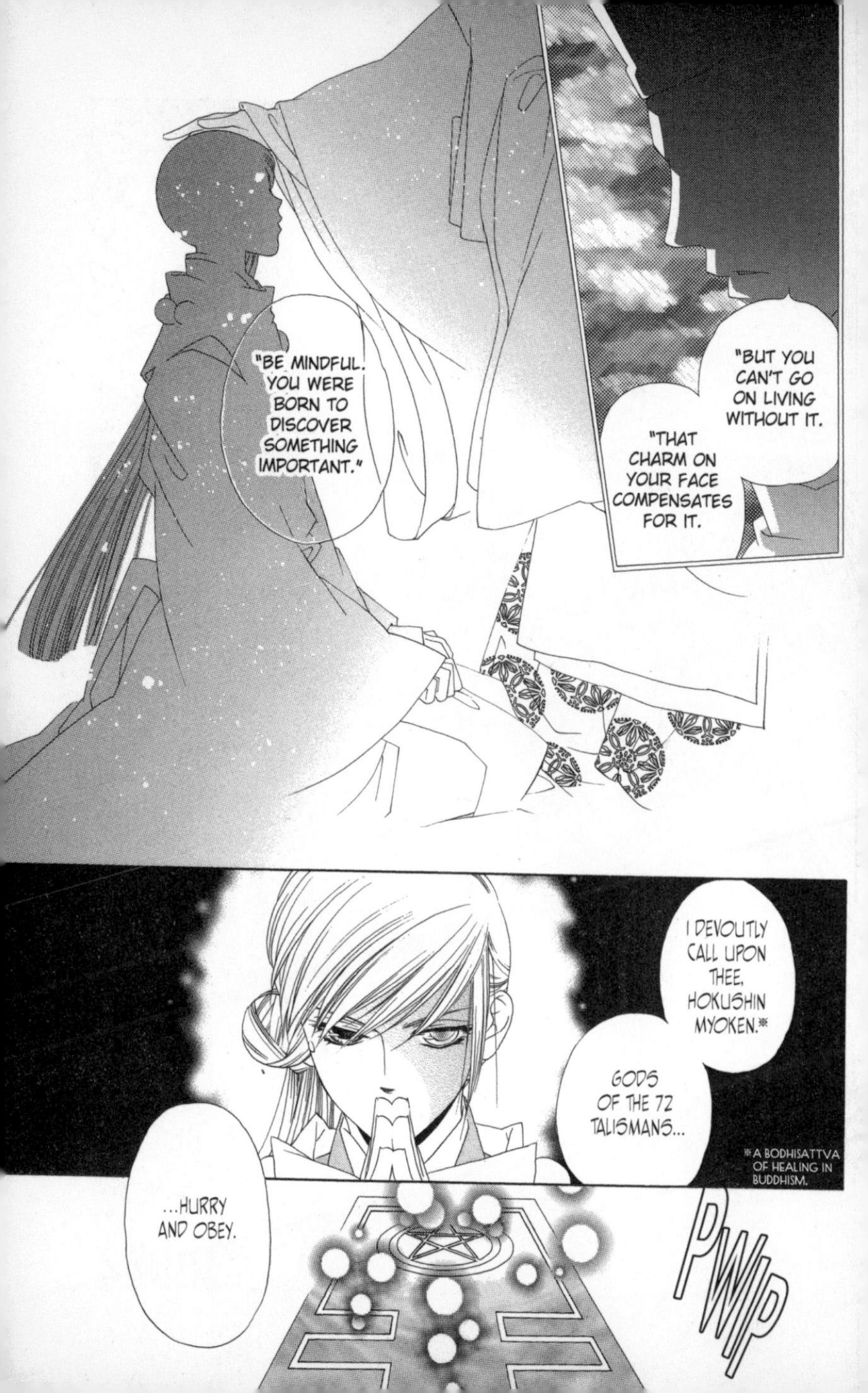
"BUT YOU CAN'T GO ON LIVING WITHOUT IT.
"THAT CHARM ON YOUR FACE COMPENSATES FOR IT.
"BE MINDFUL. YOU WERE BORN TO DISCOVER SOMETHING IMPORTANT."
I DEVOUTLY CALL UPON THEE, HOKUSHIN MYOKEN.※
GODS OF THE 72 TALISMANS...
※A BODHISATTVA OF HEALING IN BUDDHISM.
...HURRY AND OBEY.
PWIP

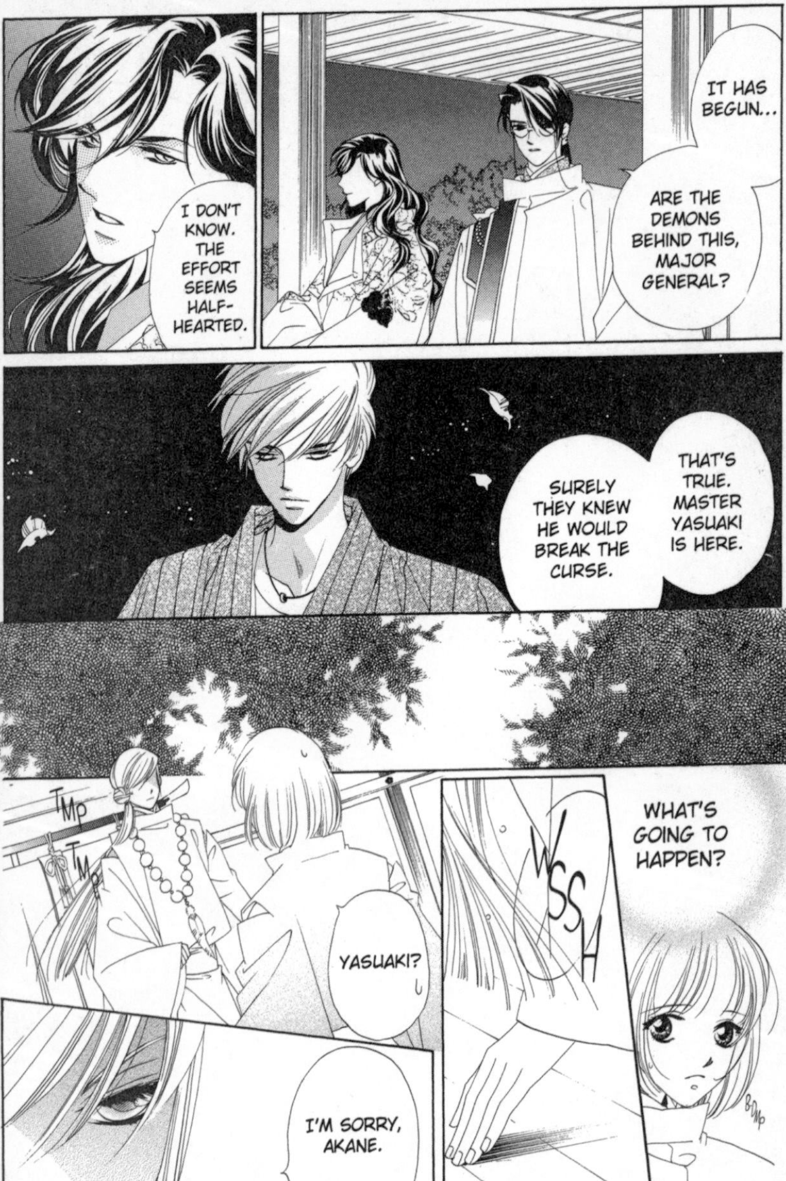
IT HAS BEGUN...
ARE THE DEMONS BEHIND THIS, MAJOR GENERAL?
I DON'T KNOW. THE EFFORT SEEMS HALF-HEARTED.
THAT'S TRUE. MASTER YASUAKI IS HERE.
SURELY THEY KNEW HE WOULD BREAK THE CURSE.
WHAT'S GOING TO HAPPEN?
WSSH
BOMP
TMP
TMP
YASUAKI?
I'M SORRY, AKANE.

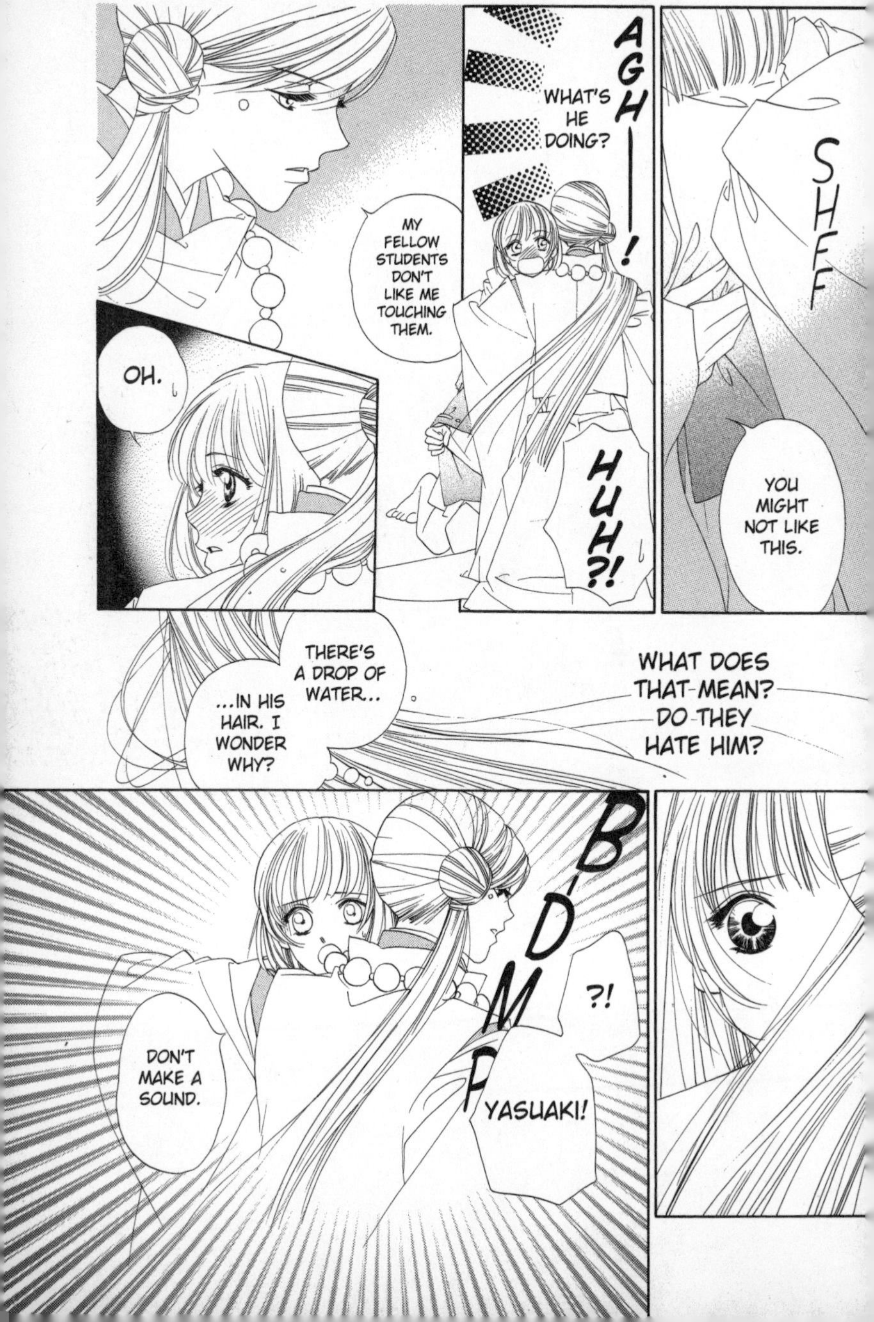
SHFF
YOU MIGHT NOT LIKE THIS.
AGH—!
WHAT'S HE DOING?
HUH?!
MY FELLOW STUDENTS DON'T LIKE ME TOUCHING THEM.
OH.
WHAT DOES THAT MEAN? DO THEY HATE HIM?
THERE'S A DROP OF WATER...
...IN HIS HAIR. I WONDER WHY?
B-DMP
?!
YASUAKI!
DON'T MAKE A SOUND.

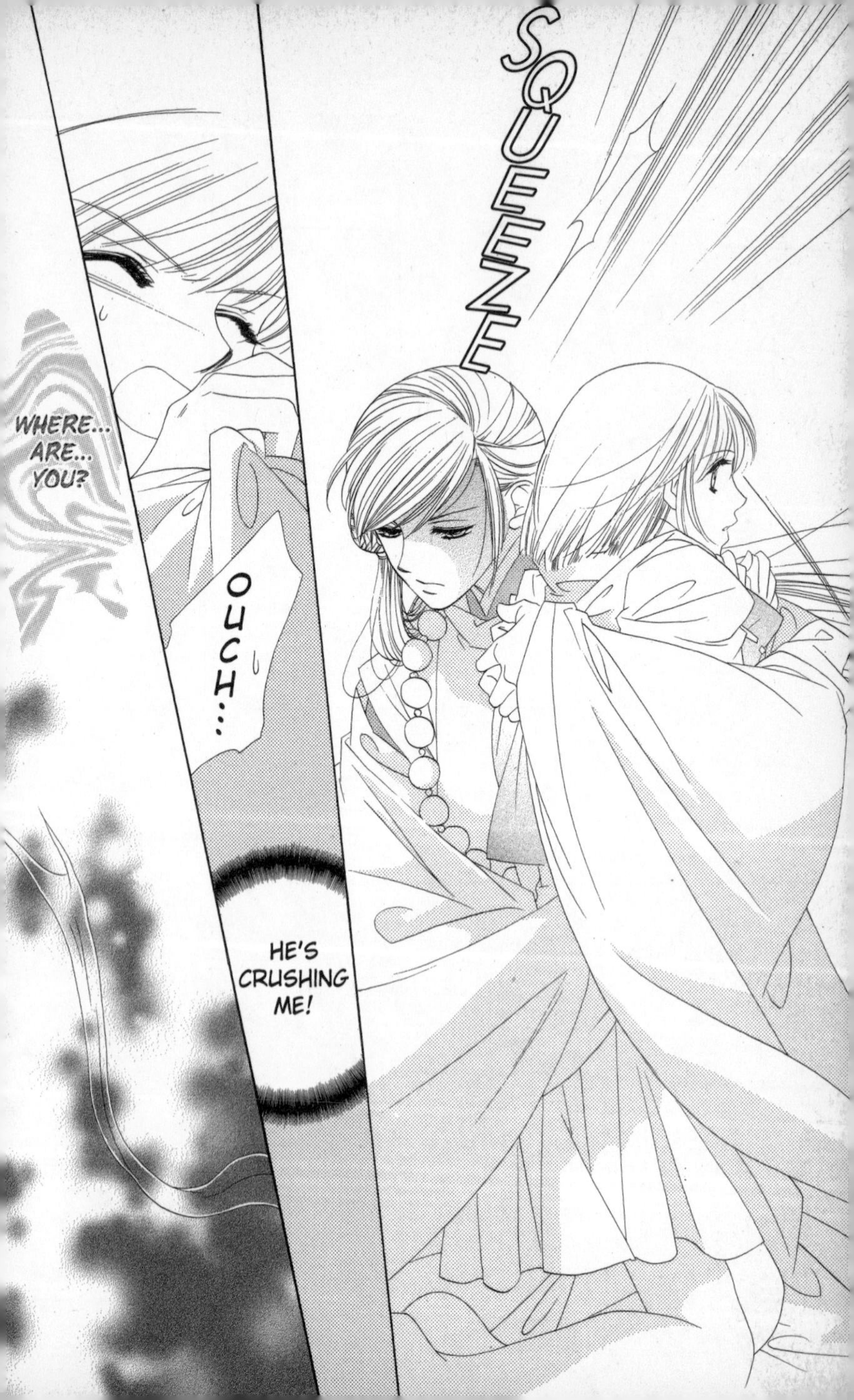
SQUEEZE
OUCH...
HE'S CRUSHING ME!
WHERE... ARE... YOU?

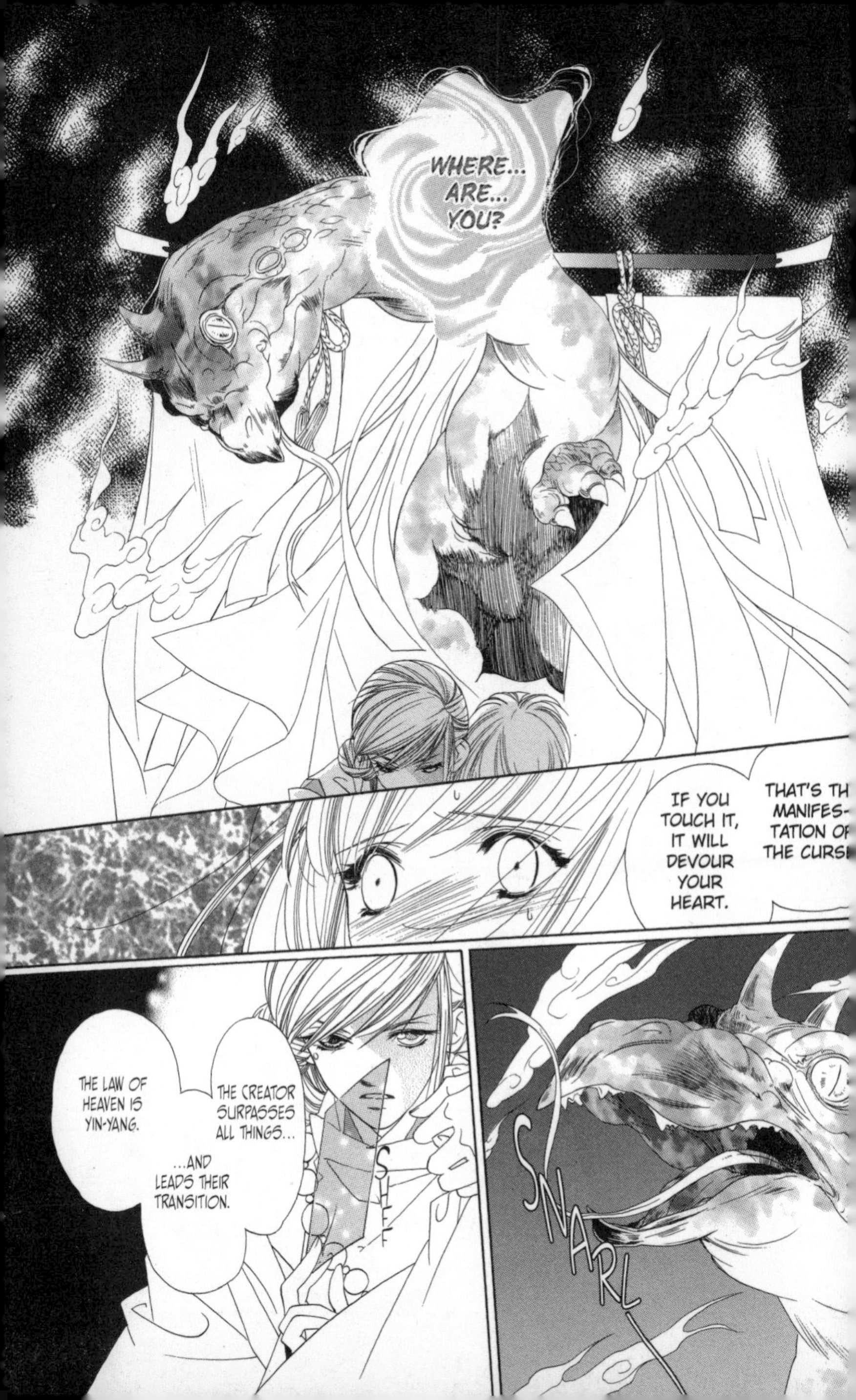

WHERE... ARE... YOU?
THAT'S TH MANIFES-TATION OF THE CURS
IF YOU TOUCH IT, IT WILL DEVOUR YOUR HEART.
SNARL
THE CREATOR SURPASSES ALL THINGS...
THE LAW OF HEAVEN IS YIN-YANG.
...AND LEADS THEIR TRANSITION.

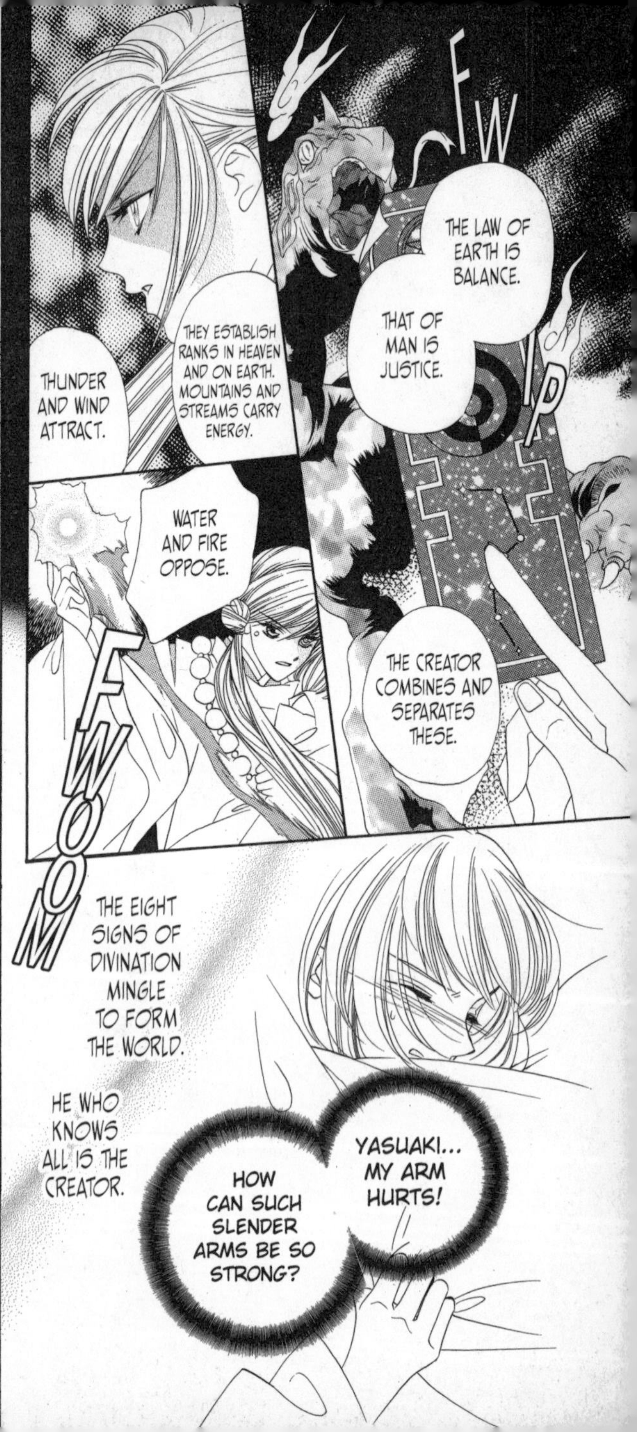
FWIP
THE LAW OF EARTH IS BALANCE.
THAT OF MAN IS JUSTICE.
THE CREATOR COMBINES AND SEPARATES THESE.
THEY ESTABLISH RANKS IN HEAVEN AND ON EARTH. MOUNTAINS AND STREAMS CARRY ENERGY.
THUNDER AND WIND ATTRACT.
WATER AND FIRE OPPOSE.
FWOOM
THE EIGHT SIGNS OF DIVINATION MINGLE TO FORM THE WORLD.
HE WHO KNOWS ALL IS THE CREATOR.
YASUAKI... MY ARM HURTS!
HOW CAN SUCH SLENDER ARMS BE SO STRONG?
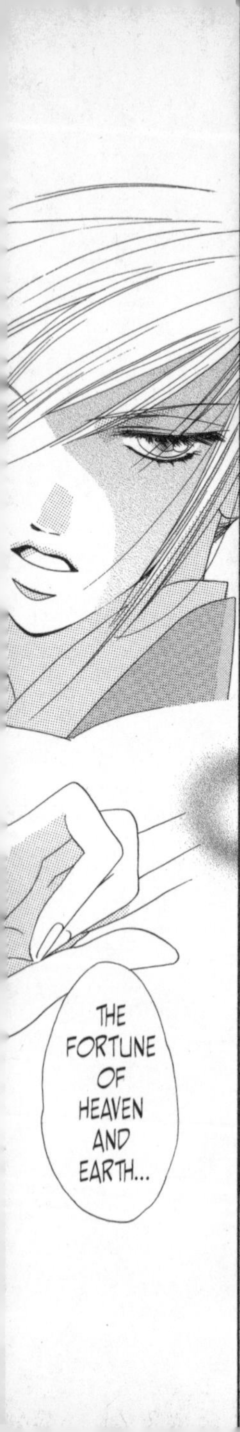
THE FORTUNE OF HEAVEN AND EARTH...

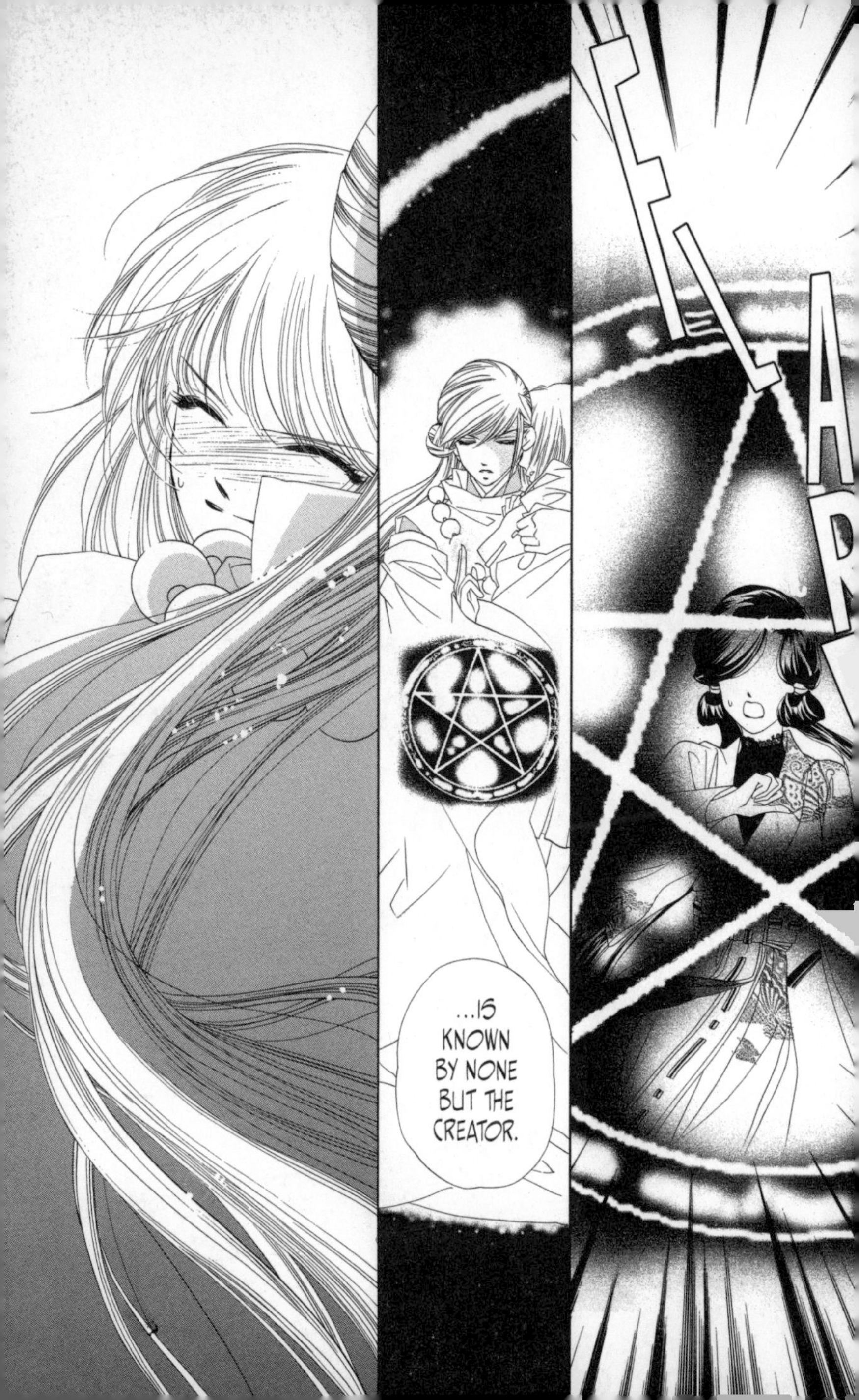
...IS KNOWN BY NONE BUT THE CREATOR.

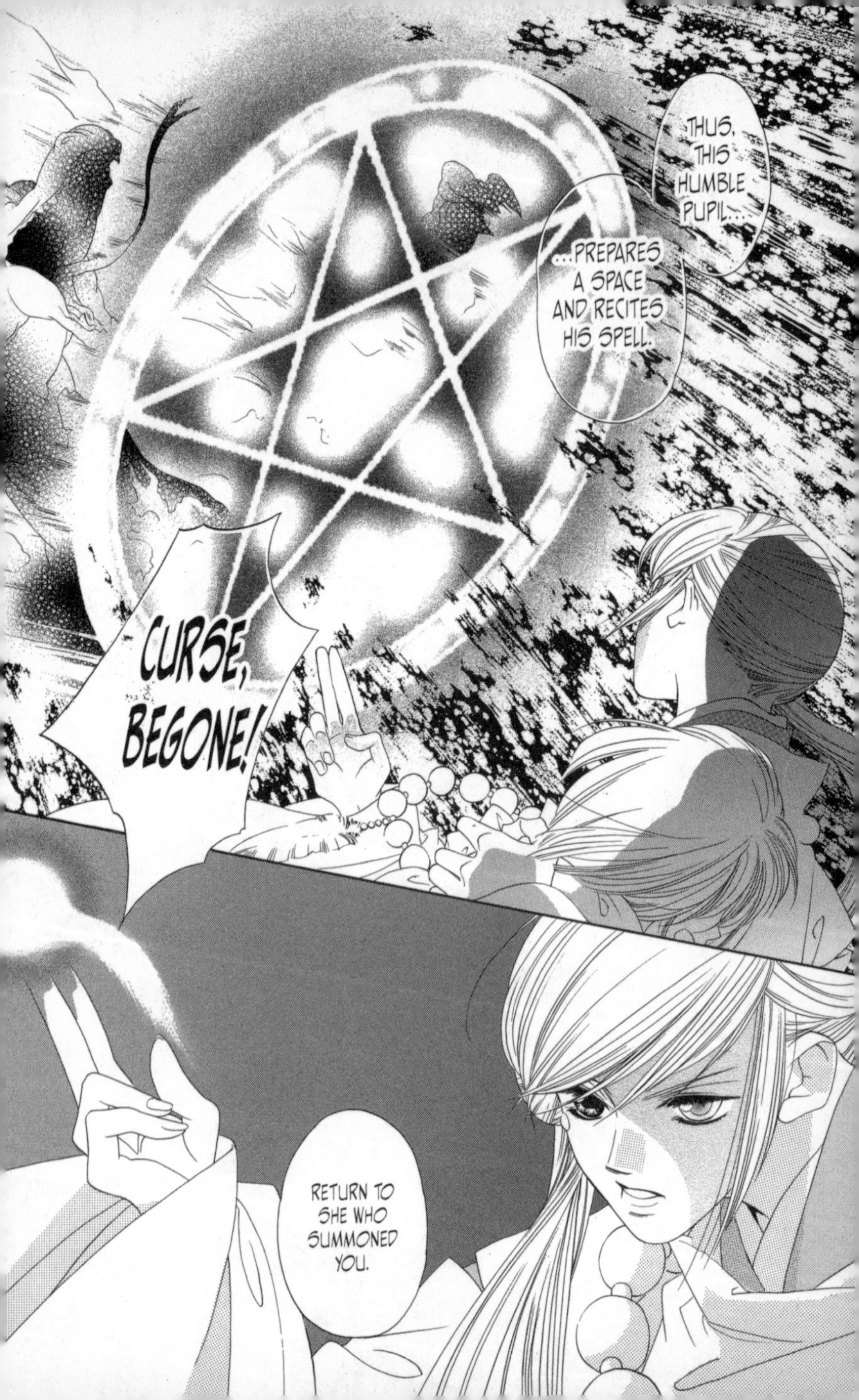
THUS, THIS HUMBLE PUPIL...
...PREPARES A SPACE AND RECITES HIS SPELL.
CURSE, BEGONE!
RETURN TO SHE WHO SUMMONED YOU.

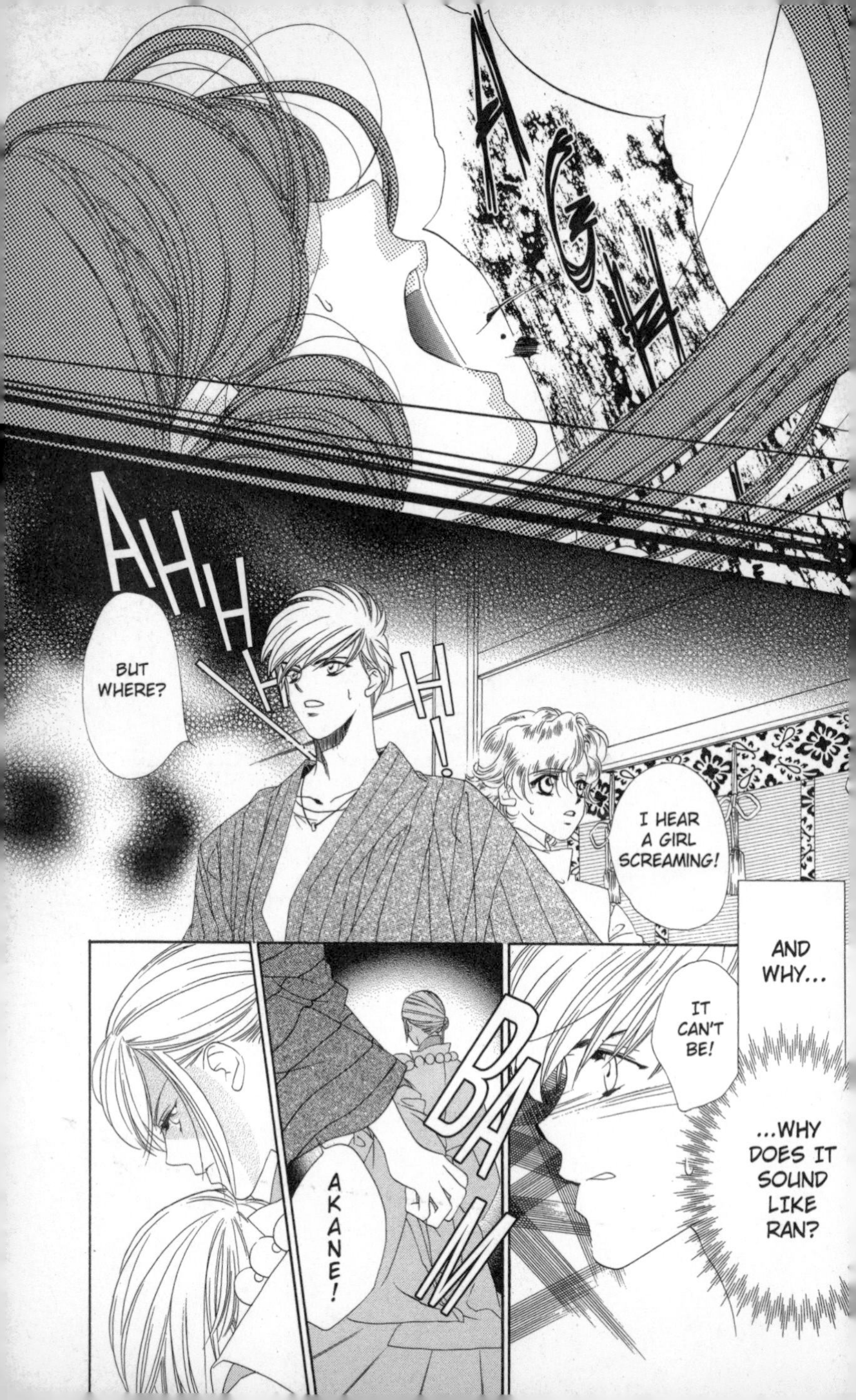
AGH
AHHHHHH!
I HEAR A GIRL SCREAMING!
BUT WHERE?
AND WHY...
IT CAN'T BE!
...WHY DOES IT SOUND LIKE RAN?
BAM
AKANE!

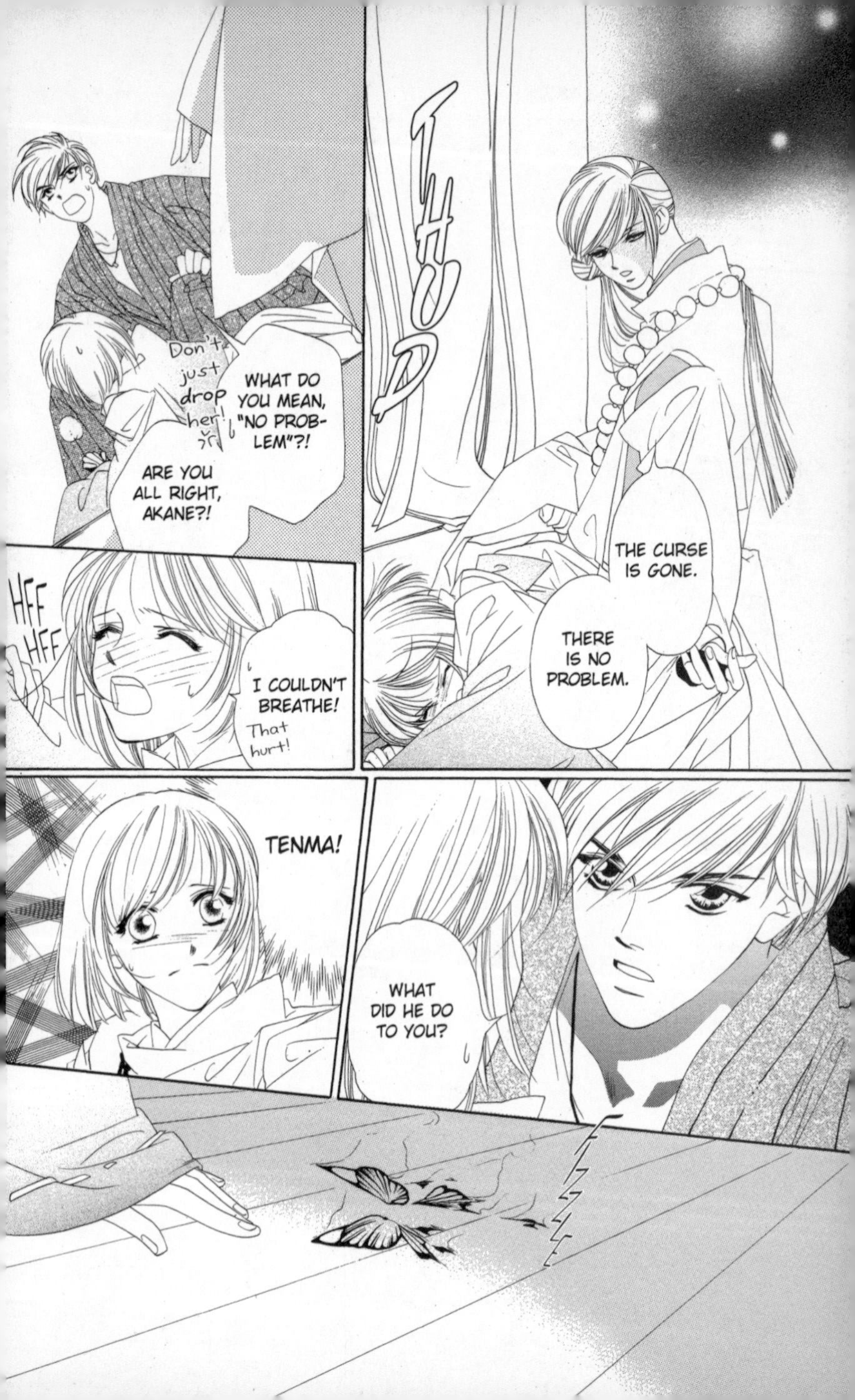
THUD
THE CURSE IS GONE.
THERE IS NO PROBLEM.
WHAT DO YOU MEAN, "NO PROBLEM"?!
Don't just drop her!
ARE YOU ALL RIGHT, AKANE?!
HFF HFF
I COULDN'T BREATHE!
That hurt!
WHAT DID HE DO TO YOU?
TENMA!

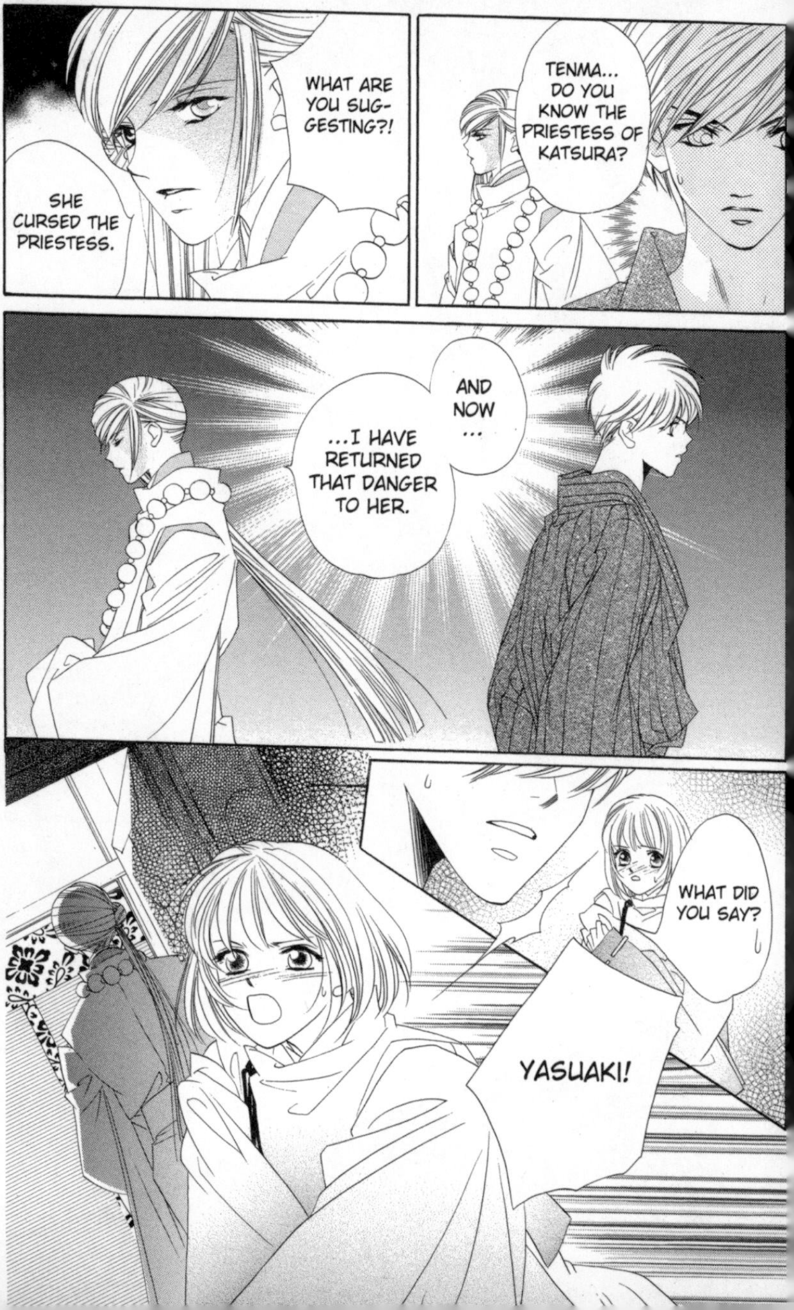
TENMA... DO YOU KNOW THE PRIESTESS OF KATSURA?
WHAT ARE YOU SUG-GESTING?!
SHE CURSED THE PRIESTESS.
AND NOW...
...I HAVE RETURNED THAT DANGER TO HER.
WHAT DID YOU SAY?
YASUAKI!

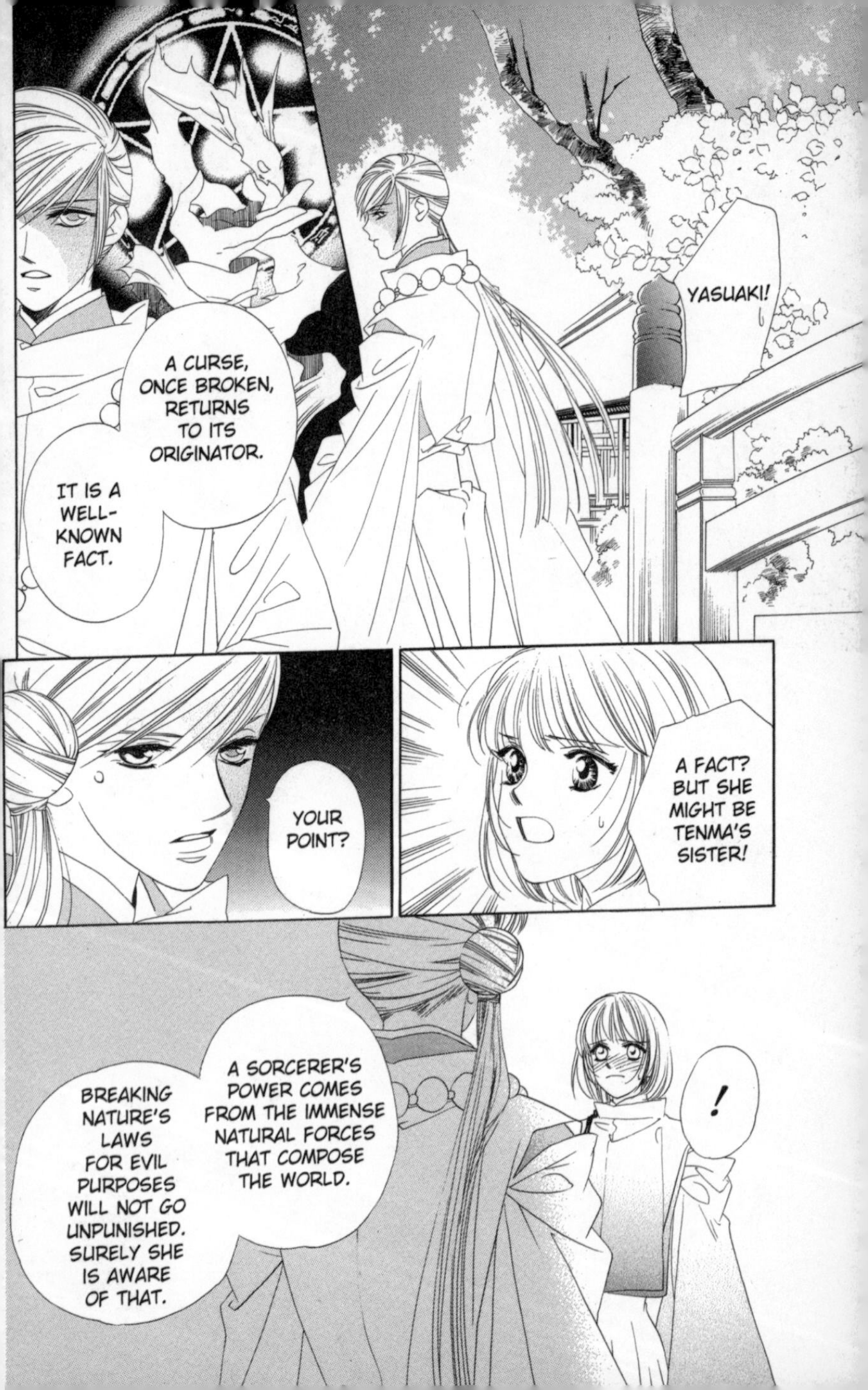
YASUAKI!
A CURSE, ONCE BROKEN, RETURNS TO ITS ORIGINATOR.
IT IS A WELL-KNOWN FACT.
A FACT? BUT SHE MIGHT BE TENMA'S SISTER!
YOUR POINT?
!
A SORCERER'S POWER COMES FROM THE IMMENSE NATURAL FORCES THAT COMPOSE THE WORLD.
BREAKING NATURE'S LAWS FOR EVIL PURPOSES WILL NOT GO UNPUNISHED. SURELY SHE IS AWARE OF THAT.

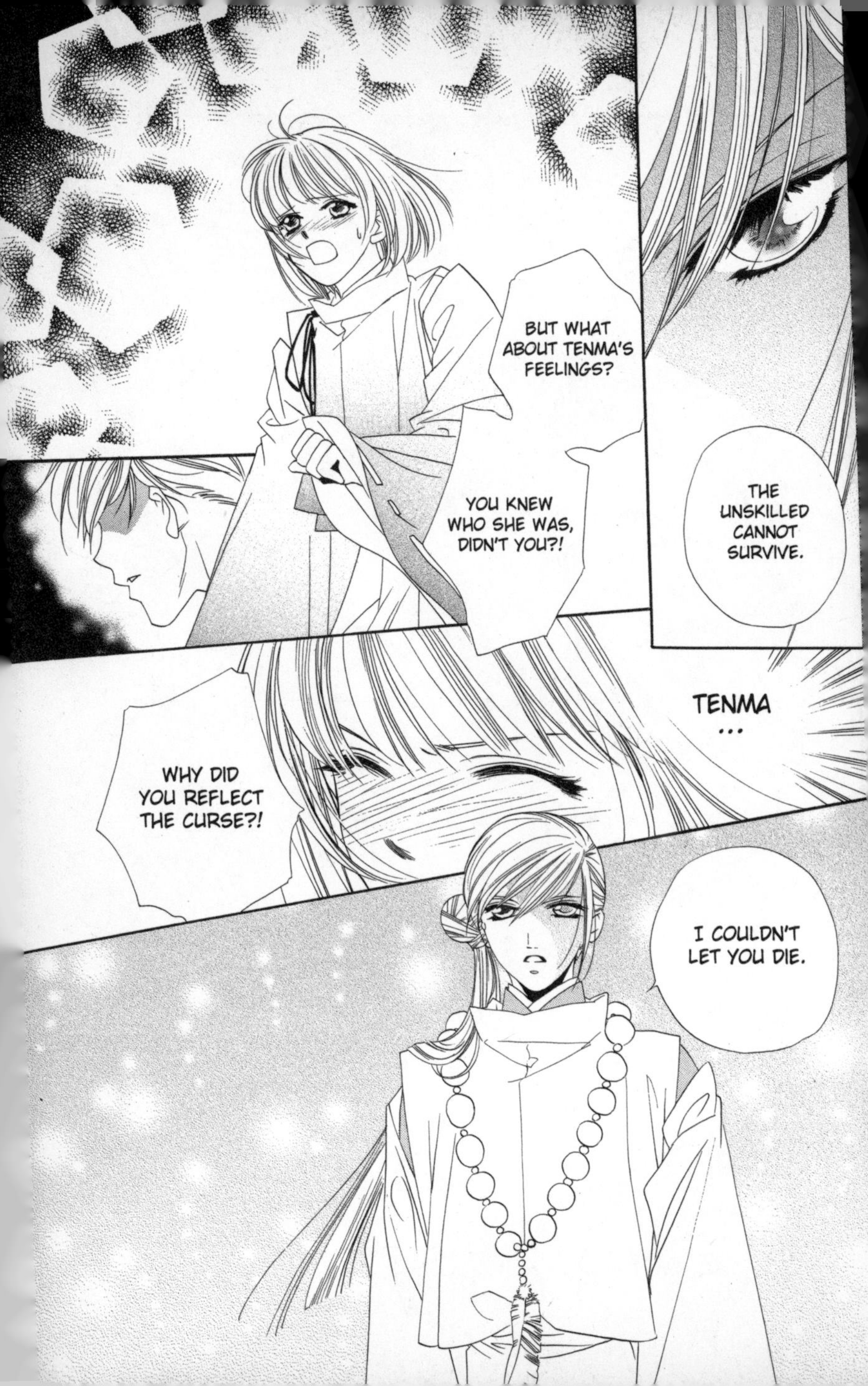
THE UNSKILLED CANNOT SURVIVE.
BUT WHAT ABOUT TENMA'S FEELINGS?
YOU KNEW WHO SHE WAS, DIDN'T YOU?!
TENMA ...
WHY DID YOU REFLECT THE CURSE?!
I COULDN'T LET YOU DIE.

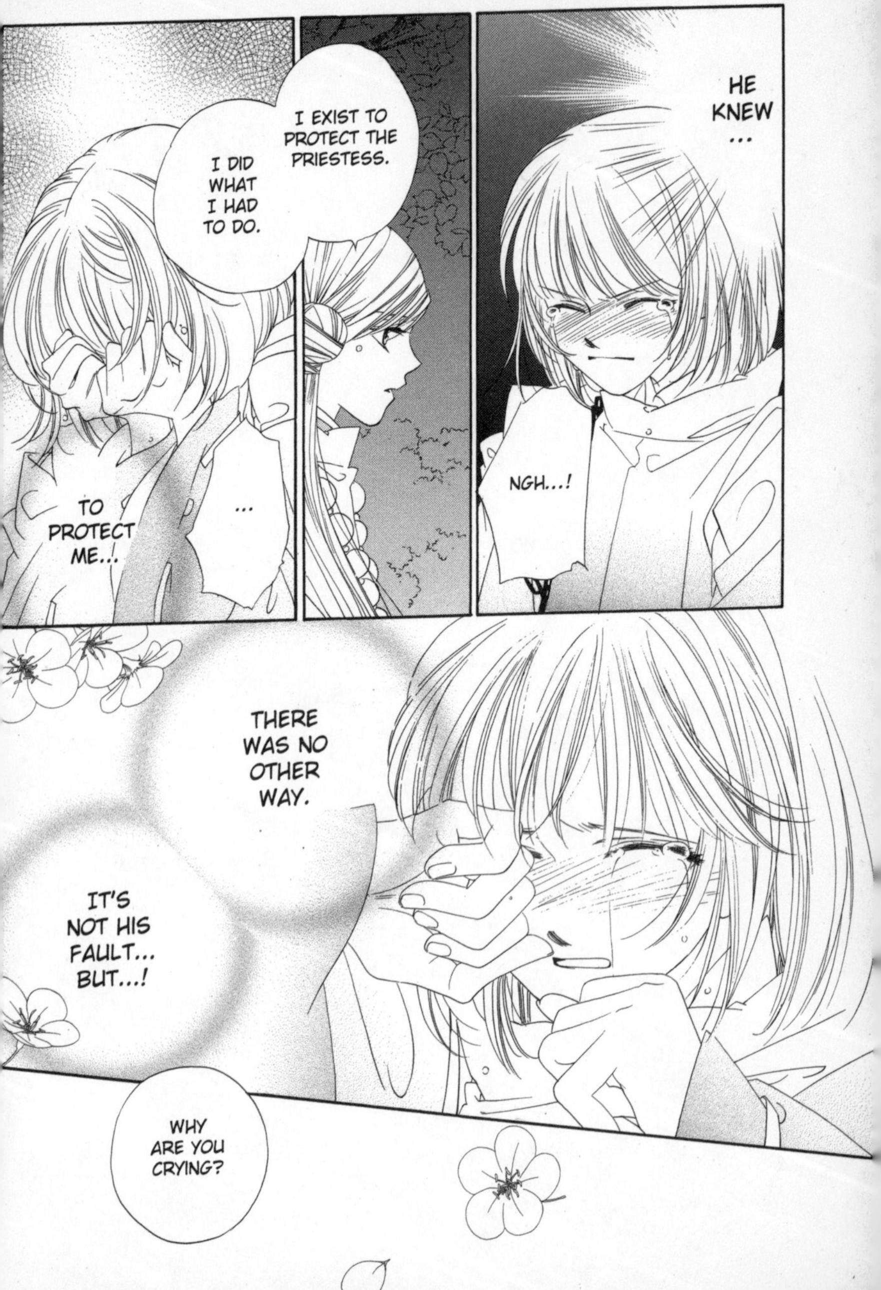
HE KNEW...
NGH...!
I EXIST TO PROTECT THE PRIESTESS.
I DID WHAT I HAD TO DO.
...
TO PROTECT ME...!
THERE WAS NO OTHER WAY.
IT'S NOT HIS FAULT... BUT...!
WHY ARE YOU CRYING?

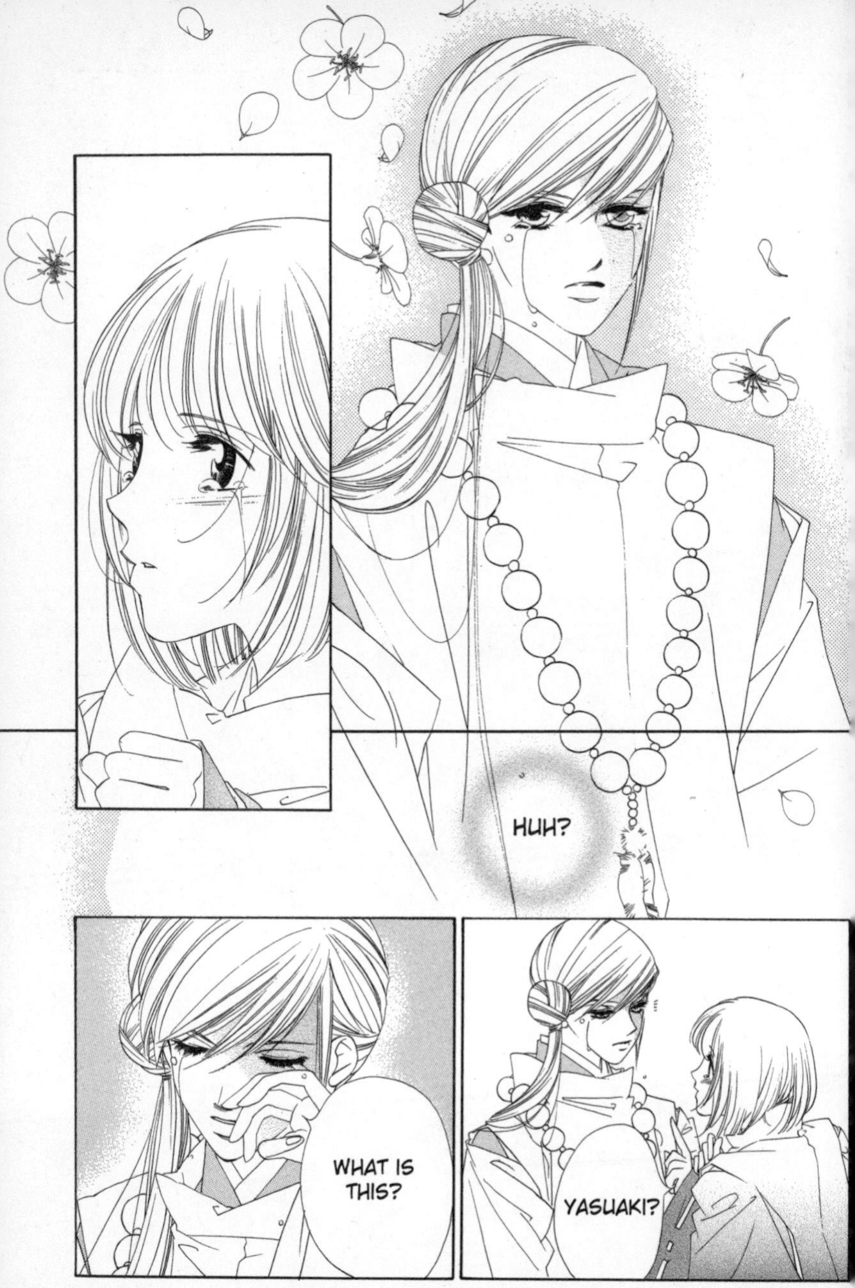
HUH?
YASUAKI?
WHAT IS THIS?

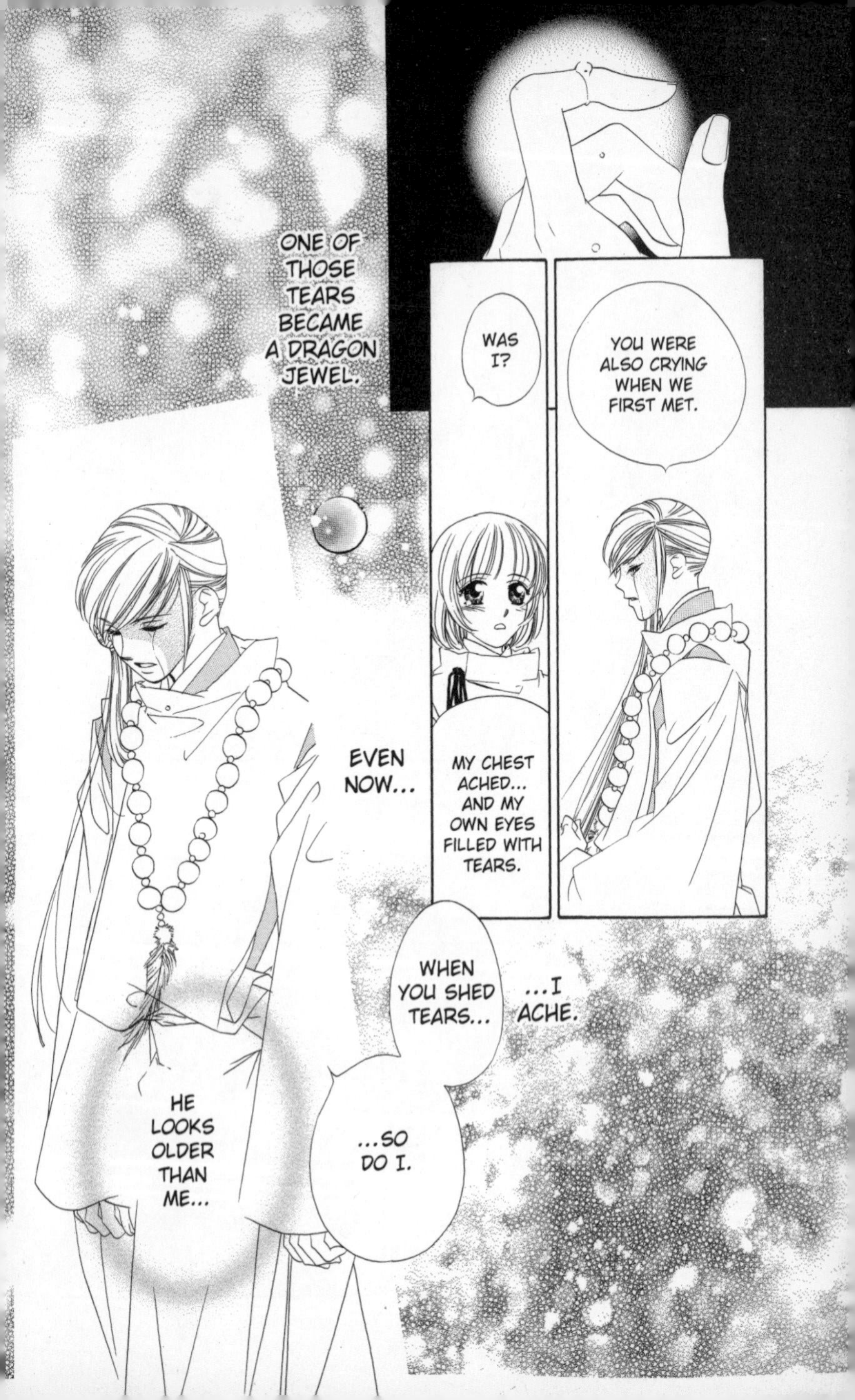

ONE OF THOSE TEARS BECAME A DRAGON JEWEL.
YOU WERE ALSO CRYING WHEN WE FIRST MET.
WAS I?
MY CHEST ACHED... AND MY OWN EYES FILLED WITH TEARS.
EVEN NOW...
WHEN YOU SHED TEARS...
...I ACHE.
...SO DO I.
HE LOOKS OLDER THAN ME...

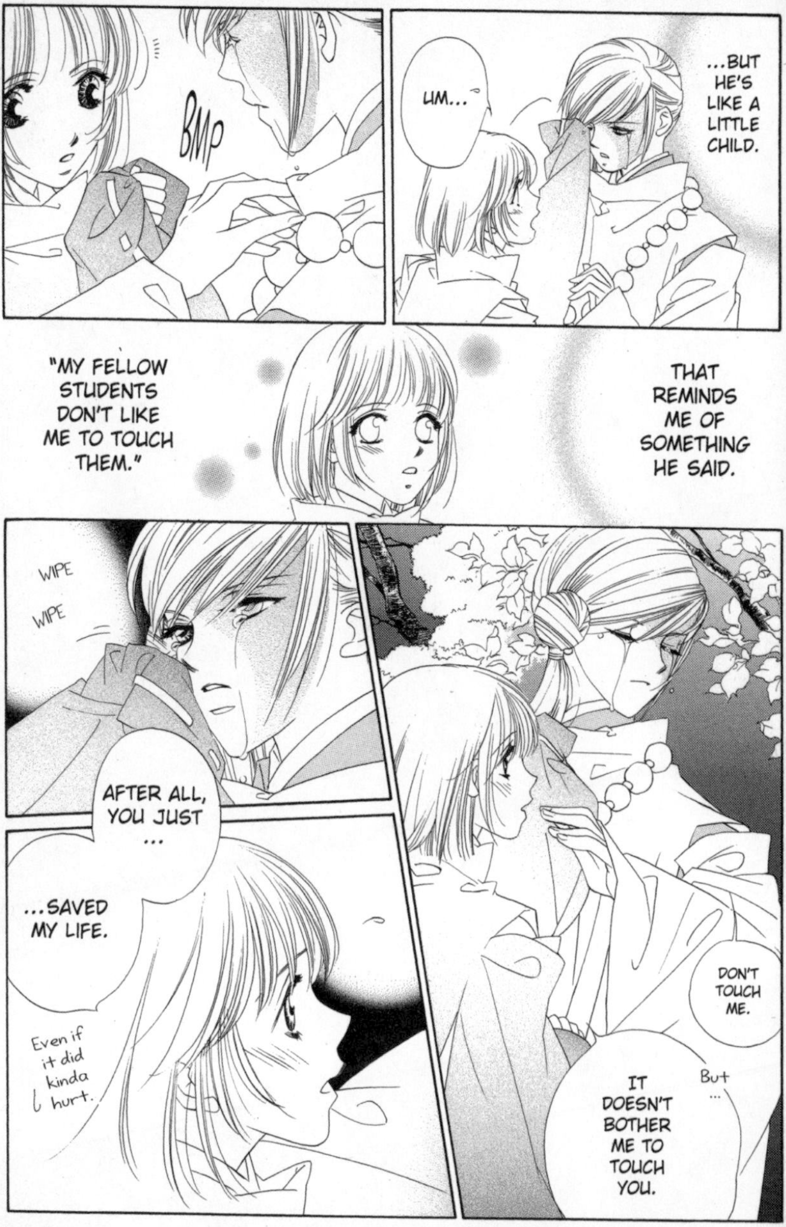
...BUT HE'S LIKE A LITTLE CHILD.
UM...
BMP
THAT REMINDS ME OF SOMETHING HE SAID.
"MY FELLOW STUDENTS DON'T LIKE ME TO TOUCH THEM."
DON'T TOUCH ME.
But ...
IT DOESN'T BOTHER ME TO TOUCH YOU.
WIPE
WIPE
AFTER ALL, YOU JUST ...
...SAVED MY LIFE.
Even if it did kinda hurt.

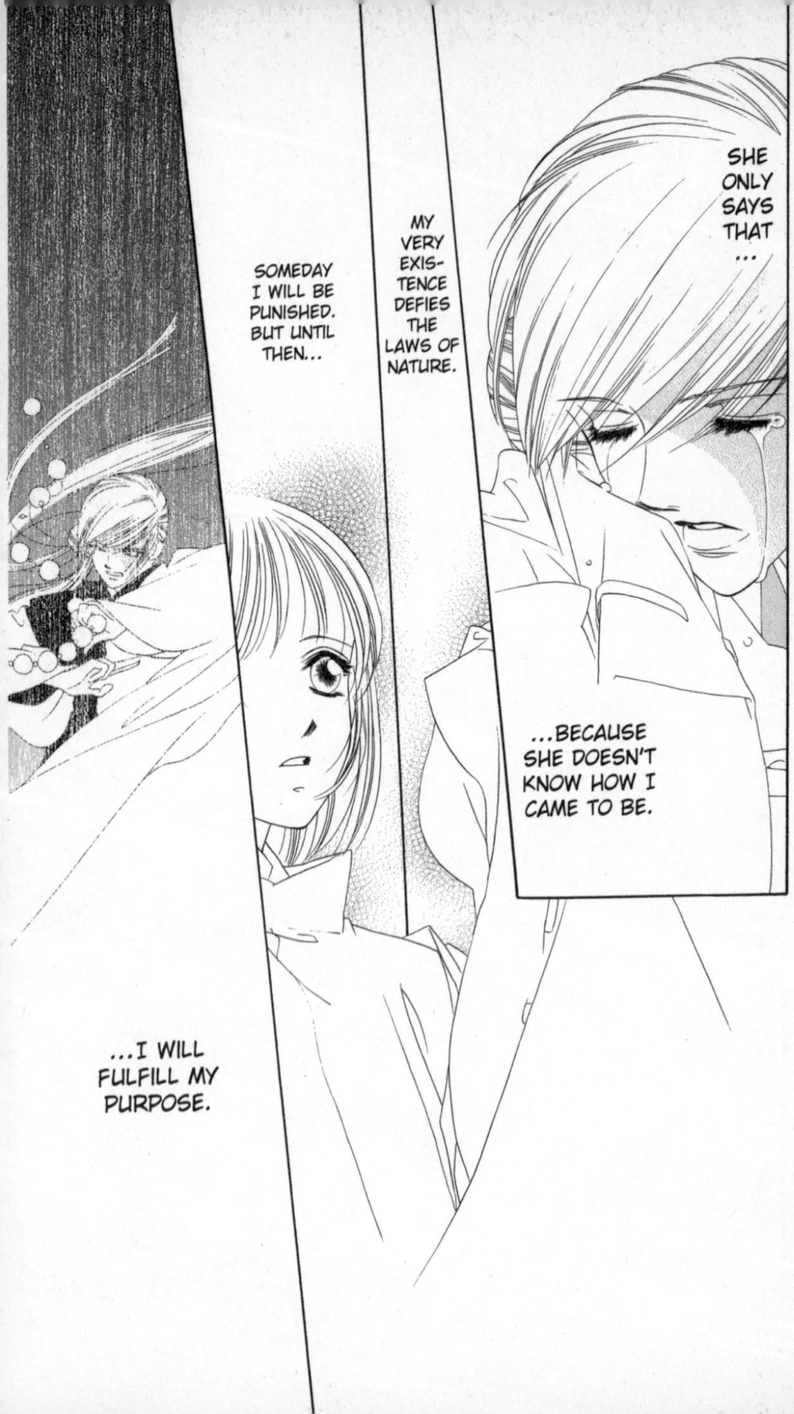
SHE ONLY SAYS THAT ...
...BECAUSE SHE DOESN'T KNOW HOW I CAME TO BE.
MY VERY EXIS-TENCE DEFIES THE LAWS OF NATURE.
SOMEDAY I WILL BE PUNISHED. BUT UNTIL THEN...
...I WILL FULFILL MY PURPOSE.

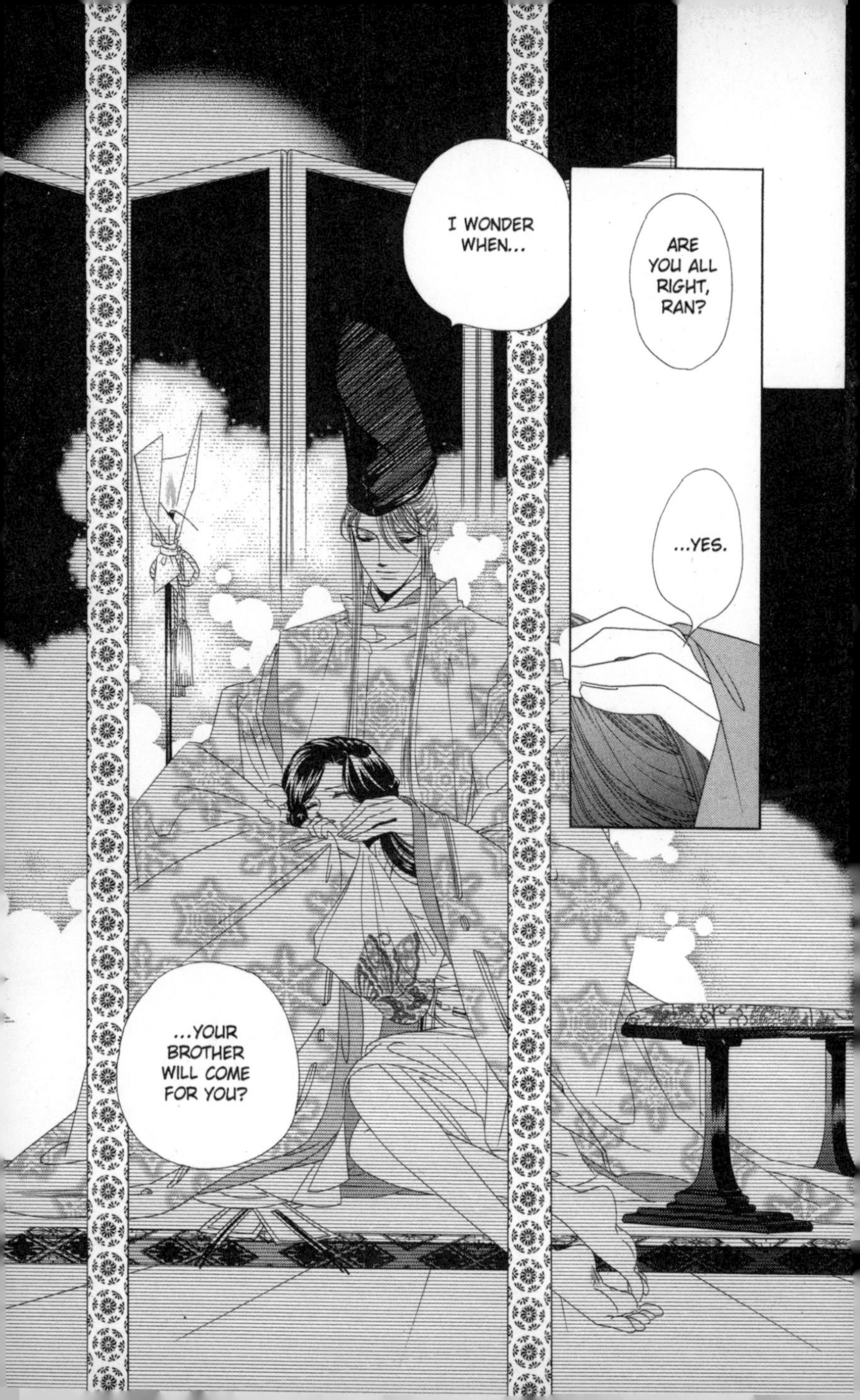
ARE YOU ALL RIGHT, RAN?
...YES.
I WONDER WHEN...
...YOUR BROTHER WILL COME FOR YOU?

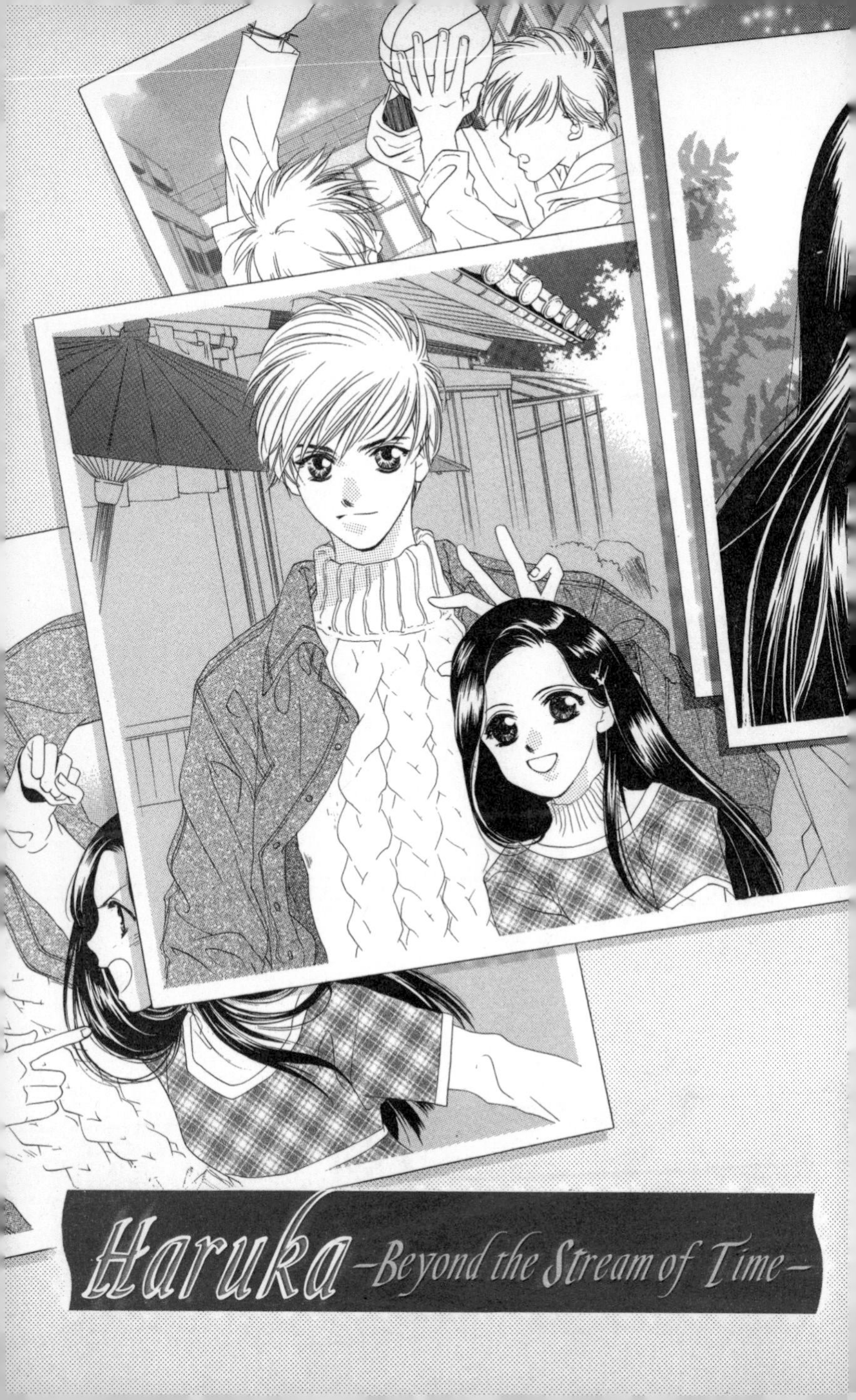

Haruka -Beyond the Stream of Time-

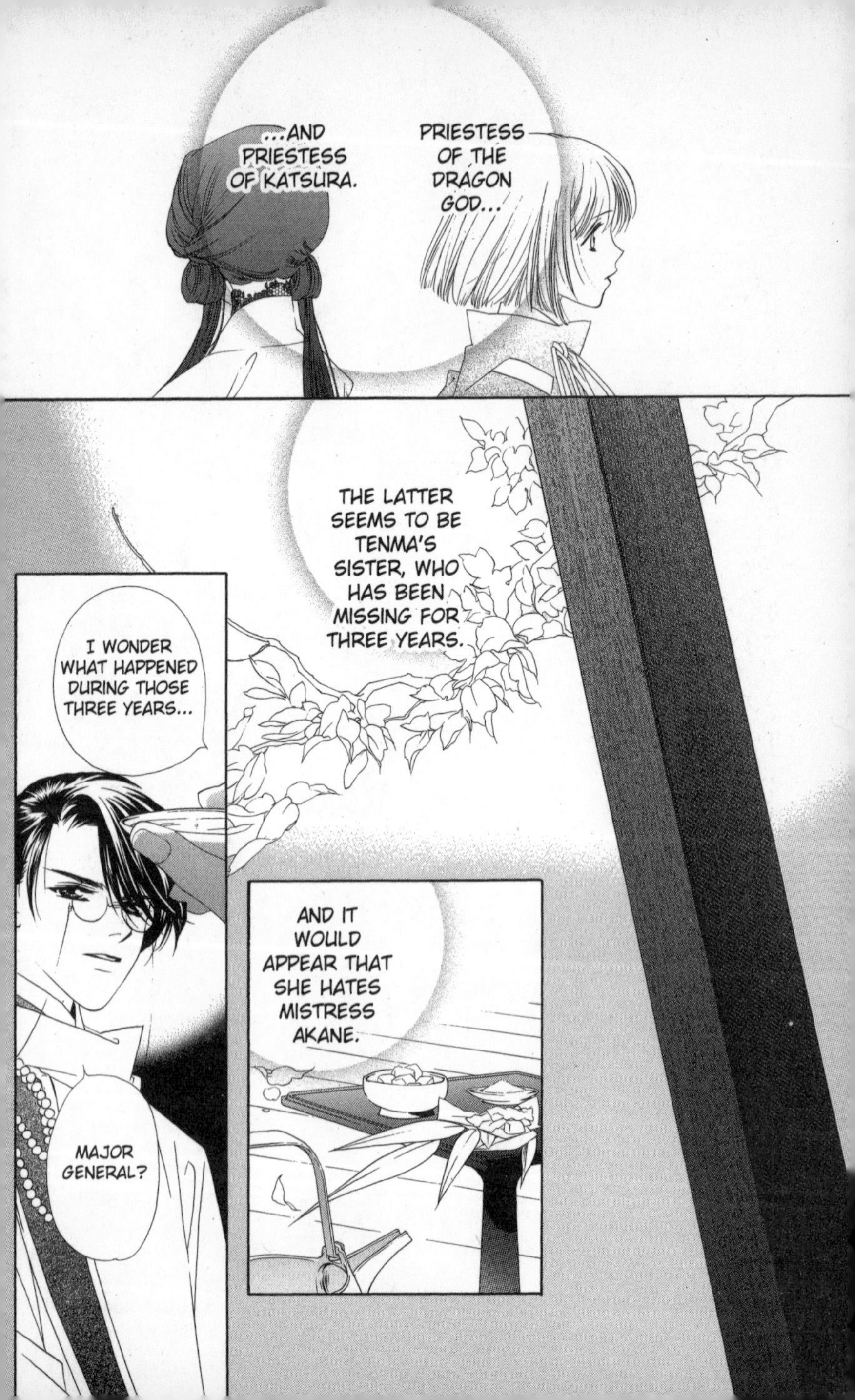
PRIESTESS OF THE DRAGON GOD...
...AND PRIESTESS OF KATSURA.
THE LATTER SEEMS TO BE TENMA'S SISTER, WHO HAS BEEN MISSING FOR THREE YEARS.
AND IT WOULD APPEAR THAT SHE HATES MISTRESS AKANE.
I WONDER WHAT HAPPENED DURING THOSE THREE YEARS...
MAJOR GENERAL?

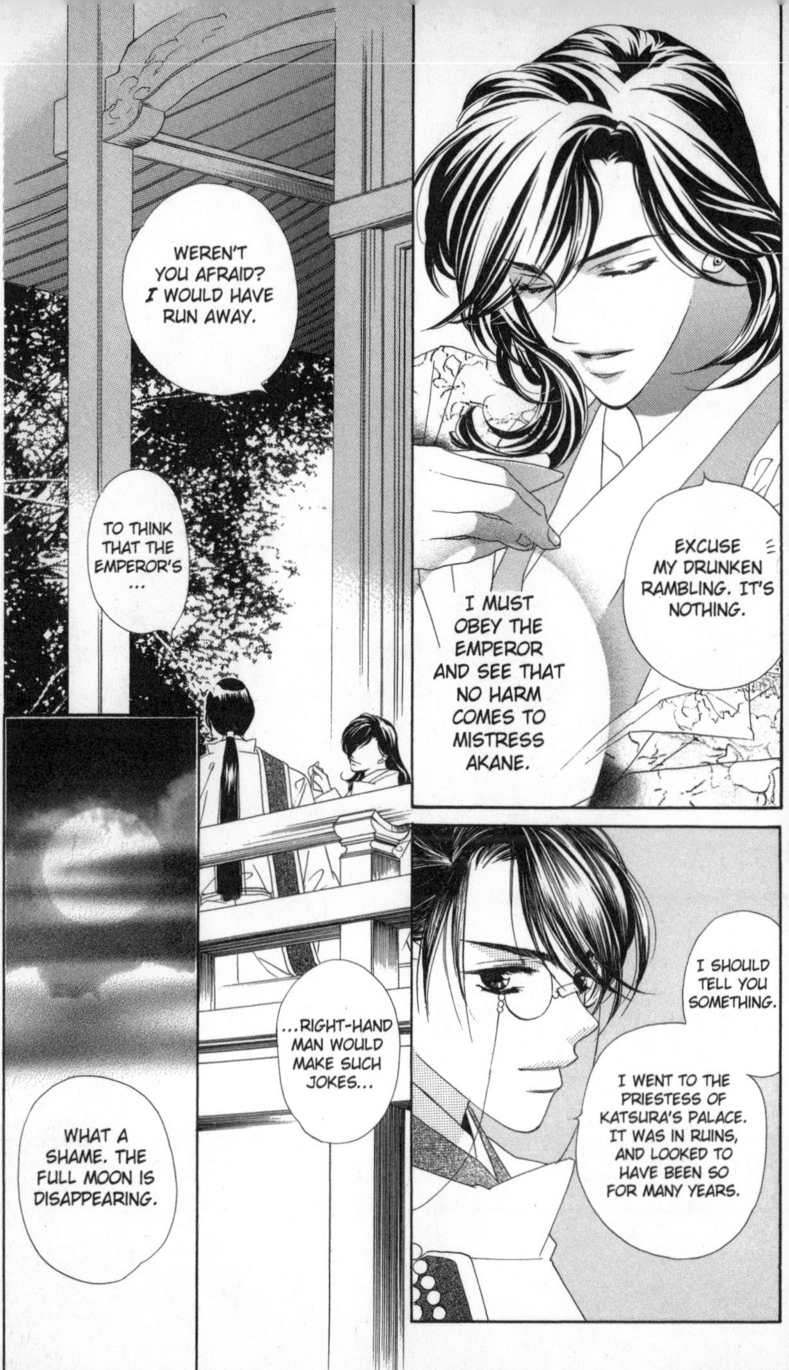
EXCUSE MY DRUNKEN RAMBLING. IT'S NOTHING.
I MUST OBEY THE EMPEROR AND SEE THAT NO HARM COMES TO MISTRESS AKANE.
WEREN'T YOU AFRAID? *I* WOULD HAVE RUN AWAY.
TO THINK THAT THE EMPEROR'S ...
...RIGHT-HAND MAN WOULD MAKE SUCH JOKES...
I SHOULD TELL YOU SOMETHING.
I WENT TO THE PRIESTESS OF KATSURA'S PALACE. IT WAS IN RUINS, AND LOOKED TO HAVE BEEN SO FOR MANY YEARS.
WHAT A SHAME. THE FULL MOON IS DISAPPEARING.

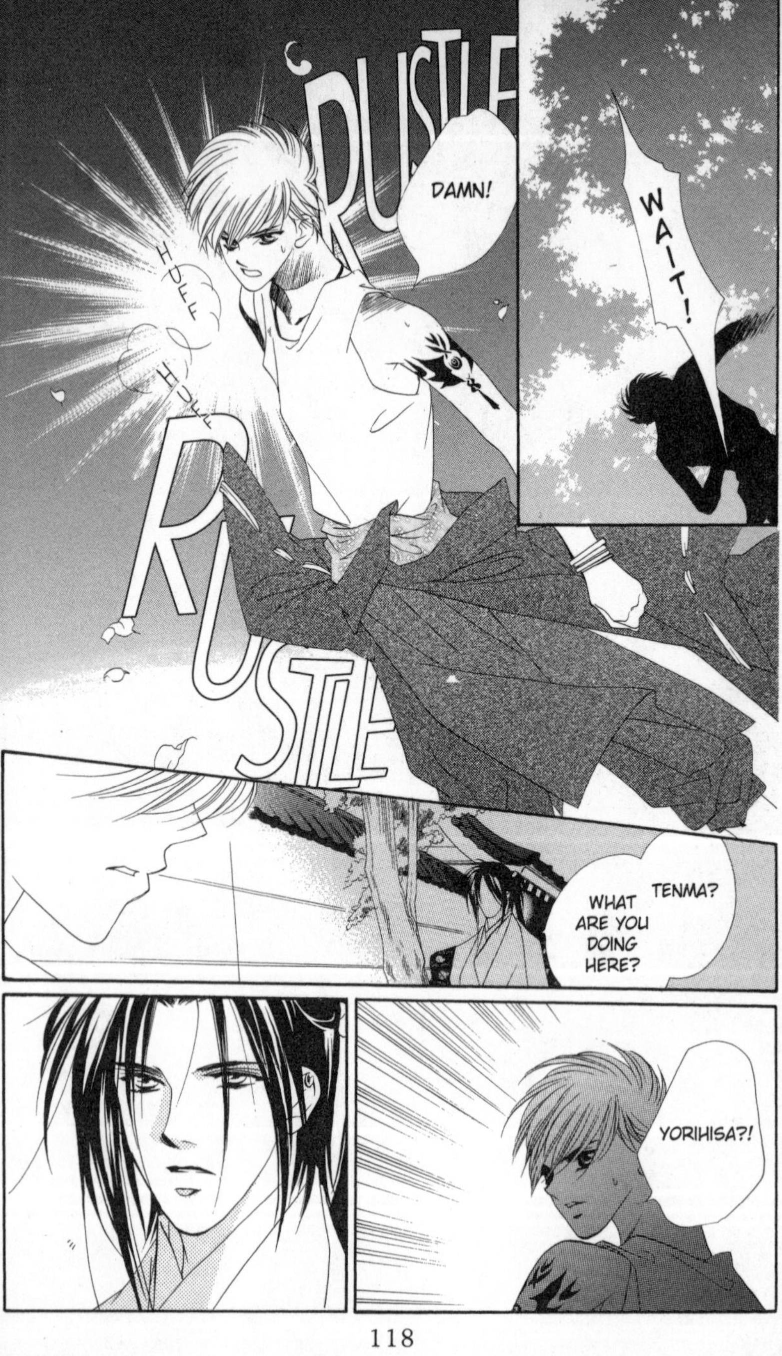
WAIT!
RUSTLE
DAMN!
HUFF HUFF
RUSTLE
TENMA?
WHAT ARE YOU DOING HERE?
YORIHISA?!

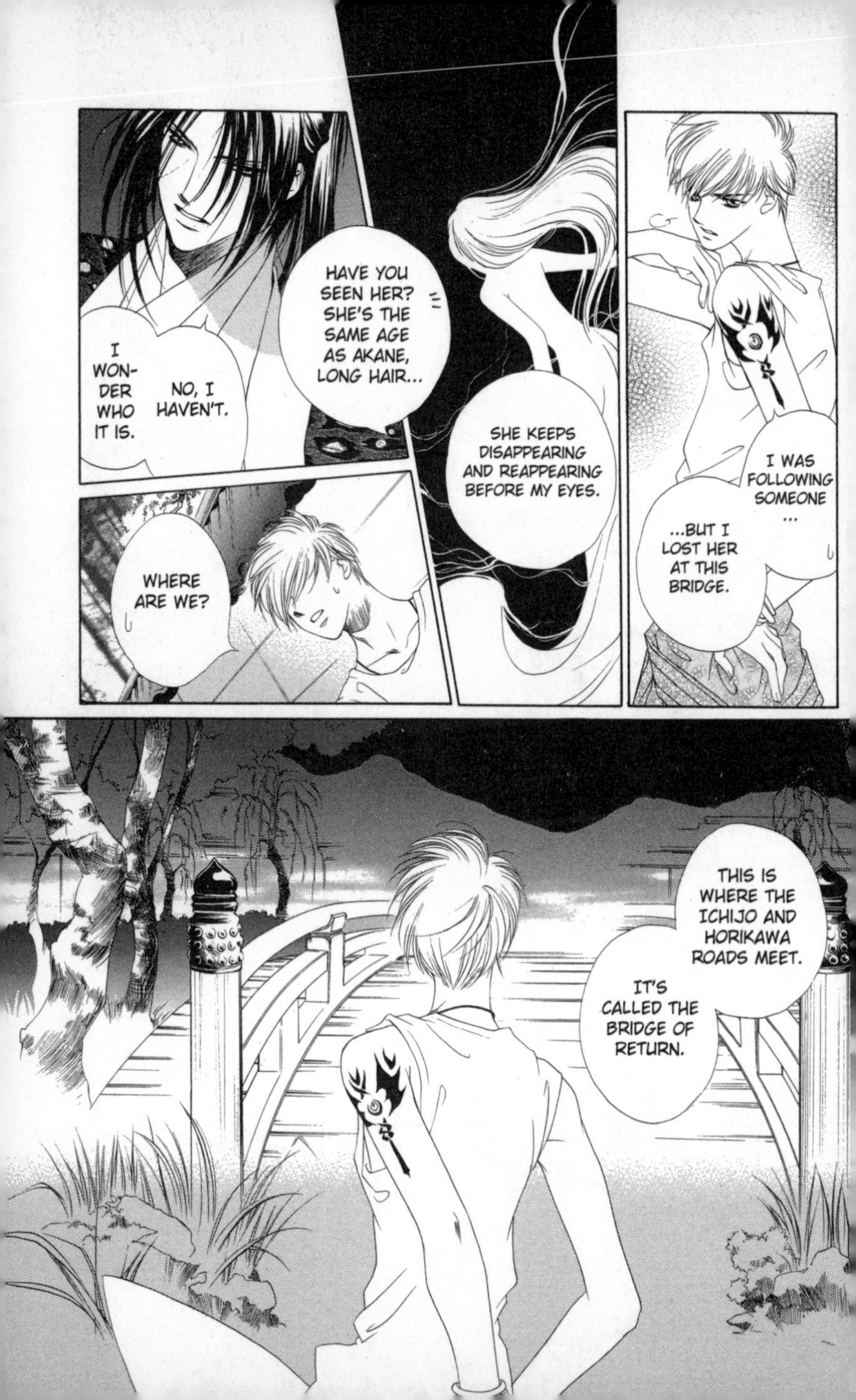
I WAS FOLLOWING SOMEONE ...
...BUT I LOST HER AT THIS BRIDGE.
SHE KEEPS DISAPPEARING AND REAPPEARING BEFORE MY EYES.
HAVE YOU SEEN HER? SHE'S THE SAME AGE AS AKANE, LONG HAIR...
NO, I HAVEN'T.
I WONDER WHO IT IS.
WHERE ARE WE?
THIS IS WHERE THE ICHIJO AND HORIKAWA ROADS MEET.
IT'S CALLED THE BRIDGE OF RETURN.

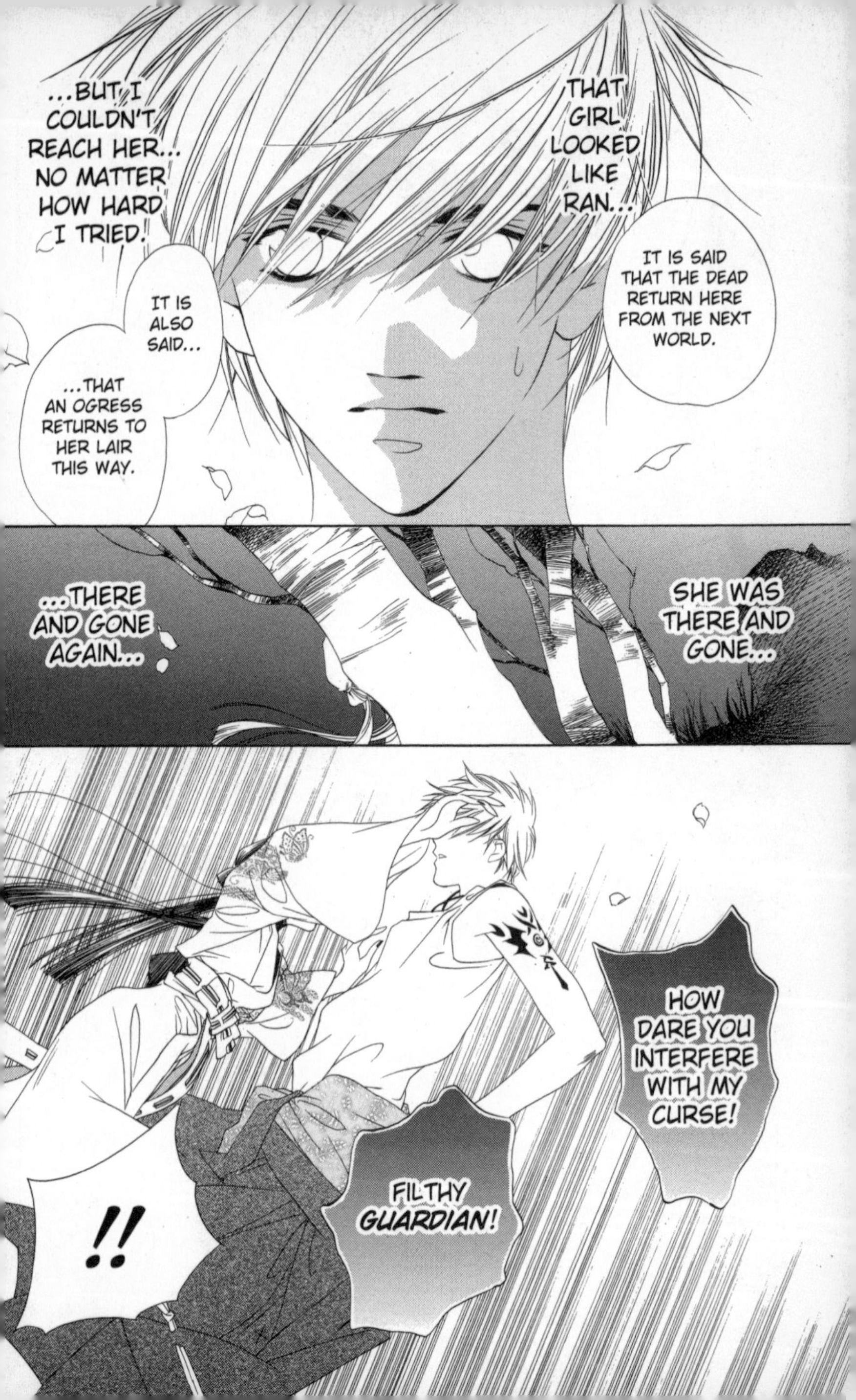
THAT GIRL LOOKED LIKE RAN...
...BUT I COULDN'T REACH HER... NO MATTER HOW HARD I TRIED.
IT IS SAID THAT THE DEAD RETURN HERE FROM THE NEXT WORLD.
IT IS ALSO SAID...
...THAT AN OGRESS RETURNS TO HER LAIR THIS WAY.
SHE WAS THERE AND GONE...
...THERE AND GONE AGAIN...
HOW DARE YOU INTERFERE WITH MY CURSE!
FILTHY GUARDIAN!
!!

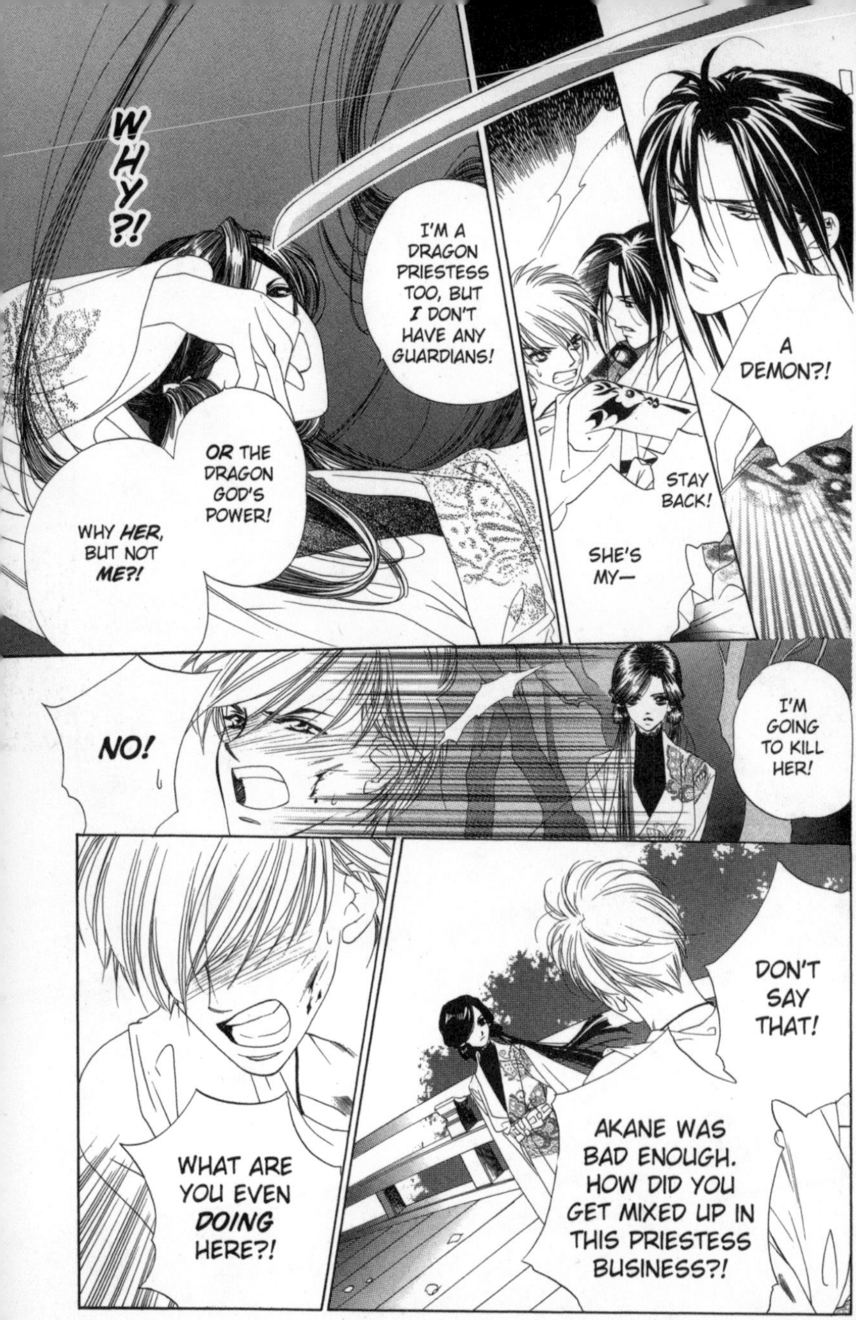
A DEMON?!
STAY BACK!
SHE'S MY—
I'M A DRAGON PRIESTESS TOO, BUT *I* DON'T HAVE ANY GUARDIANS!
WHY?!
OR THE DRAGON GOD'S POWER!
WHY *HER*, BUT NOT *ME*?!
I'M GOING TO KILL HER!
NO!
DON'T SAY THAT!
AKANE WAS BAD ENOUGH. HOW DID YOU GET MIXED UP IN THIS PRIESTESS BUSINESS?!
WHAT ARE YOU EVEN *DOING* HERE?!

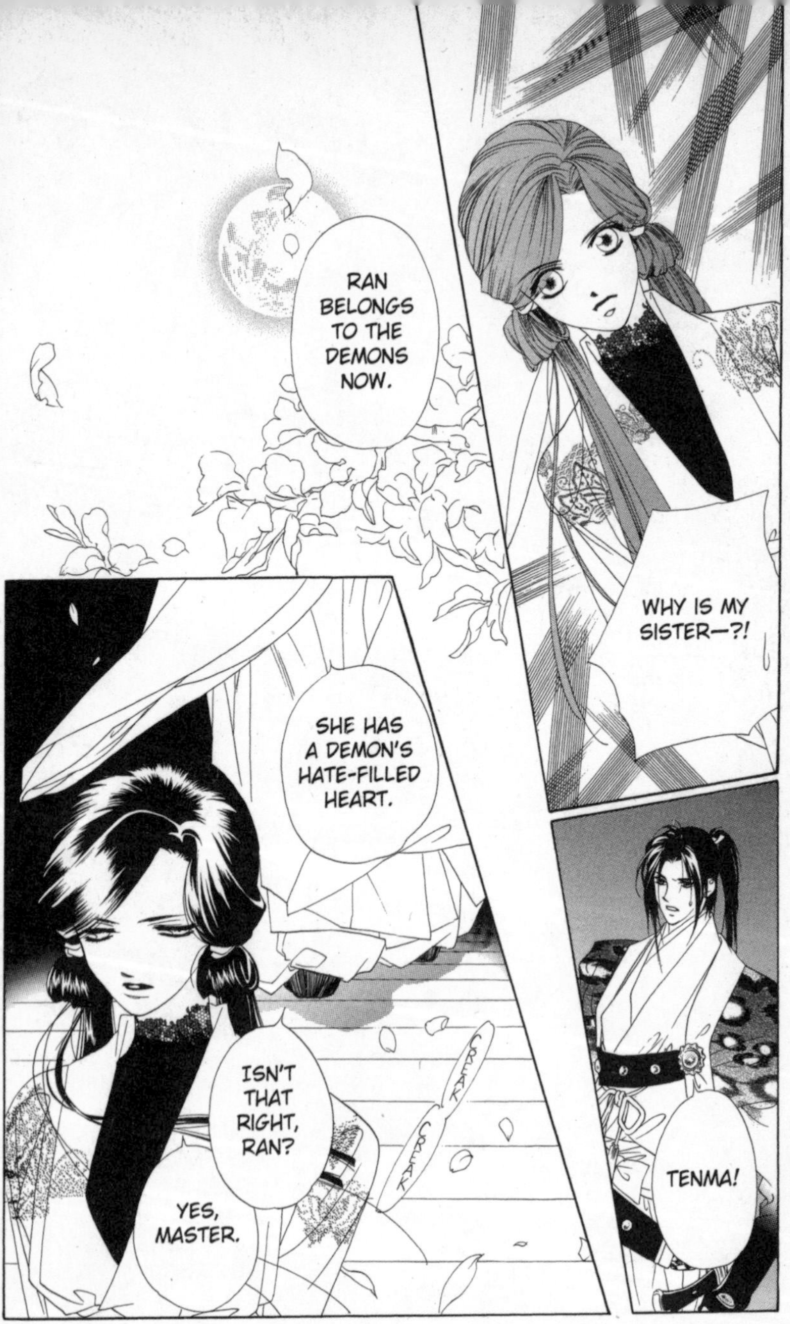
WHY IS MY SISTER—?!
RAN BELONGS TO THE DEMONS NOW.
TENMA!
SHE HAS A DEMON'S HATE-FILLED HEART.
CREAK
CREAK
ISN'T THAT RIGHT, RAN?
YES, MASTER.

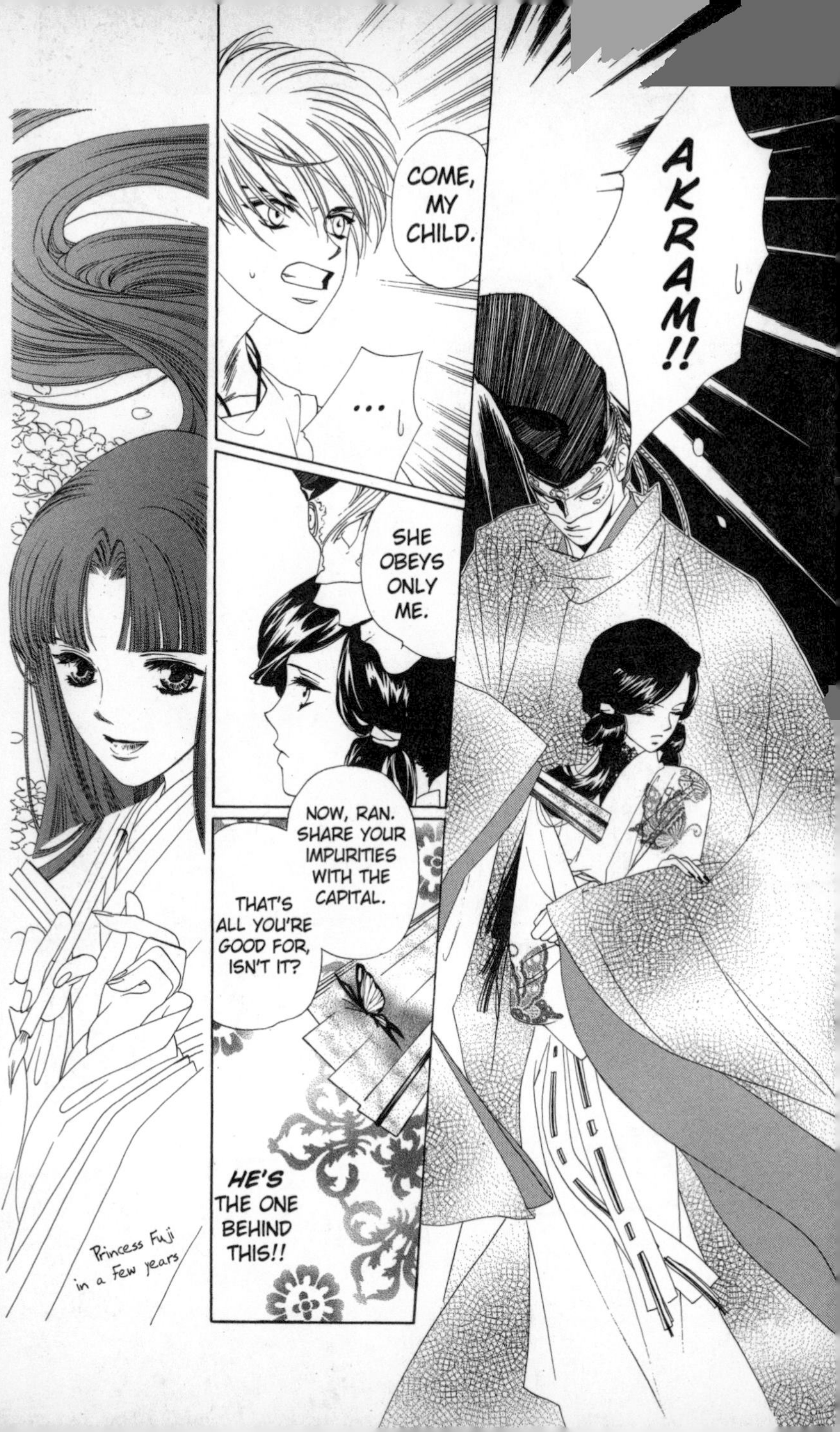
AKRAM!!
COME, MY CHILD.
...
SHE OBEYS ONLY ME.
NOW, RAN. SHARE YOUR IMPURITIES WITH THE CAPITAL.
THAT'S ALL YOU'RE GOOD FOR, ISN'T IT?
HE'S THE ONE BEHIND THIS!!
Princess Fuji in a Few years

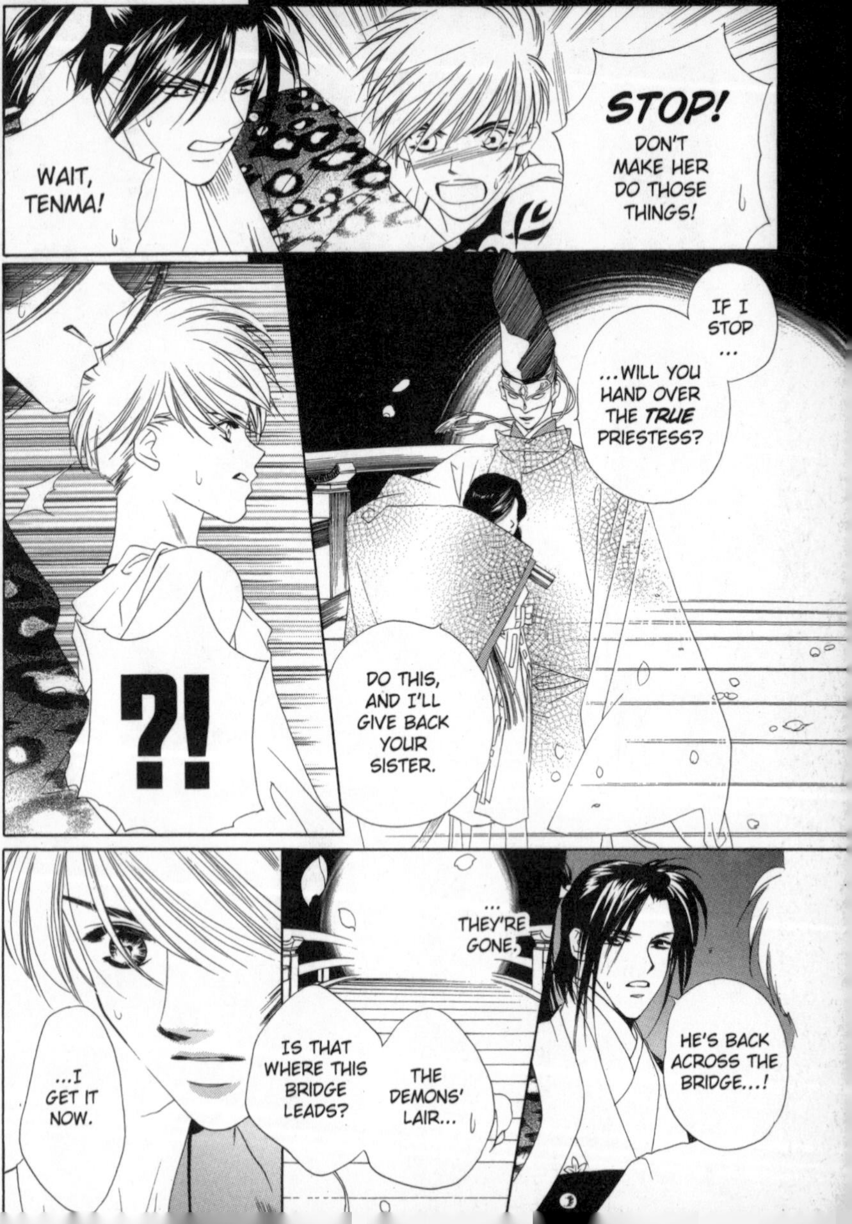
STOP! DON'T MAKE HER DO THOSE THINGS!
WAIT, TENMA!
IF I STOP ...
...WILL YOU HAND OVER THE TRUE PRIESTESS?
DO THIS, AND I'LL GIVE BACK YOUR SISTER.
?!
HE'S BACK ACROSS THE BRIDGE...!
... THEY'RE GONE.
THE DEMONS' LAIR...
IS THAT WHERE THIS BRIDGE LEADS?
...I GET IT NOW.

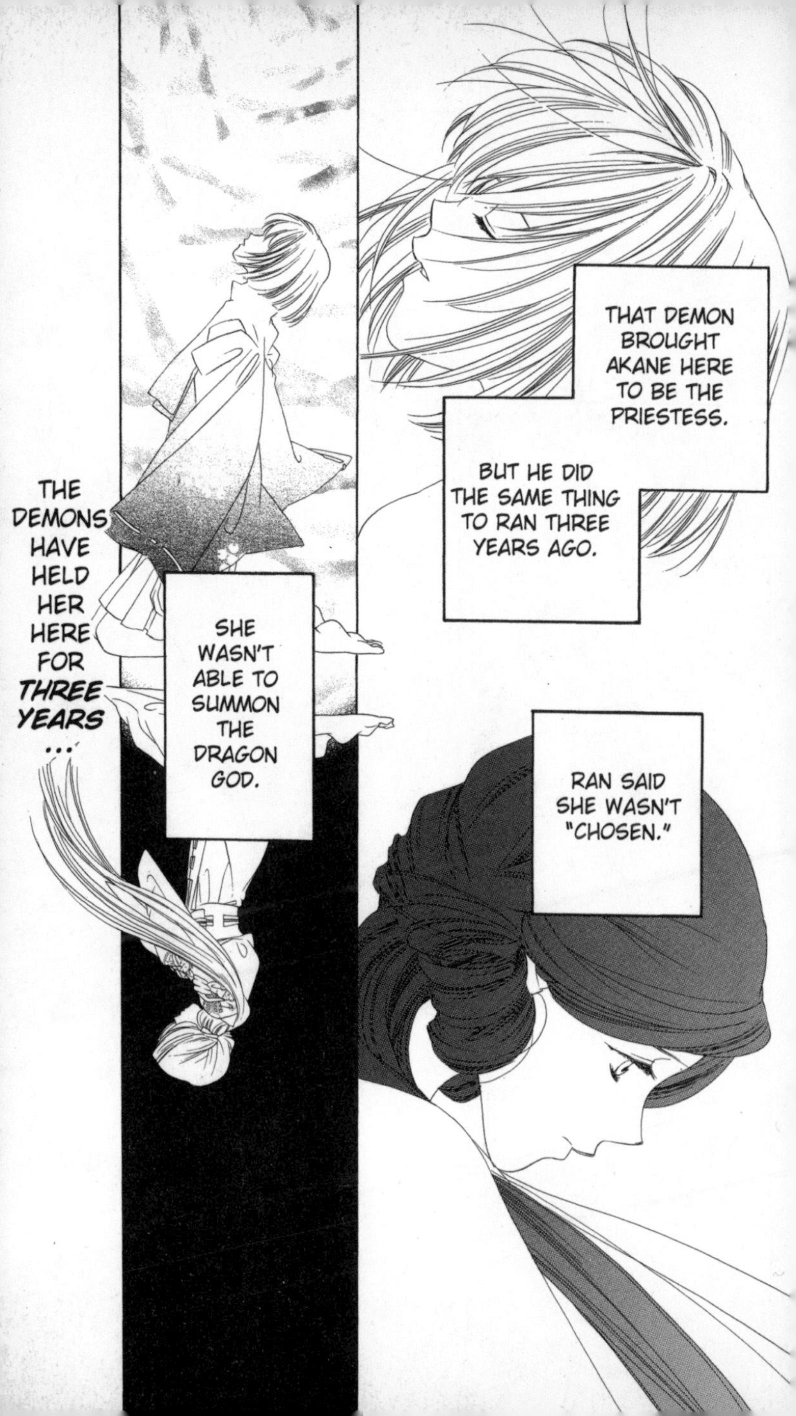
THAT DEMON BROUGHT AKANE HERE TO BE THE PRIESTESS.
BUT HE DID THE SAME THING TO RAN THREE YEARS AGO.
RAN SAID SHE WASN'T "CHOSEN."
SHE WASN'T ABLE TO SUMMON THE DRAGON GOD.
THE DEMONS HAVE HELD HER HERE FOR *THREE YEARS*...

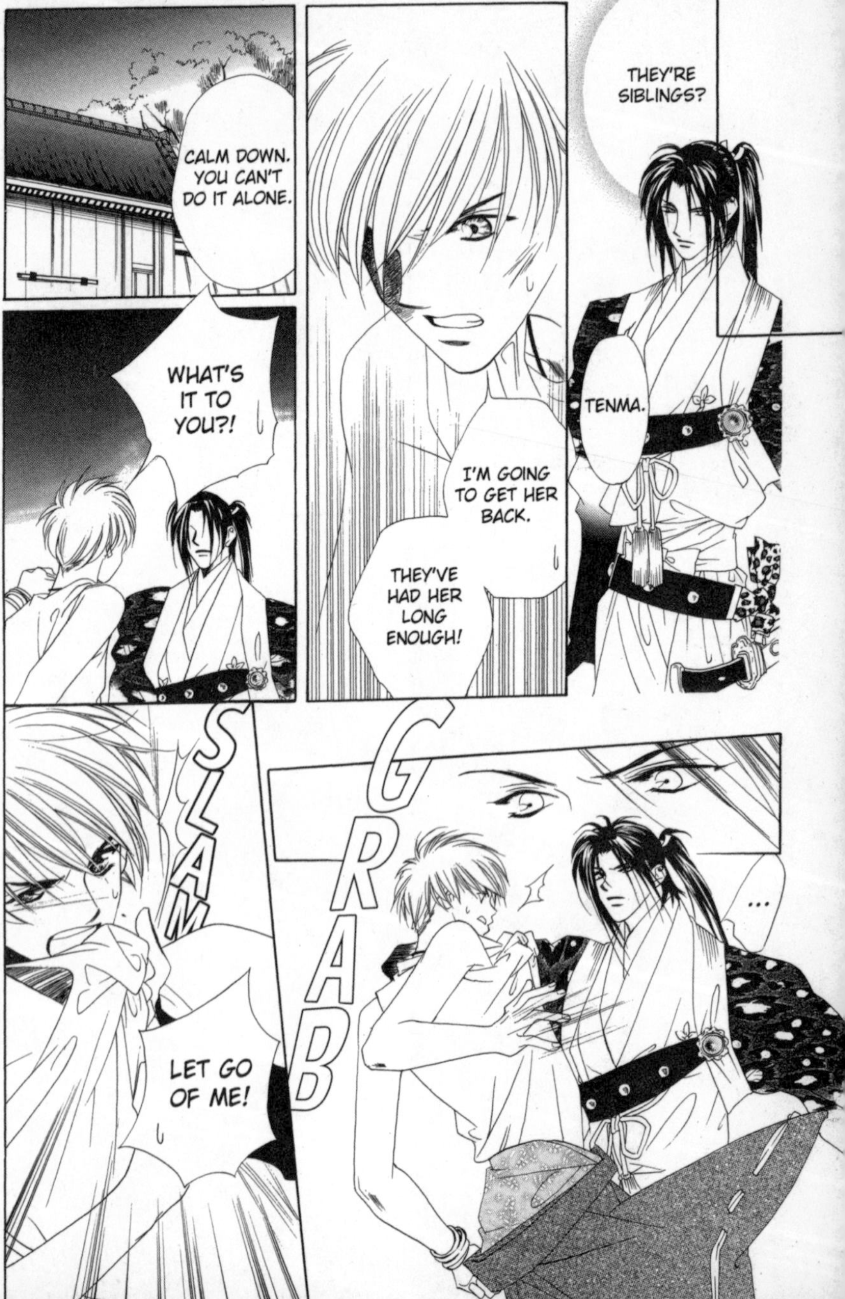
THEY'RE SIBLINGS?
TENMA.
I'M GOING TO GET HER BACK.
THEY'VE HAD HER LONG ENOUGH!
CALM DOWN. YOU CAN'T DO IT ALONE.
WHAT'S IT TO YOU?!
GRAB
...
SLAM
LET GO OF ME!

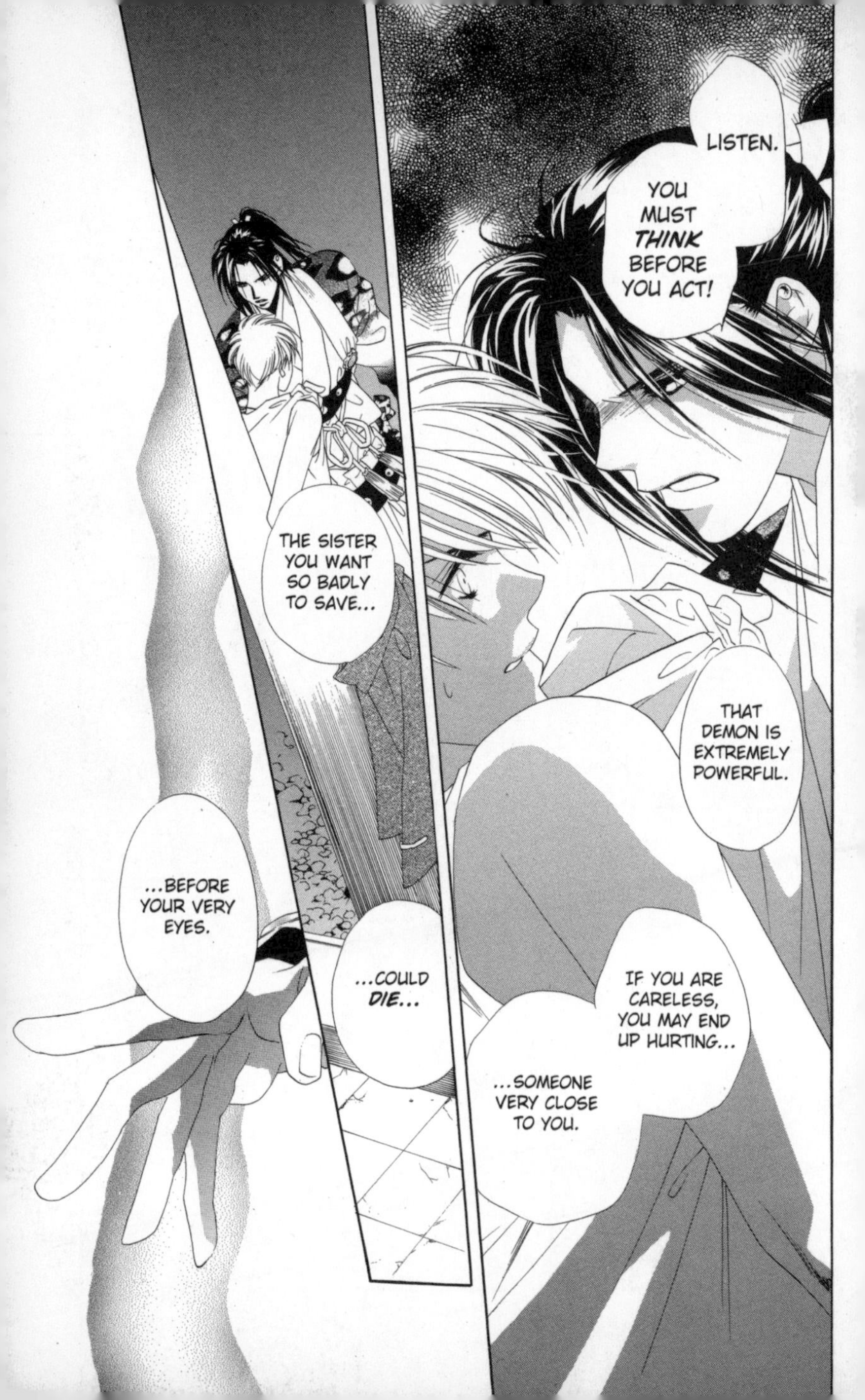
LISTEN.
YOU MUST *THINK* BEFORE YOU ACT!
THAT DEMON IS EXTREMELY POWERFUL.
IF YOU ARE CARELESS, YOU MAY END UP HURTING...
...SOMEONE VERY CLOSE TO YOU.
THE SISTER YOU WANT SO BADLY TO SAVE...
...COULD *DIE*...
...BEFORE YOUR VERY EYES.

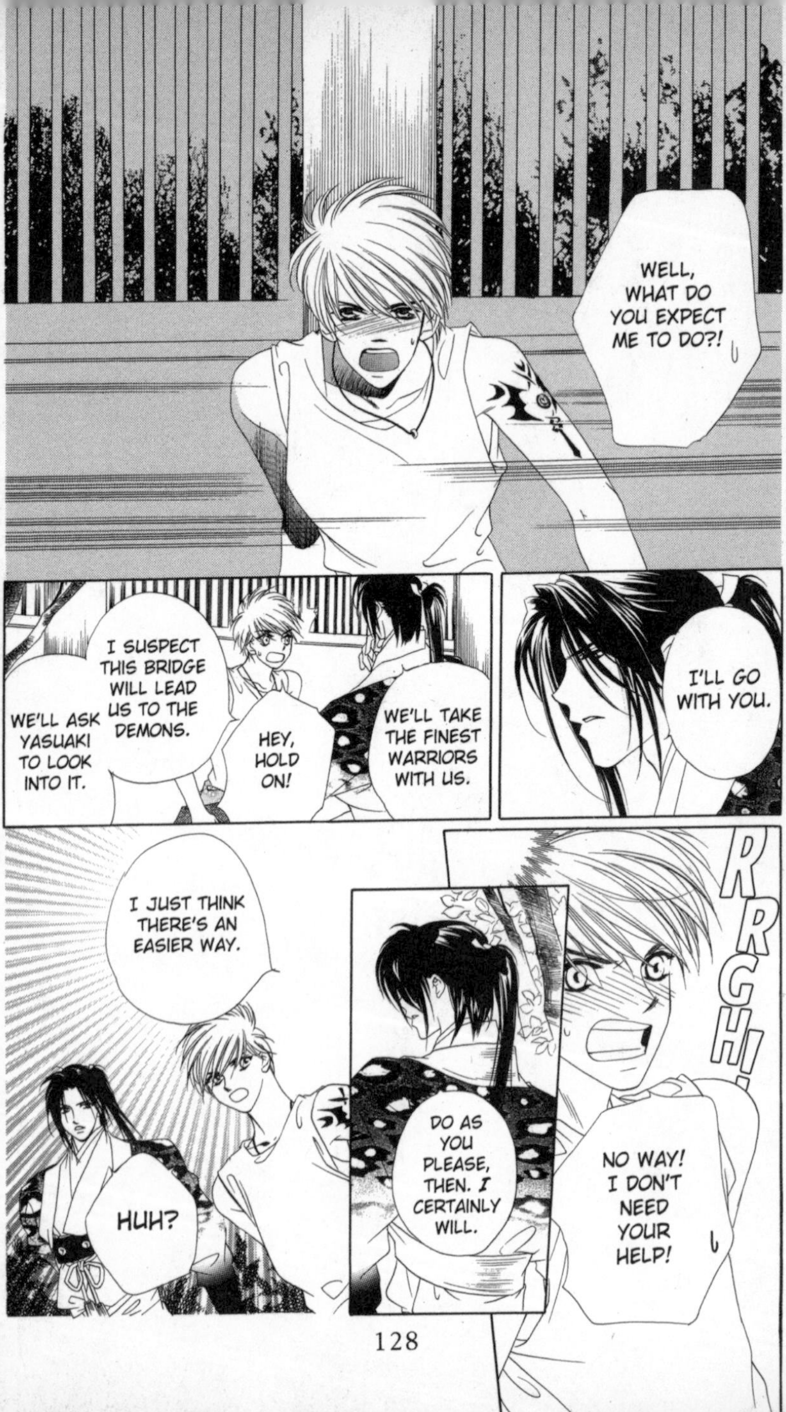
WELL, WHAT DO YOU EXPECT ME TO DO?!
I'LL GO WITH YOU.
I SUSPECT THIS BRIDGE WILL LEAD US TO THE DEMONS.
WE'LL TAKE THE FINEST WARRIORS WITH US.
HEY, HOLD ON!
WE'LL ASK YASUAKI TO LOOK INTO IT.
RRGH!
NO WAY! I DON'T NEED YOUR HELP!
DO AS YOU PLEASE, THEN. *I* CERTAINLY WILL.
I JUST THINK THERE'S AN EASIER WAY.
HUH?

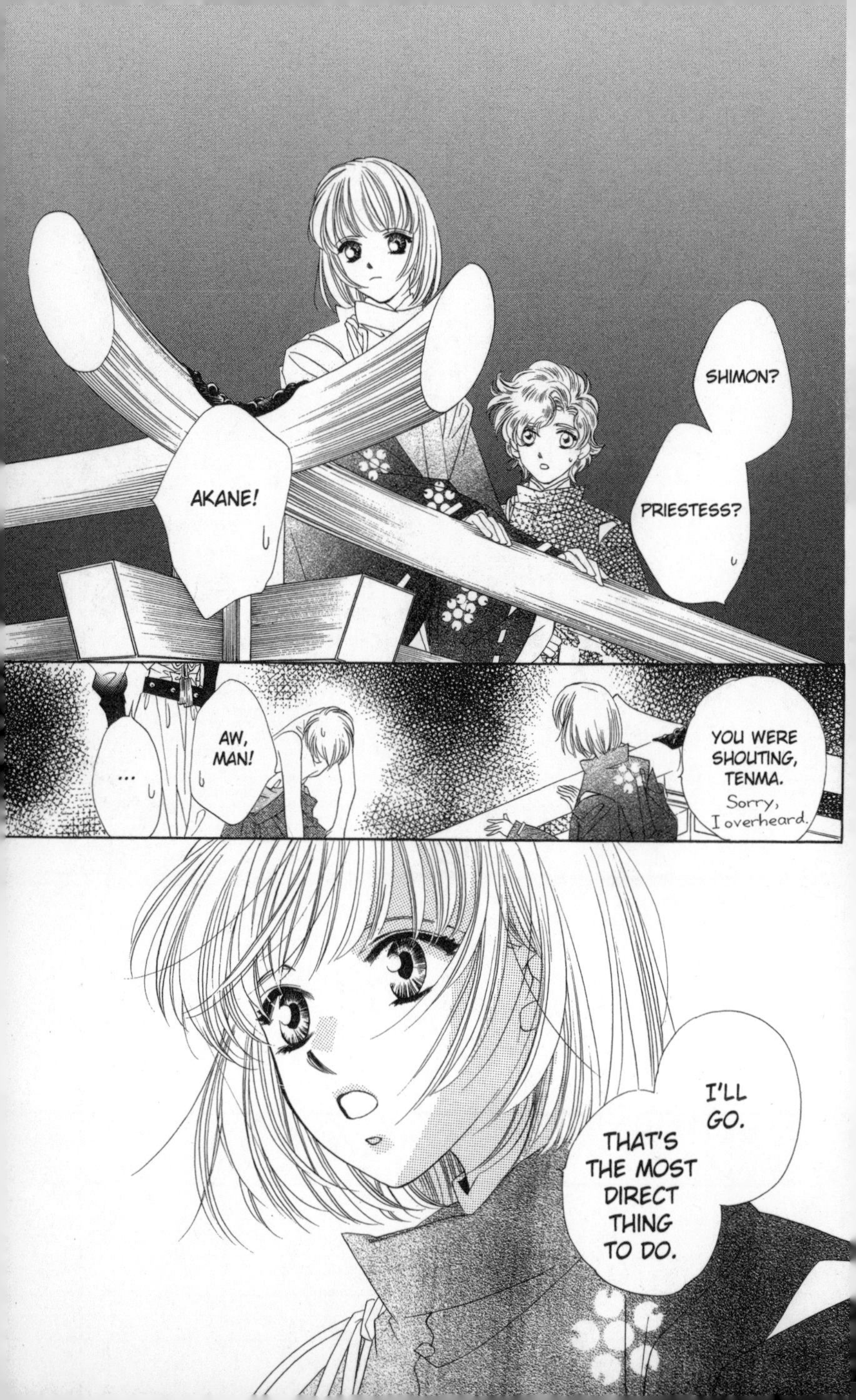
SHIMON?
PRIESTESS?
AKANE!
YOU WERE SHOUTING, TENMA.
Sorry, I overheard.
AW, MAN!
...
I'LL GO.
THAT'S THE MOST DIRECT THING TO DO.

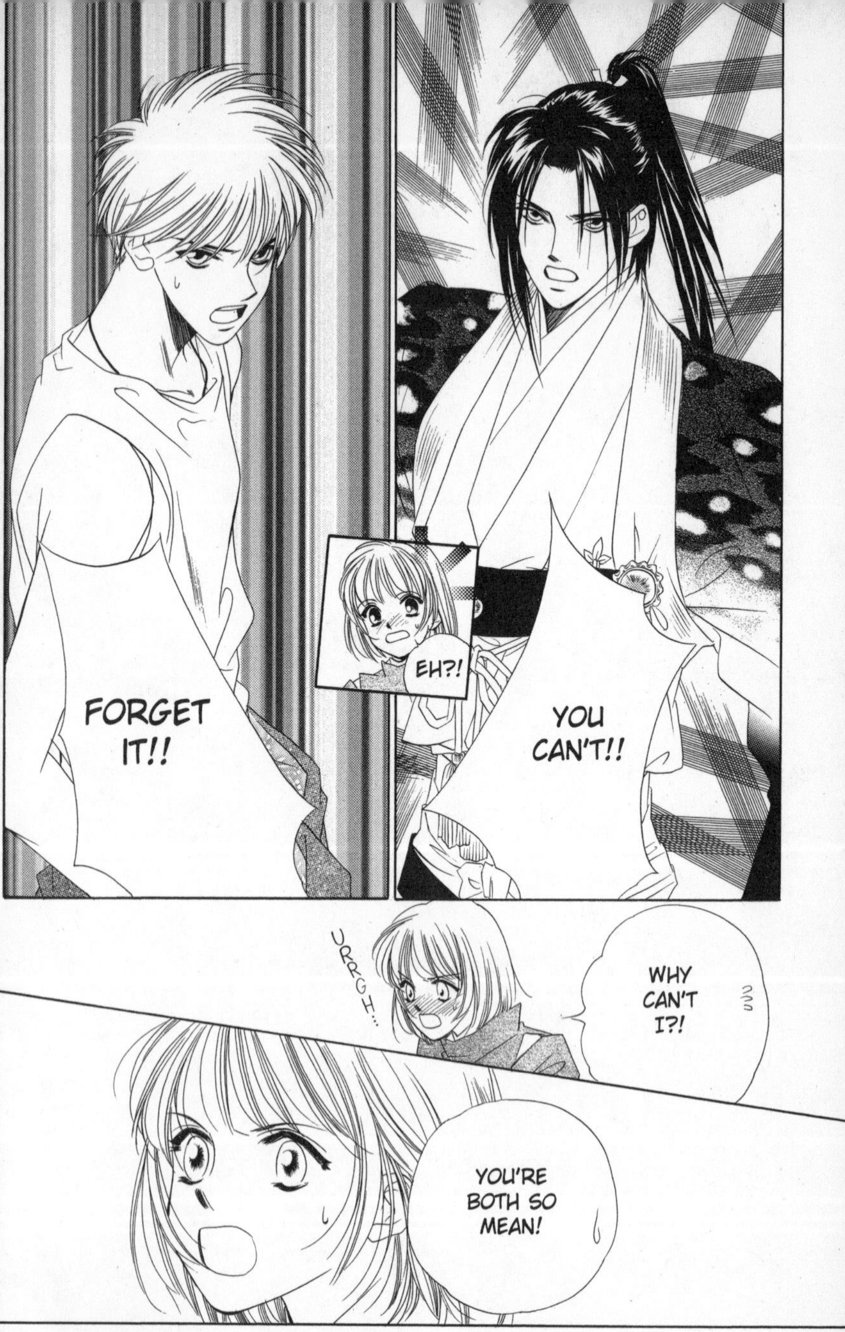
YOU CAN'T!!
FORGET IT!!
EH?!
WHY CAN'T I?!
URRGH...
YOU'RE BOTH SO MEAN!

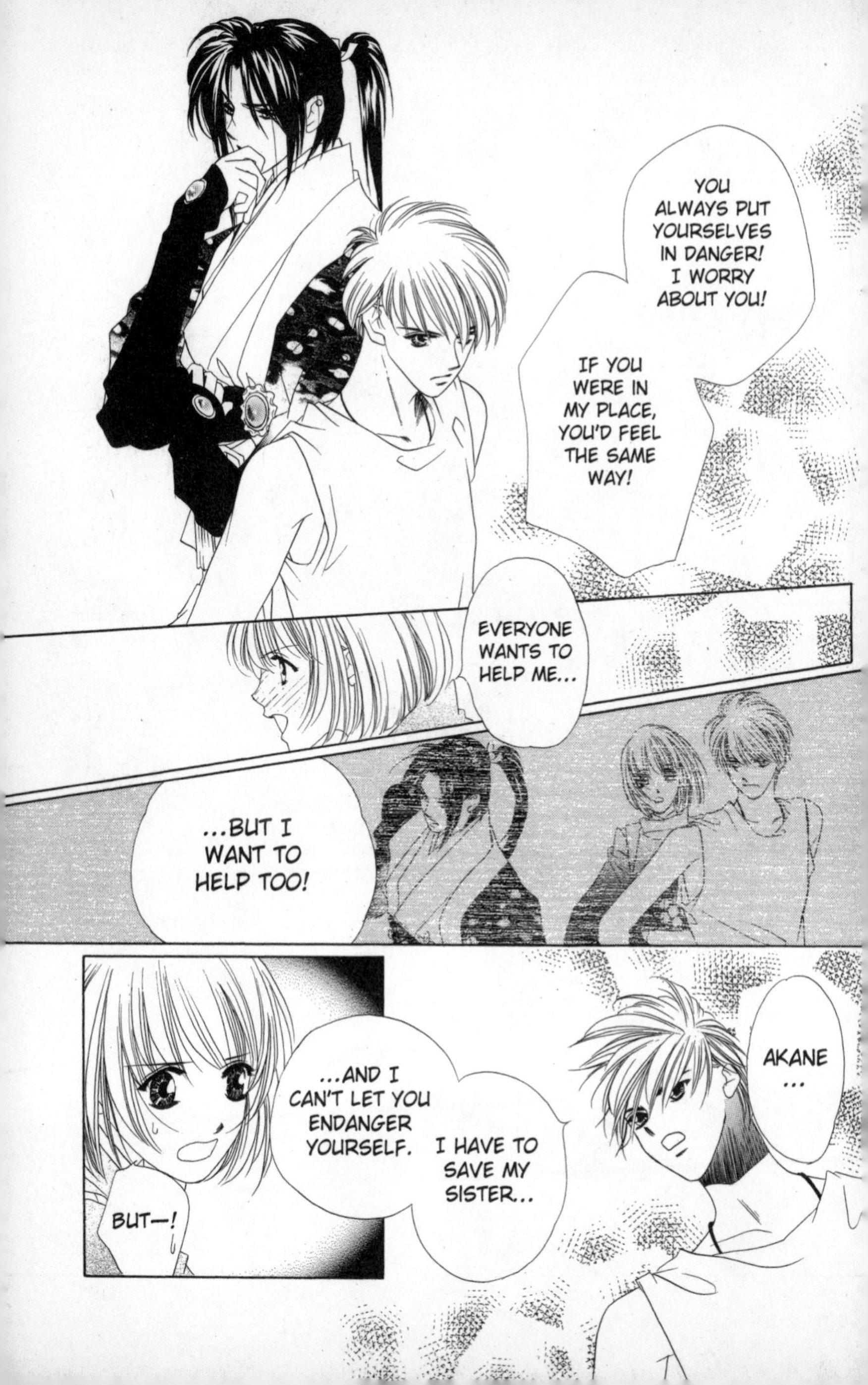
YOU ALWAYS PUT YOURSELVES IN DANGER! I WORRY ABOUT YOU!
IF YOU WERE IN MY PLACE, YOU'D FEEL THE SAME WAY!
EVERYONE WANTS TO HELP ME...
...BUT I WANT TO HELP TOO!
AKANE...
I HAVE TO SAVE MY SISTER...
...AND I CAN'T LET YOU ENDANGER YOURSELF.
BUT—!

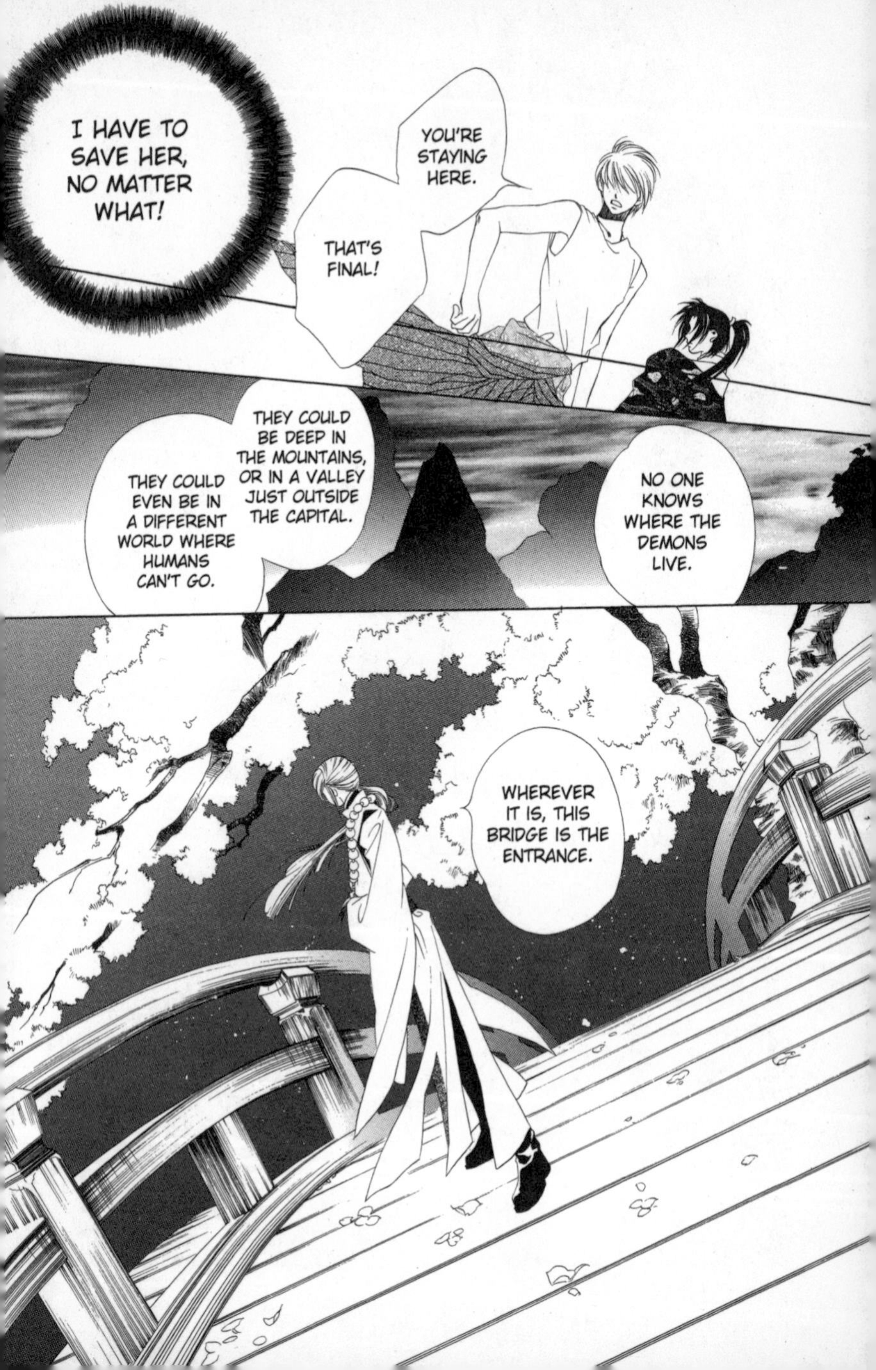
YOU'RE STAYING HERE.
THAT'S FINAL!
I HAVE TO SAVE HER, NO MATTER WHAT!
NO ONE KNOWS WHERE THE DEMONS LIVE.
THEY COULD BE DEEP IN THE MOUNTAINS, OR IN A VALLEY JUST OUTSIDE THE CAPITAL.
THEY COULD EVEN BE IN A DIFFERENT WORLD WHERE HUMANS CAN'T GO.
WHEREVER IT IS, THIS BRIDGE IS THE ENTRANCE.

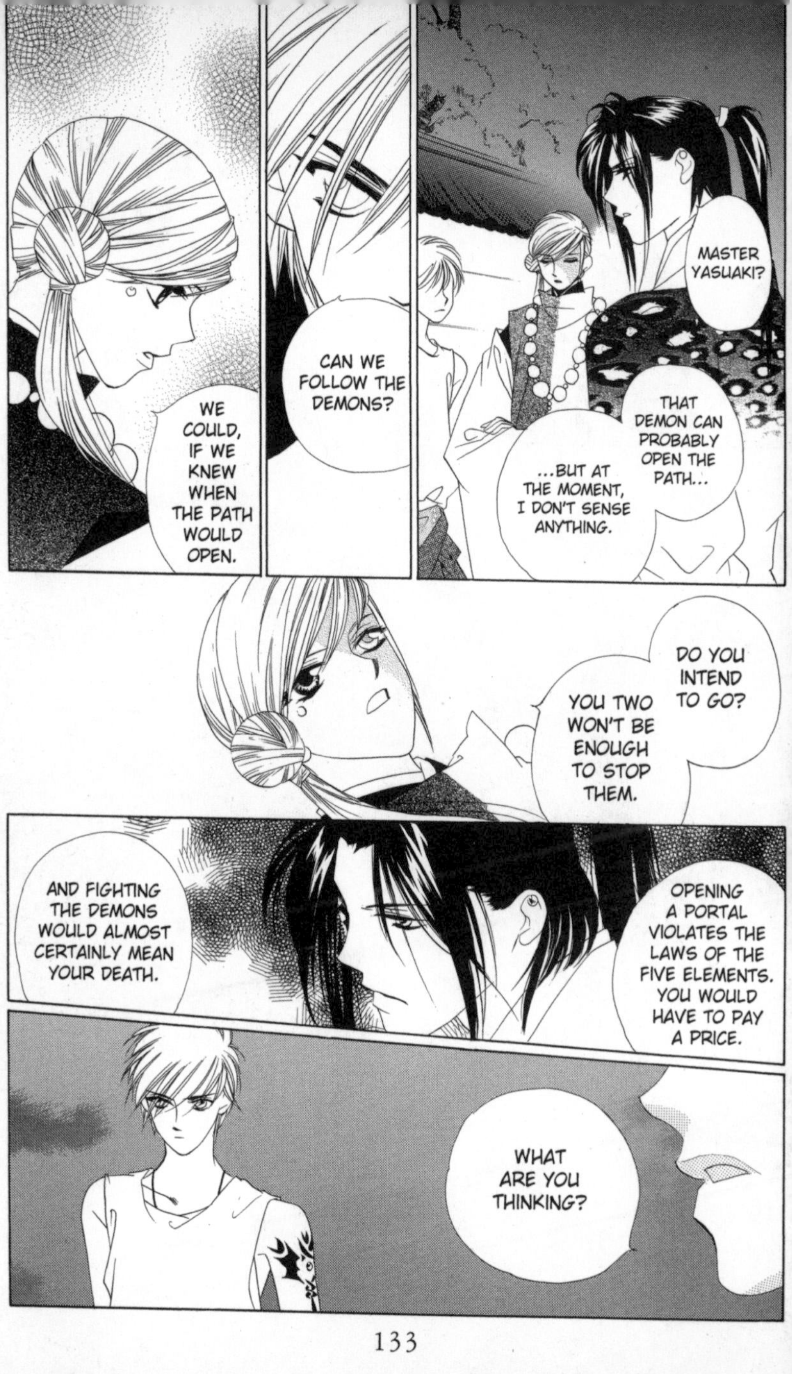
MASTER YASUAKI?
THAT DEMON CAN PROBABLY OPEN THE PATH...
...BUT AT THE MOMENT, I DON'T SENSE ANYTHING.
CAN WE FOLLOW THE DEMONS?
WE COULD, IF WE KNEW WHEN THE PATH WOULD OPEN.
DO YOU INTEND TO GO?
YOU TWO WON'T BE ENOUGH TO STOP THEM.
OPENING A PORTAL VIOLATES THE LAWS OF THE FIVE ELEMENTS. YOU WOULD HAVE TO PAY A PRICE.
AND FIGHTING THE DEMONS WOULD ALMOST CERTAINLY MEAN YOUR DEATH.
WHAT ARE YOU THINKING?

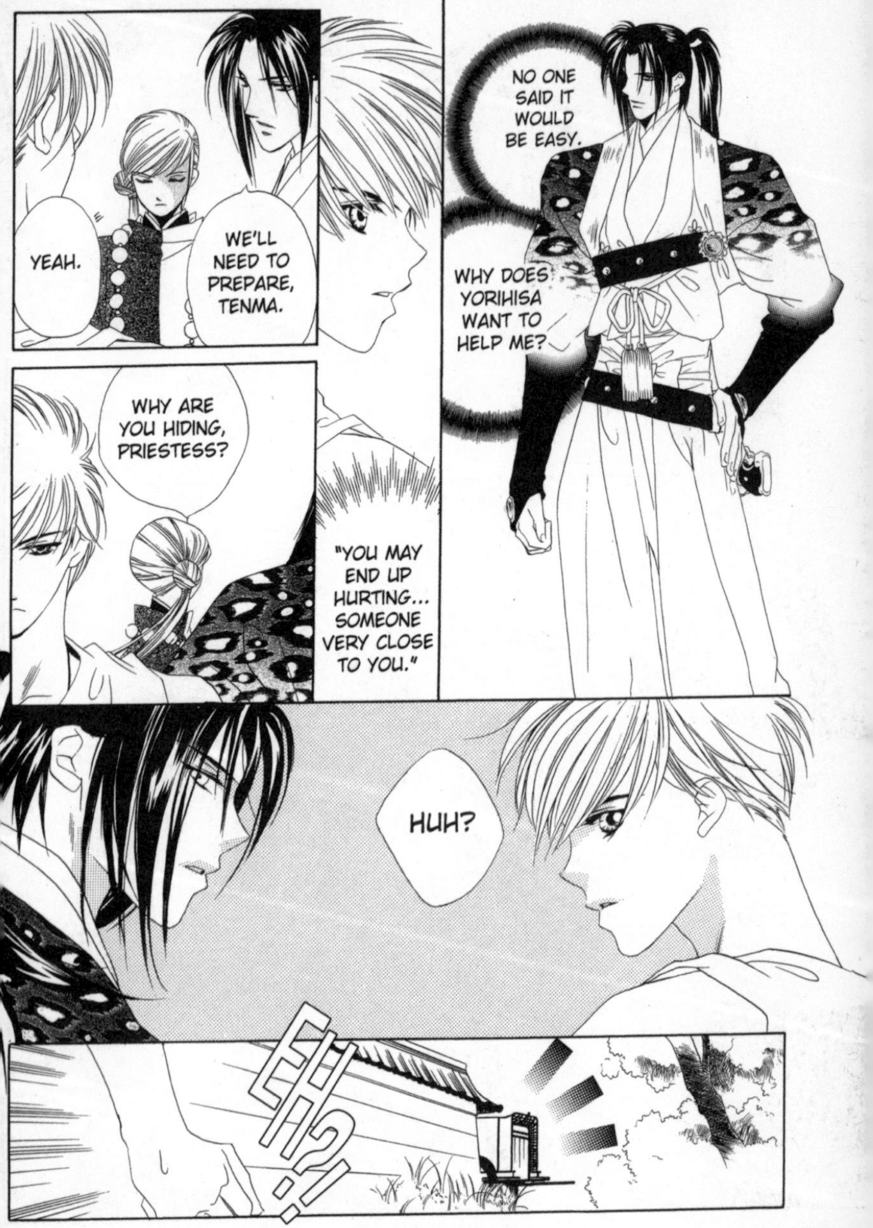
NO ONE SAID IT WOULD BE EASY.
WHY DOES YORIHISA WANT TO HELP ME?
WE'LL NEED TO PREPARE, TENMA.
YEAH.
WHY ARE YOU HIDING, PRIESTESS?
"YOU MAY END UP HURTING... SOMEONE VERY CLOSE TO YOU."
HUH?
EH?!

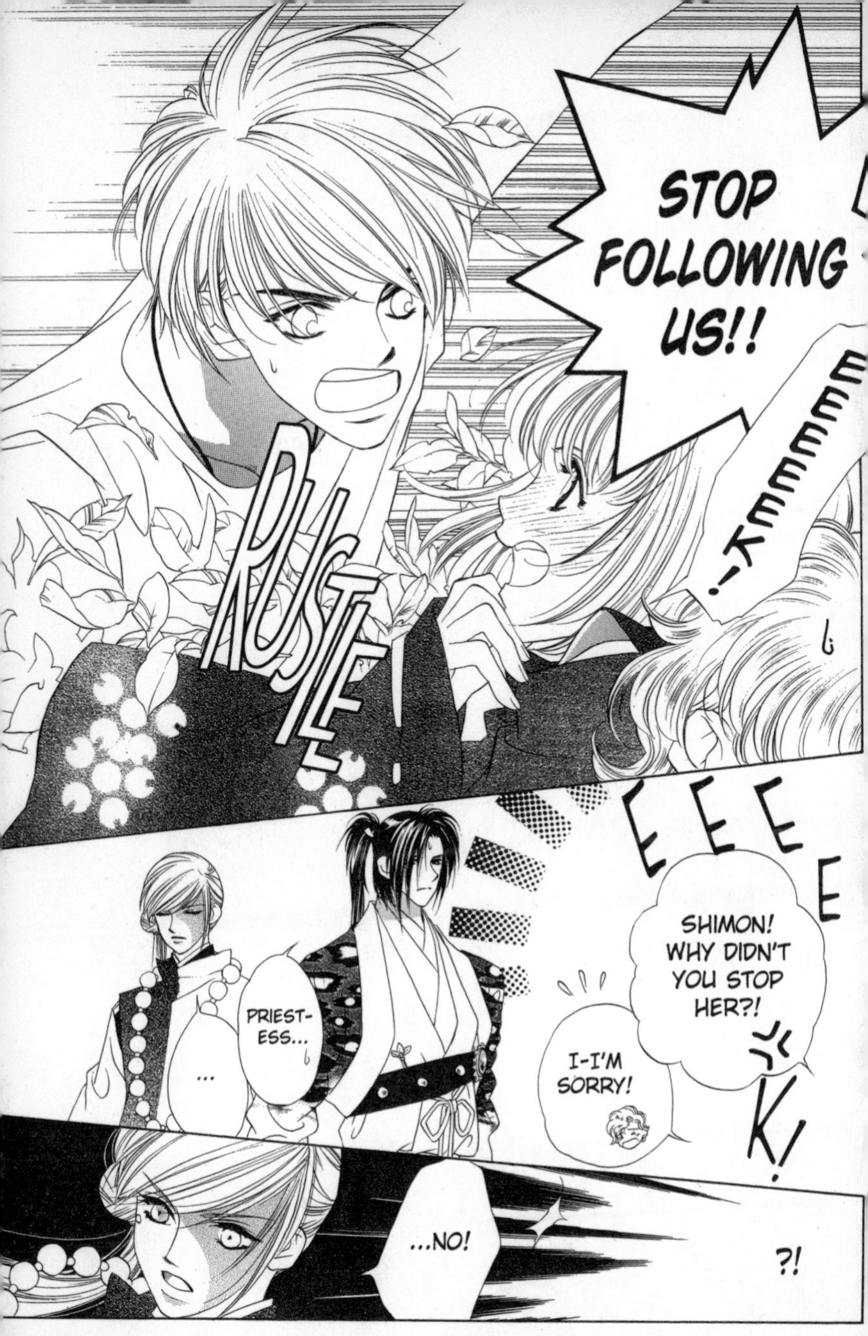
STOP FOLLOWING US!!
EEEEEEEK!
RUSTLE
EEEEK!
SHIMON! WHY DIDN'T YOU STOP HER?!
I-I'M SORRY!
PRIEST-ESS...
...
?!
...NO!

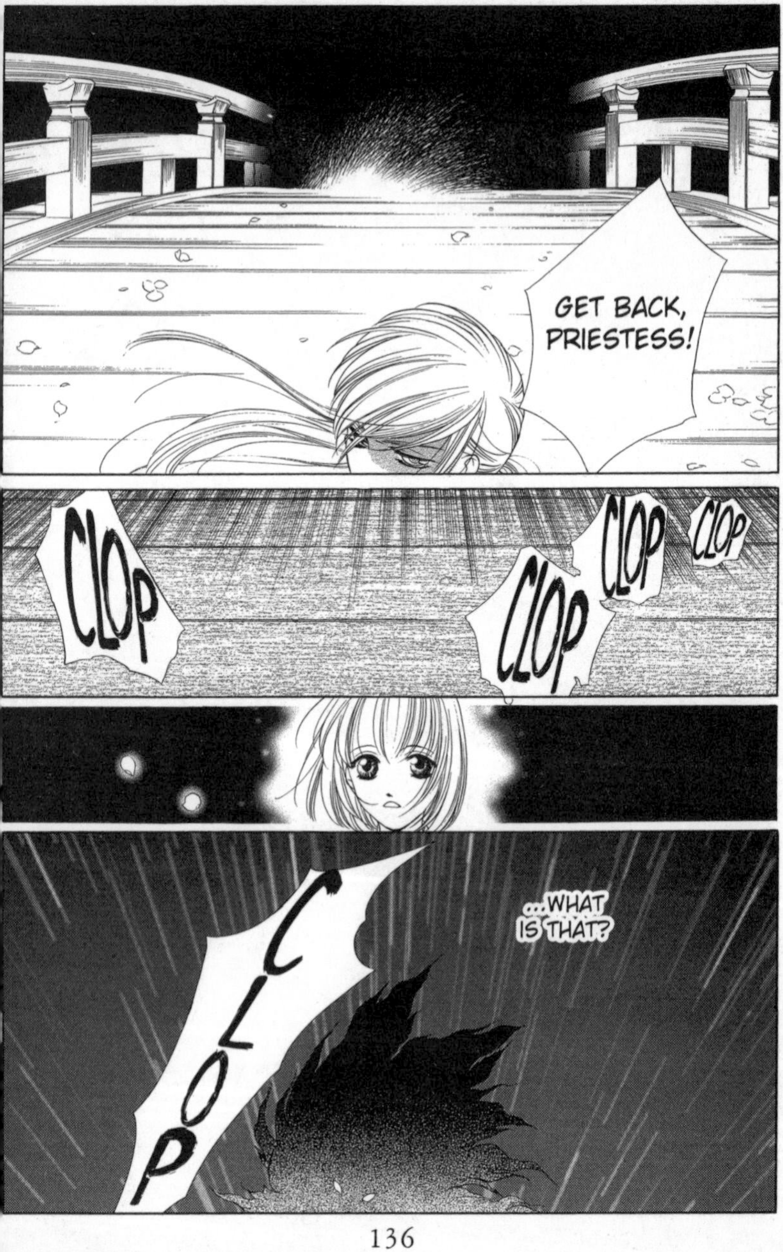
GET BACK, PRIESTESS!
CLOP
CLOP
CLOP
CLOP
...WHAT IS THAT?
CLOP

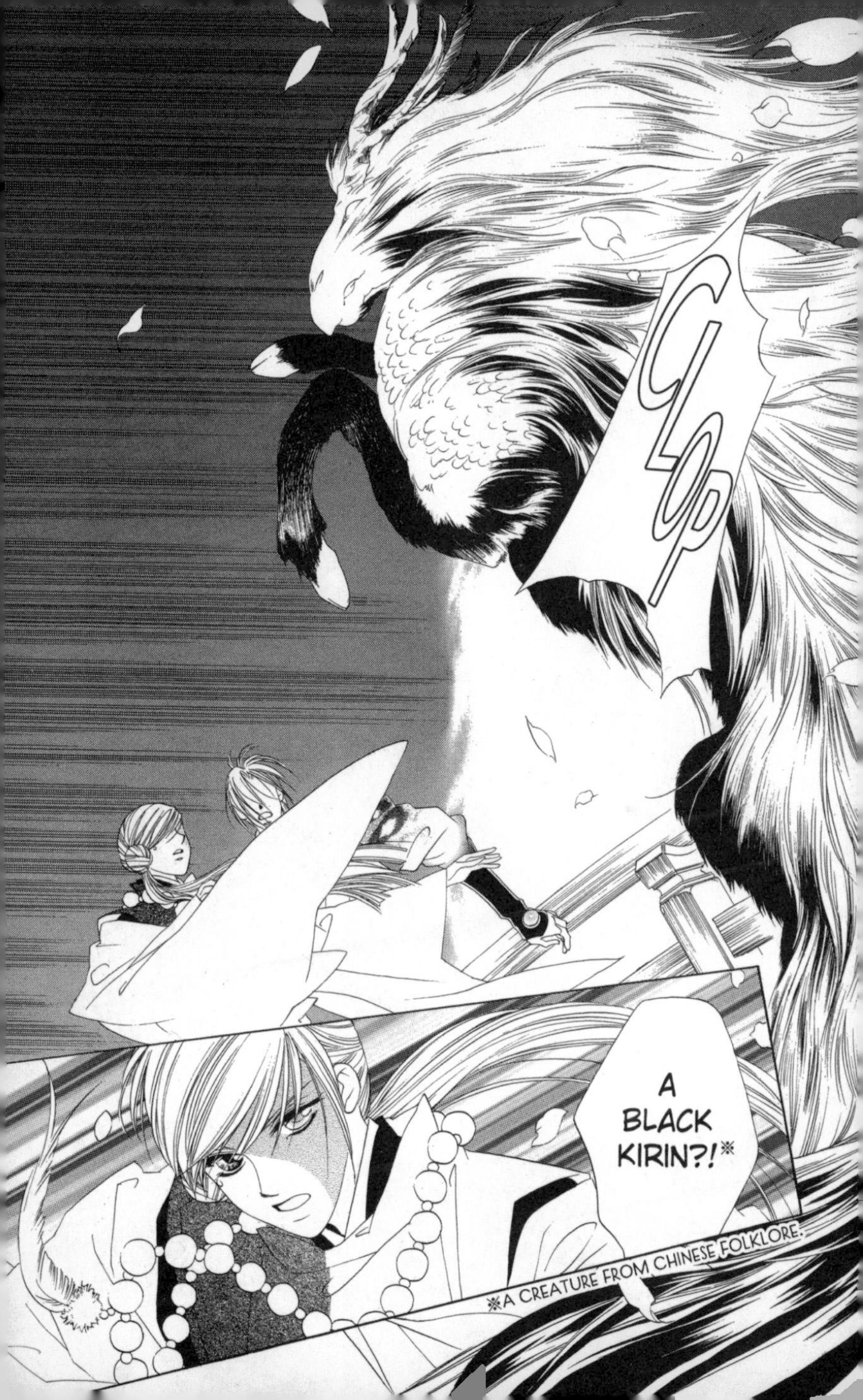
CLOP
A BLACK KIRIN?!※
※A CREATURE FROM CHINESE FOLKLORE.

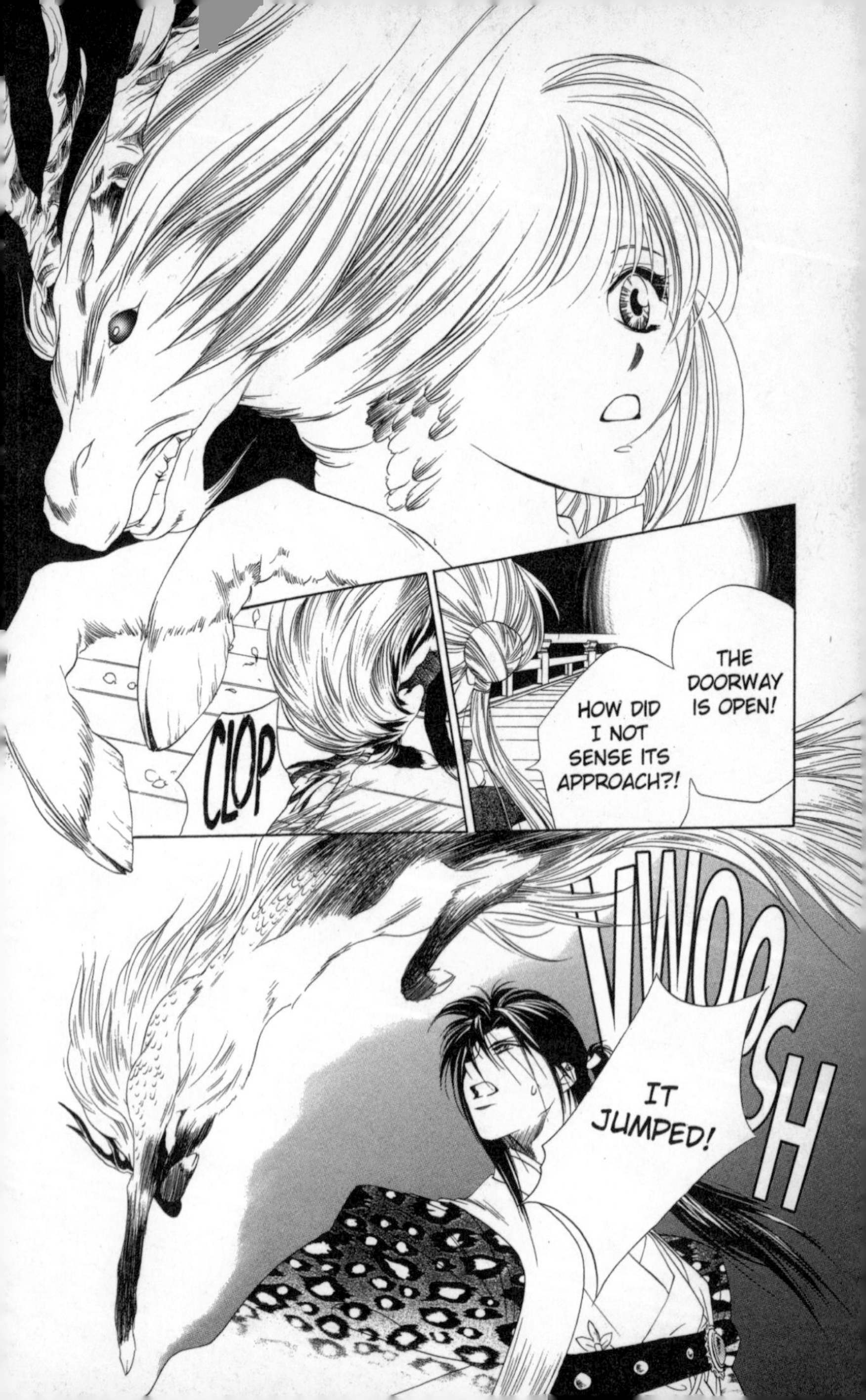
THE DOORWAY IS OPEN!
HOW DID I NOT SENSE ITS APPROACH?!
CLOP
WHOOSH
IT JUMPED!

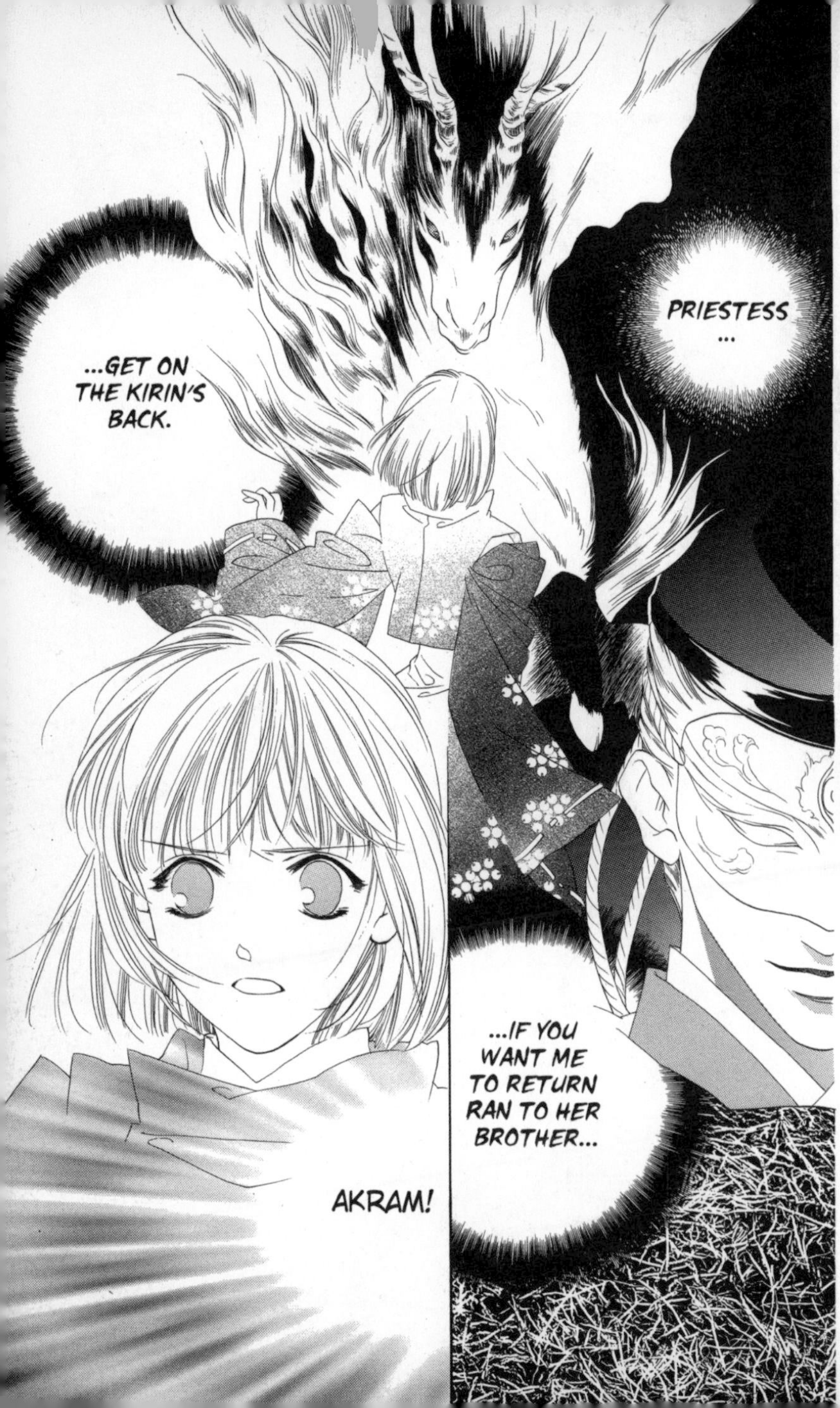
PRIESTESS...
...IF YOU WANT ME TO RETURN RAN TO HER BROTHER...
...GET ON THE KIRIN'S BACK.
AKRAM!

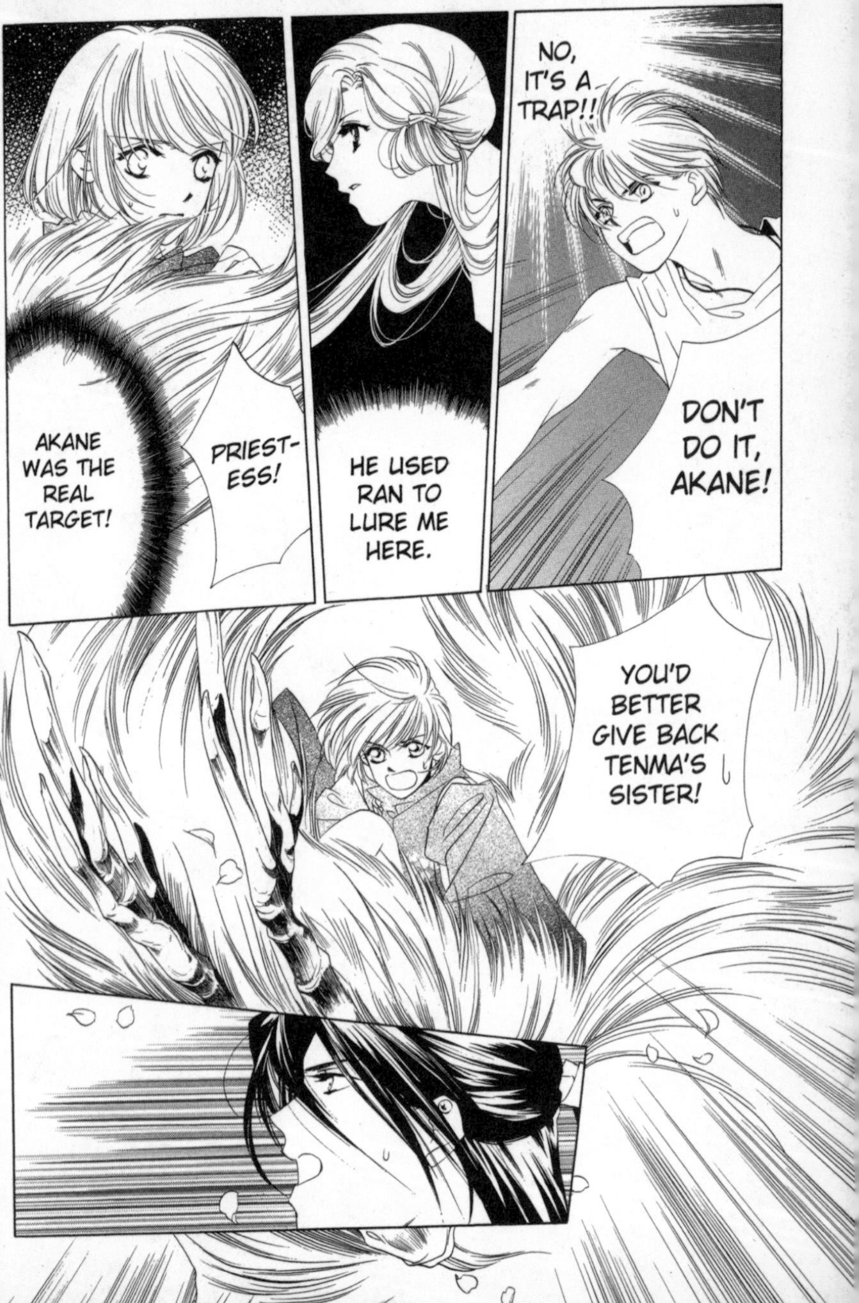
NO, IT'S A TRAP!!
DON'T DO IT, AKANE!
HE USED RAN TO LURE ME HERE.
PRIEST-ESS!
AKANE WAS THE REAL TARGET!
YOU'D BETTER GIVE BACK TENMA'S SISTER!

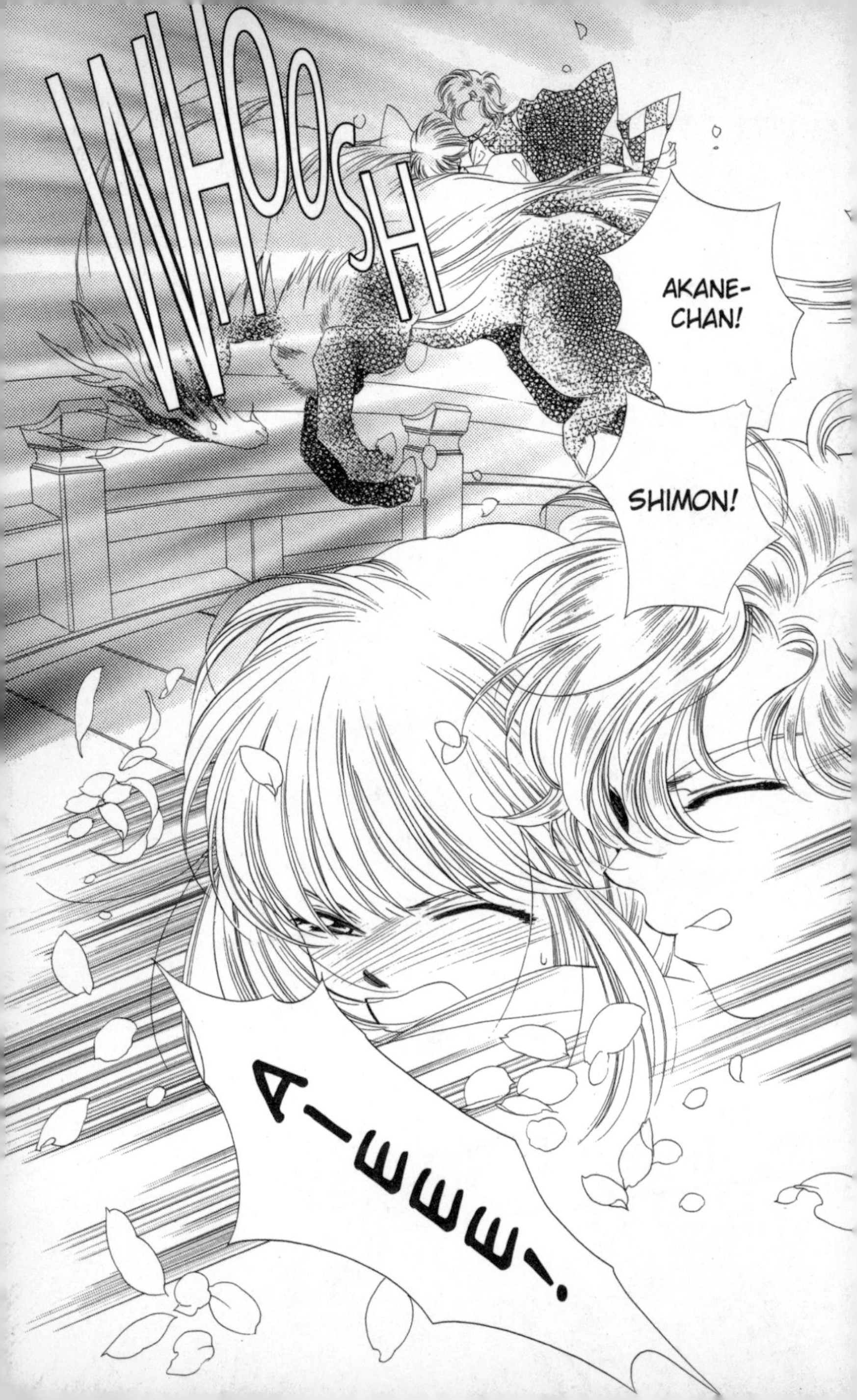
AKANE-CHAN!
SHIMON!
WHOOSH
A-EEEE-!

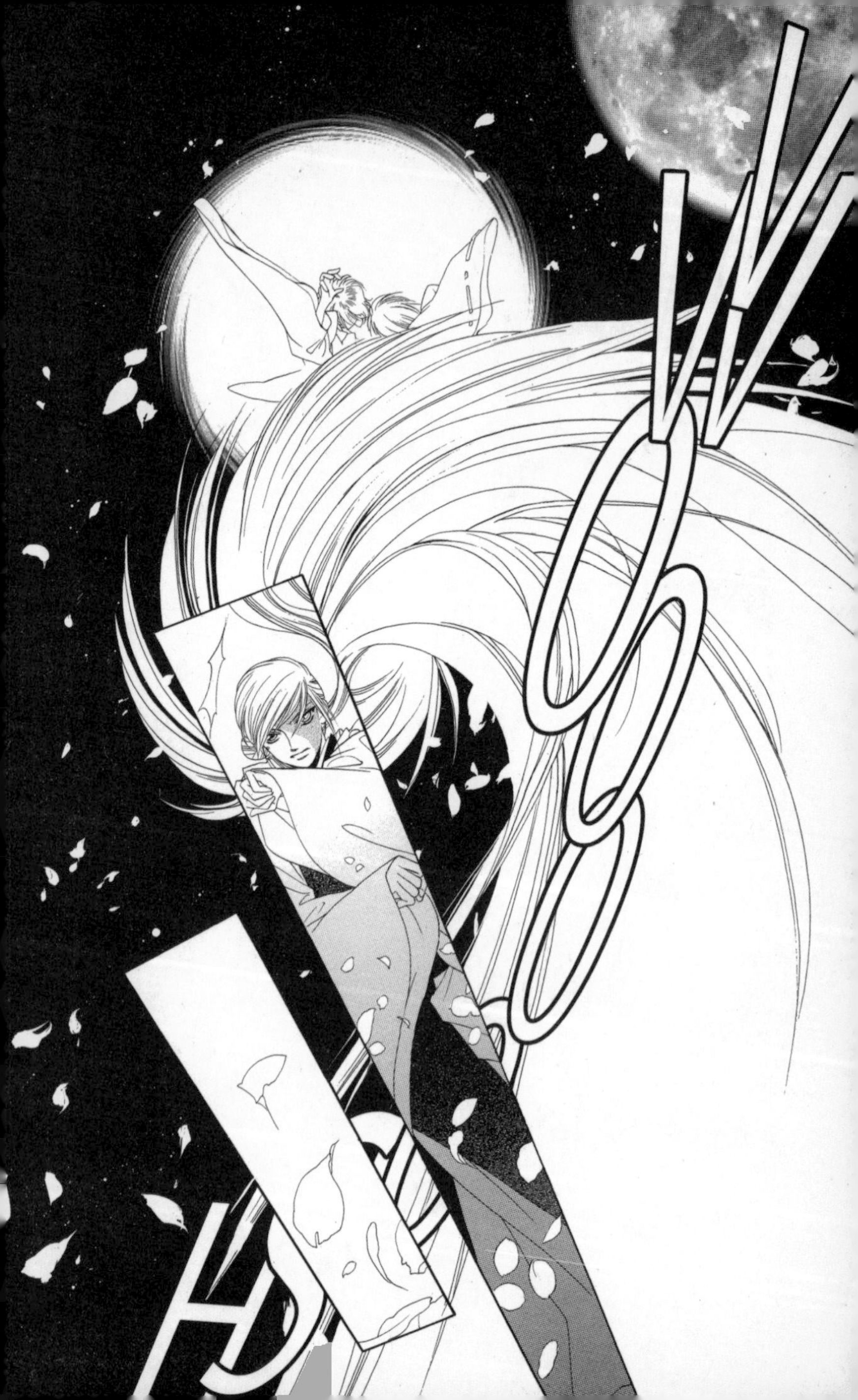

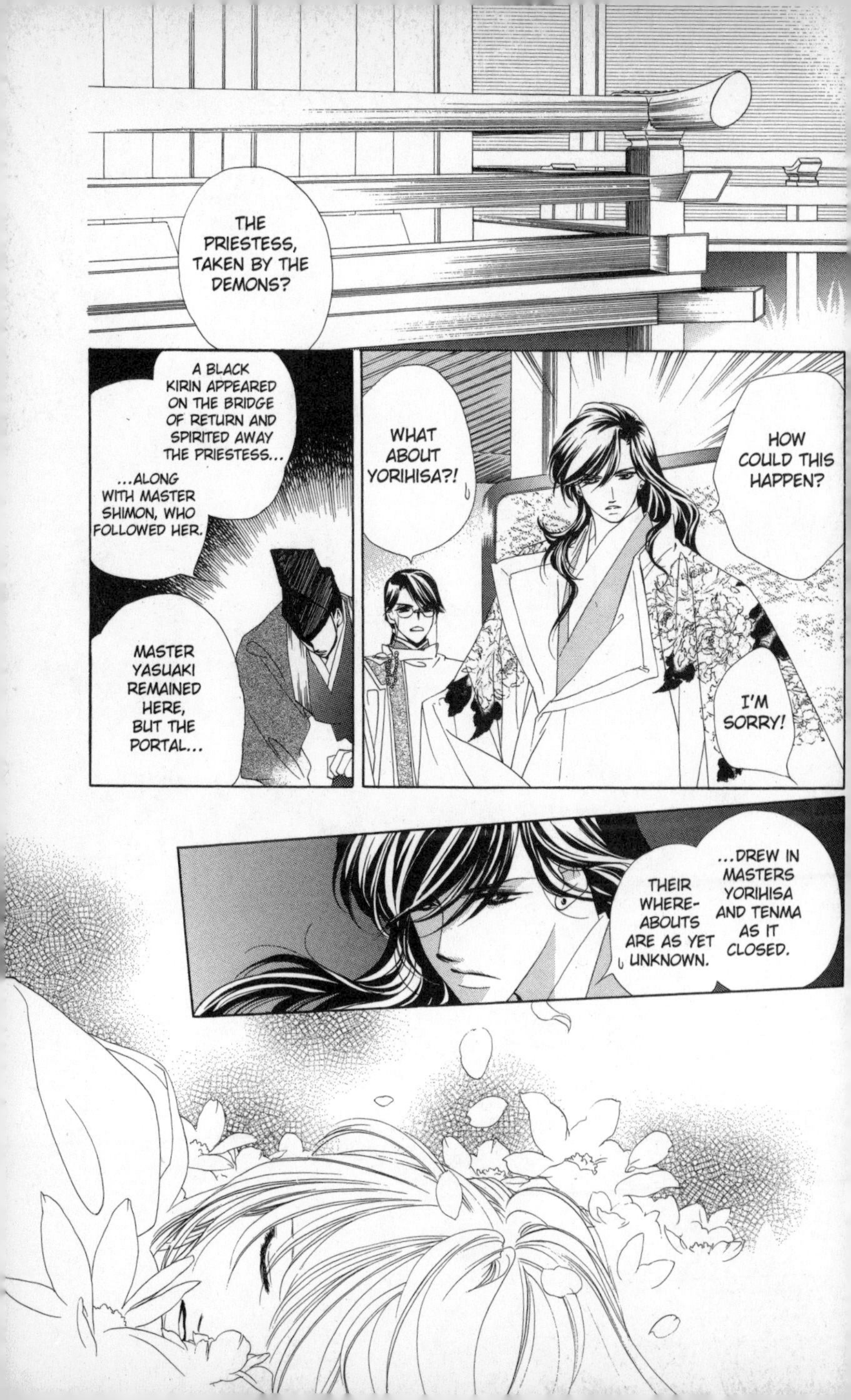
THE PRIESTESS, TAKEN BY THE DEMONS?
HOW COULD THIS HAPPEN?
WHAT ABOUT YORIHISA?!
I'M SORRY!
A BLACK KIRIN APPEARED ON THE BRIDGE OF RETURN AND SPIRITED AWAY THE PRIESTESS...
...ALONG WITH MASTER SHIMON, WHO FOLLOWED HER.
MASTER YASUAKI REMAINED HERE, BUT THE PORTAL...
...DREW IN MASTERS YORIHISA AND TENMA AS IT CLOSED.
THEIR WHERE-ABOUTS ARE AS YET UNKNOWN.

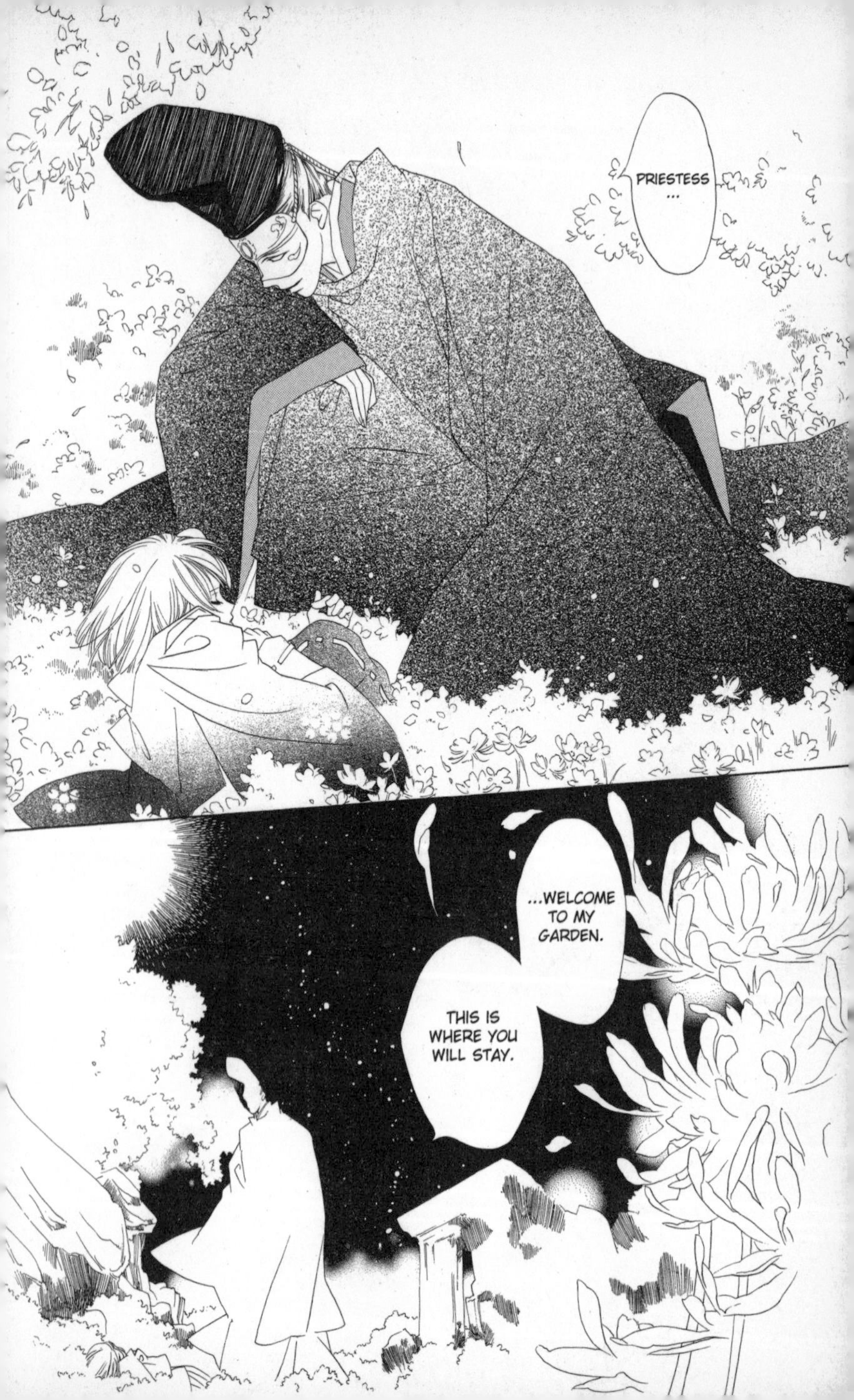
PRIESTESS ...
...WELCOME TO MY GARDEN.
THIS IS WHERE YOU WILL STAY.

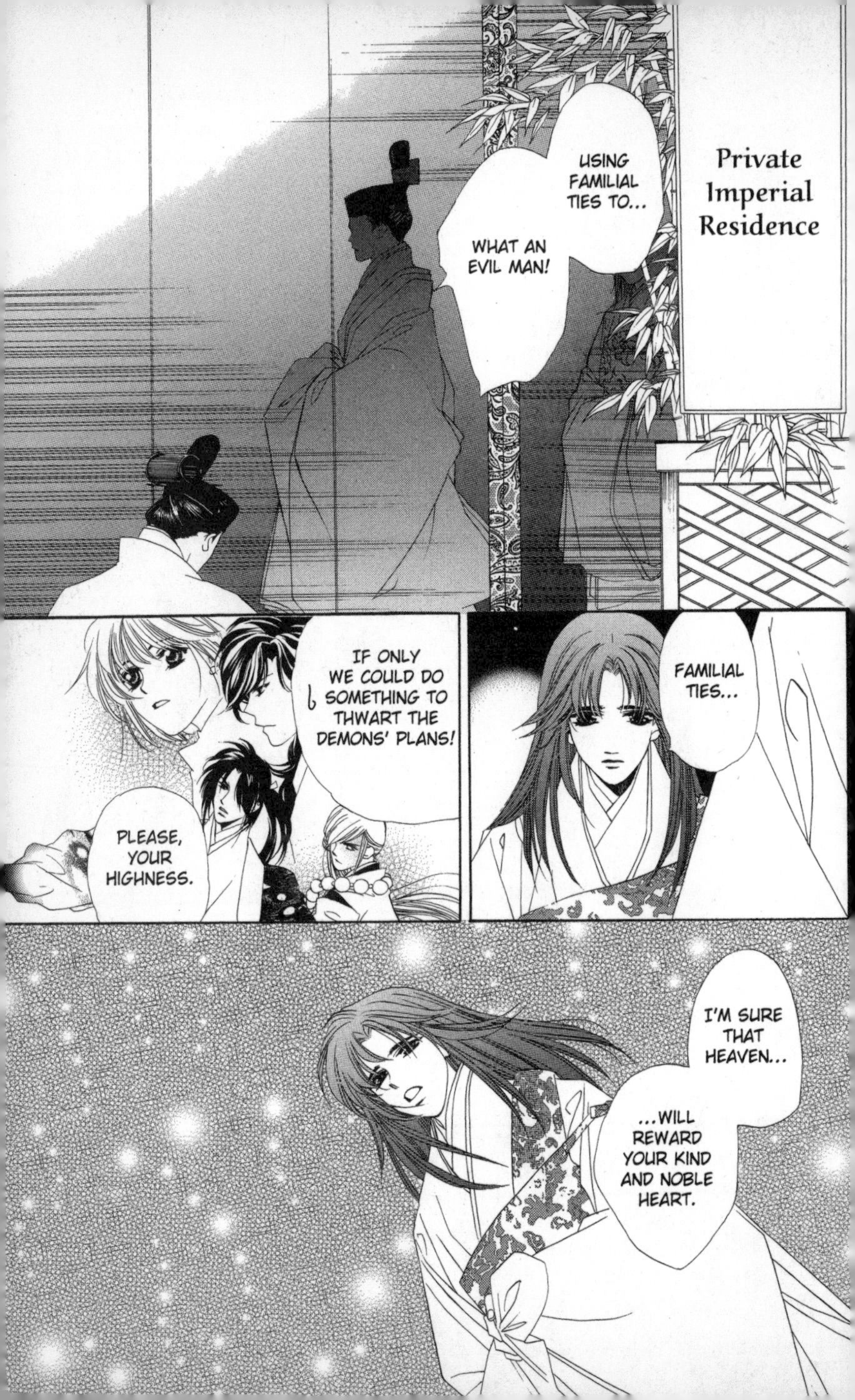
Private Imperial Residence
USING FAMILIAL TIES TO...
WHAT AN EVIL MAN!
FAMILIAL TIES...
IF ONLY WE COULD DO SOMETHING TO THWART THE DEMONS' PLANS!
PLEASE, YOUR HIGHNESS.
I'M SURE THAT HEAVEN...
...WILL REWARD YOUR KIND AND NOBLE HEART.

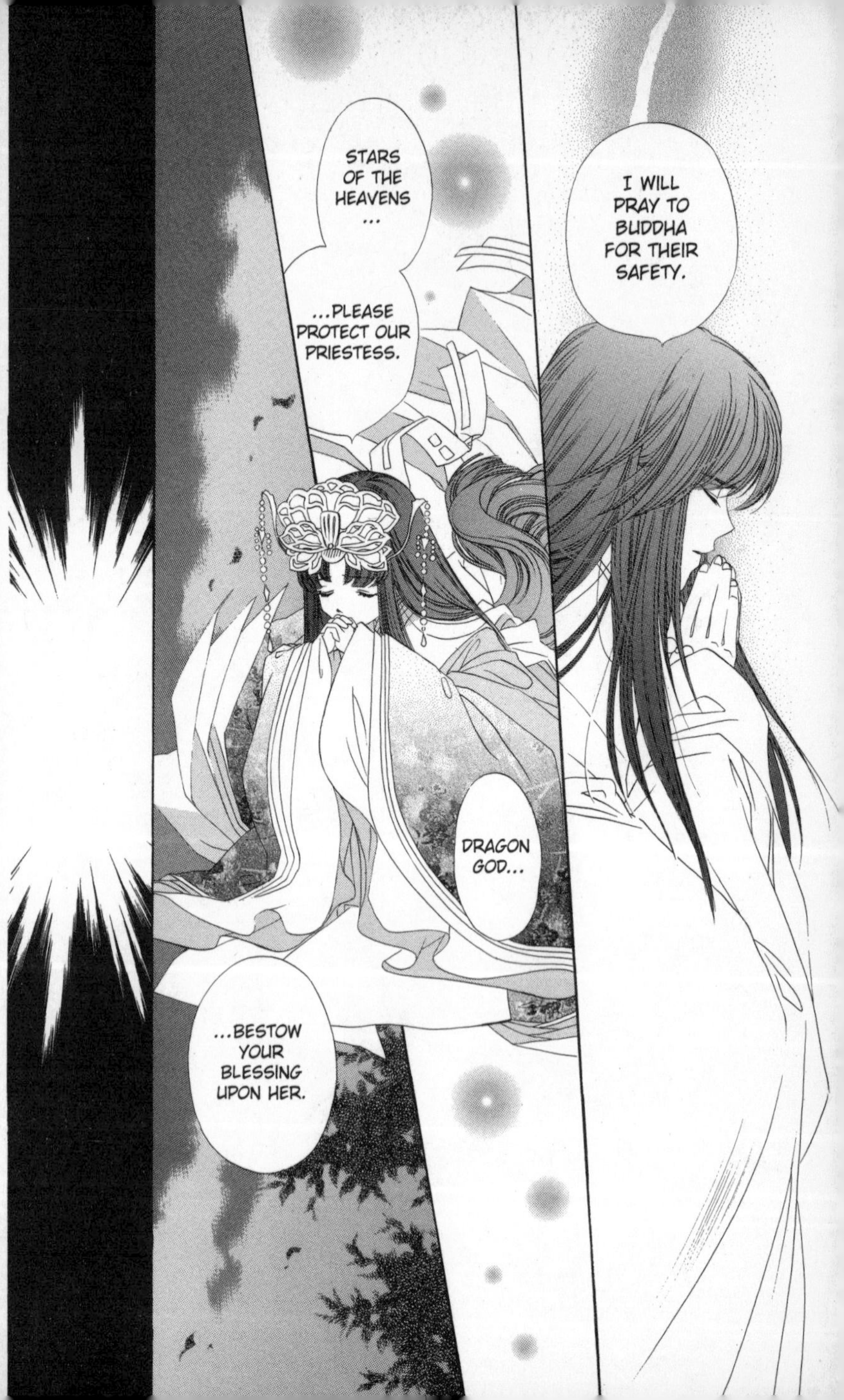
I WILL PRAY TO BUDDHA FOR THEIR SAFETY.
STARS OF THE HEAVENS ...
...PLEASE PROTECT OUR PRIESTESS.
DRAGON GOD...
...BESTOW YOUR BLESSING UPON HER.

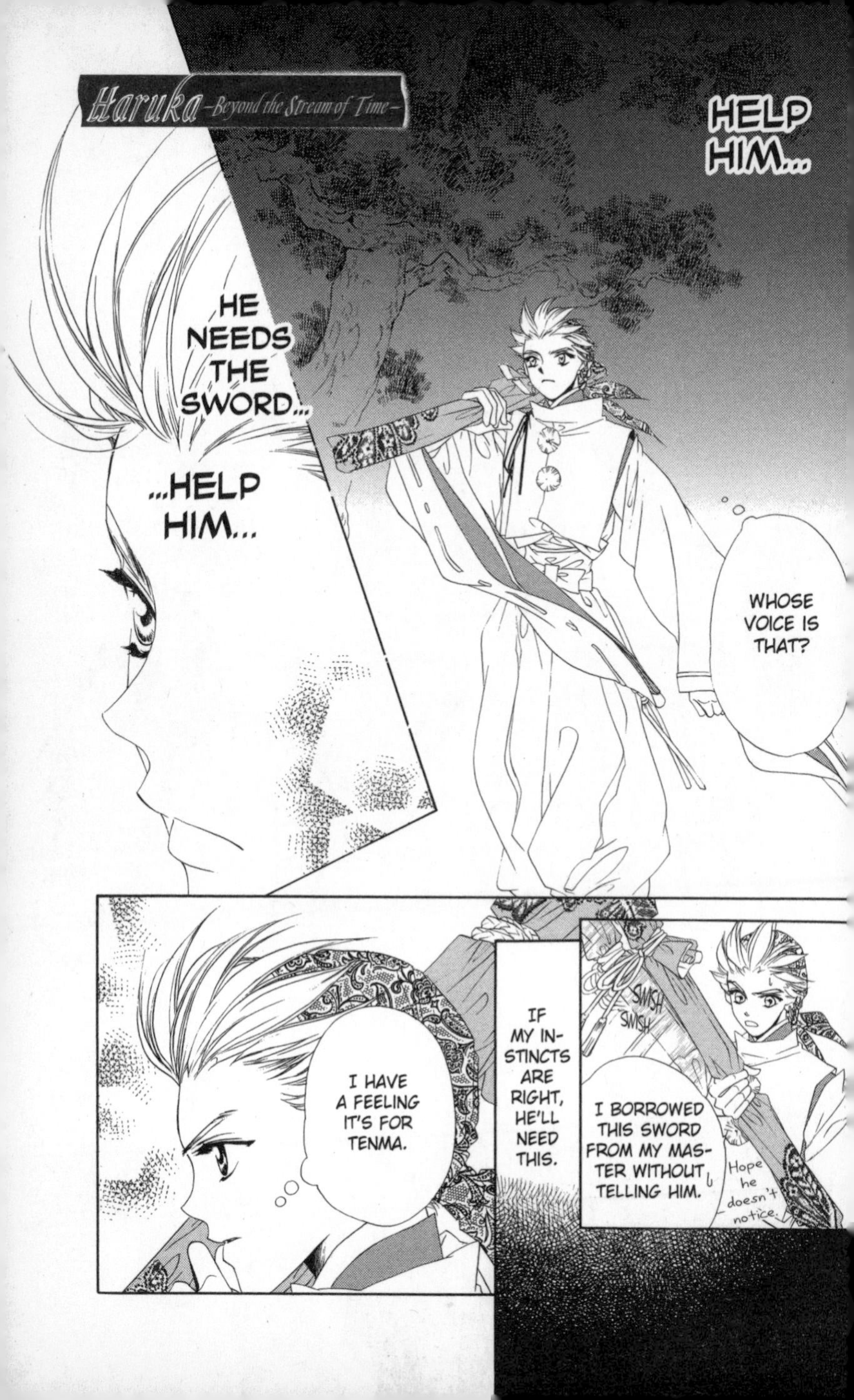
HELP HIM...
WHOSE VOICE IS THAT?
HE NEEDS THE SWORD...
...HELP HIM...
SWISH
SWISH
I BORROWED THIS SWORD FROM MY MASTER WITHOUT TELLING HIM.
Hope he doesn't notice.
IF MY INSTINCTS ARE RIGHT, HE'LL NEED THIS.
I HAVE A FEELING IT'S FOR TENMA.

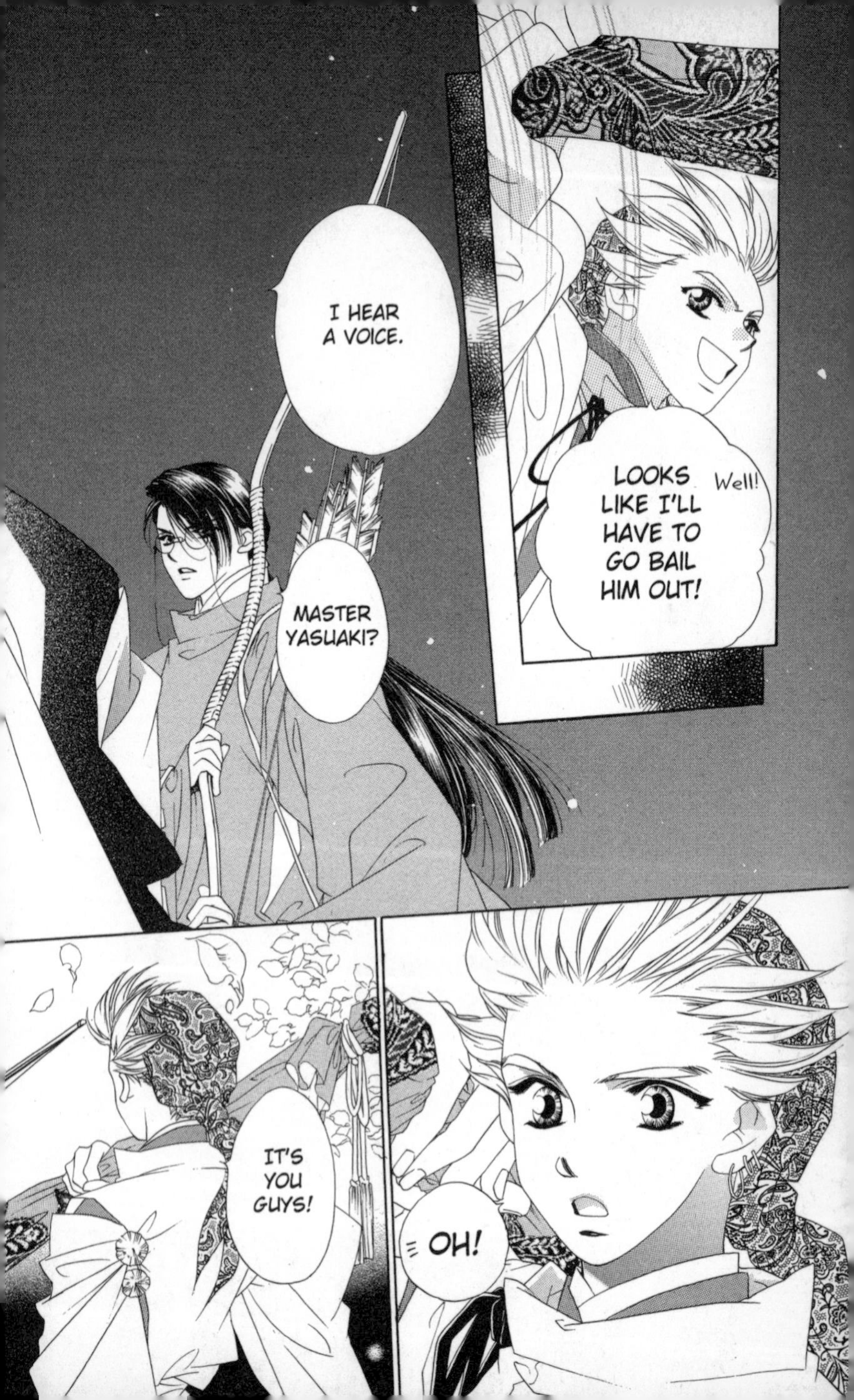
Well!
LOOKS LIKE I'LL HAVE TO GO BAIL HIM OUT!
I HEAR A VOICE.
MASTER YASUAKI?
OH!
IT'S YOU GUYS!

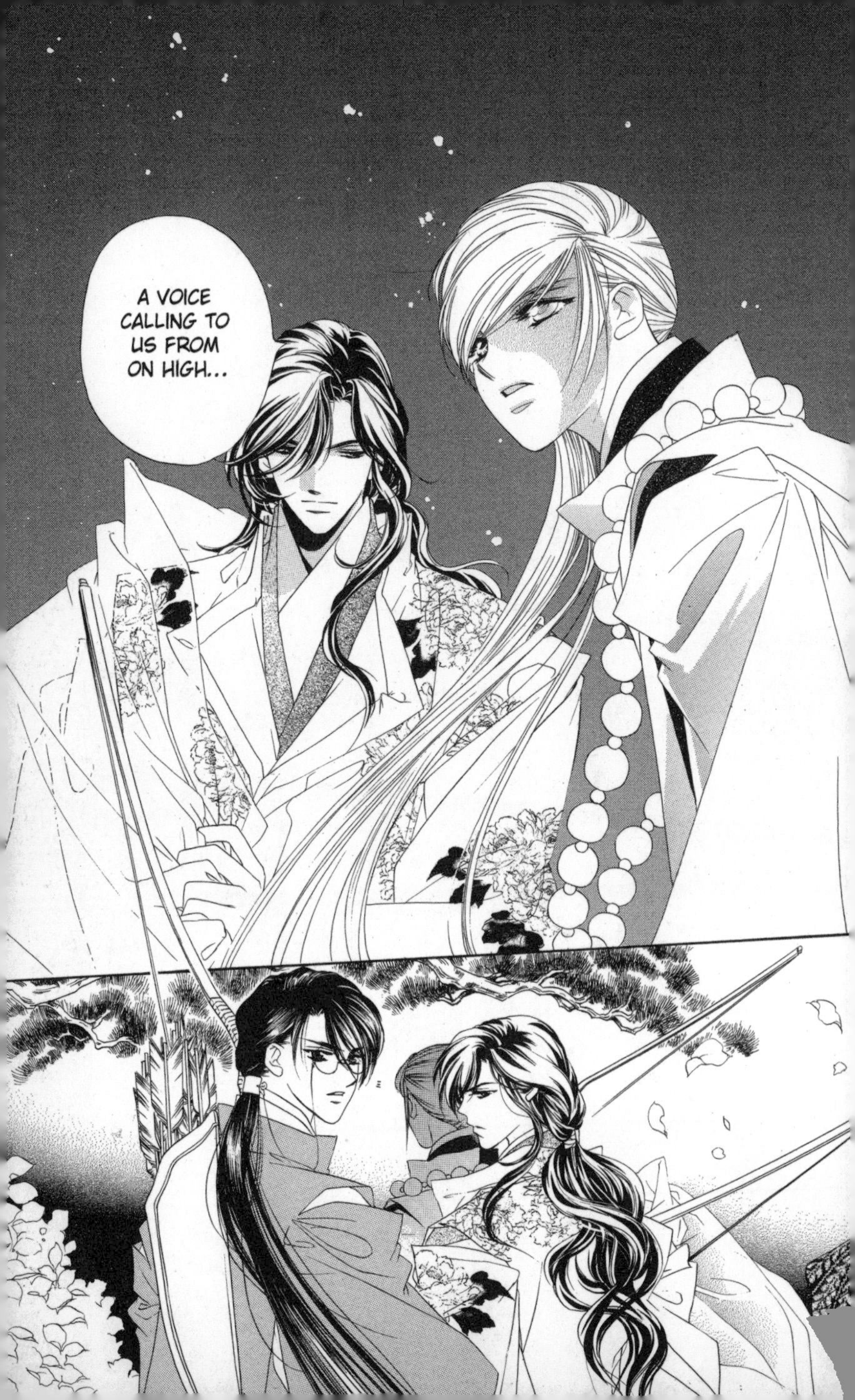
A VOICE CALLING TO US FROM ON HIGH...

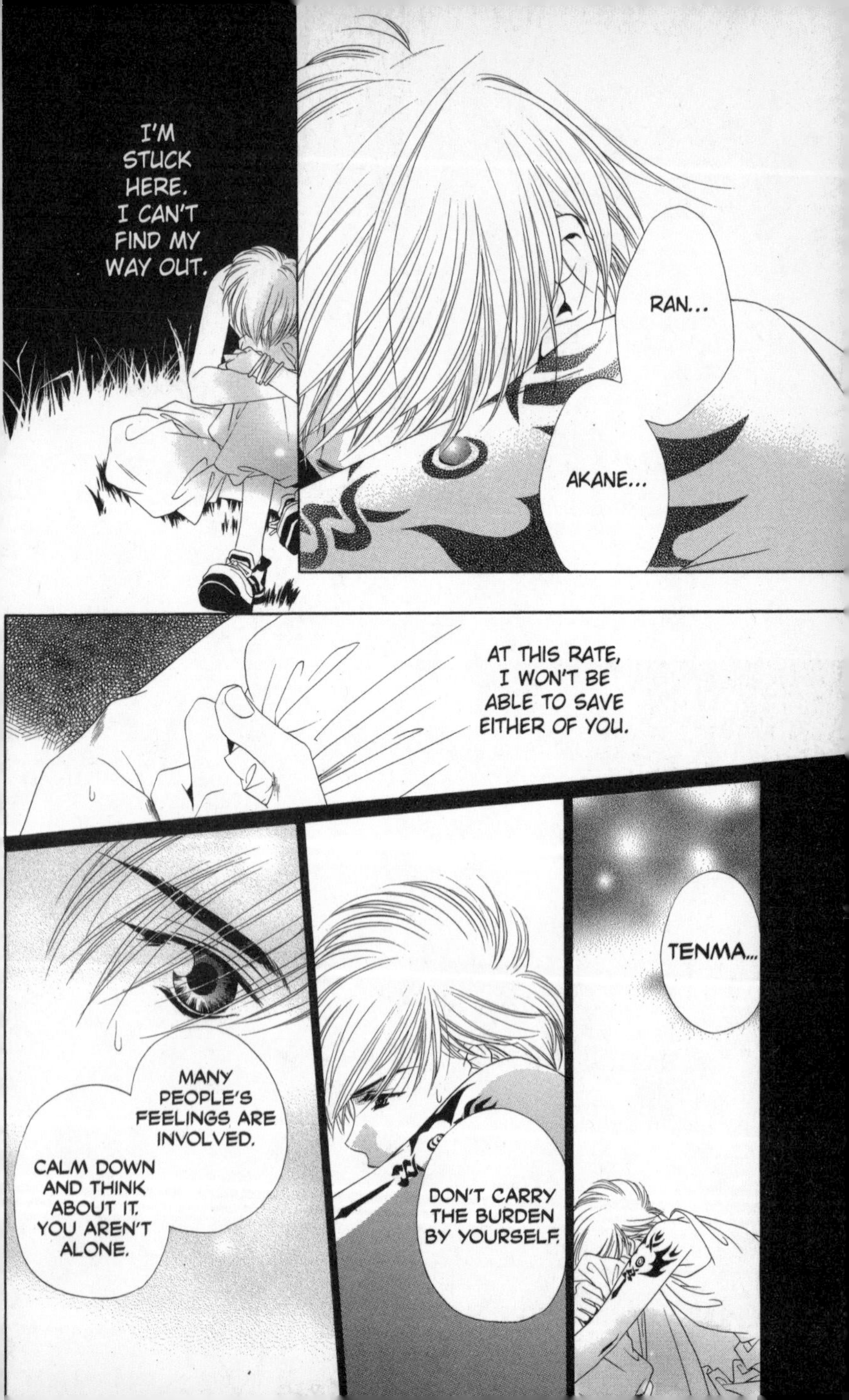
RAN...
AKANE...
I'M STUCK HERE. I CAN'T FIND MY WAY OUT.
AT THIS RATE, I WON'T BE ABLE TO SAVE EITHER OF YOU.
TENMA...
DON'T CARRY THE BURDEN BY YOURSELF.
MANY PEOPLE'S FEELINGS ARE INVOLVED.
CALM DOWN AND THINK ABOUT IT. YOU AREN'T ALONE.

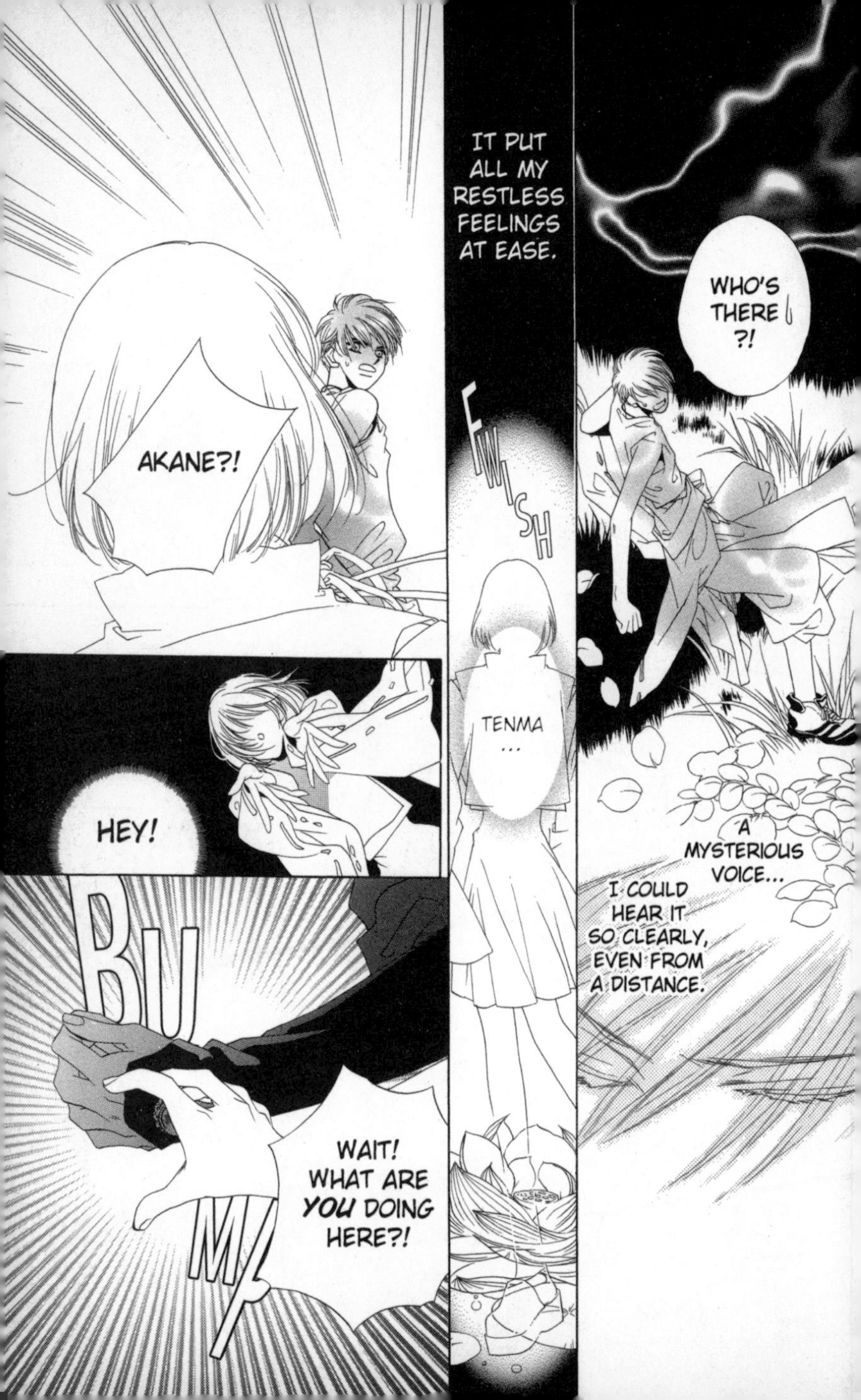
WHO'S THERE?!
A MYSTERIOUS VOICE...
I COULD HEAR IT SO CLEARLY, EVEN FROM A DISTANCE.
IT PUT ALL MY RESTLESS FEELINGS AT EASE.
FWISH
TENMA ...
AKANE?!
HEY!
BUM
WAIT! WHAT ARE *YOU* DOING HERE?!

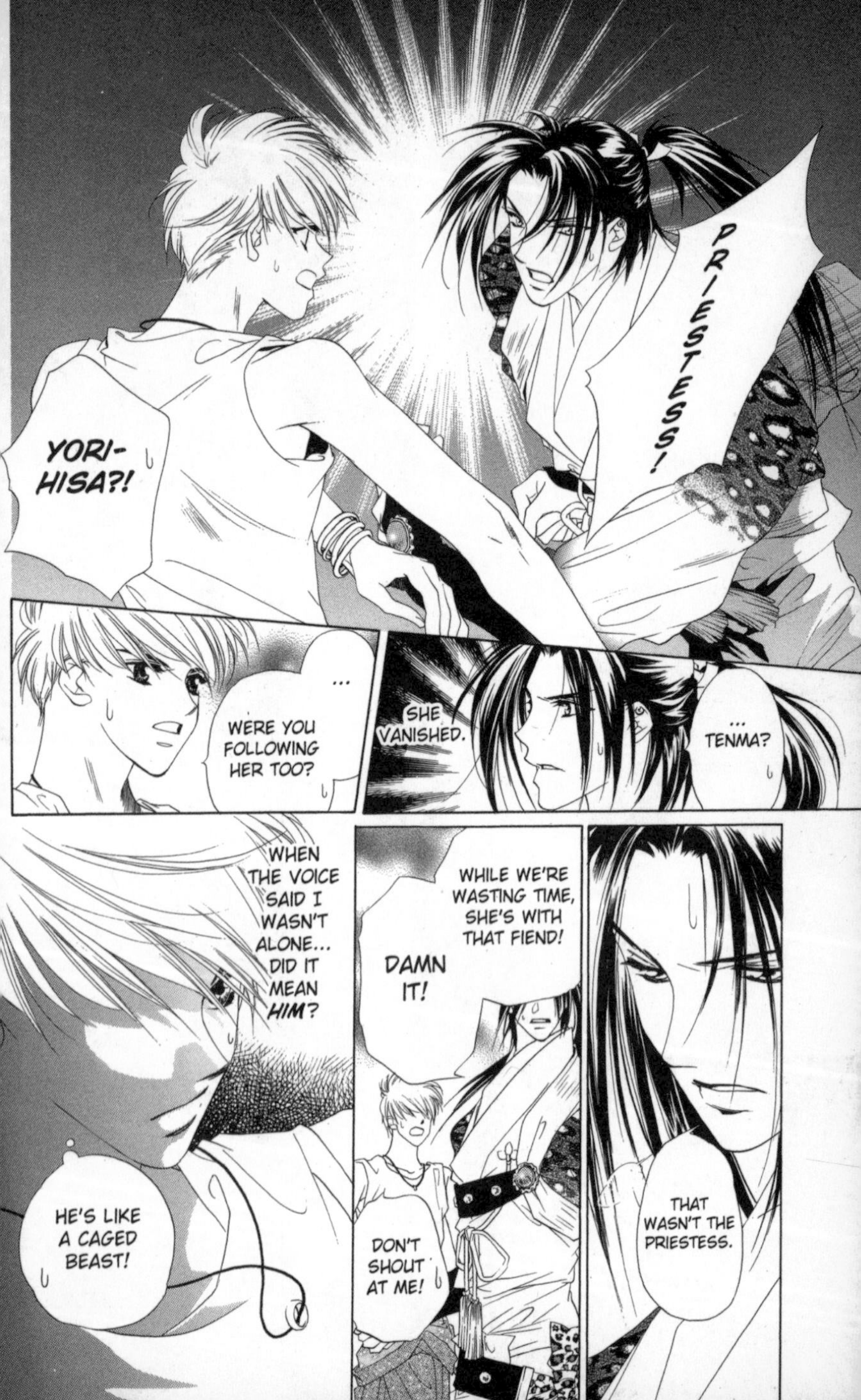
PRIESTESS!
YORI-HISA?!
... TENMA?
SHE VANISHED.
... WERE YOU FOLLOWING HER TOO?
THAT WASN'T THE PRIESTESS.
WHILE WE'RE WASTING TIME, SHE'S WITH THAT FIEND!
DAMN IT!
DON'T SHOUT AT ME!
WHEN THE VOICE SAID I WASN'T ALONE... DID IT MEAN *HIM*?
HE'S LIKE A CAGED BEAST!

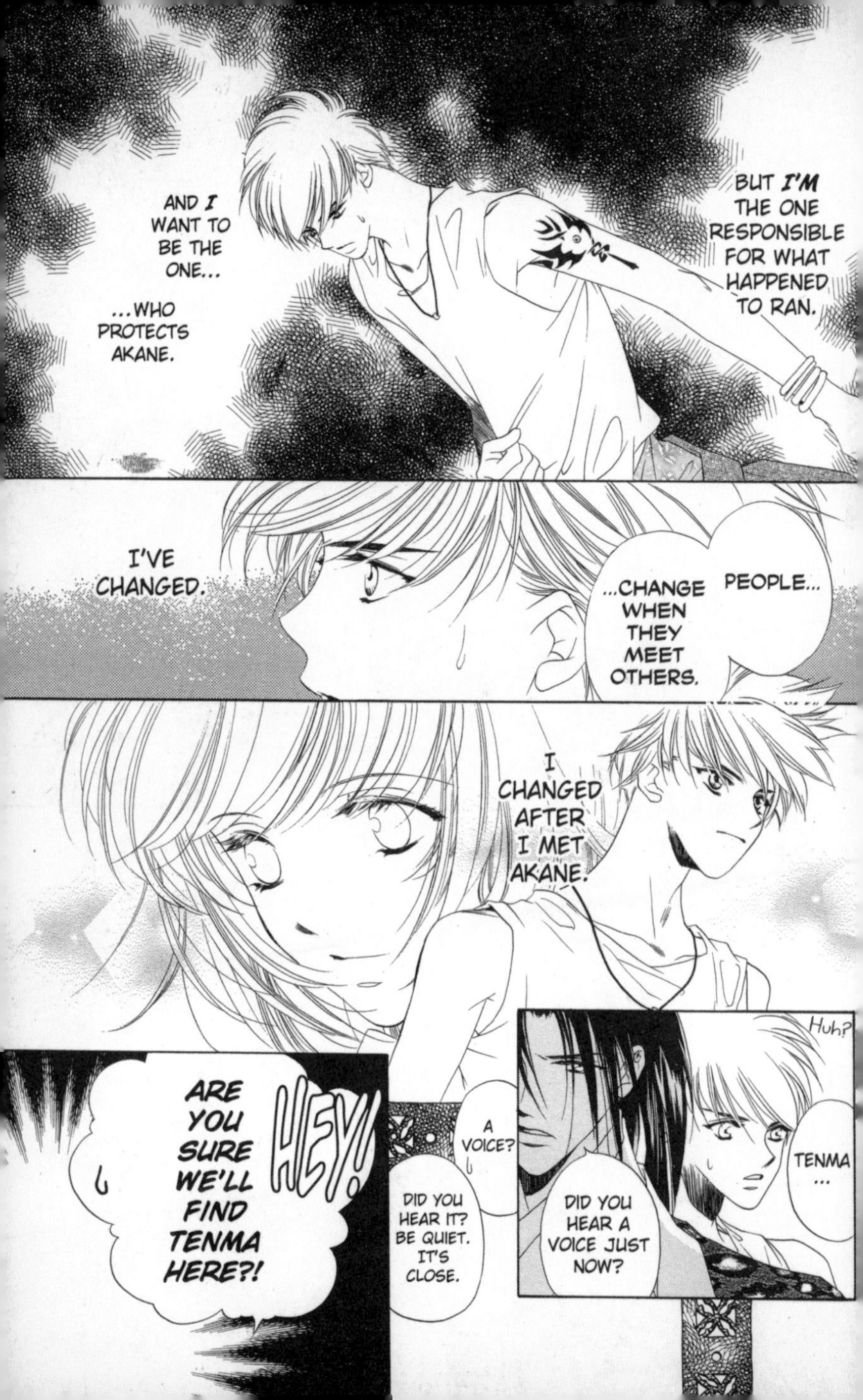
BUT I'M THE ONE RESPONSIBLE FOR WHAT HAPPENED TO RAN.
AND I WANT TO BE THE ONE...
...WHO PROTECTS AKANE.
PEOPLE...
...CHANGE WHEN THEY MEET OTHERS.
I'VE CHANGED.
I CHANGED AFTER I MET AKANE.
Huh?
TENMA ...
DID YOU HEAR A VOICE JUST NOW?
A VOICE?
DID YOU HEAR IT? BE QUIET. IT'S CLOSE.
HEY!
ARE YOU SURE WE'LL FIND TENMA HERE?!

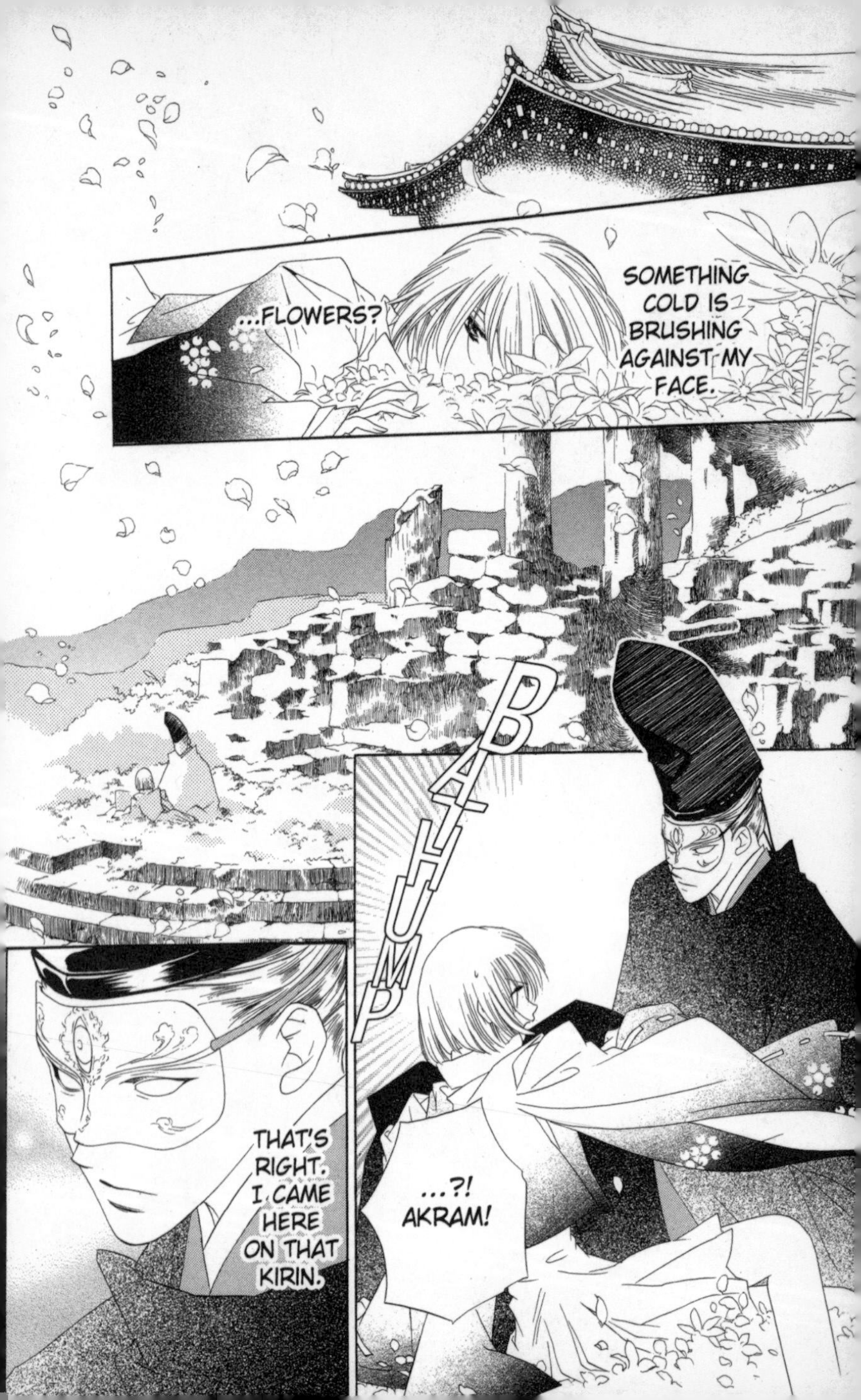
SOMETHING COLD IS BRUSHING AGAINST MY FACE.
...FLOWERS?
BATHUMP
...?! AKRAM!
THAT'S RIGHT. I CAME HERE ON THAT KIRIN.

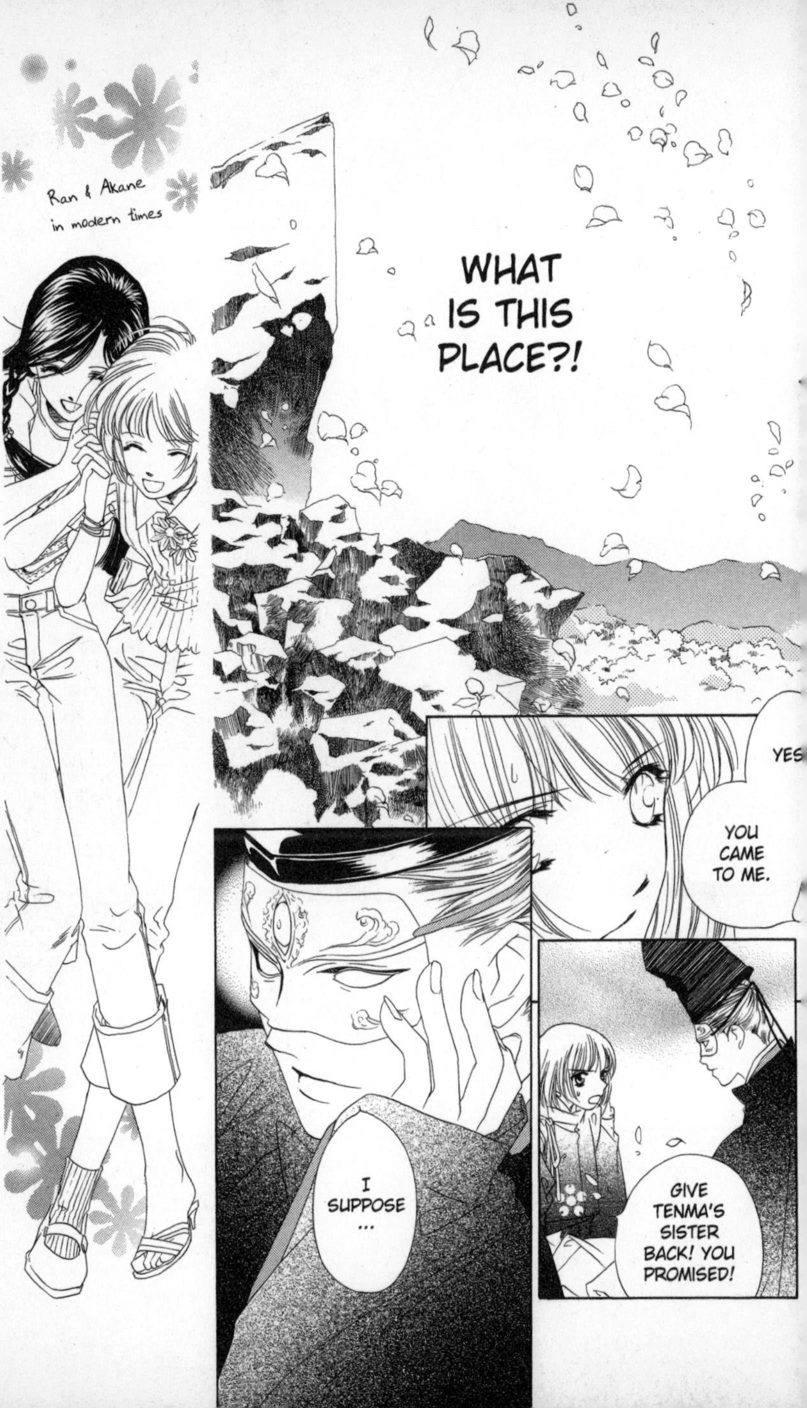
WHAT IS THIS PLACE?!
YES
YOU CAME TO ME.
GIVE TENMA'S SISTER BACK! YOU PROMISED!
I SUPPOSE ...
Ran & Akane in modern times

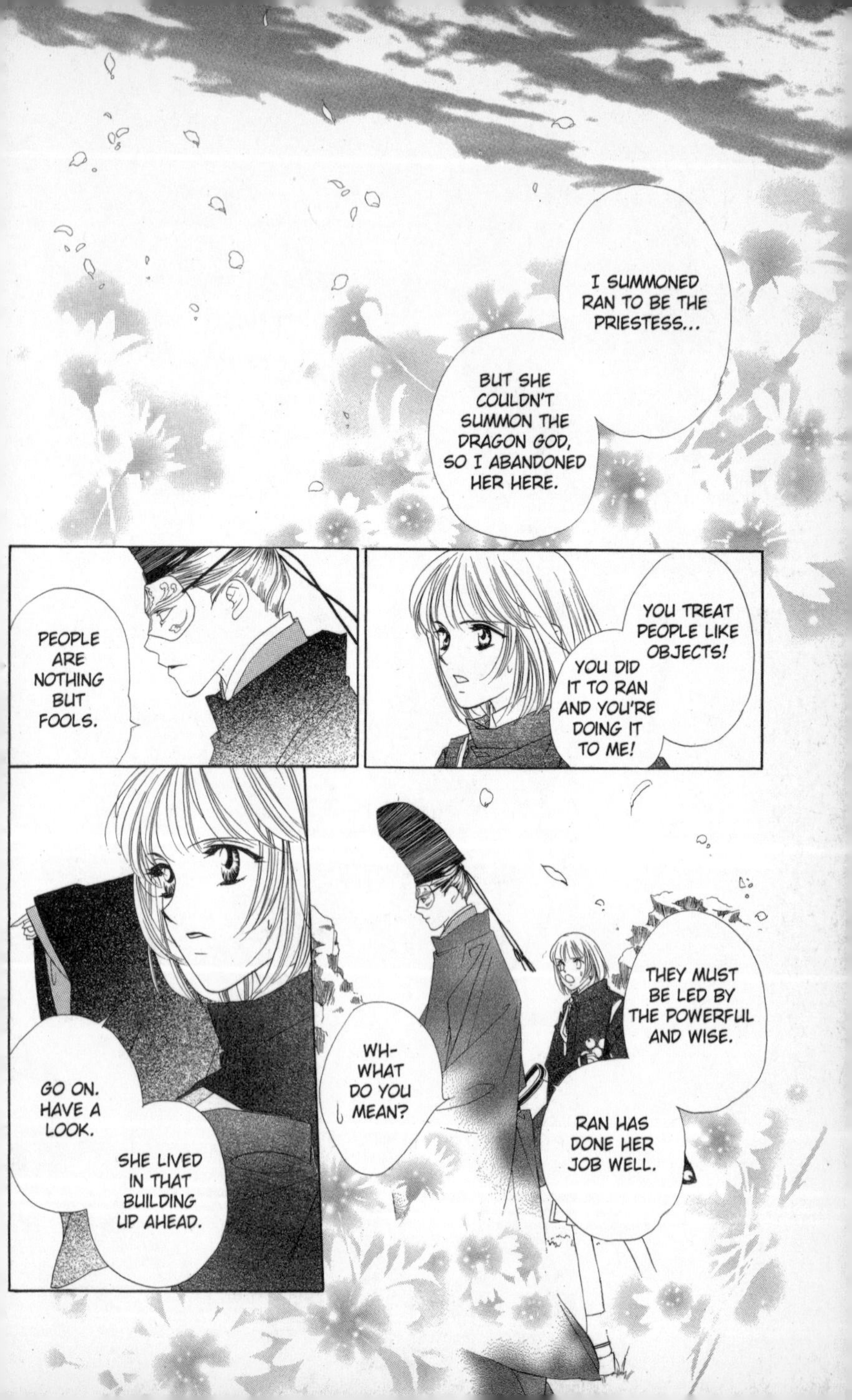
I SUMMONED RAN TO BE THE PRIESTESS...
BUT SHE COULDN'T SUMMON THE DRAGON GOD, SO I ABANDONED HER HERE.
YOU TREAT PEOPLE LIKE OBJECTS!
YOU DID IT TO RAN AND YOU'RE DOING IT TO ME!
PEOPLE ARE NOTHING BUT FOOLS.
THEY MUST BE LED BY THE POWERFUL AND WISE.
RAN HAS DONE HER JOB WELL.
WH-WHAT DO YOU MEAN?
GO ON. HAVE A LOOK.
SHE LIVED IN THAT BUILDING UP AHEAD.

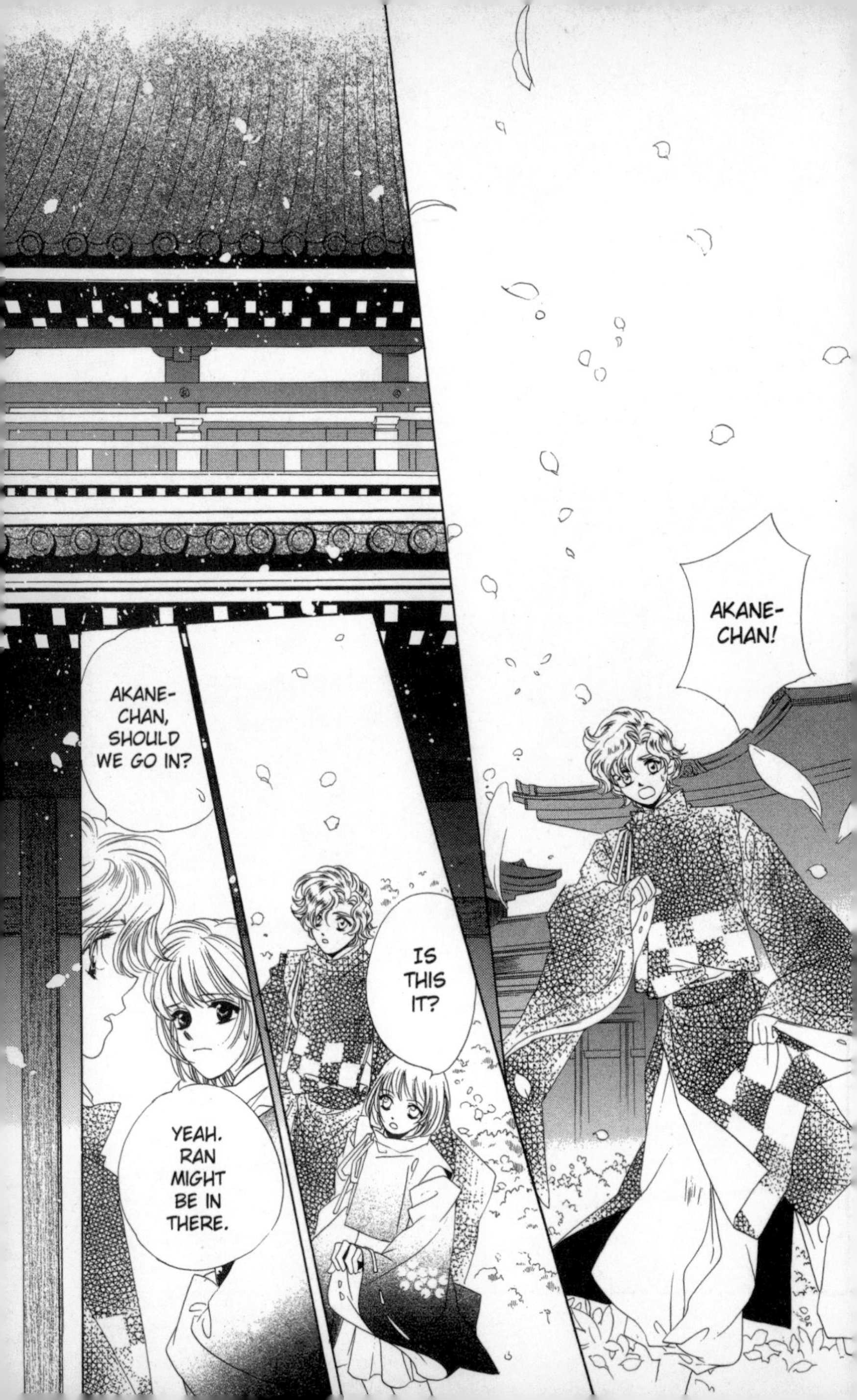
AKANE-CHAN!
IS THIS IT?
AKANE-CHAN, SHOULD WE GO IN?
YEAH. RAN MIGHT BE IN THERE.

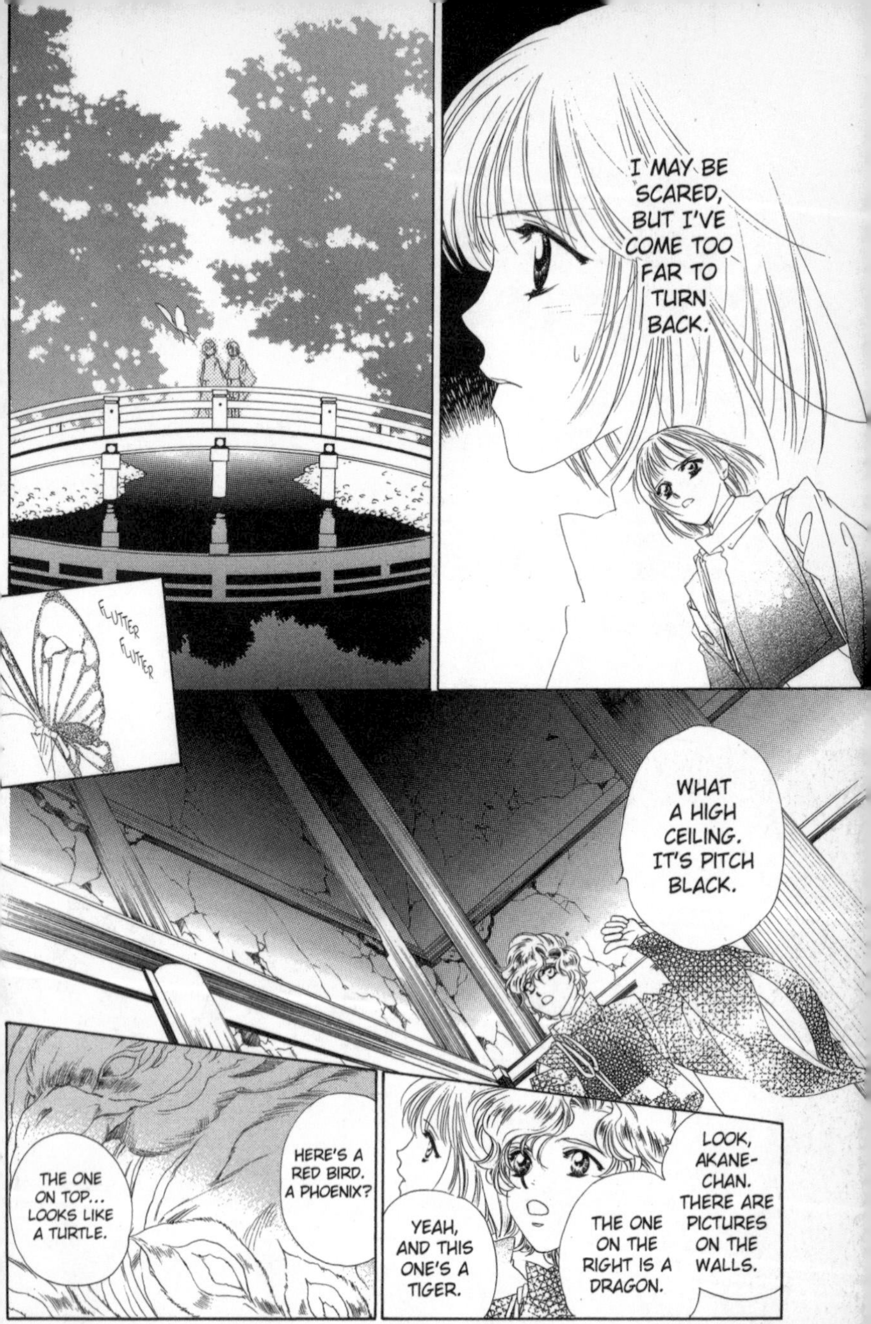
I MAY BE SCARED, BUT I'VE COME TOO FAR TO TURN BACK.
FLUTTER FLUTTER
WHAT A HIGH CEILING. IT'S PITCH BLACK.
LOOK, AKANE-CHAN. THERE ARE PICTURES ON THE WALLS.
THE ONE ON THE RIGHT IS A DRAGON.
YEAH, AND THIS ONE'S A TIGER.
HERE'S A RED BIRD. A PHOENIX?
THE ONE ON TOP... LOOKS LIKE A TURTLE.

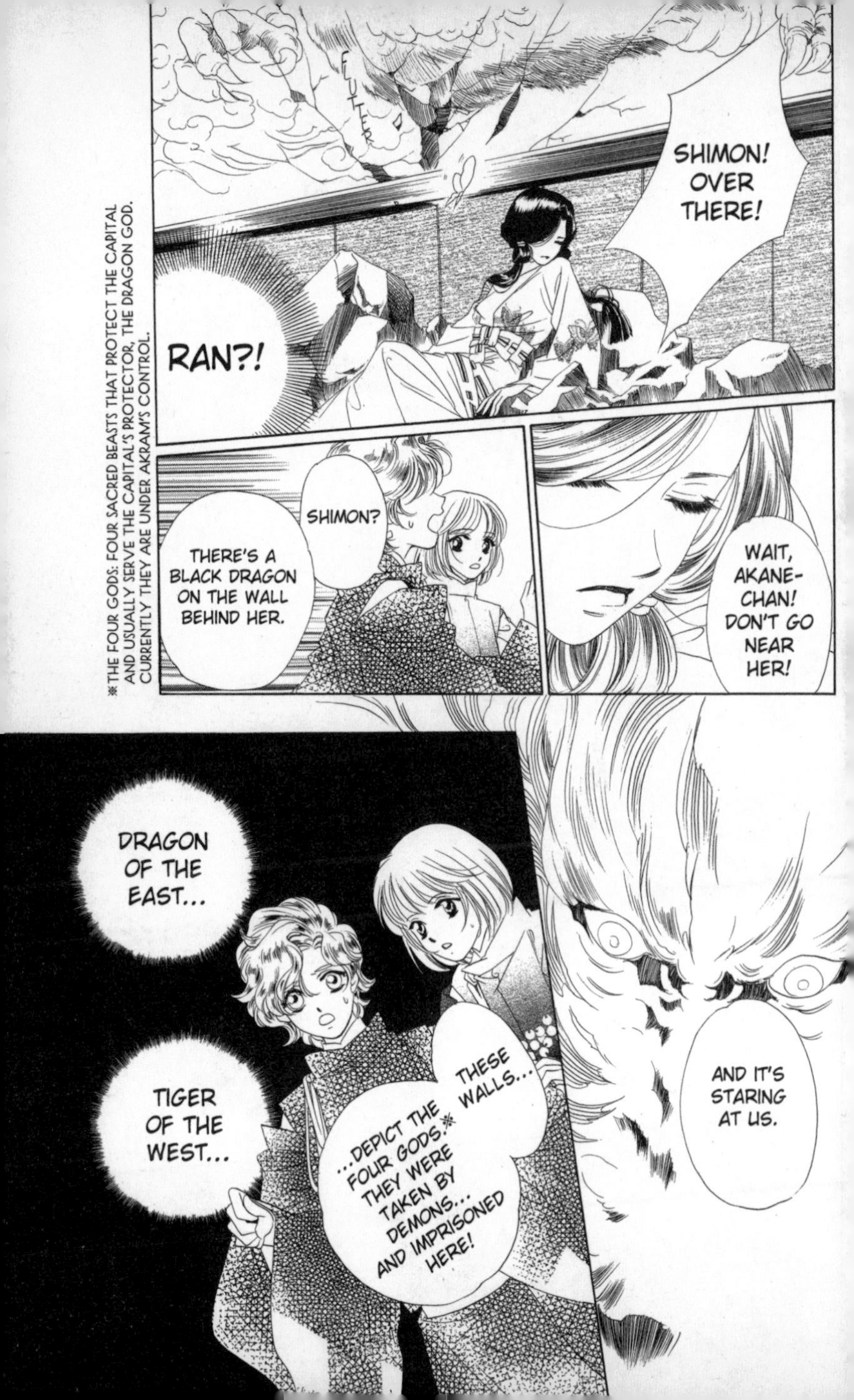
FLUTTER
SHIMON! OVER THERE!
RAN?!
WAIT, AKANE-CHAN! DON'T GO NEAR HER!
SHIMON?
THERE'S A BLACK DRAGON ON THE WALL BEHIND HER.
AND IT'S STARING AT US.
THESE WALLS...
...DEPICT THE FOUR GODS.※ THEY WERE TAKEN BY DEMONS... AND IMPRISONED HERE!
DRAGON OF THE EAST...
TIGER OF THE WEST...

※THE FOUR GODS: FOUR SACRED BEASTS THAT PROTECT THE CAPITAL AND USUALLY SERVE THE CAPITAL'S PROTECTOR, THE DRAGON GOD. CURRENTLY THEY ARE UNDER AKRAM'S CONTROL.

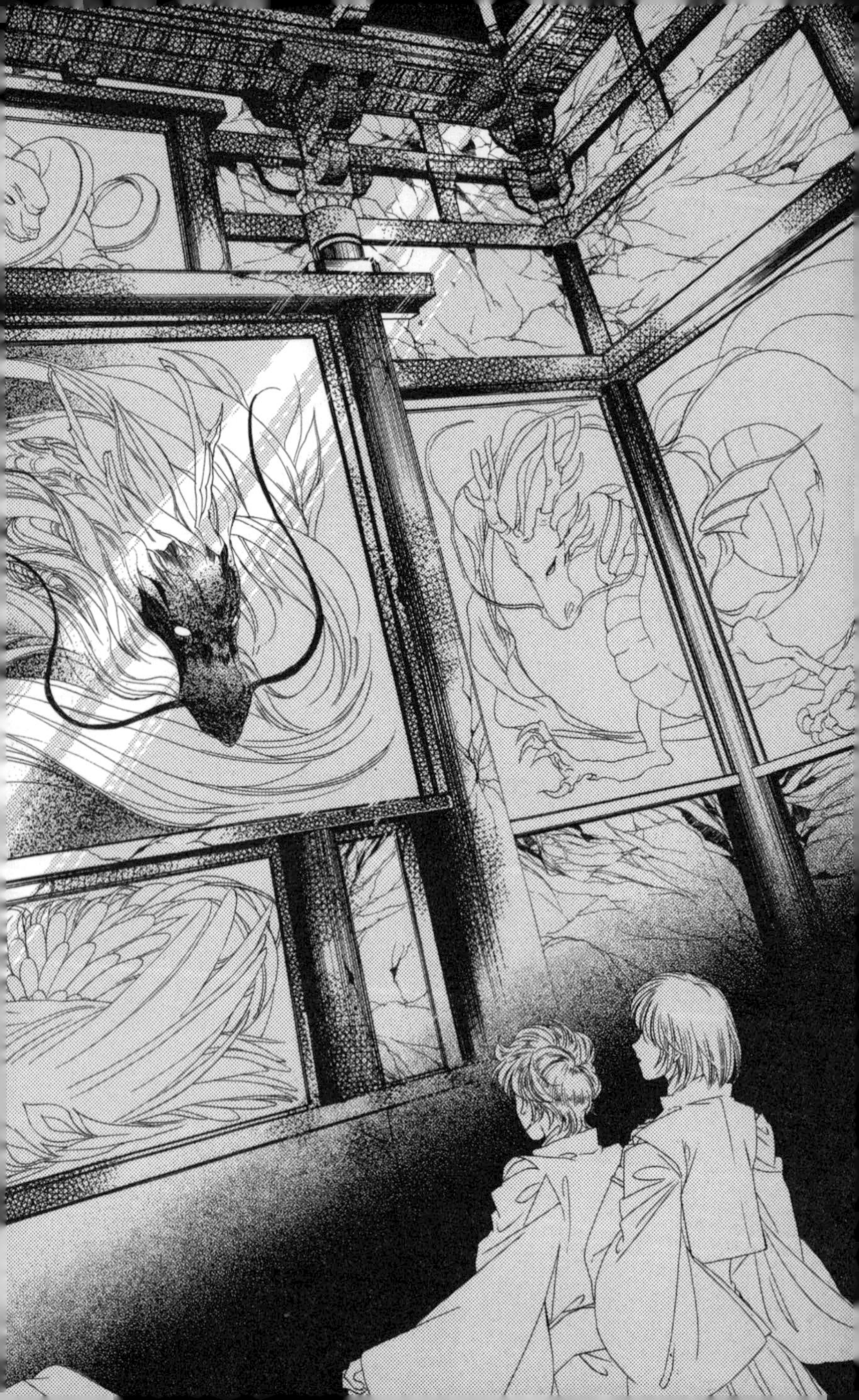

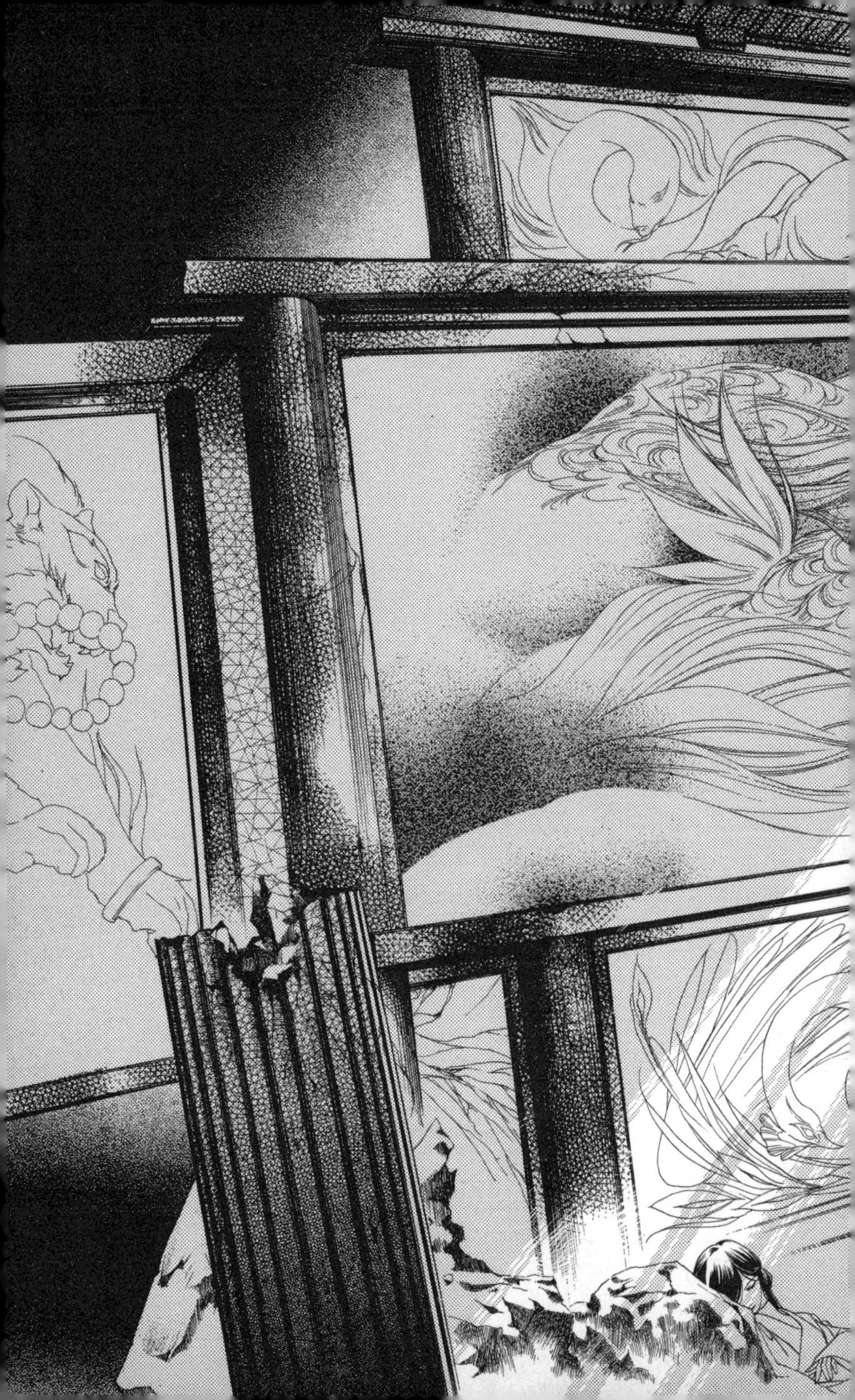

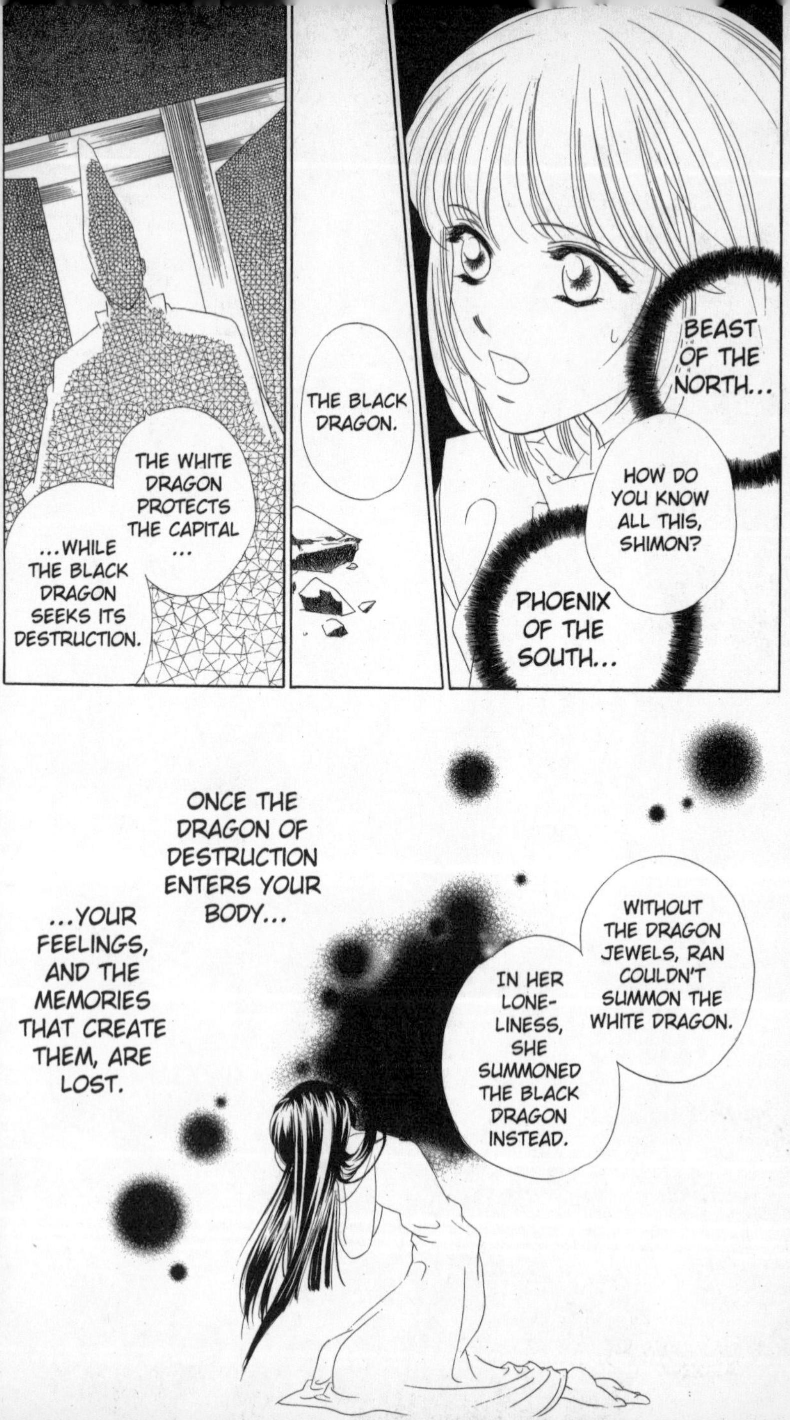
BEAST OF THE NORTH...
HOW DO YOU KNOW ALL THIS, SHIMON?
PHOENIX OF THE SOUTH...
THE BLACK DRAGON.
THE WHITE DRAGON PROTECTS THE CAPITAL...
...WHILE THE BLACK DRAGON SEEKS ITS DESTRUCTION.
WITHOUT THE DRAGON JEWELS, RAN COULDN'T SUMMON THE WHITE DRAGON.
IN HER LONE-LINESS, SHE SUMMONED THE BLACK DRAGON INSTEAD.
ONCE THE DRAGON OF DESTRUCTION ENTERS YOUR BODY...
...YOUR FEELINGS, AND THE MEMORIES THAT CREATE THEM, ARE LOST.

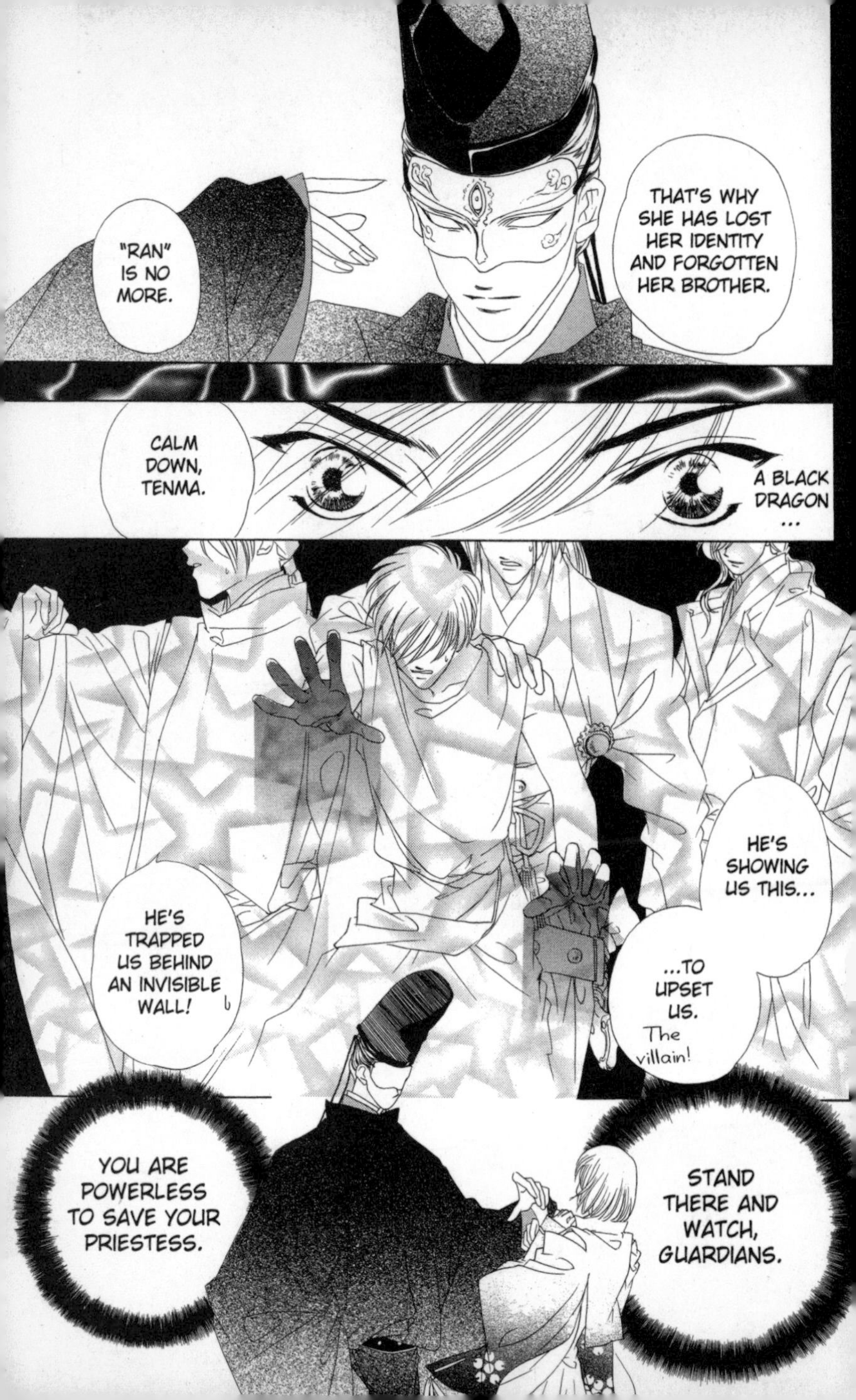
THAT'S WHY SHE HAS LOST HER IDENTITY AND FORGOTTEN HER BROTHER.
"RAN" IS NO MORE.
A BLACK DRAGON...
CALM DOWN, TENMA.
HE'S SHOWING US THIS...
...TO UPSET US.
The villain!
HE'S TRAPPED US BEHIND AN INVISIBLE WALL!
STAND THERE AND WATCH, GUARDIANS.
YOU ARE POWERLESS TO SAVE YOUR PRIESTESS.

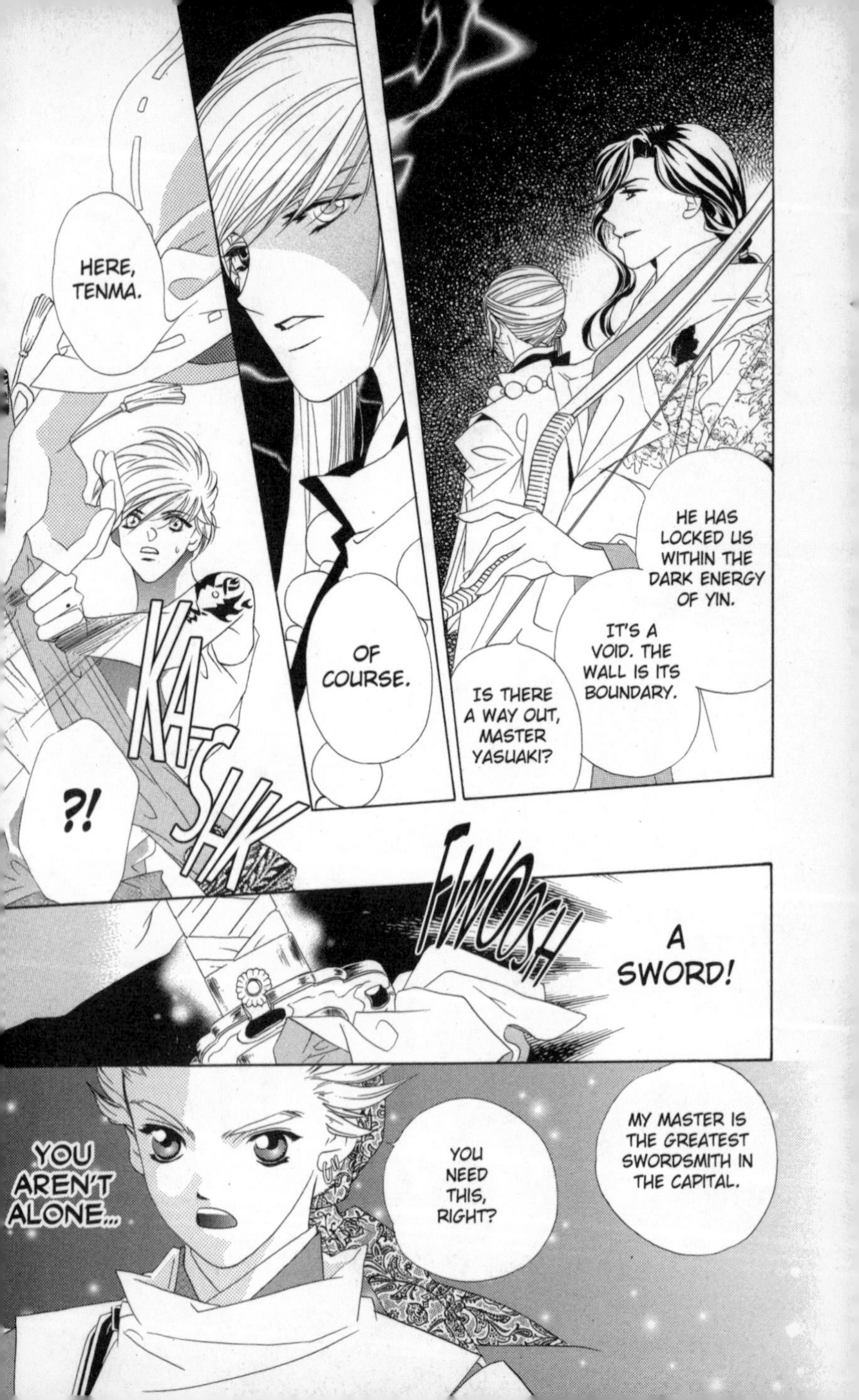
HE HAS LOCKED US WITHIN THE DARK ENERGY OF YIN.
IT'S A VOID. THE WALL IS ITS BOUNDARY.
IS THERE A WAY OUT, MASTER YASUAKI?
OF COURSE.
HERE, TENMA.
KA-SHK
?!
A SWORD!
FWOOSH
MY MASTER IS THE GREATEST SWORDSMITH IN THE CAPITAL.
YOU NEED THIS, RIGHT?
YOU AREN'T ALONE...

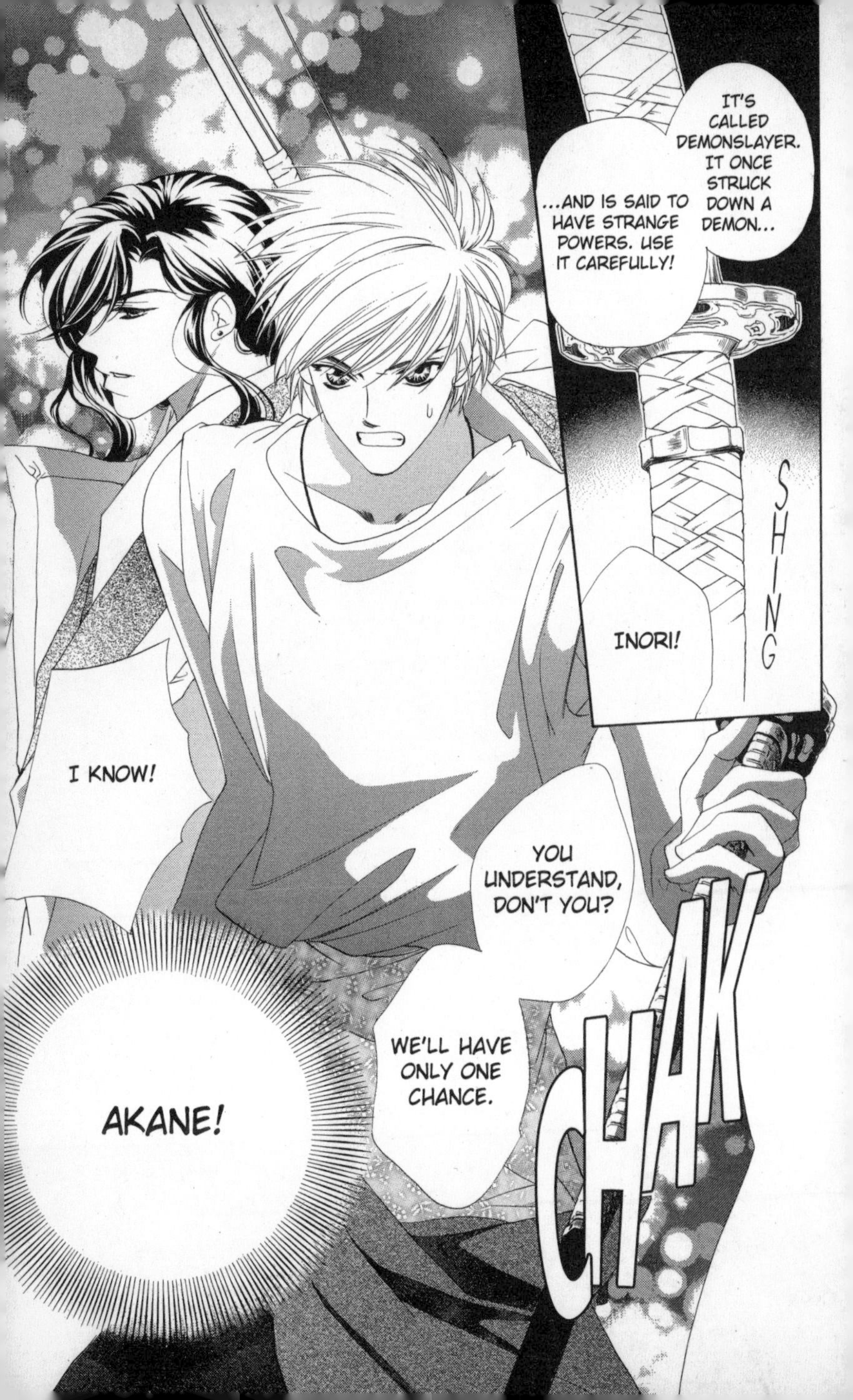
IT'S CALLED DEMONSLAYER. IT ONCE STRUCK DOWN A DEMON...
...AND IS SAID TO HAVE STRANGE POWERS. USE IT CAREFULLY!
SHING
INORI!
YOU UNDERSTAND, DON'T YOU?
WE'LL HAVE ONLY ONE CHANCE.
CHAK
I KNOW!
AKANE!

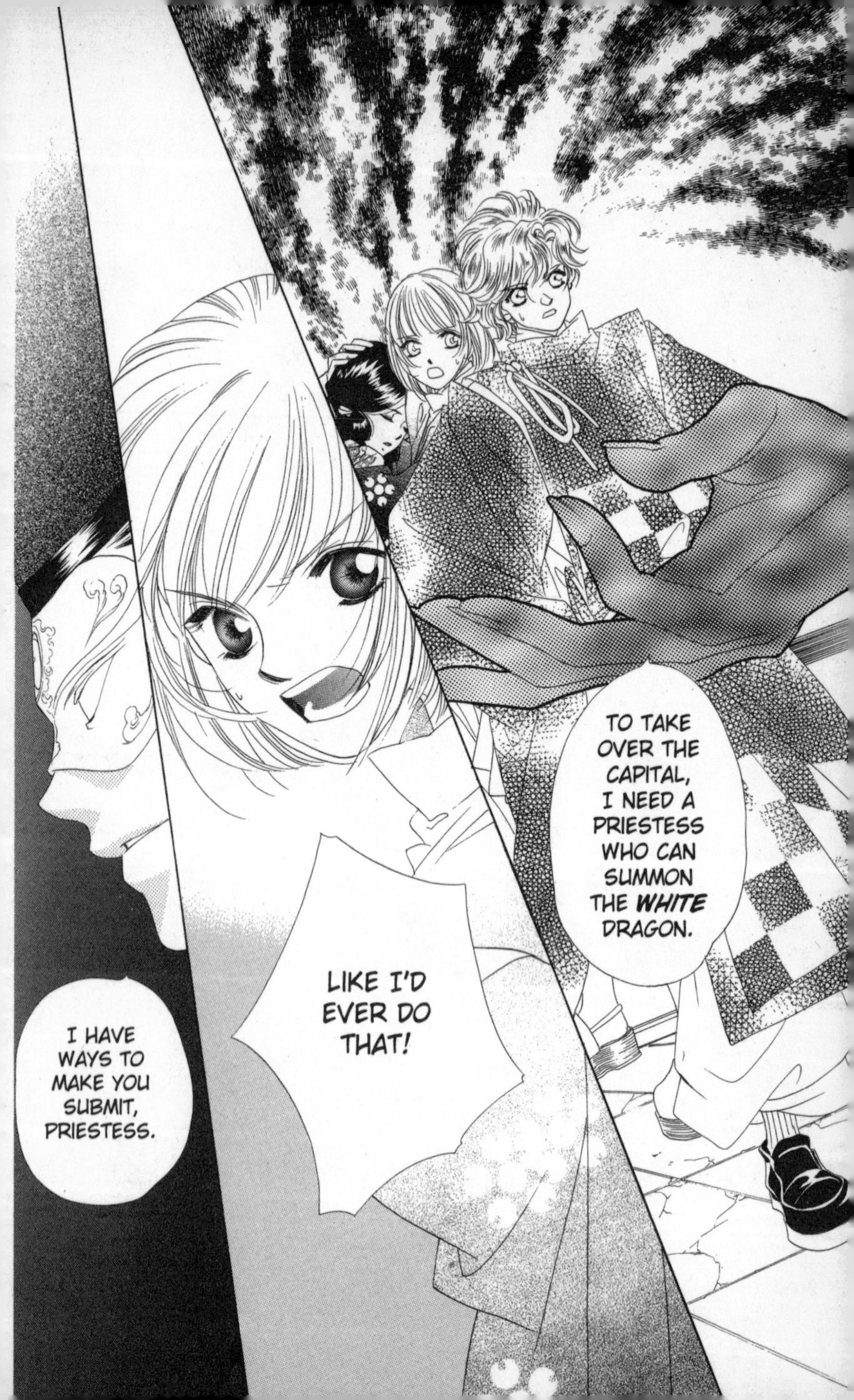
TO TAKE OVER THE CAPITAL, I NEED A PRIESTESS WHO CAN SUMMON THE *WHITE* DRAGON.
LIKE I'D EVER DO THAT!
I HAVE WAYS TO MAKE YOU SUBMIT, PRIESTESS.

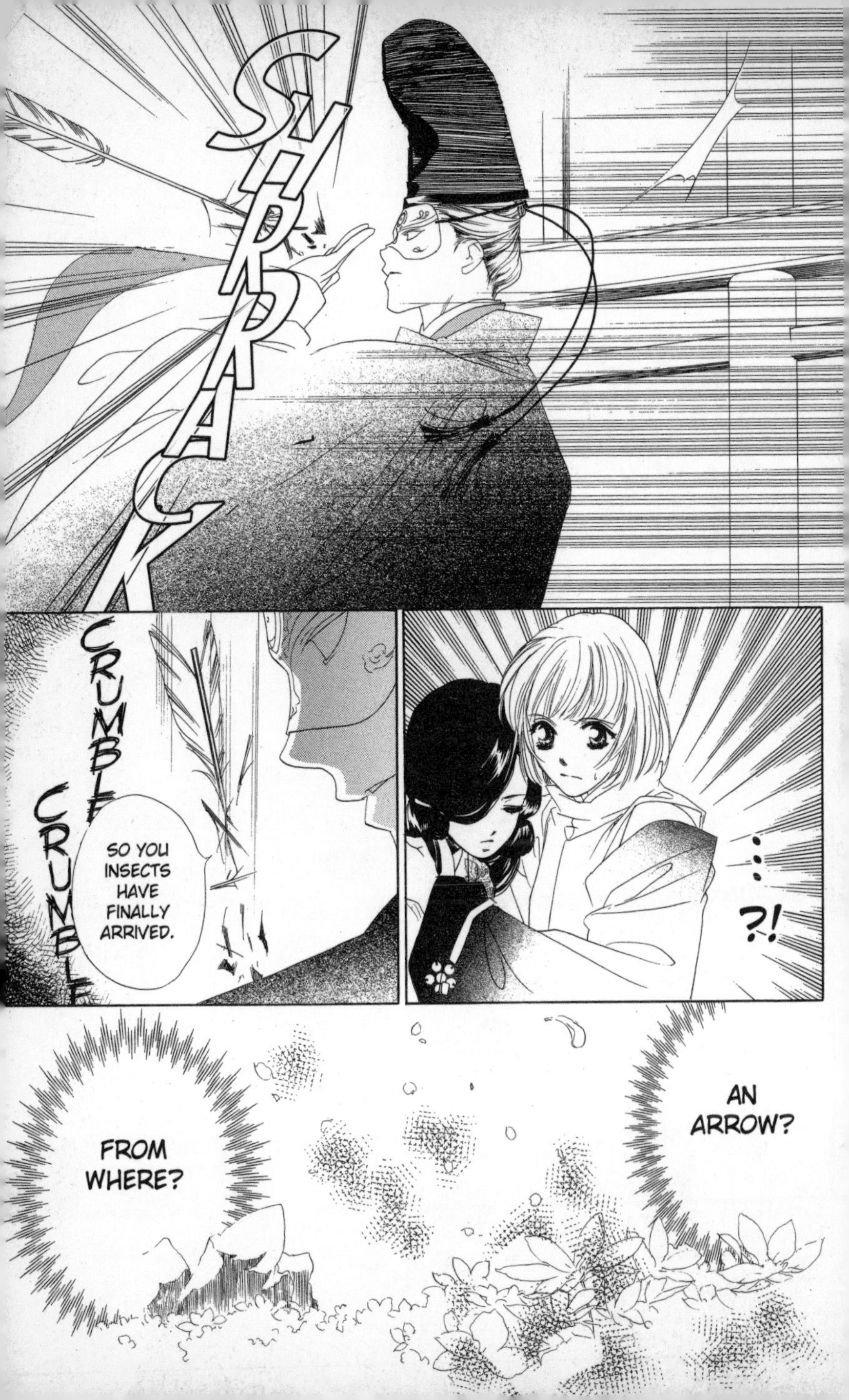
SHRRAACK
...
?!
CRUMBLE
CRUMBLE
SO YOU INSECTS HAVE FINALLY ARRIVED.
AN ARROW?
FROM WHERE?

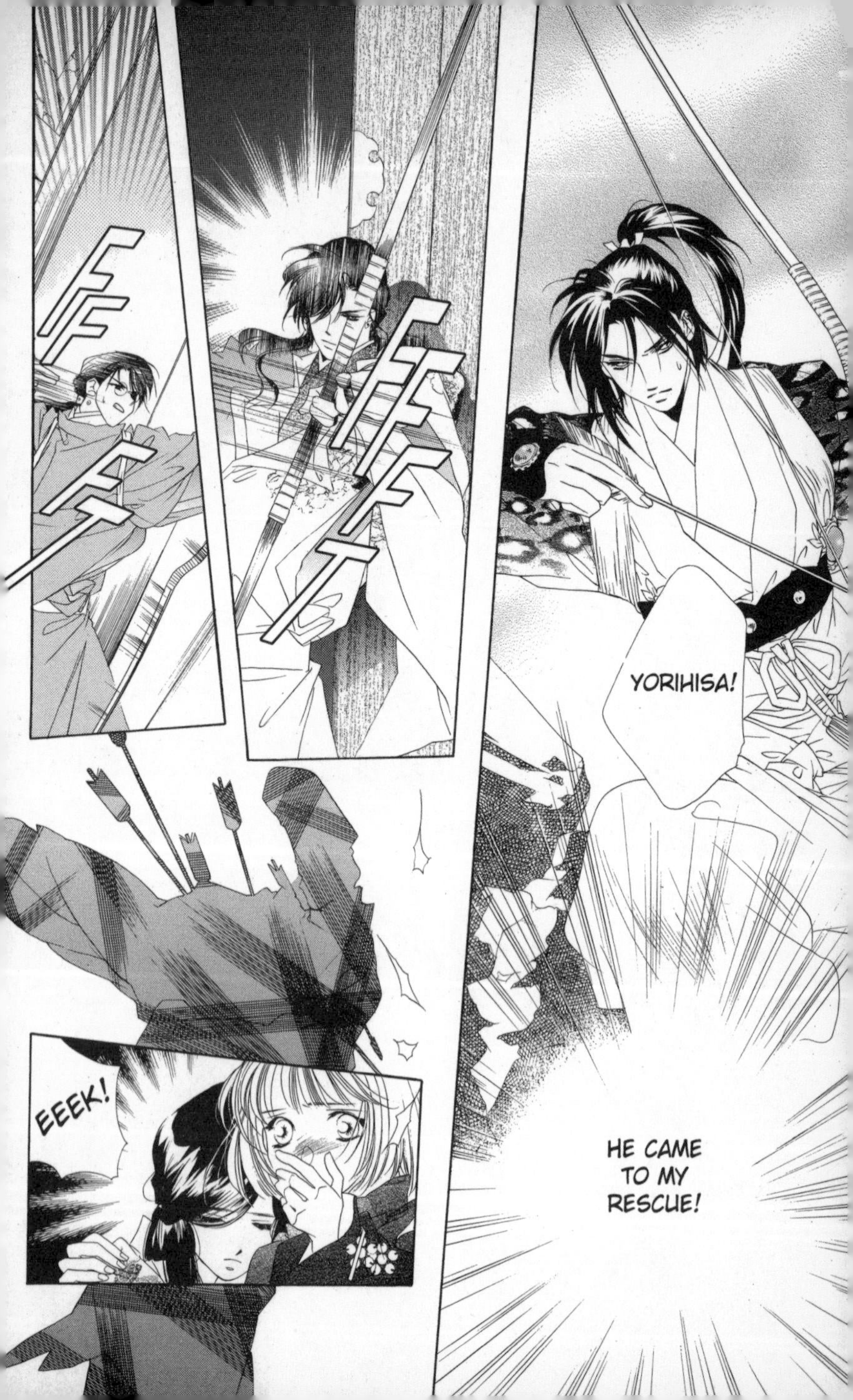
YORIHISA!
HE CAME TO MY RESCUE!
FFFFT
FFFFT
EEEK!

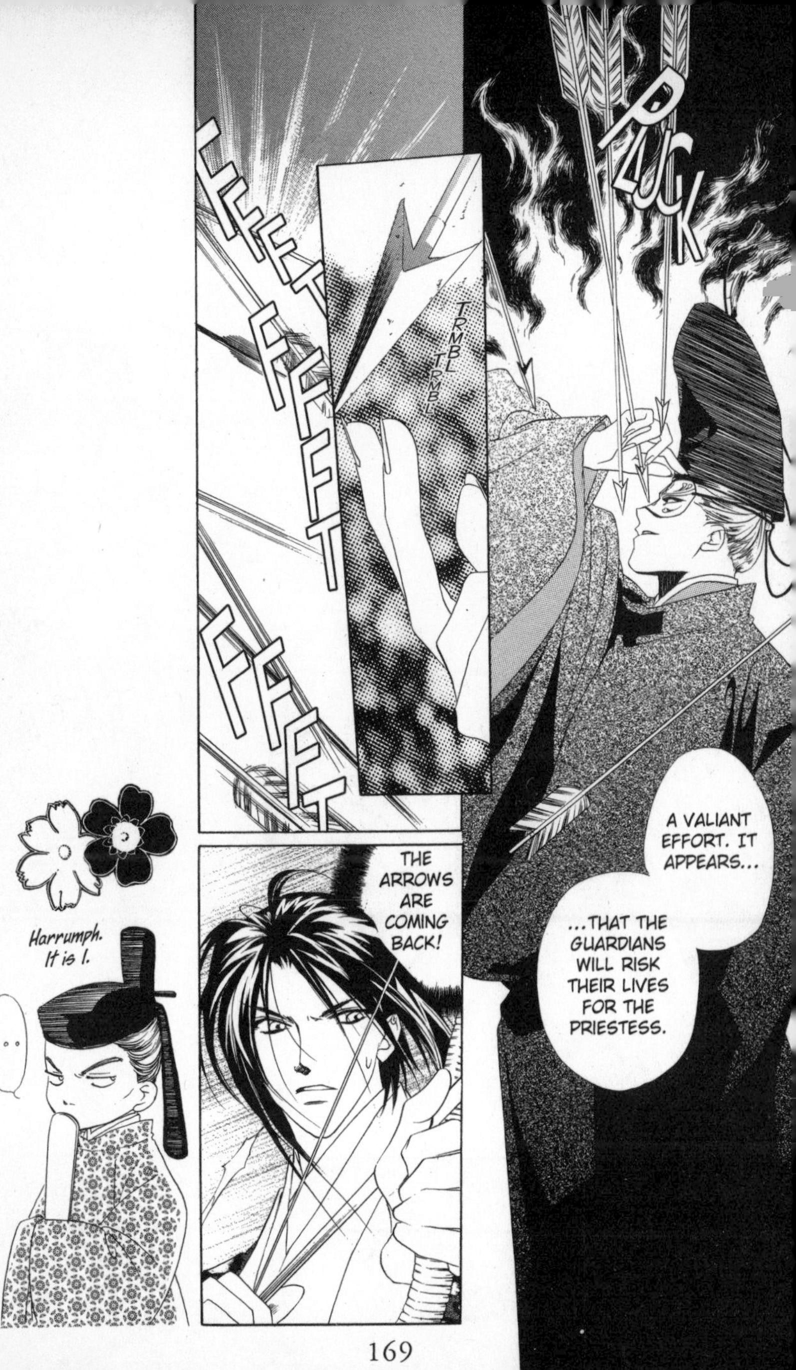
PLUCK
A VALIANT EFFORT. IT APPEARS...
...THAT THE GUARDIANS WILL RISK THEIR LIVES FOR THE PRIESTESS.
FFFFT FFFFT FFFFT
TRMBL TRMBL
THE ARROWS ARE COMING BACK!
Harrumph. It is I.
...

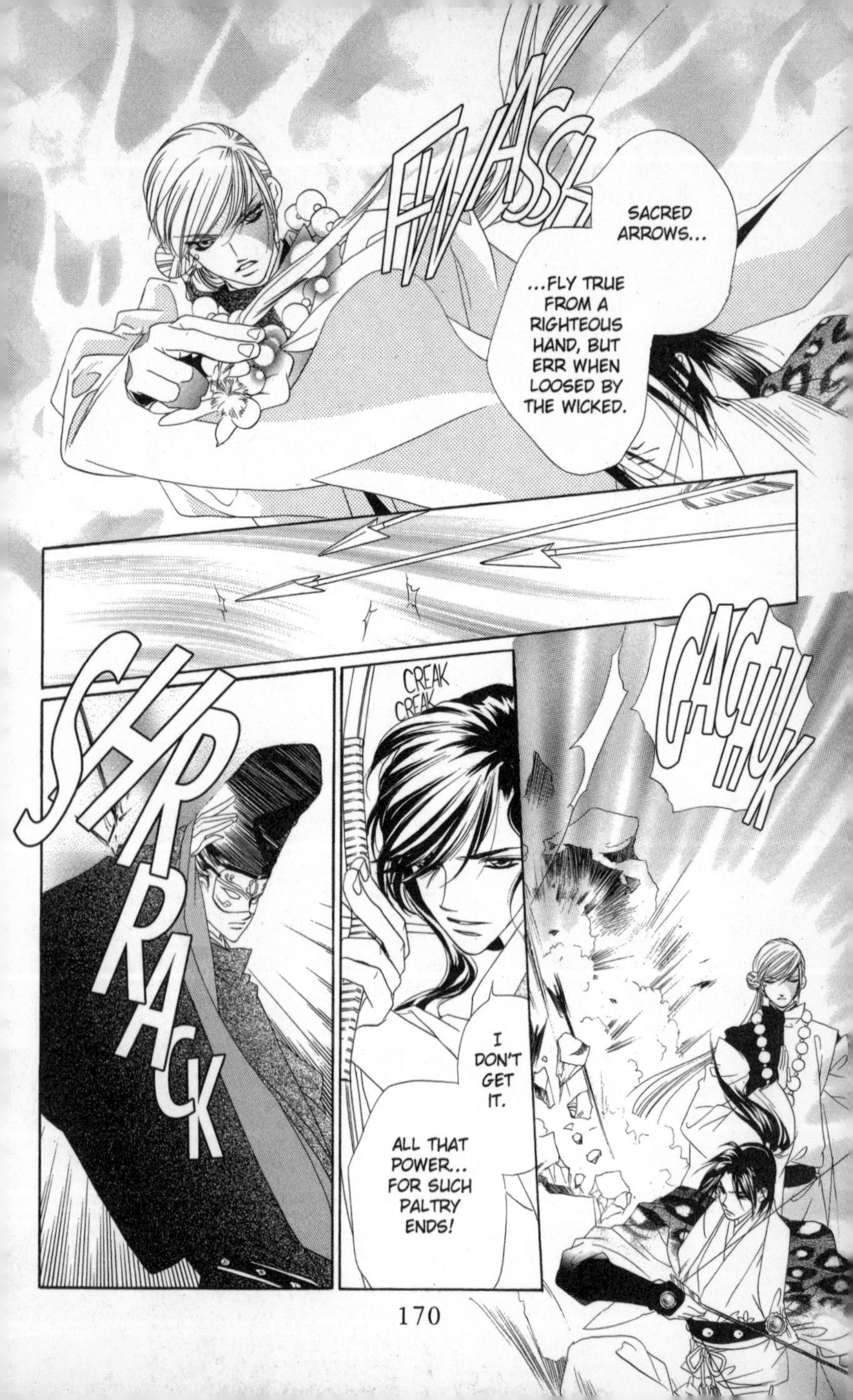
FWASSH
SACRED ARROWS...
...FLY TRUE FROM A RIGHTEOUS HAND, BUT ERR WHEN LOOSED BY THE WICKED.
CACHUNK
CREAK CREAK
I DON'T GET IT.
ALL THAT POWER... FOR SUCH PALTRY ENDS!
SHRRACK

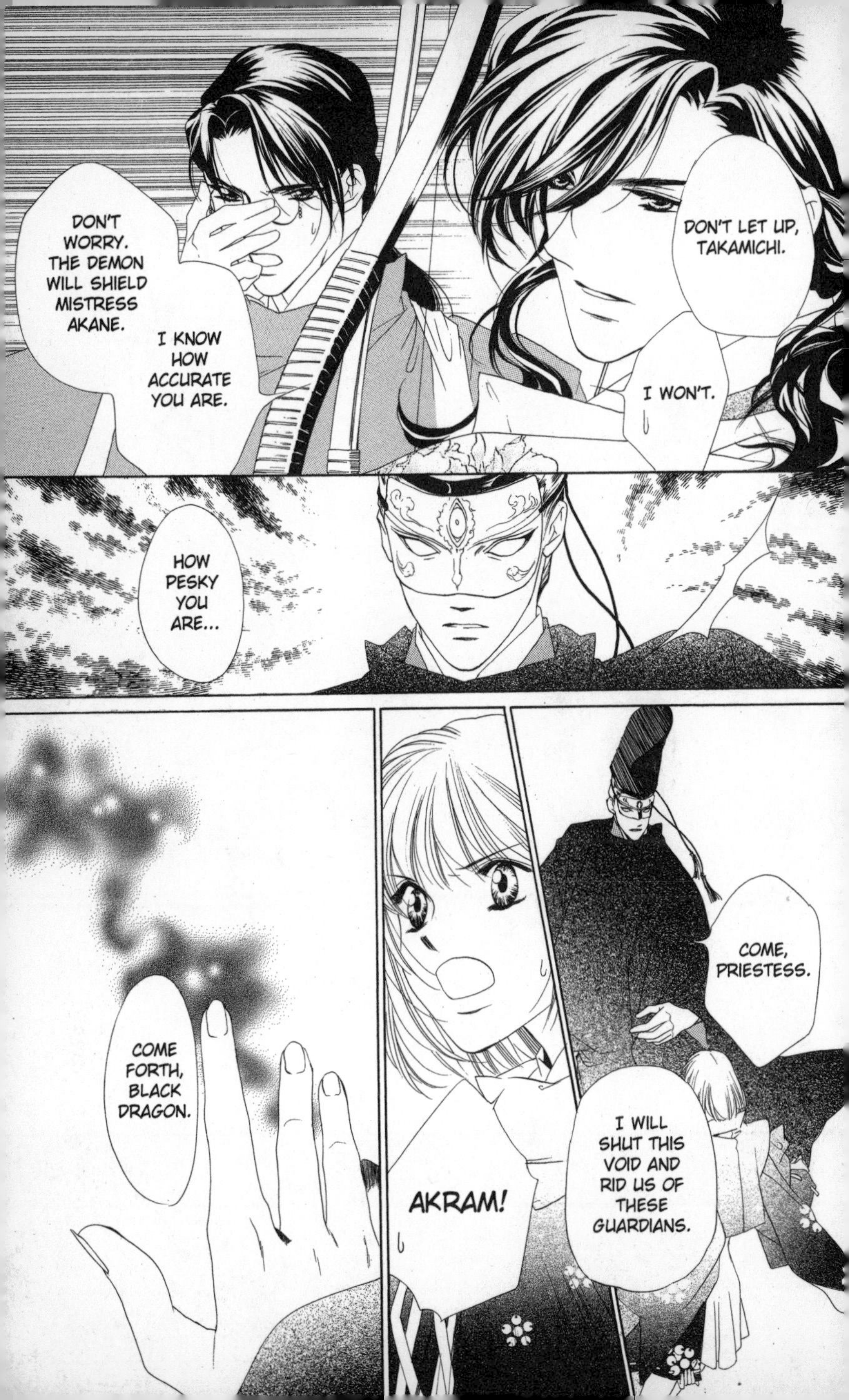
DON'T LET UP, TAKAMICHI.
I WON'T.
DON'T WORRY. THE DEMON WILL SHIELD MISTRESS AKANE.
I KNOW HOW ACCURATE YOU ARE.
HOW PESKY YOU ARE...
COME, PRIESTESS.
I WILL SHUT THIS VOID AND RID US OF THESE GUARDIANS.
AKRAM!
COME FORTH, BLACK DRAGON.

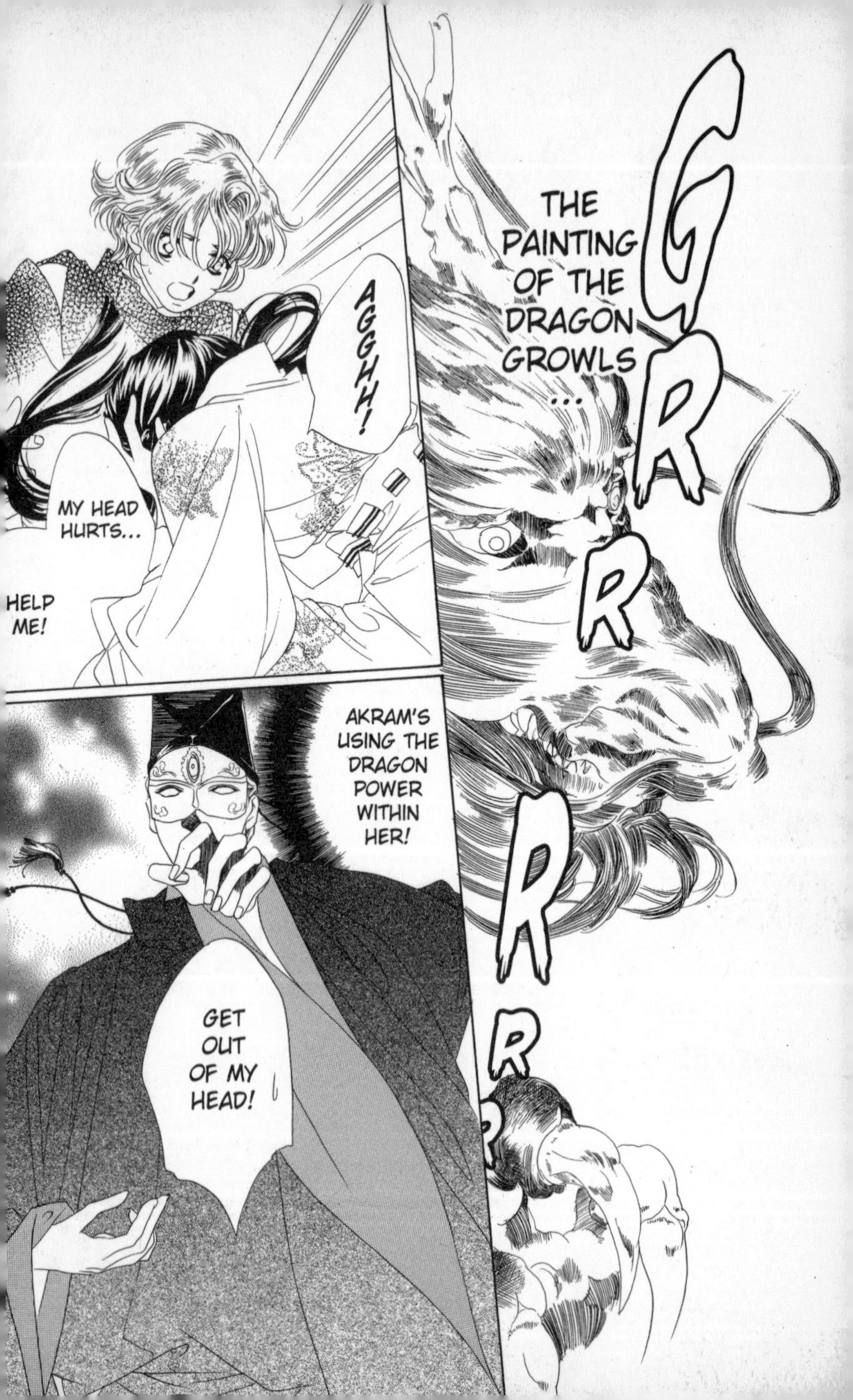
THE PAINTING OF THE DRAGON GROWLS...
GRRRRR
AGGHH!
MY HEAD HURTS...
HELP ME!
AKRAM'S USING THE DRAGON POWER WITHIN HER!
GET OUT OF MY HEAD!

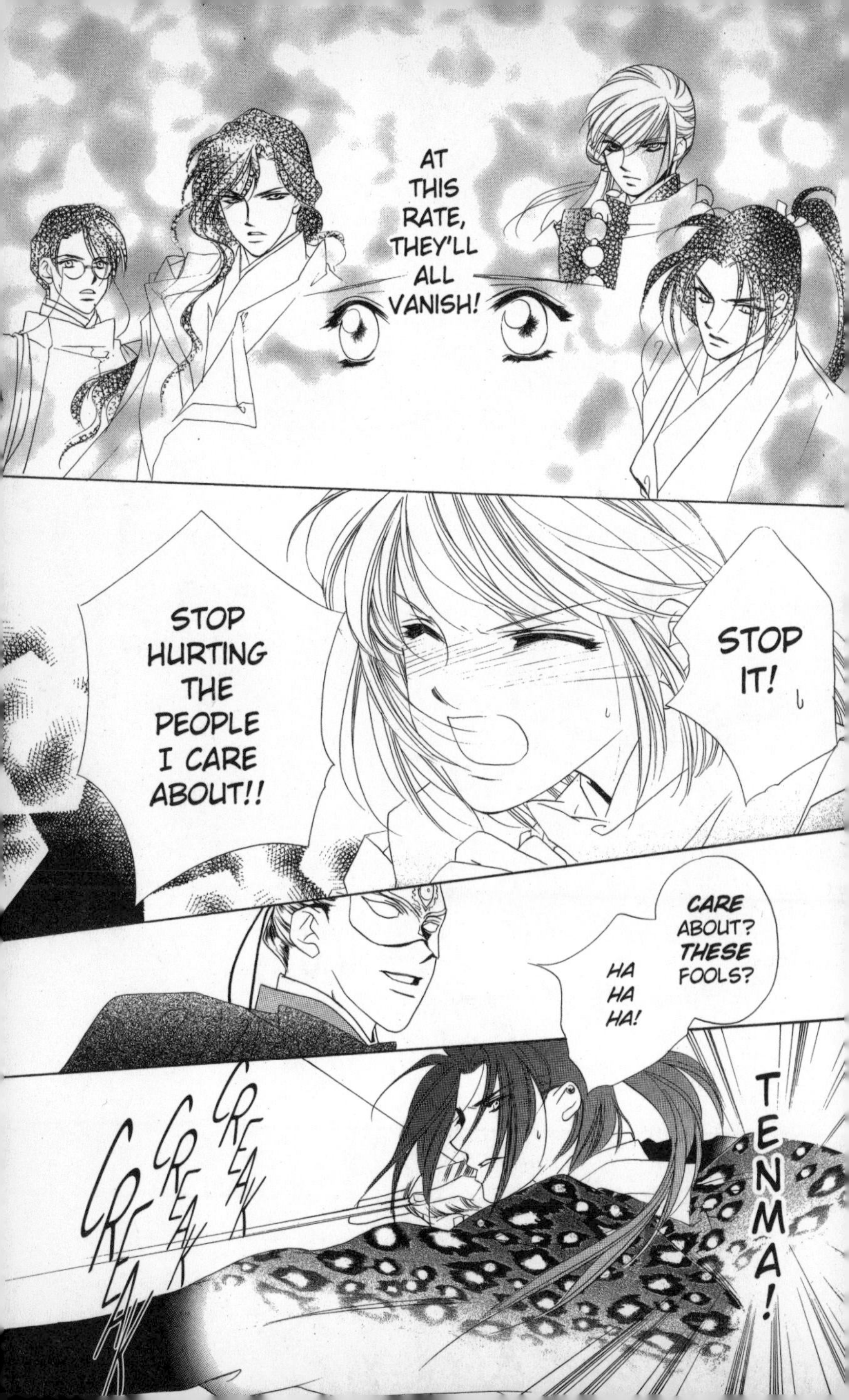
AT THIS RATE, THEY'LL ALL VANISH!
STOP IT!
STOP HURTING THE PEOPLE I CARE ABOUT!!
CARE ABOUT? THESE FOOLS?
HA HA HA!
TENMA!
CREAK
CREAK
CREAK

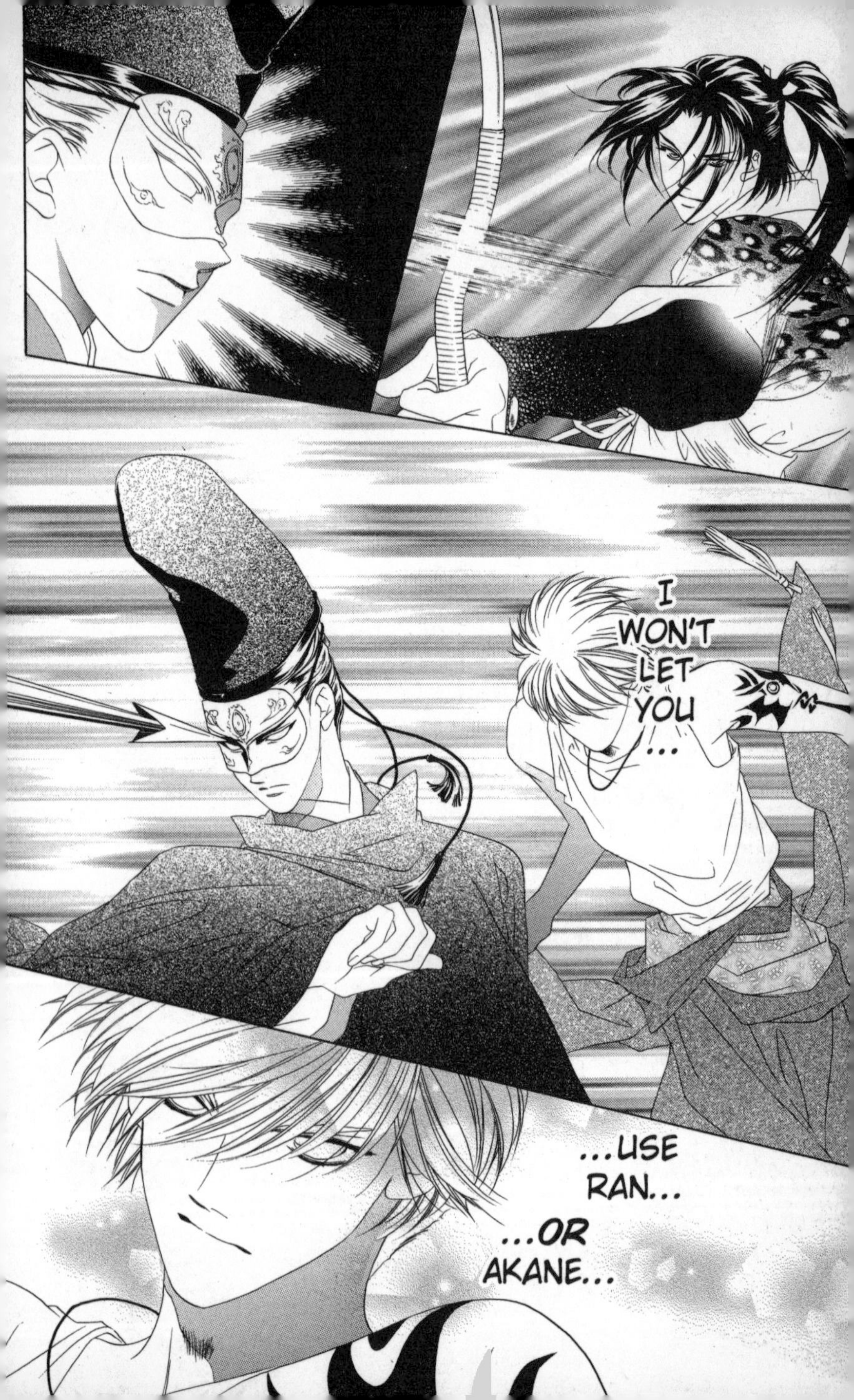
I WON'T LET YOU ...
...USE RAN...
...OR AKANE...

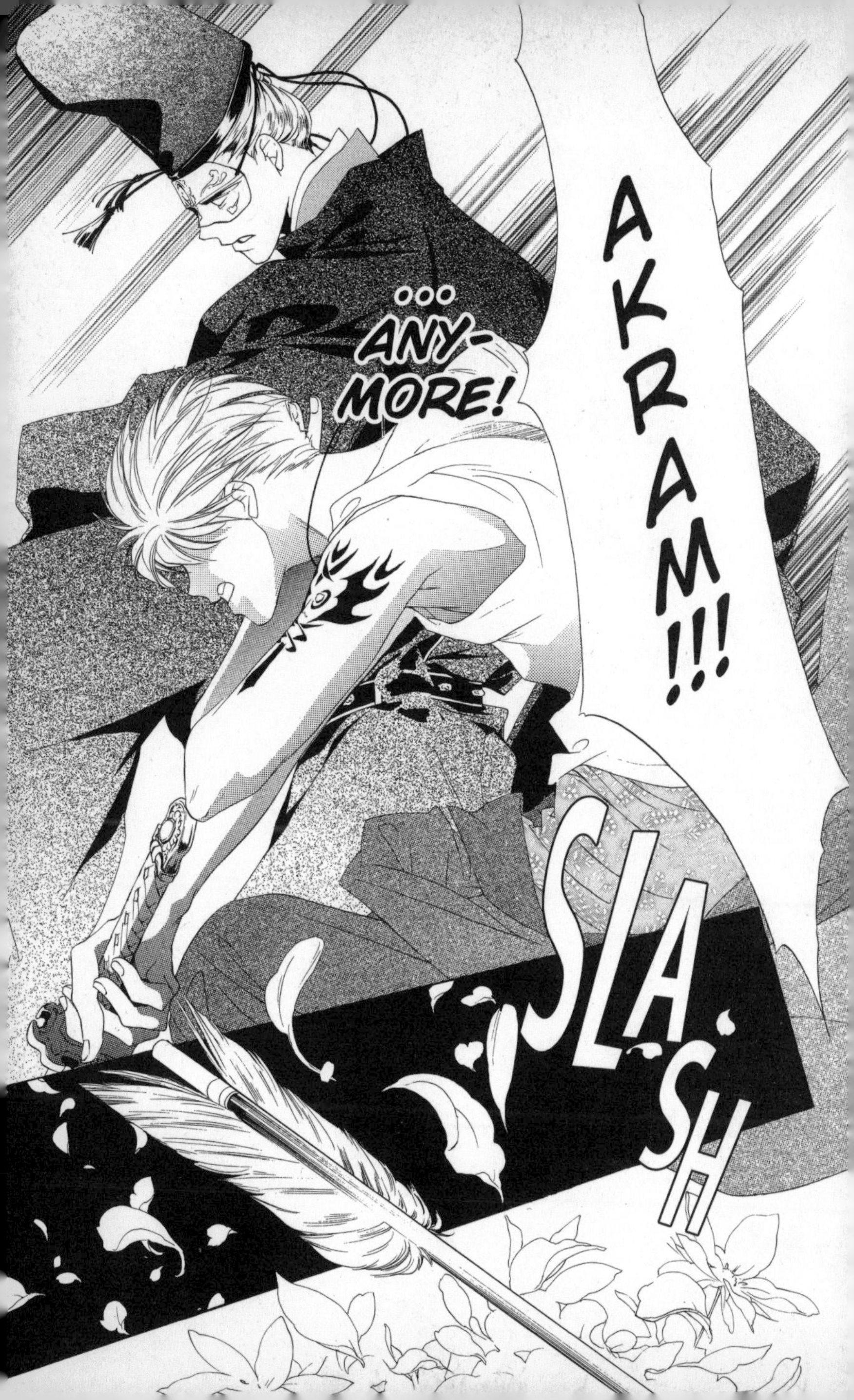
...ANY-MORE!
AKRAM!!!
SLASH

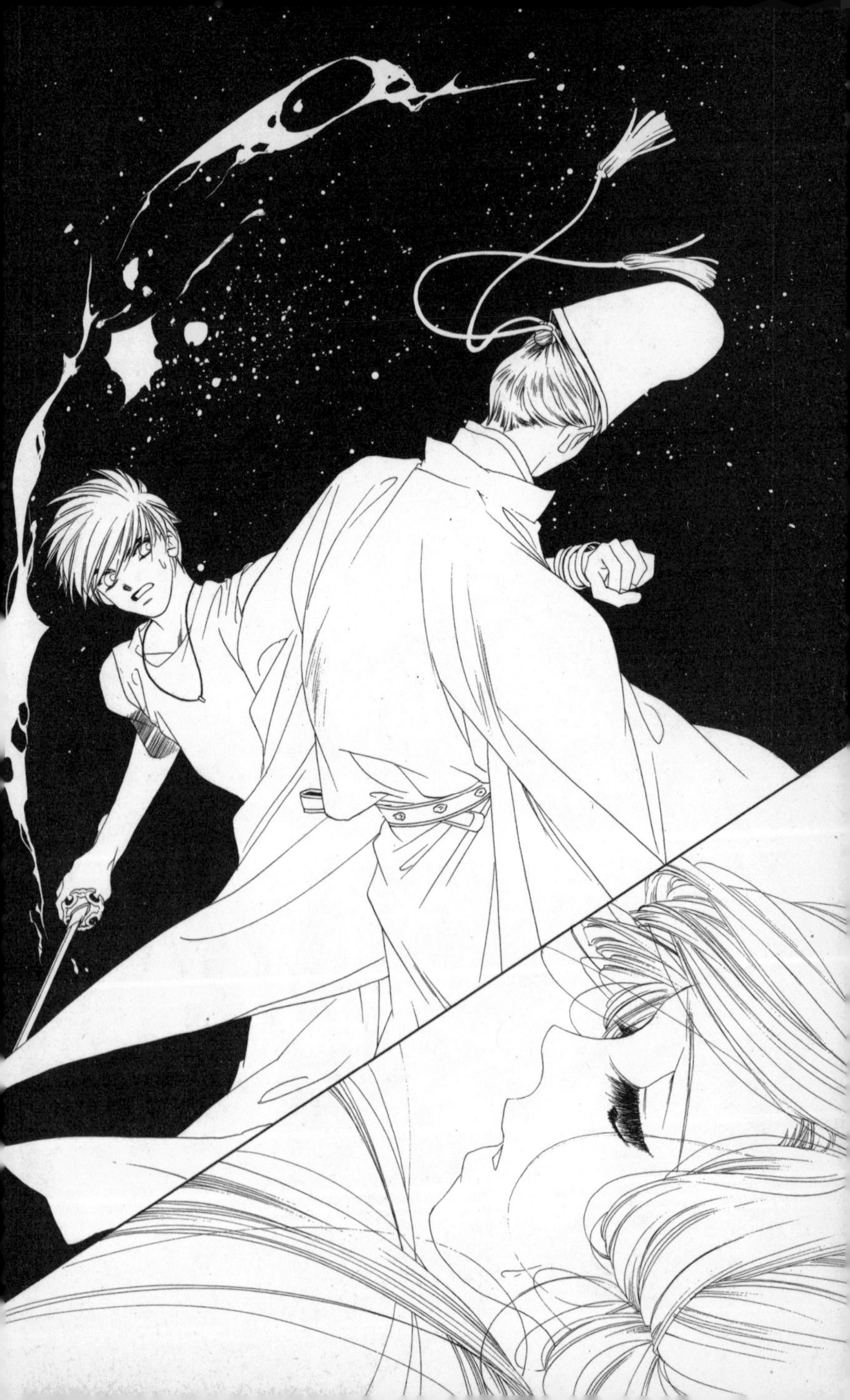

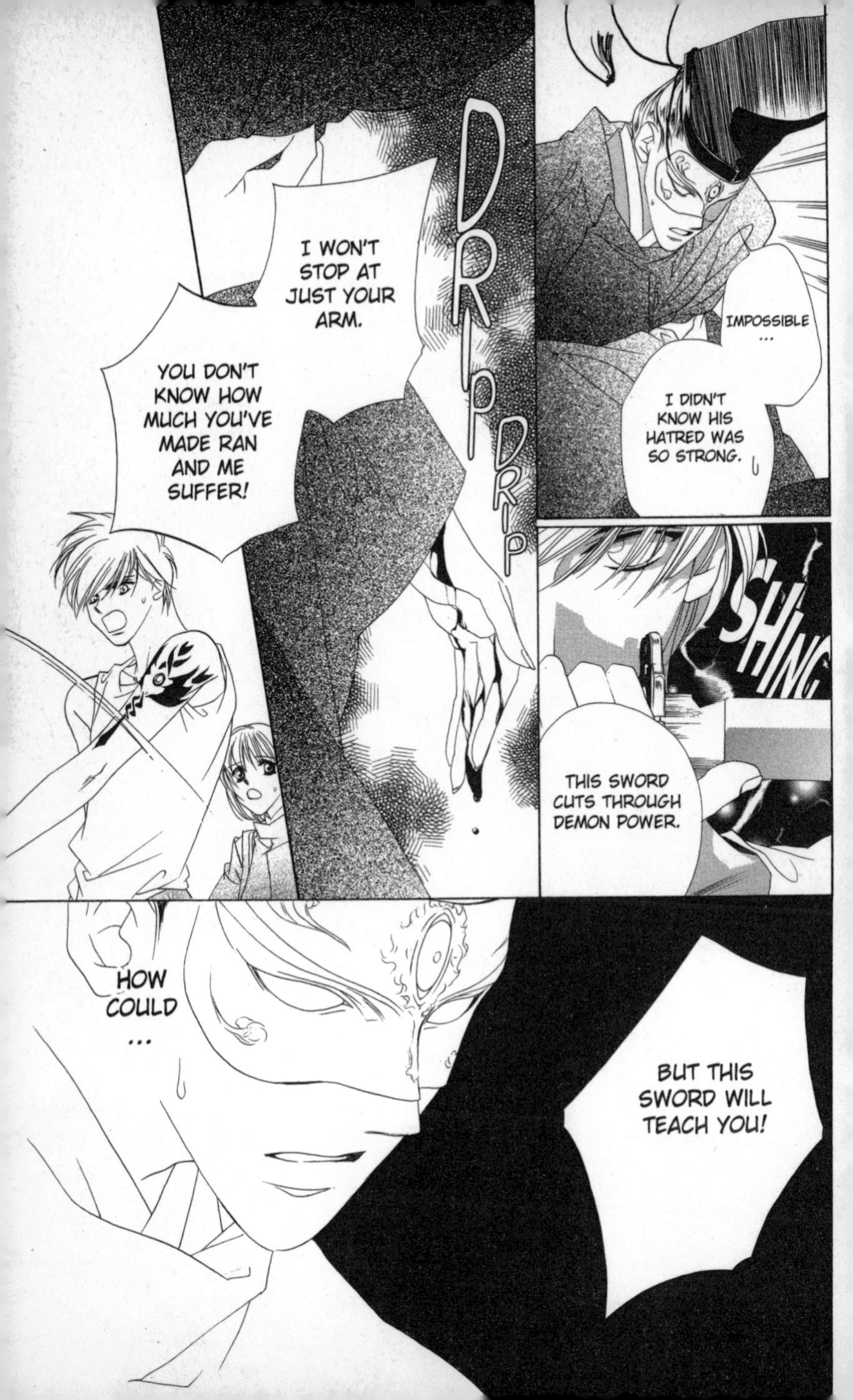
IMPOSSIBLE ...
I DIDN'T KNOW HIS HATRED WAS SO STRONG.
SHING
THIS SWORD CUTS THROUGH DEMON POWER.
DRIP DRIP
I WON'T STOP AT JUST YOUR ARM.
YOU DON'T KNOW HOW MUCH YOU'VE MADE RAN AND ME SUFFER!
BUT THIS SWORD WILL TEACH YOU!
HOW COULD ...

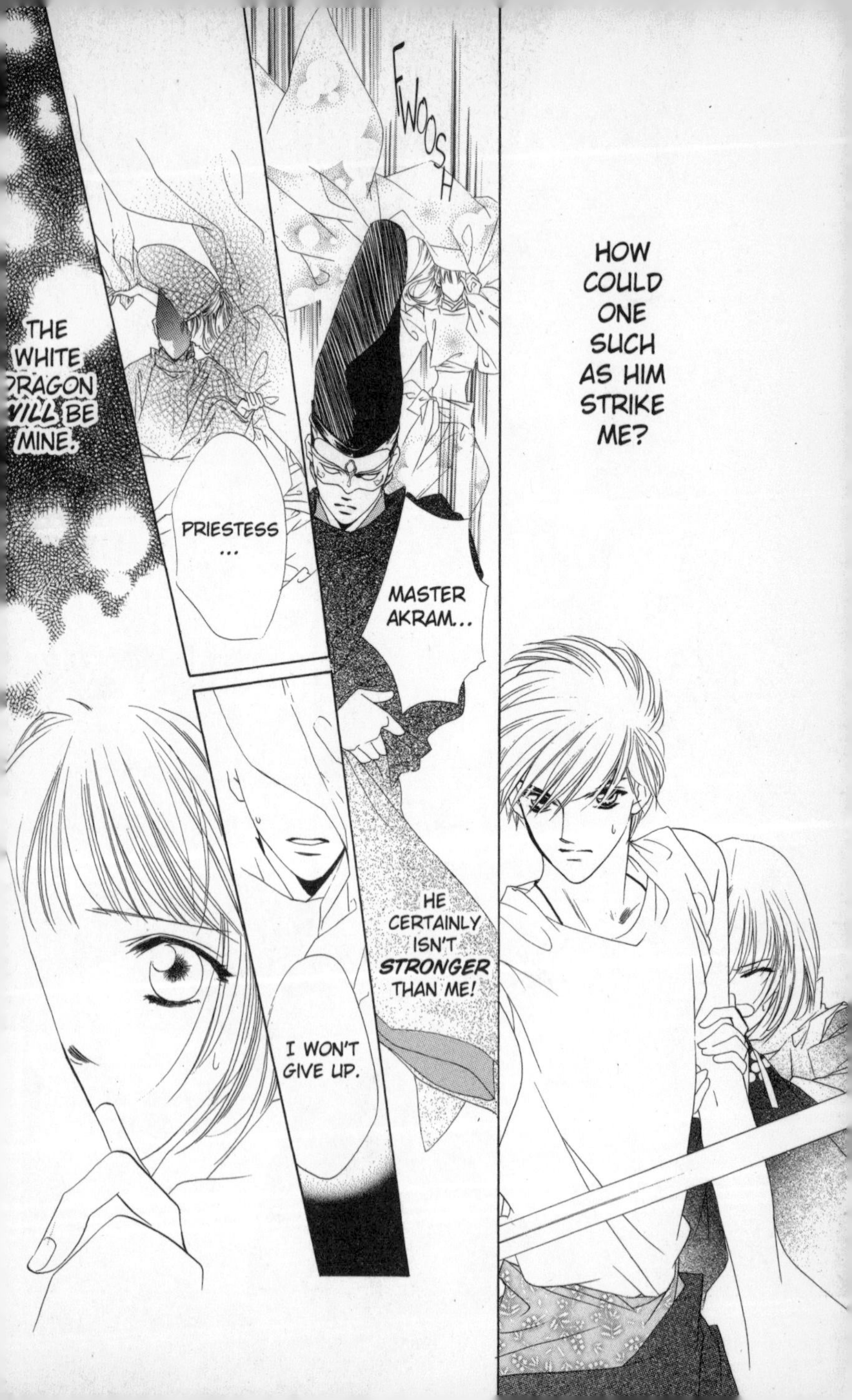
HOW COULD ONE SUCH AS HIM STRIKE ME?
FWOOSH
MASTER AKRAM...
HE CERTAINLY ISN'T STRONGER THAN ME!
THE WHITE DRAGON WILL BE MINE.
PRIESTESS...
I WON'T GIVE UP.

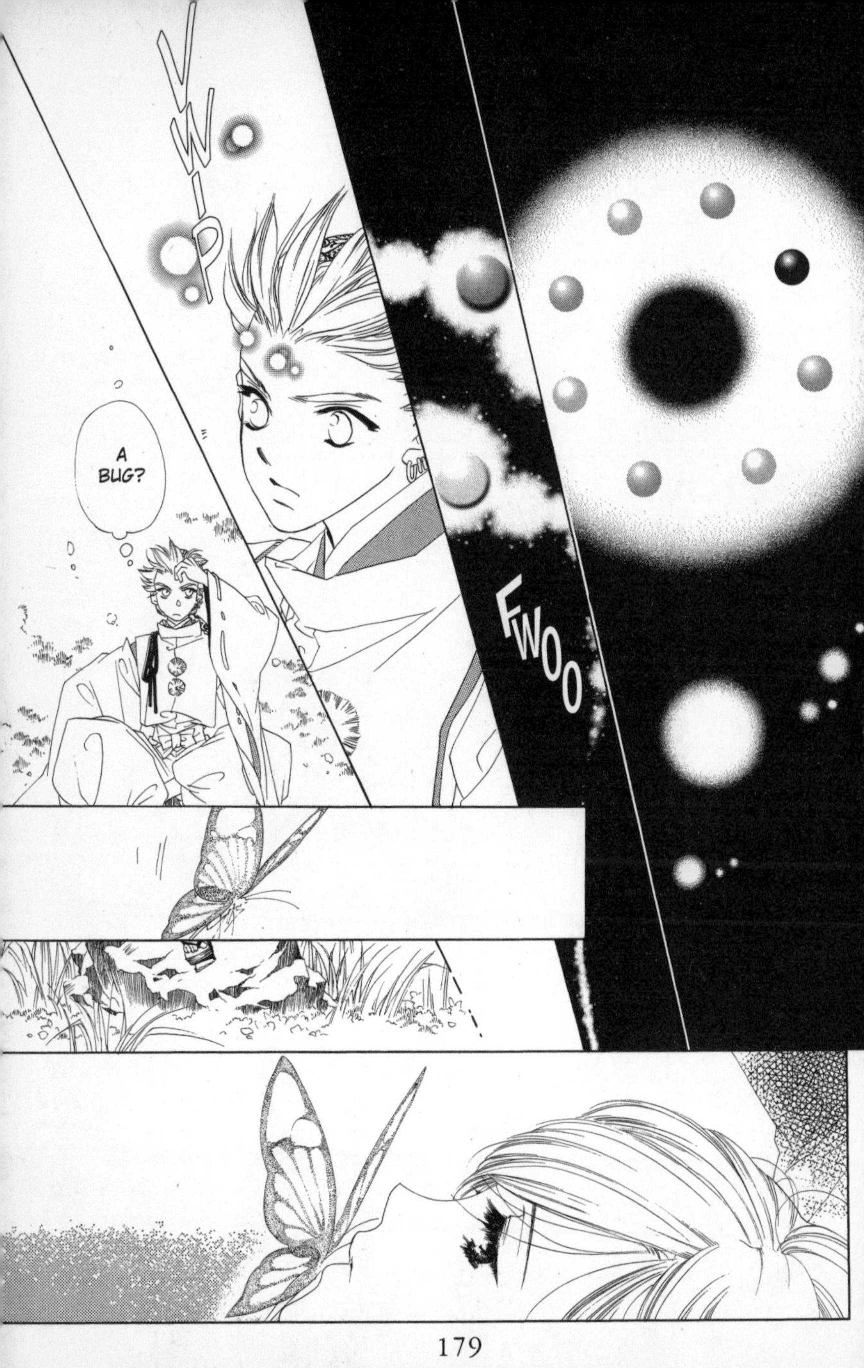
FWOO
VWIP
A BUG?

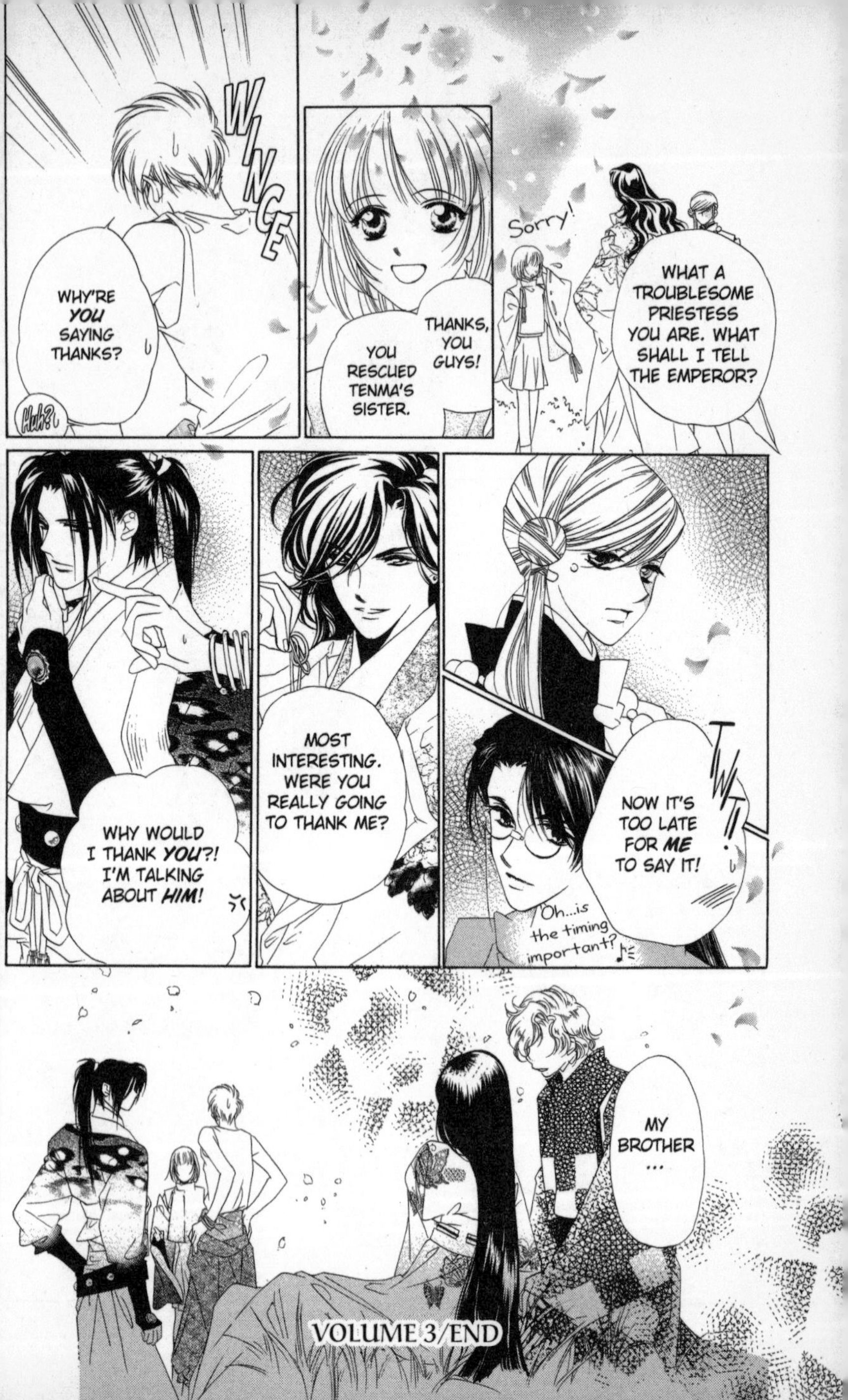
WHAT A TROUBLESOME PRIESTESS YOU ARE. WHAT SHALL I TELL THE EMPEROR?
Sorry!
THANKS, YOU GUYS!
YOU RESCUED TENMA'S SISTER.
WINCE
WHY'RE YOU SAYING THANKS?
Huh?!
TWIT!!
NOW IT'S TOO LATE FOR ME TO SAY IT!
Oh...is the timing important?
MOST INTERESTING. WERE YOU REALLY GOING TO THANK ME?
WHY WOULD I THANK YOU?! I'M TALKING ABOUT HIM!
MY BROTHER ...
VOLUME 3/END

Bonus Material

This is the third volume of *Haruka: Beyond the Stream of Time*. Thank you all so much for reading!

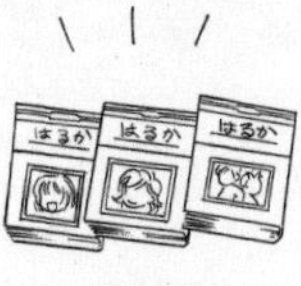
はるか
はるか
はるか

Hooray!

The video game *Haruka: Beyond the Stream of Time 2* is now in the works! ♪

Part 1

Beyond the Stream of Time

Come to think of it, the first time I saw the title of the game, *Beyond the Stream of Time*, I was surprised at how straightforward it was. Since "tentative" was written on the back, I figured it would change. This was before the first game had come out in stores. Actually, a number of different titles had been suggested.

Yep!

The reason I know this is because I racked my brain for titles and made some suggestions myself! (blush)

But I guess that's not really important!

Even the editorial department at *LaLa* made some suggestions. Combined with the comments from Koei, there were quite a few!

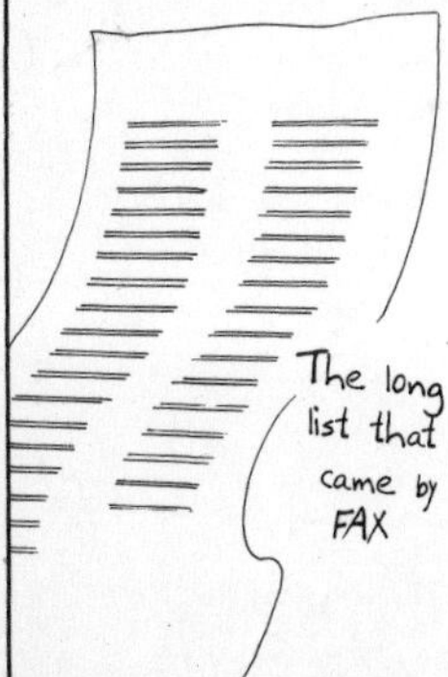
The long list that came by FAX

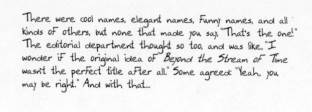

There were cool names, elegant names, funny names, and all kinds of others, but none that made you say, "That's the one!" The editorial department thought so too, and was like, "I wonder if the original idea of *Beyond the Stream of Time* wasn't the perfect title after all." Some agreed: "Yeah, you may be right." And with that...

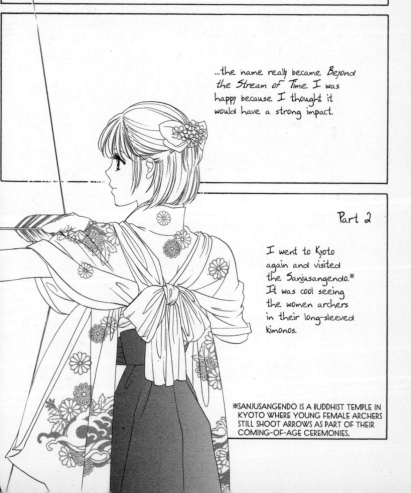

...the name really became *Beyond the Stream of Time*. I was happy because I thought it would have a strong impact.

Part 2

I went to Kyoto again and visited the Sanjusangendo.* It was cool seeing the women archers in their long-sleeved kimonos.

*SANJUSANGENDO IS A BUDDHIST TEMPLE IN KYOTO WHERE YOUNG FEMALE ARCHERS STILL SHOOT ARROWS AS PART OF THEIR COMING-OF-AGE CEREMONIES.

Since it was an event for Coming-of-Age Day,* there were tons of people.
AGH!
All the seats by the temple were full. I don't know if they were pushed, but someone fell from the stands!
*IN JAPAN, COMING-OF-AGE DAY IS CURRENTLY HELD ON THE SECOND MONDAY OF JANUARY.

No matter when I go, Kyoto is always crowded.

I've heard that everyone goes to Kyoto at least three times in their life.

A taxi driver there told me that people usually come as students on their final school trip, then on vacation as working adults, and finally with their spouses after they retire. That sounded about right.

Bonus Material / End May 2001

P.S.
Wow, I received lots of chocolates for Valentine's Day!
I was a bit surprised.
Thank you very much!
Although...is it okay for me to receive chocolates intended for Tomomasa, Yasuaki, Shimon and all the other characters?

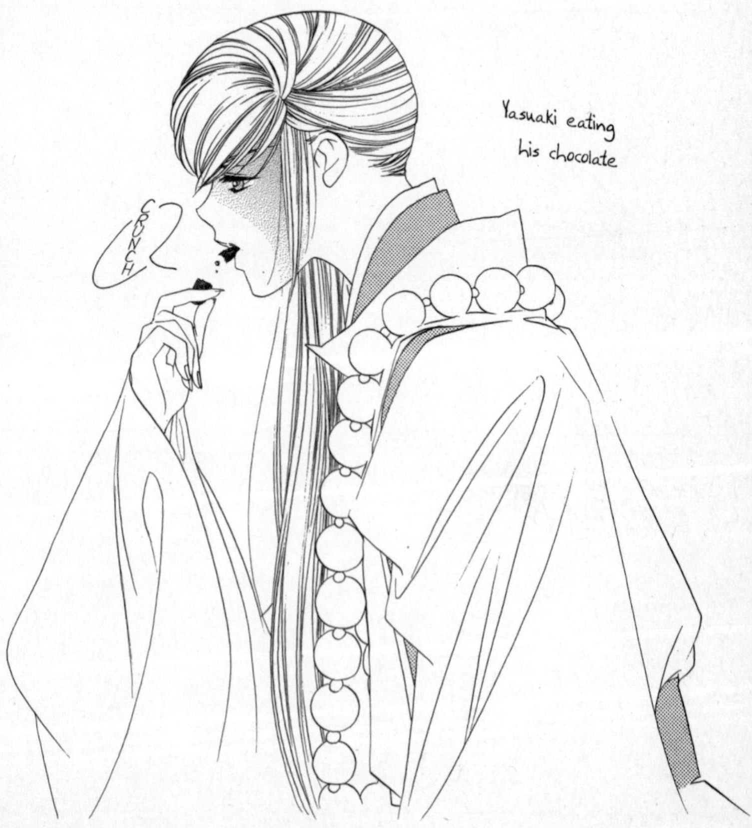
CRUNCH
Yasuaki eating his chocolate

Tohko Mizuno made her mangaka debut with *Night Walk*, which ran in *Lunatic LaLa* magazine in 1995. Showcasing her delicate line work and use of rich textures and patterns, the quasi-historical *Haruka* is Mizuno's first serialized manga and is based on a video game of the same name. It has spawned several books, including a fanbook, a super guidebook, and a collection of illustrations. Mizuno is also the author of *Mukashi, Oboronaru Otoko Arikeri* (Once Upon a Time, There Was a Hazy Man).

HARUKA
VOL. 3
The Shojo Beat Manga Edition

STORY AND ART BY
TOHKO MIZUNO
ORIGINAL CONCEPT BY RUBY PARTY

Translation/Stanley Floyd, HC Language Solutions
Touch-up Art & Lettering/James Gaubatz
Cover Design/Hidemi Dunn
Interior Design/Yuki Ameda
Editor/Carol Fox

Editor in Chief, Books/Alvin Lu
Editor in Chief, Magazines/Marc Weidenbaum
VP, Publishing Licensing/Rika Inouye
VP, Sales & Product Marketing/Gonzalo Ferreyra
VP, Creative/Linda Espinosa
Publisher/Hyoe Narita

Harukanaru Toki no Nakade by Tohko Mizuno
© Tohko Mizuno, KOEI Co., Ltd. 2000
All rights reserved.
First published in Japan in 2001 by HAKUSENSHA, Inc., Tokyo.
English language translation rights arranged
with HAKUSENSHA, Inc., Tokyo.
The stories, characters and incidents mentioned
in this publication are entirely fictional.

Printed in Canada

Published by VIZ Media, LLC
P.O. Box 77010
San Francisco, CA 94107

Shojo Beat Manga Edition
10 9 8 7 6 5 4 3 2 1
First printing, December 2008

www.viz.com

store.viz.com

PARENTAL ADVISORY
HARUKA is rated T+ for Older
Teen and is recommended for
ages 16 and up.
ratings.viz.com

FUSHIGI YÛGI
GENBU KAIDEN™
BY YUU WATASE

THIS **EXCITING**
PREQUEL TO **VIZ** MEDIA'S
BEST-SELLING FANTASY
SERIES, *FUSHIGI YÛGI*,
TELLS THE STORY OF THE
VERY FIRST PRIESTESS OF
THE FOUR GODS—
THE PRIESTESS OF GENBU!

Only **$8**⁹⁹

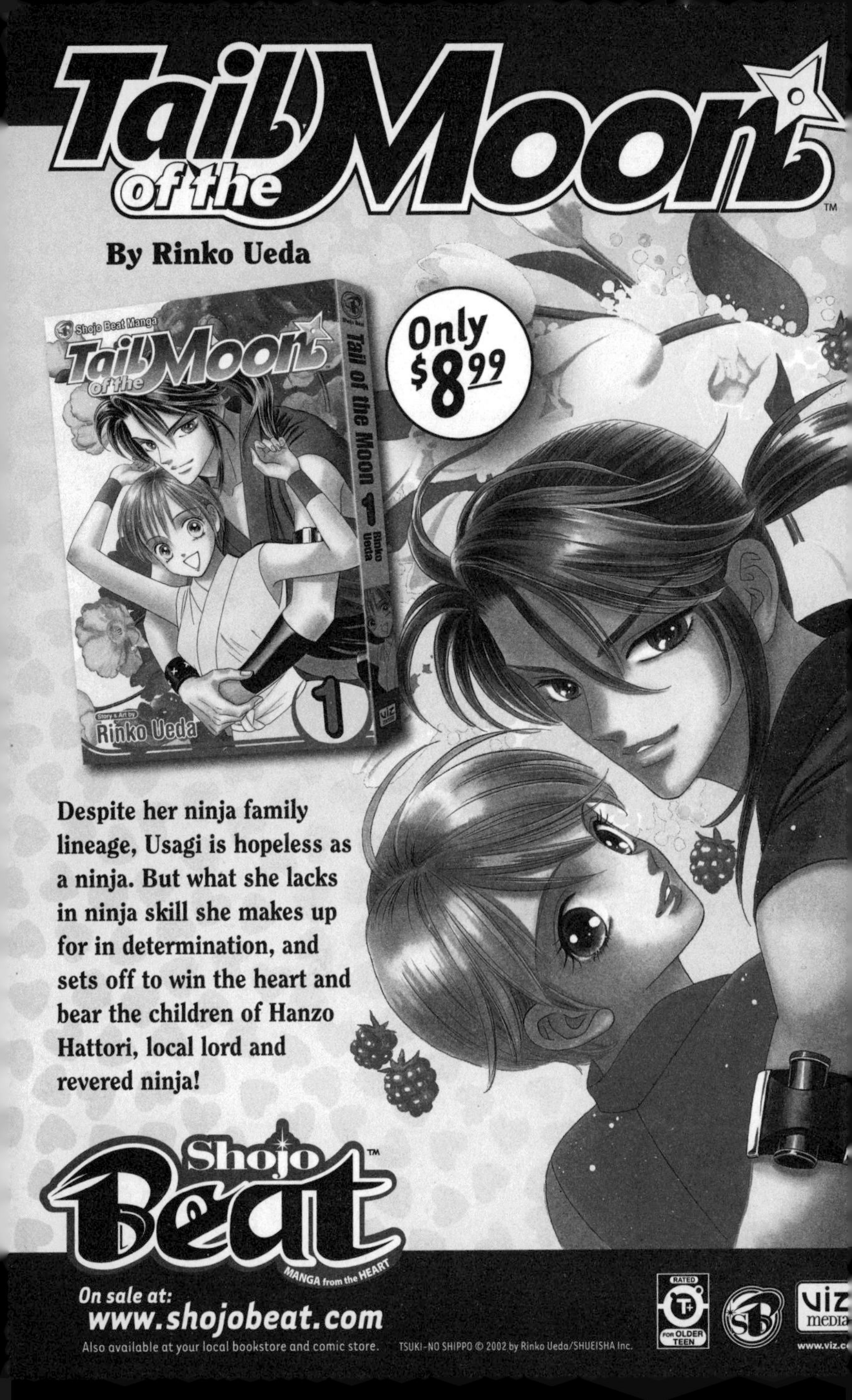
Tail of the Moon™
By Rinko Ueda
Shojo Beat Manga
Tail of the Moon
1
Story & Art by
Rinko Ueda
Only $8.99
Despite her ninja family lineage, Usagi is hopeless as a ninja. But what she lacks in ninja skill she makes up for in determination, and sets off to win the heart and bear the children of Hanzo Hattori, local lord and revered ninja!
Shojo Beat™
MANGA from the HEART
On sale at:
www.shojobeat.com
Also available at your local bookstore and comic store.
TSUKI-NO SHIPPO © 2002 by Rinko Ueda/SHUEISHA Inc.
RATED T+ FOR OLDER TEEN
viz media
www.viz.c

Save ... er price!

The Shojo Manga Authority

This monthly magazine is injected with the most **ADDICTIVE** shojo manga stories from Japan. PLUS, unique editorial coverage on the arts, music, culture, fashion, and much more!

☑ **YES!** Please enter my one-year subscription (12 GIANT issues) to *Shojo Beat* at the LOW SUBSCRIPTION RATE of **$34.99!**

Over **300 pages** per issue!

NAME

ADDRESS

CITY   STATE   ZIP

E-MAIL ADDRESS   P7GNC1

☐ MY CHECK IS ENCLOSED (PAYABLE TO *Shojo Beat*)   ☐ BILL ME LATER

CREDIT CARD: ☐ VISA   ☐ MASTERCARD

ACCOUNT #   EXP. DATE

SIGNATURE

CLIP AND MAIL TO ➡

SHOJO BEAT
Subscriptions Service Dept.
P.O. Box 438
Mount Morris, IL 61054-0438

Canada price for 12 issues: $46.99 USD, including GST, HST and QST. US/CAN orders only. Allow 6-8 weeks for delivery. Must be 16 or older to redeem offer. By redeeming this offer I represent that I am 16 or older.

Vampire Knight © Matsuri Hino 2004/HAKUSENSHA, Inc. Nana Kitade © Sony Music Entertainment (Japan), Inc. CRIMSON HERO © 2002 by Mitsuba Takanashi/SHUEISHA Inc.

RATED **T+** FOR OLDER TEEN ratings.viz.com